POLYTECHNIC UNIVERSITY

CHANGING THE WORLD

THE FIRST 150 YEARS

ROSTER / BROOKLYN POLYTECHNIC ALUMNI ASSOCIATION /

ROSTER / BROOKLYN POLYTECHNIC ALUMNI ASSOCIATION

ROSTER

Brooklyn Polytechnic Alumni Association, In

AS OF OCTOBER, 1967

POLYTECHNIC UNIVERSITY

CHANGING THE WORLD

THE FIRST 150 YEARS

Jeffrey L. Rodengen

Edited by Mickey Murphy
Design and layout by Sandy Cruz

Write Stuff Enterprises, Inc.
1001 South Andrews Avenue
Second Floor
Fort Lauderdale, FL 33316
1-800-900-Book (1-800-900-2665)
(954) 462-6657
www.writestuffbooks.com

PUBLISHER'S CATALOGING IN PUBLICATION
(PREPARED BY THE DONOHUE GROUP, INC.)

Rodengen, Jeffrey L.
   Changing the World : Polytechnic University, The First 150 Years / Jeffrey L. Rodengen ; edited by Mickey Murphy ; design and layout by Sandy Cruz.

   p. : ill. ; cm.
   Includes index.
   ISBN: 1-932022-08-2

1. Polytechnic University (Brooklyn, New York, N.Y.)—History. 2. Technical institutes—New York (State)—History. I. Murphy, Mickey. II. Sandy Cruz. III. Title. IV. Title: Polytechnic University

T171.P65 R63 2005
378.04/09747   2005929712

Library of Congress
Catalog Card Number 2005929712

Completely produced in the
United States of America
10 9 8 7 6 5 4 3 2 1

ALSO BY JEFFREY L. RODENGEN

The Legend of Chris-Craft

*IRON FIST:
The Lives of Carl Kiekhaefer*

*Evinrude-Johnson
and The Legend of OMC*

*Serving the Silent Service:
The Legend of Electric Boat*

The Legend of Dr Pepper/Seven-Up

The Legend of Honeywell

The Legend of Briggs & Stratton

The Legend of Ingersoll-Rand

*The Legend of Stanley:
150 Years of The Stanley Works*

The MicroAge Way

The Legend of Halliburton

The Legend of York International

The Legend of Nucor Corporation

*The Legend of Goodyear:
The First 100 Years*

The Legend of AMP

The Legend of Cessna

The Legend of VF Corporation

The Spirit of AMD

The Legend of Rowan

*New Horizons:
The Story of Ashland Inc.*

The History of American Standard

The Legend of Mercury Marine

The Legend of Federal-Mogul

*Against the Odds:
Inter-Tel—The First 30 Years*

The Legend of Pfizer

*State of the Heart:
The Practical Guide to Your Heart
and Heart Surgery*
with Larry W. Stephenson, M.D.

*The Legend of
Worthington Industries*

The Legend of IBP, Inc.

The Legend of Trinity Industries, Inc.

*The Legend of
Cornelius Vanderbilt Whitney*

The Legend of Amdahl

The Legend of Litton Industries

The Legend of Gulfstream

The Legend of Bertram
with David A. Patten

*The Legend of
Ritchie Bros. Auctioneers*

The Legend of ALLTEL
with David A. Patten

*The Yes, you can of
Invacare Corporation*
with Anthony L. Wall

*The Ship in the Balloon:
The Story of Boston Scientific
and the Development of
Less-Invasive Medicine*

The Legend of Day & Zimmermann

The Legend of Noble Drilling

*Fifty Years of Innovation:
Kulicke & Soffa*

*Biomet—From Warsaw
to the World*
with Richard F. Hubbard

NRA: An American Legend

*The Heritage and Values
of RPM, Inc.*

*The Marmon Group:
The First Fifty Years*

The Legend of Grainger

*The Legend of
The Titan Corporation*
with Richard F. Hubbard

The Legend of Discount Tire Co.
with Richard F. Hubbard

The Legend of Polaris
with Richard F. Hubbard

The Legend of La-Z-Boy
with Richard F. Hubbard

The Legend of McCarthy
with Richard F. Hubbard

*InterVoice:
Twenty Years of Innovation*
with Richard F. Hubbard

*Jefferson-Pilot Financial:
A Century of Excellence*
with Richard F. Hubbard

The Legend of HCA
with Richard F. Hubbard

The Legend of Werner Enterprises
with Richard F. Hubbard

The Legend of J. F. Shea Co.
with Richard F. Hubbard

True to Our Vision
with Richard F. Hubbard

The Legend of Albert Trostel & Sons
with Richard F. Hubbard

The Legend of Sovereign Bancorp
with Richard F. Hubbard

*Innovation is the Best Medicine:
The extraordinary story of Datascope*
with Richard F. Hubbard

The Legend of Guardian Industries

*The Legend of
Universal Forest Products*

TABLE OF CONTENTS

FOREWORD

BY

WM. A. WULF, PhD

PRESIDENT OF THE NATIONAL ACADEMY OF ENGINEERING

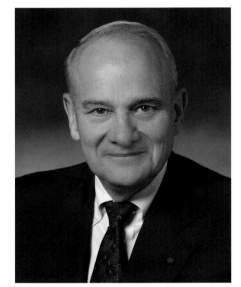

ENGINEERS, ARGUABLY, have had more impact on our quality of life than have any other professionals during the last 100 years. Yes, this is a fairly bold statement—especially from an otherwise cautious engineer. But it is the only conclusion I can draw from the list of the twenty greatest engineering achievements of the 20th Century compiled by the National Academy of Engineering (see the list by following the link at www.nae.edu).

In 1900, almost no one had access to electricity, telephone, or an automobile—but just think how they pervade your life today. The first airplane hadn't flown in 1900. There were no radios, televisions, refrigerators, household appliances, computers, or Internet. There were only a few miles of paved road in the entire country, and certainly no interstate highways. In 1900, half of the population lived on farms, and it took that many to feed the rest of the population; today two percent of the population feeds both us and a good part of the rest of the world because of agricultural mechanization. How remarkably the world has changed!

But clean water is my favorite. The average life span in 1900 was only 46 years. Today it's 77-plus, and something like 20 of those 30+ years are due simply to the general availability of clean water.

Waterborne diseases were the third major cause of death in the country in 1900.

Imagine, too, that in 1900, Polytechnic University had already been granting degrees to professional engineers for more than 50 years, providing a constant stream of visionaries and innovators destined to forever change the world.

One measure of the impact of Poly is the number of its faculty and students that have been elected to the National Academy of Engineering (NAE)—65 in total. Election to the NAE is generally considered the highest honor that can be bestowed on an engineer by his or her peers. Poly's students and professors have been so honored for groundbreaking discoveries in microwave technology, aeronautics, barcode technology, polymer science, and telecommunications, to name just a few. They have helped to invent the VCR, the camcorder, the laser, and to put men on the moon.

Though it is very difficult to single out individuals among Poly's distinguished engineers and scientists, a few must be mentioned to honor so many: Dr. Jasper H. Kane, class of 1928, was instrumental in the development of the mass production of penicillin during World War II. Professors Raymond E. Kirk and Donald F. Othmer released the *Kirk-Othmer Encyclopedia of Chemical Technology*—the fourth edition of this classic 27-volume work is used worldwide. Professor Antonio Ferri, founding director of Poly's Aerodynamics Laboratories, was one of the developers of the world's first jet-engine-powered aircraft. Dr. Ernst Weber and his colleagues were instrumental in refining microwave technology for radar applications. Dr. Gertrude B. Elion, who studied at Poly, was awarded the Nobel Prize in Medicine in 1988, along with her partner, George H. Hitchings. Their work contributed to the development of drugs treating AIDS, leukemia, gout, malaria, autoimmune disorders, and for the prevention of the rejection of donated organs; and she is featured in a chapter of Tom Brokaw's book, *The Greatest Generation.*

Polytechnic University has earned the respect and admiration of the worldwide engineering community. For 150 years, it has provided the talent, ingenuity, and academic crucible to advance the principles and frontiers of engineering and science which have improved the lives of the vast majority of the earth's inhabitants. All who have been associated with this venerable and celebrated university can be proud of its unparalleled accomplishments. It can be said with some certainty that significant future innovations in the fields of engineering will also come from the graduates, faculty, and alumni of this remarkable institution.

Congratulations, Polytechnic University, on your first 150 years—but the best is yet to come!

—September 2005

ACKNOWLEDGMENTS

NUMEROUS INDIVID-
uals and organizations
assisted in the sponsor-
ship, research, development, and
publication of *Polytechnic University: Changing the World, The First
150 Years*.

Sponsors

Thanks to their generosity, the following spon-
sors helped make this book possible.

William L. Friend
Francis J. Hallenbeck
Charles O. Klimas
Daniel S. Leickhardt
Robert A. Linoki
Alfred C. Maevis
Craig G. Matthews
George H. Neugebauer
Polytechnic Alumni
Steven M. Rittvo
Hubert W. Schleuning
John J. and Adele F. Steinke Trust
John M. Trani
Wilfred R. Violette
Ingersoll-Rand Co. Ltd.
Pfizer Inc.
The Stanley Works

Contributors

Vital to this endeavor was
the work of Richard Thorsen,
Polytechnic vice president of
development and university relations, who served as primary catalyst and managing editor; and Lea
Bowie, who served as editorial
assistant. Numerous Polytechnic
alumni and professors, past and present, along
with other members of the Polytechnic community, enriched the book by discussing their experiences. The author extends particular gratitude to
these men and women, many of whom also assisted
as contributing editors, for their candid recollections and guidance.

Stephen Arnold
Henry Bertoni
Holly Block
Martin Bloom
Lea Bowie
George Bugliarello
Irving Cadoff
Cecilia Chang
David Chang
David Doucette
Gloria Fazio
Leopold Felsen

Robert Flynn
Ivan Frisch
Christopher Hayes
Charles Hinkaty
Mel Horwitch
Donald Ivanoff
Joseph Jacobs
James Jarman
Beverly Johnson
Ray Katzen
John Kelly
Michelle Kerr
Erwin Lutwak
Rudolph Marcus
Hans Mark
Arthur Martinez
Joe Martini
Carmine Masucci
Bill McShane
Henry Middendorf
Jovan Mijovic
Herbert Morawetz
William Murray
Stewart Nagler
Shiv Panwar
Eli Pearce
Jana Richman
Roger Roess
George Schillinger
Misha Schwartz
Benjamin Senitzky
Leonard Shaw
Leonard Shustek
Henry Singer
Harold Sjursen
Stuart Steele
Charles Strang
Richard Thorsen
Therese Tillett
Carolyn Tobias

Alair Townsend
Richard Van Slyke
Hermann Viets
Victor Wallach
Heather Walters
Helen Warren
Harry Wechsler
Donald Weisstuch
Beh Sue Yuen

Others

Other key contributors also played crucial roles in the book's development. The principal research and assembly of the narrative time line was accomplished by Research Assistant W.B. King. He also coordinated with Polytechnic to secure all photos, illustrations, and other graphical items. Senior Editor Mickey Murphy was responsible for text editing and photo placement, as well as overall book project coordination. The graphic design of Senior Art Director Sandy Cruz brought the story to compelling visual life.

Additionally, these other Write Stuff Enterprises Inc. professionals also helped make this book a reality.

Mary Aaron
Kevin Allen
Constance A. Angelo
Amy Blakely
Dianne Cormier
Rachelle Donley
Sherry Hasso
Lars Jessen
Barbara Koch
Dawn LaVoir
Bill Laznovsky
Amy Major
Marianne Roberts
Dennis Shockley
Sam Stefanova

A plaque in memory of Polytechnic University's founders was erected in 1928 by the class of 1912.

CHAPTER ONE

BIRTH OF AN INSTITUTE
1853–1876

The Collegiate and Polytechnic Institute is established with a view to aid the intellectual development of our youth; to place Brooklyn in the front rank of our cities ... and promote that mental discipline, intelligence, and refined taste which are the real glory of a people.

—*Brooklyn Daily Eagle,* September 6, 1855

WHEN THE SUN ROSE on New Year's morning in 1853 on Joralemon Street, the Brooklyn Female Academy had been reduced to ashes. The only school of higher learning in the city was destroyed by an uncontrollable fire that ripped through its corridors.[1]

In the days that followed, Harriet Putnam Packer, a widow of an academy trustee, wrote a check for $65,000 that was eventually used to rebuild the academy, which was renamed Packer Collegiate Institute in her husband's honor and still exists today. Packer had one stipulation regarding her bequest: a similar institute of higher learning was to be constructed for young men, which paved the way for Polytechnic.[2]

Little would Packer know that in the 150 years that followed, Polytechnic University, the nation's second oldest private science and engineering institution, would employ world renowned professors to produce graduates who changed the course of science and engineering, physics, polymer chemistry, aerospace, telecommunications, biotechnology, and information science. Additionally, distinguished alumni have been awarded Pulitzer and Nobel Prizes for their varied accomplishments.

The roughly 44,000 alumni and countless professors all share a common experience, defined by the pursuit of educational excellence and the yearning for discovery and innovation; an experience continually faced with vigor and progressive evolution, despite episodic challenges.

THE EARLY YEARS

In the years and decades that preceded the birth of Polytechnic, the city of Brooklyn went through considerable changes. First developed by European settlers, Brooklyn was predominately influenced by the Dutch, who opened the first free denominational schools before the turn of the 19th century.[3] Dutch was still being taught in school in 1819, when Brooklyn, which included Gowanus and Bushwick, was incorporated. The resulting tax levied on properties helped establish Brooklyn's first public school, Public School No. 1. At this time, Brooklyn was mainly a farming community, with cornfields dominating what is now Montague Street. The city's center was moved in 1849 with the erection of a new City Hall on what had been the Remsen family farm. This transferred the business quarter from "The Ferry" to what is now the Borough Hall district.[4]

Bylaws for the Brooklyn Female Academy, which burned down in 1853. From its ashes, Polytechnic Institute was born.

It was during this period that Brooklyn experienced significant growth, most notably marked by the construction of the Brooklyn Navy Yard, which created the need for housing and commerce. Across the river, New Yorkers were seeking refuge from the tremendous growth Manhattan was experiencing; to this end, they began buying land and building homes. Many would capitalize on Brooklyn's prime location, which resulted in the city's population growing by the thousands each year. Wealthy Dutch and British families began building mansions in the Brooklyn Heights area and selling parcels of land along the river to entrepreneurs from Long Island.[5]

Horse cars began replacing stage coaches, and railway lines began bisecting fields, woods, and farms. Block-paved streets and gaslight street lamps quickly added to the emerging landscape, and in 1852 alone 2,500 new structures were constructed.[6] As Brooklyn grew, so did industry, and many business leaders, especially those concerned with consumer goods, began looking past the streets of Manhattan to the budding city of Brooklyn. By this time, Brooklyn was educating approximately 18,000 students daily.

By 1853, Brooklyn's population was 145,000, which was a nearly 700 percent increase from 1834.[7] With intensive commercial, civic, and cultural growth, education became a paramount concern, and the leaders of the community understood that an institute of higher learning for young men was needed.

GROUNDS BROKEN—MINDS OPENED

On May 17, 1853, a group of 14 distinguished Brooklyn residents drew up the charter to create the Brooklyn Collegiate and Polytechnic Institute.

THE FIRST SETTLERS

CURRENTLY, THE LAND WHICH POLY-technic occupies has significant history that includes the first European settlement and lineage and a now vanished Native American tribe.

More than 400 years ago, the Rinnegaconck Tribe, part of the Canarsie Indian Federation, inhabited the area. The second largest village, known as Marechkawick, subsequently became the site of the first European settlement in Brooklyn and was in the vicinity of what are now Lawrence and Jay Streets.[1]

In 1637, Joris Jansen Rapelje, a 33-year-old French sailor and weaver, purchased the Rinnegaconck territory. Rapelje and his wife had emigrated 13 years earlier with 30 other families, the first colonists of Nieuw Netherlands (which then covered present-day New York, New Jersey, Delaware, and parts of Connecticut). Rapelje's daughter, Sarah, was the first European female child born in Nieuw Netherlands.[2]

The site for Polytechnic was mainly rolling farmland. In 1694, the pastoral land was sold to two brothers, Isaac and Jeremiah Remsen. Jeremiah's son inherited the parcel of land and during the Revolutionary War deeded the property to a relative, Barent Johnson, who was commander of the Kings County Militia. Johnson left the property to his son, Jeremiah, a major general during the War of 1812 and the third mayor of the city of Brooklyn. For many years thereafter, the Polytechnic site was referred to as the Johnson Farm.[3]

In the early months of 1822, Jeremiah Johnson divided the land into various lots and streets. In 1836, the first wood-frame house was constructed on the west side of Jay Street, a location approximately where the Marriott Hotel stands today. In 1849, the Centenary Methodist Episcopal Church was built where the Joseph J. Jacobs Administration Building now stands.[4]

THE NAMING OF BROOKLYN

IN 1646, THE VILLAGE OF BREUCKELEN was authorized by the Dutch West India Company and became the first municipality in what is now New York State. (The predecessors of the cities of Albany and New York were numbers two and three, respectively.)

In 1683, which was almost 20 years after the English had removed the Dutch from power, the General Assembly of Freeholders took the step of reorganizing the governmental structure in all of the province of New York into 12 counties, each of which was subdivided into towns.

Brooklyn was one of the original six towns of Kings County when the county and town system was established in 1683.[1]

The founders of the Institute were prominent Ivy League graduates and businessmen who wanted their sons to study closer to home.

The trustees mostly lived in Brooklyn Heights, but also hailed from Gowanus, South Brooklyn, and Bedford Corners. They were represented by the city's largest employers: the Brooklyn White Lead Factory (George S. Howland); the Atlantic Dock Company (James S. T. Stranahan); the Hydraulic Works in South Brooklyn (Henry R. Worthington); a lawyer with a diploma in civil engineering from Paris who worked on the surveying of the North East Boundary of Maine (J. Carson Brevoort); a physician connected with the Brooklyn City Hospital (Dillon S. Landon); and several other prominent merchants whose businesses were located in New York. Among them were Isaac H. Frothingham, who was connected with over a half dozen financial concerns on both sides of the river; and Josiah O. Low, of the family firm of A. A. Low and Bros., which operated the fastest fleet of flat-bottomed clipper ships for the China trade and the California Gold Rush. They were able to purchase tea in China a full three weeks after harvest sales, at considerably lower costs, and still beat the earlier purchasers of tea back to American markets, thereby pocketing the difference in costs between their competitors, who bought early when the price was high.[8]

Polytechnic was modeled in part after the New York Free Academy, which educated the poor and disadvantaged from the greater New York area. The Free Academy was located on the southeast corner of 23rd Street and Lexington Avenue in Manhattan. It opened in 1847 and experienced great success. By 1866 it was renamed City College of New York.[9]

While Polytechnic's Board of Trustees wanted to offer a similar institution of higher learning in Brooklyn, they weren't in the business of providing free education; thus tuition in the early years of Polytechnic was set at $20 to $40 (depending on age) per quarter for preparatory students and $40 for collegiate students. The school year began in September and concluded in July. The

This early drawing shows Brooklyn's Fulton Street, between Bridge and Lawrence Streets, circa 1776.

scholastic day would begin at 8:30 A.M. and end at 2:30 P.M.[10]

On January 20, 1854, the first meeting of the board of trustees of the Institute was held. That same day the board elected Isaac H. Frothingham as chairman, a position he would hold for the next 43 years. Eleven days later the board agreed to pay $16,000 for land at 99 Livingston Street.[11] The trustees took the initial steps to construct the building that would house the Institute. They secured Fredrick A. Peterson to design the building, an accomplished architect who is now perhaps best known for his design of the Cooper Union building in Manhattan.[12]

In March 1854, the board of trustees drafted a circular that was published and distributed to the Institute's stockholders, as well as to residents in Brooklyn, requesting money to meet construction costs. While some residents purchased shares, the majority of shareholders were successful businessmen from Manhattan and Brooklyn.

According to the *Brooklyn Daily Eagle*'s March 20 edition, Polytechnic intended to serve approximately 150 students; however, this number would be exceeded by the end of the first academic year. The shares were issued in $100 increments. The stockholders mainly consisted of Brooklyn's elite; however, it was stipulated that the profits of their investments were never to exceed 5 percent so that mercenary motives were not in conflict with the enterprise of the Institute.[13]

Despite their best intentions, the trustees failed to meet their intended goal and were forced to take a partial mortgage in the amount of $20,000 while managing minor floating debts. This was a minor setback, and in April the New York Board of Regents granted the Institute's charter, which speaks to the perseverance of the trustees.[14] This

This is an original stock certificate in the amount of $100, issued on October 10, 1855, one month after the Institute opened. The certificate was signed by the Institute's first chairman of the board of trustees (later known as "The Corporation"), Isaac Frothingham.

spirit of overcoming obstacles, no matter the effort needed, would be passed along from administration to administration, class to class, and generation to generation.

The location of Polytechnic was chosen because of its proximity to Brooklyn's City Hall and the railway station that offered access from all points in the greater New York area. This was essential because the Institute did not offer boarding.

"No location could be selected the country over, embracing so many advantages for the successful establishment of such a department as our own city...." Polytechnic board members wrote in the Institute's first annual report that was published on October 11, 1854.[15]

While faced with a great challenge of creating an institute of higher learning, the trustees clearly spelled out the mission in the first annual report. In part, the report stated:

A view of Brooklyn City Hall in Brooklyn Heights, 1860.

An educational institution in our midst, which, while it should not only meet the present and pressing wants of the members, would at the same time enable us to give our sons, under our own inspection, and surrounded by all the saving influences of home and the family circle, such an education as would qualify them in a far higher degree, through an enlarged, liberal and thorough training in a course of practical, scientific and classical studies, to enter successfully upon the active pursuits and duties of life.[16]

During this time, Brooklyn, the country's third-largest city, held the distinction as the nation's leader in public education, with 78 schools under the supervision of the Board of Education, which was incorporated in 1853. The city was also home to 30 private schools. Across the river in Manhattan, there were already three successful institutions for higher learning, including the New York Free Academy, the University of the City of New York, which later became known as New York University, and Columbia College, which eventually became Columbia University.[17]

Aside from the rebuilt Brooklyn Female Academy, Brooklyn could now boast an institution of higher learning for men, which made Polytechnic a beacon of educational light. The leaders of Brooklyn's business community understood that

the city needed cultivated, educated, and trained young men to manage the increasingly complex operations of the city's developing business and industries. These leaders, some of them fathers, also wanted better-educated husbands for the graduates (their daughters) of the Brooklyn Female Academy and, above all, needed a distinct group of young men who would be sensitive to the cultural and social needs of a rising metropolis.[18]

THE FIRST BELL RINGS

In August of 1855, the *New York Independent* described Polytechnic as "spacious and airy, [affording] ample accommodations for five or six hundred students." The article also noted, "the plan combines all the modern improvements in style of building, form of furniture, methods of warming, and ventilation ... designed to promote the health and comfort of the pupils, and secure the greatest possible efficiency in the business of instruction."[19]

On September 10, 1855, Polytechnic opened its doors to 265 young men, ages 9 to 17. The first academic year was under the guidance of the Reverend John H. Raymond, who was also instrumental in establishing the University of Rochester. Raymond was Polytechnic's first president. He would employ his vast experience in designing the curriculum and personally selecting the faculty.[20]

A distinguished educator, Raymond was assisted in the first year by 11 professors. They collectively were charged with sorting and sizing the student body that attended Polytechnic, most of whom came from the elite neighborhoods of Brooklyn, which included the Heights, the Hill, and the Eastern District.[21] Because the name of the Institute was so long, many people began calling it by shorter names like "The Polytechnic" or simply "The Poly."

In its first year, the Institute was divided into academic and collegiate departments, with a principal and superintendent for each. Edward C. Seymour was named Principal of the Academic Department, which is equivalent to today's elementary educational system. The Collegiate Department was guided by Robert Foster, who served as superintendent. He oversaw the junior and senior sections, which are the equivalent of freshmen and sophomores in today's university setting.[22]

At this time, courses offered included Classical or Preparatory Collegiate; the Scientific; and the

Commercial. All were designed to meet specific aptitudes and objectives. The subjects of study included English language and literature, mathematics, history and geography, penmanship and bookkeeping, ancient languages, modern languages, physical sciences, philosophy, drawing, and vocal music.[23]

With a solid faculty, curriculum, and growing student body, Polytechnic quickly became a leading academic institution. This was achieved in no small part by strict academic standards and an advanced philosophy of discipline in which corporal punishment was outlawed. The founders' motto was to establish a "Polytechnic Department second to none" in the country, and judging by its first year of success, their declaration was coming to fruition.[24]

AN INSTITUTE ON THE RISE

As the streets of Brooklyn grew and expanded, so did Polytechnic. The enrollment doubled after its first year, and education standards grew with each passing day. The school soon became known by yet another nickname, "Brooklyn Poly." With its close proximity to many leading engineering and industrial firms, the focus of the Institute leaned toward the collegiate division rather than the preparatory. One account of its early history noted:

A technical school where the employees of over one thousand engineering and industrial firms gain the theoretical knowledge that gives meaning and scope to their practical experience, and where the faculty, regular and adjunct, works hand in glove with the many varied industries and research enterprises of the metropolitan area.[25]

Polytechnic's first few years developed with great excitement as the Brooklyn community embraced it with open arms. Polytechnic professors would often give lectures to the student body as well as to curious residents concerning the latest technological advances. For example, one of the many lectures at the Institute explained the principles of telegraphy, which at the time was a truly newfangled development.[26]

The Institute's first president, Reverend John H. Raymond.

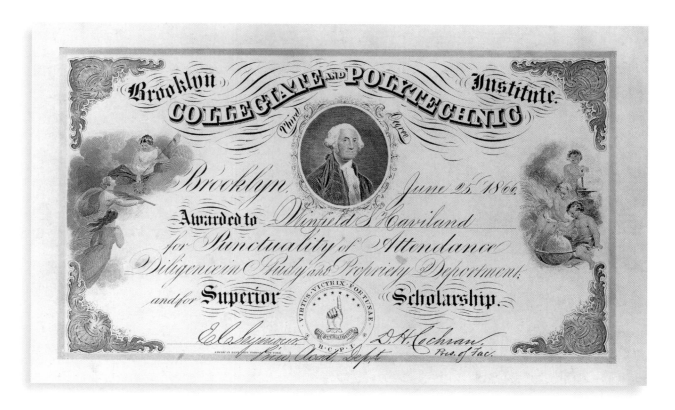

This certificate was awarded to Winfield S. Haviland on June 23, 1866. It was signed by Dr. David H. Cochran and Professor Edward C. Seymour.

By including the community, Polytechnic also gained the attention of many business owners and industry leaders, a relationship that continues today. Perhaps the best declaration of the Institute's mission was written in the pages of the *Brooklyn Daily Eagle*, which held no bias but was beneficial to the growth and vitality of the Institute.

If it [Polytechnic] had been established as a profitable investment for surplus capital, no word of ours should have recommended it to public favor, however beneficial to [the] public the effects it might produce; but coming with such claims as it presents we deem it a duty to bear our humble testimony in its behalf.[27]

In another glowing report, the newspaper commented about the Institute:

The Collegiate and Polytechnic Institute is established with a view to aid the intellectual development of our youth; to place Brooklyn in the front rank of our cities in point of educational facilities, and promote that mental discipline, intelligence and refined taste which are the real glory of a people.[28]

BROOKLYN ACADEMY OF MUSIC

Polytechnic's founders wanted to support community growth because they believed it would benefit the Institute. For that and related reasons, in 1858 Polytechnic hosted the first meeting for the formation of the Brooklyn Academy of Music. Raymond was appointed secretary of the committee. At the first meeting, the committee noted the value of the planned institution to Brooklyn.

The time has full come when Brooklyn, already provided with religious and educational institutions, should have also a place where her citizens can obtain the benefit to be derived from innocent amusements, and the other influences which promote social happiness … instead of being obliged, as they now are, to go beyond the bounds of their

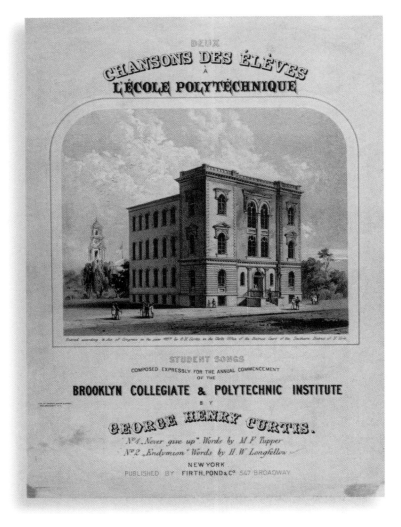

advantages for the training of boys 10 years old and upwards," with a faculty consisting of "gentlemen possessing superior abilities in their professions, aided by a numerous corps of competent instructors."[31]

As enrollment grew, so did Polytechnic's facilities, which included a new gymnasium in 1859 and plans to expand its building on Livingston Street. During its first 10 years, the Institute annually served approximately 500 students from Brooklyn and nearby towns and villages. Polytechnic also expanded its physical science and civil engineering curricula, with continued focus on business and the arts.[32]

CIVIL WAR

While Polytechnic expanded its educational programs for young men from Brooklyn and environs, other young men were getting a different type of education on Civil War battlefields north and south. But Poly students also played their part during the war. Indeed, approximately 100 Poly men saw active service during the war.

In answering a call of duty, the Institute took a semimilitary stance by forming the Polytechnic Cadets. The able students who joined this rank were adorned in a uniform of blue trousers, frock coats with brass buttons, and military caps. The

own city, and for that purpose, she should have a building adapted to musical performance, literary and scientific objects, and the exhibitions of works of art and nature.[29]

Beginning in 1871, most of the commencement exercises for graduates were held at the Academy of Music.[30]

SUCCESS IN NUMBERS

By 1859, enrollment at Polytechnic was increasing significantly. In order to meet the educational demands of the Institute, the Brooklyn Juvenile High School was established to prepare young boys for competitive entrance into Polytechnic. The Institute advertised that "[Polytechnic] possesses unusual

Above left: Pictured here is the Institute's original building in the 1870s located at 99 Livingston Street. This once underdeveloped neighborhood is a five-minute walk from the MetroTech Center, Brooklyn's $1 billion office complex.

Right: Seth Low was graduated from Poly's Classical Course in 1866. His plan of municipal administration while he was mayor of the City of Brooklyn was copied by a number of cities throughout the country—and used again when he became mayor of the City of Greater New York. He is shown in the cadet uniform worn by Poly students during the Civil War.

cadets were organized in a military corps forming a complete battalion and regularly practiced their drilling exercises in Polytechnic's backyard. Polytechnic granted half-day holidays when the North was victorious in battle.[33] In addition to the many Poly men who served their nation with valor during the Civil War, the wartime achievements of two of them, Professor Joshua W. Sill and alumnus George W. Melville, were recognized and immortalized by the United States government.

Oklahoma's Fort Sill, the largest artillery center in the world, was named after Brigadier General Joshua W. Sill, who was the youngest general appointed to lead Northern forces. The USS *Melville* and the oceanographic research ship *Melville* were both named in honor of Rear Admiral George W. Melville. (Please see sidebar on pages 20–21 concerning Polytechnic's Civil War heroes.)

As the Civil War pressed on, Polytechnic was emerging as one of the leading academic institutions in the greater New York area. The summer of 1862 brought educational change across the nation as the United States Congress authorized the grant of land to states, maintaining colleges offering courses in agriculture and mechanic arts. In 1865, as the Civil War came to an end, Polytechnic adopted the colors blue and gray to symbolize the unification of the nation.

The Institute formally organized its Alumni Association in 1862. The first annual alumni banquet was held the following year. The sponsorship of the annual alumni reunions included both the alumni of the college and preparatory school. All members were required to hold a degree, and those who did were afforded membership and benefits, which usually took the form of job placements upon graduation. In today's vernacular, membership was considered a "networking" tool, which still exists as students accept internships and jobs from businesses that partner with the Institute.[34]

These advances were due in no small part to the guidance Polytechnic received under Raymond's leadership. However, after five years of academic success, Raymond wanted the Institute to expand the college aspect of the curricula. The trustees

A view of the original Brooklyn Academy of Music. Beginning in 1871, the Academy hosted most of the Institute's commencement ceremonies, a practice that continued through the early 1900s.

wavered, and Raymond threatened to resign. It was clear that Raymond needed a break from Polytechnic and his dealings with Polytechnic's trustees, so in 1863 he took an extended leave of absence. When he returned months later, Raymond continued to express his disappointment with the direction the Institute was taking. The following year, Raymond left Polytechnic and accepted the position of president at Vassar College, a women's school located in Poughkeepsie, New York, which embraced his progressive educational views.[35]

THE REIGN OF DAVID

Raymond was succeeded by Polytechnic's second president, Dr. David H. Cochran, who arrived from the only school in New York State for the training of teachers, the Albany State School, known today as the University at Albany. He would lead Polytechnic for 35 years. Cochran's tenure was commonly known as "the Reign of David." Cochran was highly regarded in academic circles nationwide

POLY'S CIVIL WAR HEROES

ONE YEAR AFTER GRADUATING FROM Polytechnic, in 1861, George W. Melville left an entry-level engineering position and joined the U.S. Navy in the rank of third assistant engineer.[1]

He spent his first year in the navy on the Great Lakes gunboat *Michigan*; later that year he was promoted to second assistant engineer. Melville served on the warships *Dacotah* and *Wachusett* from mid-1862 until late in 1864, when he took part in the capture of CSS *Florida* in October 1864. He finished the Civil War in Hampton Roads, Virginia, working with torpedo boats and as an engineer on the gunboat *Maumee*.[2]

After the Civil War, First Assistant Engineer Melville served aboard several ships, among them the experimental cruiser *Chattanooga*, gunboat *Tacony*, steam sloop *Lancaster*, and Asiatic squadron flagship *Tennessee*. In 1873 he was chief engineer of the steamer *Tigress* during an Arctic cruise searching for survivors of the exploration ship *Polaris*. He returned to the Arctic in 1879 as chief engineer of the steamer *Jeannette* and assumed leadership of the survivors of the ill-fated expedition after they landed in Siberia in 1881.[3]

Melville was promoted to chief engineer during his time on the *Jeannette* and again went to the Arctic aboard the USS *Thetis* in 1884. He was an inspector of coal from 1884 to 1886, then performed his final duty aboard the new cruiser *Atlanta*. In August 1887, Melville became chief of the Bureau of Steam Engineering, with the relative rank of commodore and, after 1899, rear admiral. During more than a decade and a half in that post, he was responsible for the navy's propulsion systems during an era of extraordinary force expansion, technological progress, and institutional change. He is credited for establishing the first Naval Research Laboratory at Annapolis. Also, he was a founding member of the National Geographic Society. After leaving active duty in 1903, Melville spent his last years in Philadelphia, Pennsylvania, where he died on March 18, 1912.

In his memory, the U.S. Navy named two ships in his honor: the USS *Melville* (Destroyer Tender No. 2, later AD-2), which was in commission from 1915 to 1948; and the oceanographic

A portrait of George W. Melville around the turn of the century. Among the medals he proudly wears is the Congressional Gold Medal (far left), which was awarded to him in 1890 for his bravery on the Arctic explorer the *Jeannette*. The U.S. Navy established The George W. Melville award to recognize outstanding engineering advances.

research ship *Melville* (AGOR-14), which was launched in 1969.[4] A statue of Melville is located at the Philadelphia Naval Base.

JOSHUA W. SILL

While Melville's service was aboard ships, Joshua W. Sill served in the fields and trenches. An Ohio native, Sill began as a professor of mathematics and civil engineering at Polytechnic at the age of 29. Before arriving at the Institute, he was a career military man who ranked third in his class at West Point. However, Sill would spend only one year at Polytechnic. In August 1861 he was commissioned a colonel with the 33rd Ohio volunteers and accompanied General Nelson in the Eastern Kentucky expedition. His regiment was then assigned to General Mitchell's division, and Sill was placed in command of a brigade and was promoted to the rank of brigadier general. At age 30, Sill was the youngest brigadier general, and later, commanding general of a division.[5]

His leadership of the division during frequent skirmishes with the enemy was outstanding, and he was noted for having accomplished missions with very few losses to his troops.[6]

He was soon given command of a brigade under General Sheridan and shortly thereafter took part in the bloodiest battle of the Civil War, the Battle of Stone's River, just outside of Murfreesboro, Tennessee. During the second day of this battle, on December 31, 1862, while leading his men forward, he was killed by rifle fire. His body was found by Confederate troops, who buried it in a battlefield cemetery near the scene of his death. A few years later his body was moved to the Grandview Cemetery at Chillicothe, Ohio. Although he was only 31 years old and despite the brevity of his military career, he had carved a record for outstanding performance of duty that few have equaled.

FORT SILL

In 1869, General Sheridan officially established a military post in the Wichita Mountains of Oklahoma, which he named in memory of his West Point classmate, Joshua W. Sill. Today, Fort Sill is the largest artillery center in the world.

In recent years an interesting anecdote concerning General Sill surfaced. According to the memoirs of General Sheridan's sister, Nelly Sheridan Wilson, on the eve of the Battle of Stone's River, General Sill was in conference with General Sheridan. When they left the conference, General Sill and Sheridan mistakenly put on each other's coats. Sill was thus wearing Sheridan's coat at the time he was killed. Nelly Sheridan claimed that the riflemen that killed Sill mistook him for Sheridan.[7]

Joshua W. Sill became the youngest brigadier general of the Union Army during his service in the Civil War. In 1869, Fort Sill, presently the largest artillery center in the world, was named in his honor. *(Photo credit: Ross County Historical Society.)*

CONSTANTINE HERTZBERG.

THREE members of the Institute Faculty have served the Polytechnic longer than Constantine Hertzberg. His practised hand has guided the trembling pencils of class after class, each with the same task, each with the same emotions. The students of bygone days will recall the curiosity and awe with which they used to watch the professor dive into the labyrinths of the enchanted garret, and reappear serenely with the mystic design next to be drawn. The younger students have the same recollections. But that delightful spot, which always had a mediæval air, has been forsaken now for the new studio, as lofty as the professor's art, and the mystery is no more.

Leipzig was the birthplace of Professor Hertzberg. Each year, as the 6th of September swings round, the professor puts on his hat and flees the building, to escape the congratulations which have marked the day ever since 1833, when as yet he knew no art, nor dreamed of future conquests in a distant world.

He received his education for what was to be his profession, at the Royal school of Design, in Dresden, Saxony, the school being under the direction of Herr Julius Schnorr von Carolsfeld, the eminent artist. Four years were spent here, during which he passed all the examinations, studying from the antique and from life, portrait and nude, for which he early developed a prediliction. Here also he learned perspective drawing, known as his forte.

He soon joined the studio of Professor Ludwig Richter, the famous landscape painter. After a year had gone he severed his connection with Herr Richter and came with his parents to America. He arrived on this side in July, 1853, and commenced to lay the foundations upon which his success has been built.

When the Cooper Institute was opened, November, 1859, Professor Hertzberg was in charge of the evening art classes. To the courses already prescribed, perspective drawing was added under his direction. He also instructed in the various branches that year, the Cooper Union day classes for women. In September, 1860, he was offered an appointment in the Brooklyn Polytechnic Institute, then under the direction of Dr. Raymond. This was the most eventful period of his history, for the professor had not fairly settled in his new position, when Dr. Raymond was called away to Vassar College, Poughkeepsie. Professor Hertzberg was invited to undertake the charge of the art department of that institution. Vassar, however, had no attractions for him. His loyalty to the Polytechnic was too strong to yield to the advances of the Hudson River students. He remained with us, and in 1874, married Miss Marietta Porter—a circumstance, no doubt, the anticipation of which was of weight in enabling him to resist the temptation of becoming a citizen of fair Poughkeepsie.

He now resides in South Oxford Street, and besides himself and wife, the family circle includes one daughter, Miss Abbie Hertzberg.

Professor Hertzberg is particularly strong in the departments of mechanical drawing. It has always excited the wonder of his pupils to see the ease and rapid intuition with which he solves the most difficult problems in construction. In addition to his other virtues, the professor is not only one who always himself remains young, but in whose eyes all others appear as if they had bathed in the fountain of perpetual youth. His "little" scholars will always remember with pleasure the hours spent with him.

Above: Charles Robert Knight, the great artist, and Poly alumnus, who became world famous for his drawings and paintings of prehistoric animals, stated that Constantine Hertzberg, a professor of drawing at Polytechnic from the 1860s on, greatly inspired him in his work. Born in Leipzig, Germany, Hertzberg attended the Royal School of Design in Dresden, Germany. He came to the United States with his parents in 1853, first teaching at Cooper Union, then joining Polytechnic in 1860 to set up its Art Department. The above description of Hertzberg, typically ornate of the times, is taken from an early, unidentified Polytechnic publication. In it, his students are described as watching Hertzberg "dive into labyrinths of the enchanted garret, and reappear serenely with the mystic design next to be drawn."

Right: President David H. Cochran was the Institute's second president and taught history and philosophy. His 35–year tenure was often referred to as "the Reign of David."

liked and respected by faculty and students. "Poly boys" came to know Old Davy as a strict disciplinarian and an excellent detective, "equal to if not surpassing Sherlock Holmes."[37] Cochran held education in the highest regard and would not tolerate any horseplay. His creed was "a man needs to be well set upon to be well trained."[38]

While Cochran's early vocation was chemistry, his teachings focused on history, philosophy, and law. This was due, in part, to Sir Henry Bessemer, who discovered in 1856 a more economical process for the production of steel, which Cochran was also researching at the time. It was at this point that he gave up on research and turned his focus to the education field. However, Cochran never lost his love for research and science and set up a private laboratory off one of his classrooms at the Institute. The students were continually intrigued by his research and "were curious as to what 'Cockey' was concocting in there for their confusion."[39]

He was a cultured gentleman, a versatile teacher, and a student of boys, or as one historian noted, "he understood boys better than he did men."[40] If a

and held the distinction of being one of the first two people in the nation to receive a PhD, which he earned in 1862.[36]

Cochran held many nicknames, including "the Doctor," "Old Davy," and "Cockey." He was generally

The above photo shows one of the Institute's early classrooms and laboratories at 99 Livingston Street. Poly eventually installed wooden armchairs (right) in place of benches.

teacher called in sick or was not able to teach a class on any given day, Cochran could step in to teach, whether the subject was logic, moral philosophy, international law, history, or chemistry.[41]

Cochran's love for research and science would ultimately change the focus of the Institute.

Three years into his presidency, Cochran revised the curriculum extensively. The most noted expansion was in the Physical Science Department, which included theoretical and applied physical science, practical chemistry, geology, and mineralogy. Advanced laboratory practices were added in qualitative analysis of inorganic compounds—the assay of ordinary ores: iron, lead, copper, silver, and gold. The following year, these new practices led to toxical examinations and commercial testing of paints, drugs, and medicines. In 1868, the Department of Mathematics was divided into pure and applied

Opposite: This photo shows Poly's original building from the outside. Note the early gaslight lamps on the stoop. An addition to the right side of the building was constructed during the early 1880s.

mathematics, and applied physical science was included as an option for qualifying students.[42] In many ways, Cochran was able to accomplish what Raymond couldn't during his tenure.

Perhaps one of Cochran's best accomplishments took place in 1869, when the Board of Regents of the University of the State of New York, recognizing the high level of the Polytechnic program in the collegiate department, authorized the conferral of bachelor of science degrees to those students who completed the scientific course, and bachelor of arts degrees to those finishing the liberal arts course.[43]

Cochran continued to develop Polytechnic's educational curriculum while addressing financial woes that hindered the Institute during its formative years. But it wasn't until 1870 that Cochran and the administration took the necessary steps to erase Polytechnic's debt and began investing surplus funds each year thereafter for the school's development, which began with the expansion of the main building's rear section that same year.[44]

Polytechnic's main source of income was tuition, although some state aid was obtained from the Literature Fund, restricted to payment of teachers' salaries, and from the Library and Apparatus Fund, which matched monies raised by the Institute for books and equipment.[45] Since the bylaws of Polytechnic were designed to "meet a public want and not to become a source of private gain," the trustees and officers of the board were not paid.[46]

This policy of financing the school almost exclusively through tuition, and later through research, would prove untenable in the years to come. Indeed, the fact that the founders and trustees didn't believe in endowments would set the stage for future financial hardships. However, money problems aside, milestones were continually reached as the Institute expanded. In 1871, the first graduation exercise was held, conferring degrees by the chancellor of the University of the State of New York, assisted by Cochran.[47]

During the next three years, Polytechnic students, faculty, and alumni saw the city flourish as Brooklyn became an increasingly attractive business destination. In 1874, the Society for the Promotion of Engineering Education held its first meeting at Polytechnic, establishing the lasting relationship between the Institute and nearly every professional society devoted to the advancement of engineering and science.[48]

TIME MARCHES ON

The hardships of the Civil War left deep wounds throughout the nation, but America would soon celebrate its 100th anniversary. As the year 1876 approached, Polytechnic began preparing for another milestone, its 25th anniversary.

While academics were of paramount concern, the boys of Polytechnic and the girls of the Packer Collegiate Institute began sharing more than the history that started with a check written by Harriet Putnam Packer more than 20 years earlier.

During the winter months, the students would often enjoy their favorite wintertime activity— ice skating at Capitoline Lake, known today as Prospect Lake, located in Brooklyn's Prospect Park.

"It is much to be feared that the youthful minds of the juveniles were more intent on the anticipation of said skating during school hours, than upon the mysteries of algebra, geometry, [and] trigonometry with which boys' brains are clouded in our prominent academics nowadays," a reporter from the *Brooklyn Daily Eagle* wrote.[49]

Skating jaunts and extracurricular events aside, in the years and decades that followed, Polytechnic alumni, professors, and students would put Brooklyn's new Institute of higher learning on the map with groundbreaking discoveries and innovations.

The 99 Livingston Street building in the late 1880s. Some Preparatory School students can be seen in knickerbockers on the far left, while older Collegiate Department students are on the right.

CHAPTER TWO

THE NEW ERA
1876–1899

It was an audience worthy of the Institution and worthy of the city of which Polytechnic is one of its brightest ornaments.

—Brooklyn Daily Eagle, June 15, 1887

AS THE INSTITUTE APPROACHED its 25th anniversary, its reputation had grown beyond Brooklyn's city limits. Students were now drawn from New York, Boston, and other cities, some from as far away as Canada. This new migration, a historian noted, was due in part to the outstanding faculty.

It was undoubtedly the fact that within its walls there was a living breathing spirit of service among a strong and devoted group of teachers who were striving, in what might be termed the true Poly spirit, to do their best for the boys entrusted to their care and guidance.[1]

A defining characteristic of the faculty was its persistence. The first teachers were revered for their talent and superb leadership. While there was constant shifting among the instructors of the lower academic grades, with some staying only a year or two, the average span for the majority of the faculty was 30-plus years.

Constantine Hertzberg, professor of drawing, held a record for service. He began teaching at the Institute in 1860 and retired 47 years later. George W. Plympton, professor of physical science and later head of the Civil Engineering Department, and Orville B. Stacy, instructor of mathematics and natural philosophy, both also served

for more than 40 years. Principal of the Academic Department, Dr. Edward C. Seymour, served 36 years, while Dr. Cochran served 35 years. One graduate from this period reflected:

There is hardly an alumnus who in reminiscing about his school days has not mentioned with affection the majority of these members of the faculty as being the most vivid recollections of his years at Poly.[2]

While the Institute was molded and guided by men, the students revered their second-grade teacher Mary Jane Baggs, who came to Poly in 1869, and would remain for 36 years. She, not unlike Dr. Cochran, was an inflexible disciplinarian who instilled respect due to her warm personality. When she passed away in 1905, the students eulogized her by saying: "Polytechnic has had many able teachers, but none better, none more loved, none who will be more missed than Mary J. Baggs."[3]

Polytechnic's cement-testing laboratory, shown above, is representative of the Institute's early classrooms and workrooms during the latter part of the nineteenth century. Note the arched windows in the rear of the lab, typical of those in the old building.

THE COUNTRY'S 100-YEAR CELEBRATION

The growth of the Brooklyn Collegiate and Poly-technic Institute, along with the city of Brooklyn, was mirrored by exciting advancements emerging across the country and around the world.

The 1876 Philadelphia Centennial Exposition, the first exposition of its kind in the United States, marked the 100th anniversary of the Declaration of Independence. This celebration highlighted the country's recovery from reconstruction, the Civil War, and its emergence as a world industrial power.[4]

Ten years in the planning, the Centennial cost more than $11 million and covered more than 450 acres of Philadelphia's Fairmount Park. Approximately 10 million visitors viewed the works of 30,000 exhibitors during its six–month stand. The focal point of the exposition was Machinery Hall, where visitors marveled at engineering wonders: electric lights, elevators powered by the 1,400-horsepower Corliss steam engine, locomotives, fire trucks, printing presses, and mining equipment. Introduced to the public for the first time were type-writers, a mechanical calculator, Bell's telephone, and Edison's telegraph.[5]

The Centennial Fair Exposition of scientific and technological advances would soon be equaled by accomplishments made by alumni of the Institute. To this end, in 1876, the Institute's science courses were expanded to include theoretical and applied physical science, practical chemistry, geology, and mineralogy.

BROOKLYN BRIDGE

In 1855, the same year the Institute opened its doors for the first time, John Roebling, the owner of a wire-rope company and a famous bridge designer, proposed a suspension bridge over the East River after becoming impatient with the Atlantic Avenue–Fulton Street Ferry. Roebling worked out every detail of the bridge, from its massive granite towers to its four steel cables. Roebling designed the bridge "to be ranked as a national monument … a great work of art."[6]

The Roebling family had significant experience, having constructed bridges along the Delaware, Niagara, and Ohio Rivers. Initially, Roebling's plans were met with skepticism by city officials representing New York and Brooklyn. However, when he approached William C. Kingsley, the publisher of the *Brooklyn Daily Eagle*, his idea was met with praise.

THE POLY CONNECTION

Kingsley was the same man who firmly supported Dr. Cochran and the Institute. Kingsley was connected to many politicians and businessmen and enlisted the support of Henry Murphy, a state senator and former mayor of Brooklyn. Murphy then drafted a bill in the New York state legislature that would enable a private company to build a bridge connecting Manhattan and Brooklyn.[7]

In 1867, a group of prominent leaders formed the New York Bridge Company "for the purpose of constructing and maintaining a bridge across the East River."[8] Among these leaders was alumnus Seth Low, then mayor of Brooklyn, and board member James S. T. Stranahan. Kingsley served as president of the committee.[9]

Stranahan is considered one of the most important financial, political, managerial, and visionary forces behind the construction of the bridge. As one of the earliest investors and trustees, he altered the original structural plans to support the weight of the Pullman cars. If this step was not implemented, the usefulness of the bridge would have been significantly reduced.

In addition to Stranahan's contributions, another graduate, Arthur V. Abbott, class of 1875, was an assistant engineer. It was Abbott's creation of an anchorage wire, and his invention of a coupling device for the steel cables, that enabled the bridge to be completed.[10]

Under the enabling act, the city of Brooklyn subscribed for $3 million of the capital stock while the city of New York subscribed for $1.5 million. The company was permitted to fix toll rates for pedestrians and all types of vehicles, receiving a profit of no more than 15 percent per year.[11]

At this time, some prominent businessmen and government officials doubted the importance of the bridge; however, Roebling retorted that projected growth in the cities of New York and Brooklyn would require not only the construction of the Brooklyn Bridge, but the future construction of what would eventually become the Williamsburg and Queensboro Bridges.[12]

A SYMBOL OF AMERICAN INGENUITY

EVEN BEFORE IT OPENED, THE BROOK-lyn Bridge became a symbol of the greatness of New York and the power of American ingenuity. While the engineering feat of spanning the East River was spectacular, what impressed people most was the overall arc of the bridge. An editor from *Scientific American* remarked:

> *The bridge is a marvel of beauty viewed from the level of the river. In looking at its vast stretch, not only over the river between the towers, but also over the inhabited, busy city shore, it appears to have a character of its own far above the drudgeries of the lower business levels.*[1]

The bridge stands as tall and proud today as it did in 1883. The Brooklyn Bridge was designated a National Historic Landmark by the federal government and a National Historic Civil Engineering Landmark by the American Society of Civil Engineers. The bridge, which now accommodates six lanes of automobile traffic, carries approximately 145,000 vehicles per day. After nearly 120 years, the bridge still has the 44th longest main span among the world's suspension bridges.[2] It should be noted that the improvements in steel cable technology perfected during the building of the Brooklyn Bridge were used to improve cable-lift elevators, thus making high-rise buildings possible.

A view of the Brooklyn Bridge today, at dusk. James J. Wood, class of 1879, was responsible for the machinery that produced the cables of the Brooklyn Bridge. In 1973, Polytechnic's alumni magazine would be renamed *Cable,* representing the importance of the bridge, not only to New York City, but also to Polytechnic University. *(Photo: Jeff Greenberg/NYC & Company.)*

Finally, two years later in June 1869, the New York City Council and the Army Corps of Engineers approved Roebling's design. Later that month, the first of many tragedies occurred. While examining locations for a Brooklyn tower site, Roebling's foot was crushed on a pier by an incoming ferry. Roebling later died of tetanus as a result of this injury. Immediately following Roebling's death, his son, Washington, took over as chief engineer of the Brooklyn Bridge.[13]

During construction, fires, explosions, and caisson disease (the "bends," caused by changes in air pressure that affect nitrogen levels in the bloodstream) took the lives of 20 men. As if there was a curse on the family, Washington Roebling became paralyzed in an accident.

Despite his paralysis, Roebling, with assistance from his wife Emily, directed the remaining construction of the bridge from his Brooklyn Heights residence. Emily Roebling studied higher mathematics and bridge engineering and soon made daily visits to the bridge to oversee her husband's staff of engineers and builders. Between 1873 and 1877, work continued on the anchorages, towers, and cables under Roebling's direction. The 276-foot neo-Gothic granite towers, which feature two arched portals, were built to withstand strong winds and provide support for rail lines.[14]

The first elements of the bridge debuted in August 1876, when two anchorages were linked across the East River for the first time by a wire rope. To commemorate this occasion and to demonstrate the integrity of the wire rope, one of the mechanics crossed the East River riding on a boatswain's chair tied to the rope.[15]

Roebling deviated from tradition and introduced the use of steel, which he called "the metal of the future," for the four cables. At the time, steel was being used for construction of the railroads, but it had not yet been used for major structures. Until the Brooklyn Bridge was constructed, iron wire was used for suspension cables. Roebling would defend his use of steel wire in an article published in the *American Railroad Journal*, where he discussed the weaknesses of earlier iron-wire and chain suspension bridges and their vulnerability to destructive oscillation caused by high winds.[16]

While the construction of the bridge was staggered at times, Mayor Low, James S. T. Stranahan, and other members of the committee continually offered their guidance to assure the project would be a success. Stranahan had experience in such endeavors. In 1866, he was the driving force behind the creation of Brooklyn's Prospect Park. Today, a statue of Stranahan looks out over Grand Army Plaza at the park's northern entrance.

MORE THAN 14,400 MILES OF WIRE

In February 1877, work began on spinning the four massive cables at the Manhattan and Brooklyn anchorages. The four steel cables, which can each hold 11,200 tons, connect the anchorages with the Manhattan and Brooklyn towers, where the cables pass over saddles within the towers. Each main cable, which has a diameter of 15 inches, is comprised of 19 strands containing a total of 5,434 steel wires. Once the spinning of the four main cables was completed in October 1878, workers strung wire ropes from the cables down to the bridge floor. More than 14,400 miles of wire were used for the suspension ropes.

Above: An artist's rendering of the celebration of the opening of the Brooklyn Bridge. The view looks toward Fulton Ferry.

Opposite: When the Brooklyn Bridge opened in 1883, its 1,595.5-ft span broke all of the world's records—indeed, it was almost half-again longer than the world's longest bridge at the time. As such, it was the eighth wonder of the world.

After the suspending ropes and deck beams were in place, the diagonal stays were installed.[17]

From one end to the other, the Brooklyn Bridge measures 6,016 feet, including approaches. The long river span passes the tower arches at an elevation of 119 feet, gradually rising to 135 feet above the East River at mid-span to accommodate passage of even the tallest ships. (The 135-foot clearance soon became the standard for bridge construction.)[18]

The Brooklyn Bridge was designed to have a load capacity of 18,700 tons. This included two elevated railroad tracks, which were to connect to elevated railroad systems in New York and Brooklyn, down the center of the bridge. On either side of the tracks, four lanes were designed—two lanes on two outer roadways—for use by carriages and horseback riders. Directly over the tracks, Roebling also provided an elevated promenade for pedestrians and bicyclists. To support the load and to protect the span from high winds and vibrations, deep stiffening trusses were also constructed, which delayed the grand opening.[19]

Construction of the bridge's understructure, the stiffening trusses, and the roadway began in March 1879 and continued for roughly four more years. The 1,595-foot main span would be the longest for any suspension bridge in the world at that time and would be more than 500 feet longer than the bridge Roebling's father, John, constructed, the Cincinnati-Covington Bridge, which was completed in 1867 and remains in service today.[20]

When the Brooklyn Bridge was officially completed, it cost $15.1 million to build, $3.8 million going toward the purchase of land for approaches and the remainder going toward construction. This was more than twice the original estimated cost.[21]

On May 23, 1883, Chester A. Arthur, the president of the United States, and Governor Grover Cleveland of New York officially dedicated the Brooklyn Bridge before more than 14,000 invitees. Many men from the Institute were on hand, including Mayor Low and Stranahan.

INNOVATION AND INVENTION

As Polytechnic's Science Department expanded, so did other areas, including the arts. In 1877, Professors Alonzo Reed and Brainerd Kellogg published *A Work of English Grammar and Composition*, which is still used in classrooms today. Professor Kellogg was described at this time as "an enthusiast for good English whose face would shine as he read some favorite passages so that it lighted up the dull understandings of many pupils until they, too, learned to love the great masterpieces of English literature."[22] Reed and Kellogg would team again in 1882 to coauthor *Graded Lessons in English: An Elementary English Grammar*.

In 2002, 125 years after the first publication of *A Work of English Grammar and Composition*, the *Washington Post* featured a story on a teacher who discovered the book and developed a lesson plan based on its grammatical theory. She eventually introduced the book to other teachers through a national teaching association, and months later, the book was incorporated into lesson plans nationwide.[23]

From textbooks to invention, the Institute reveled in many successes. Three years after the U.S. Centennial Exposition, in 1879, alumnus Robert G. Brown, class of 1868, and then living in France, invented the modern telephone instrument

Above: In 1879, while living in France, alumnus Robert G. Brown, class of 1868, invented the modern telephone instrument commonly referred to as the "French" telephone. Pictured above is Brown (holding one of his inventions) with colleagues.

Below: This photo depicts an early dynamo laboratory classroom at Polytechnic.

commonly referred to as the "French" telephone. This groundbreaking innovation combined the mouthpiece and receiver on one handset. His invention is essentially the same concept that is used in today's modern telephone.

Brown also designed and installed the first central telephone system in Paris and other French cities. In addition to his revolutionary invention, in 1880 Brown broke new ground for the women's movement by hiring the first female telephone operator, a policy which established a tradition of employment in the years and decades that followed.[24]

SOUND PRACTICES

During this time, the Institute became financially solvent. The mortgage and floating debts were retired, and surplus funds were invested each year thereafter for future development.

In 1878, the board recorded:

Extensions of the course of study and elevation of the grades has involved large expenditures for instruction. The policy was adopted and proclaimed 14 years since by the trustees that it was their wish to raise standards of the school as high as it could be carried by the use of learning. The faculty have borne this in mind and from year to year have extended the course as in their judgment the condition of the school

warranted. They now have the satisfaction of feeling that the Polytechnic is giving a more extended and completed course of instruction than is given by any other institution which is self-sustaining in the world.[25]

In the late 1870s, professors and students from the Collegiate Department gather for a class photo behind the Institute's building. Photography was still in its infancy when this photo was taken. Less than one hundred years later, alumnus Leonard Bergstein, class of 1959, invented the original zoom lens and patented several variations on it. This single invention has revolutionized photography and film forever—a zoom lens is now standard on almost every camera made worldwide. Two distinguished leaders from Poly's past are included in this photo: Isaac Frothingham, Poly's first chairman, is the stately looking individual with the white beard sitting in the middle; sitting in the same row on the far right is James How, one of Poly's first two founders. How met with John H. Prentice at Brooklyn Institute the day after the Female Academy burned down to discuss convening a meeting to establish a board of directors to form an academy for boys.

While the Institute prided itself on self-sufficiency, this set the stage for financial hardship. In 1975, President George Bugliarello wrote in an address to the Newcomen Society:

This policy of financing the school exclusively through tuition, and later through research—valid perhaps at the time, for it did provide high value for low expenditure—was to prove near fatal by the 1970s.[26]

The founding fathers and the board of trustees were steadfast in their commitment to provide elevated and advanced scholastics to the young men of Brooklyn.

BROOKLYN EXPANDS

During the 1870s and 1880s, major changes were also taking place in the district surrounding the Institute. First, a new County Court House and a Municipal Building were erected behind the Institute on Joralemon Street facing City Hall. Warehouses and factories began to line the shores

from Bay Ridge to Hunter's Point, and U.S. engineers recommended the extension of the pier line from the Fulton Ferry to the Atlantic Docks.

Building and rebuilding increased with each passing year, and the real estate movement extended from the pier line for the Fulton Ferry to adjacent towns. During this period, the City of Brooklyn introduced gas and electric lighting to businesses and homes. Streetcar lines and elevated railroads provided improved transportation to the fringes of the city and to the towns and villages of Long Island.[27]

In 1880, the Institute proudly celebrated its 25th year and completed the addition of the right-hand wing of the original building, which was needed due to an increase in enrollment.

ATHLETICS AND ORGANIZATIONS

By 1882, approximately 800 boys were enrolled at the Institute. While academics were of paramount concern to the administration and faculty, no effort or encouragement was given to student organizations. The majority of students went home after school and had no interaction with their classmates or teachers except during school hours.[28]

Like most young men, the students craved new experiences, some of which they were forced to discover outside the classroom on their own. This took many forms, including developing relationships with girls at their sister school, Packer Collegiate Institute. But for the most part, the boys were eager to establish team sports.

While Cochran "frowned on athletics of any type" he did not prevent the formation of the football and baseball teams, or playing tennis and lacrosse … all such extracurricular activities being pursued by students. At the beginning of the school year in 1880, there were three organizations: the Poly Baseball Club, the Poly Bicycle Club, and the Fraternity of Sigma Xi.

The first football team was organized in 1879, and there was a team every year except 1887 and 1888 when Cochran stated, "No more football at

Members of the Institute's Athletic Club, circa 1885.

Members of the class of 1887 pose on the front steps of the Institute.

Poly." However, the team would reemerge in subsequent years.[29]

Other activities soon followed. In 1882, the Brooklyn Agassiz Association debuted, a glee club was started, and the Polytechnic Critique Club held its first meeting. In 1884, the Poly orchestra was formed; and in 1885 the Collegiate Debating Society, the Academic Debating Society, the Poly Gun Club, and the Mock Senate were born.[30]

While Cochran frowned on athletics, he supported extracurricular activities that exercised the brain. He put it this way: "Debating was the best means of becoming a good speaker and a good leader."[31]

Perhaps Cochran's educational philosophy regarding oration was best realized in alumnus Seth Low, who in 1885 was elected mayor of Brooklyn. Low was reelected and served a second term before leaving to accept the presidency of Columbia University. Later he became the second mayor of the Greater City of New York.[32]

It may be that Low's accomplishments further fueled the student body to unite and start the first school newspaper, the *Polytechnic*. The brothers of Sigma Xi were credited with its founding. The paper made its debut in 1880 and was a vehicle for school news, literary essays, and what the faculty and administration deemed an aggressive editorial policy. In October 1886, the board faulted the publication for "giving too great liberty of criticism."[33] The paper would not be published again until four years later in 1890.

Despite the growing pains that the student body was experiencing, Poly continued to excel academically. In 1885, scientific courses were divided into engineering and applied chemistry. The following year, bachelor of science degrees in engineering

Henry Rogers Codwise, B.S.

Does married life agree with him? We think not, for he never smiles.

and chemistry were established; and separate courses in electrical engineering began. These strides were due in no small part to the leadership of Cochran, who was praised in the pages of the *Brooklyn Daily Eagle* after a commencement exercise in 1887.

It was an audience worthy of the Institution and worthy of the city of which the Polytechnic is one of its brightest ornaments. A graduating class of 22 received their diplomas from the hand of the honored President, Dr. David H. Cochran who has been identified for so many years with the Polytechnic, and to whom so much of its fame and excellence is due.[34]

In 1887 the students also published the Institute's first yearbook, the *Polywog*. Their goal

In Polytechnic's early days, students needed to work very hard on their demanding lessons and studies, just as they do in current times. But also, Poly students during the nineteenth century still found time to inject a little collegiate humor into their affairs, as evidenced by these humorous profiles of some Poly professors in an early *Polywog*. Shown clockwise, beginning from the upper left-hand corner of page 36, are Henry Rogers Codwise, BS (a member of Poly's 1899 graduating class, who, the students claimed, "never smiles"); John Charles Olsen, AM, PhD (who went on to become professor emeritus at Polytechnic and a founder of the American Institute of Chemical Engineers); Magnus C. Ihlseng, CE, EM, PhD; and Brainerd Kellogg, BA, AM.

was to "embody in permanent form the interesting matter pertaining to our school." The editor, Henry Sherman Loud, wrote in the preface:

Brainard Kellogg, B. A., A. M.

Alliteration is one woe
Organ-grinders thy veritable foe
The best of them but feel thy big toe
And hear thee shout—"Get out,
Thou representative foul, thou clout,
Of a foreign tongue ; or with me bout."
The Salvation lassies better fare
For they are native with golden hair
And to their yearly checks say, " Haben Sie
mehr ? "

John Charles Olsen,, A.M. Ph.D.

What would he be sans laugh, sans teeth, sans everything?

We are aware that other institutions have attempted publications of this nature, and envious college men may accuse us of imitation. But men sang before Homer's age and molded clay pots before Phidias was born; plays were written before Shakespeare was out of swaddling clothes ... We hope that this is sufficient answer to any charge of imitation or plagiarism ... We knew we could produce an annual which should be to other college annuals as our president is to their presidents, as our faculty is to their faculties, and our janitors are to their janitors.[35]

The *Polywog* suffered a fate similar to the *Polytechnic*, and after four years was also suspended, only to be resurrected in 1898.[36]

In March 1886, an editorial was written in the last issue of the *Polytechnic* that expressed the students yearning for a formal college. The article stated in no uncertain terms that there was a need to separate the Collegiate Department from the Academic Department, which was a frowned upon topic to discuss, at least in a public forum.

These, we think, would work a reform in the Polytechnic that would double her power of usefulness and afford many the opportunity to obtain a college education and live at home. The city certainly needs a college, and there is no organization that could at present supply this need so fully and completely as the Polytechnic.[37]

INDEPENDENCE

After maintaining itself in the course of instruction in greater length than any other private

Magnus C. Ihlseng, C.E., E.M., Ph.D.

What Dr. Munyon would have looked like had he been an Engineer.

self-sustaining school in the nation, in 1890 Polytechnic would officially separate into two schools after the commencement.

Aside from the desire for a college, the logistics of operating both schools under one roof had become difficult. The reputation of the school raised enrollment numbers; the addition of scientific equipment led to further space restrictions, and it became apparent that the advanced courses could no longer be adequately accommodated.[38]

THE CORPORATION

Another occurrence that led to the separation was the death of several board members. These trustees were replaced by men who held more progressive views, among them William Augustus White, class of 1859, who later became secretary, and Henry Sanger Snow who received his bachelor of arts degree in 1878, and went on to be elected treasurer and later, president.

The decision to divide the schools was troubling to some, but debates resulted in a balanced approach, and it was determined that the original stockholders should surrender the charter of the academy and form a "corporation" in its place. This new corporation, officially called "The Corporation," would have equal power to the original charter, particularly with respect to the acquisition of property.[39]

The trustees, who included five original members, Charles S. Baylis, Isaac H. Frothingham, Josiah O. Low, John T. Martin, and James S. T. Stranahan, contemplated "that the new corporation should afford scope for growth and devel-

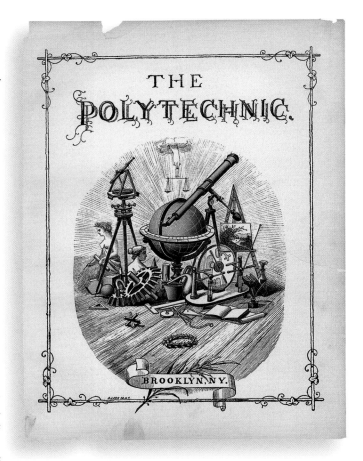

Above: Pictured here is the cover of the Institute's publication, the *Polytechnic*, circa 1888.

Left: The Poly Gun Club was one of many extracurricular clubs supported and established at the Institute before the turn of the century and into the 1900s.

THE POLY GUN CLUB.

opment; should gain the power and the right to acquire and receive property by purchase, gift, or will; and should conduct as formerly the Academic Department which had always been an important part of their work."[40]

However, the transition wasn't as smooth as expected. There was a widespread feeling that the Institute's entire reputation rested on the Preparatory school's achievements and that the original idea of the founders was being displaced, or as one historian reflected, "that in doing this the trustees had sold their birthright for a mess of pottage."[41]

This feeling was the least of the Institute's problems. The trustees did not realize that New York State would be incapable of granting a charter for the new Collegiate Department in due time. In order to provide for the dissolution of the old stock academies, an act of legislation would be required. After months of uncertainty, the two schools were officially divided, and the newly renamed Polytechnic Institute of Brooklyn was born.

The new Institute received a provisional charter of incorporation on August 8, 1889. After fulfilling the required recruitment of 21 trustees, of which seven would be a quorum, the formal charter was delivered on January 30, 1890. With this charter, the Institute would forever be changed, not only in name, but in academic direction.[42]

NEW NAMES, NEW SCHOOLS, AND A NEW DIRECTION

The division excited many because a new college was born in the streets of Brooklyn, but the announcement was made without great fanfare. The June 1890 catalog simply announced that the Institute was now comprised of two departments: the Institute and the Academic Department. These were "in all respects, separate and distinct from each other," and their work was to be conducted in separate buildings.[43] To students and residents, two new names emerged: "the Institute" for the Collegiate Department; and "the Poly" for the Academic Department.

Now the Institute needed a new building, so the college began to attempt to raise funds. Colonel Charles F. Crocker responded to this call. Crocker attended the Institute from 1873 to 1875 but left because of poor health. In Crocker's estimation, the Institute would become an outstanding scientific institution. He therefore donated $10,000. Crocker went on to become president of the Southern Pacific Railroad. Also, he became one of the legendary players during the historic rivalry between the Central Pacific Railroad and the Union Pacific Railroad.

Crocker's generous gift was followed by another when Captain Elihu Spicer presented the Institute with $20,000 for the establishment of a reference library in the memory of his son, Uriah D. Spicer, who received a bachelor of arts in 1873.

With these funds and others, a neighboring plot of land, which had been home to a church for decades, was purchased, and construction quickly commenced at 85 Livingston Street.[44]

During the first year of separation, the two schools operated in tandem, as usual. However, there was confusion because of changing course descriptions, and departments. In time, these lines would become clearly defined, but this would take almost 10 years.

The conditions for admission to the Institute corresponded in general with those of the freshman classes of the leading schools of arts and sciences.

Dr. Samuel Sheldon was appointed a professor of physics and electrical engineering at Polytechnic in 1889. One of the very first researchers to experiment with X-rays, Sheldon is reported to have employed this nascent technology to take a photo of a student's foot through his shoe around the same time (1895) that Wilhelm Röntgen is credited with discovering X-rays. Polytechnic eventually became distinguished throughout the world for its leading work in X-rays.

Samuel Sheldon A. M., Ph. D.

IN the order of appointment, the name of Dr. Sheldon stands thirteenth on the books of the Faculty. He was constituted Professor of Physics and Electrical Engineering at the Polytechnic Institute in 1889.

Born in Middlebury, Vermont, he graduated at the college which takes its name from the town, in the Spring of '83. He remained at Middlebury as instructor in Mathematics two years longer. While at that institution he must have come under the benign influence of Prof. Kellogg, who, it will be remembered, is the guardian angel of the place. Whether this influence had any share in inducing him to continue his studies thereafter in Germany, it is impossible to tell. It is certain that he crossed the Atlantic.

At Würzburg University, Professor Sheldon was Assistant in Physics to Kohlrausch throughout 1886 and 1887. Here he became engaged in experiments and investigations of extreme delicacy. Upon departing from Würzburg he received the degree Ph. D. from that university, just as he had been given A. M. by Middlebury when leaving that college in '86. Returning, Dr. Sheldon came as far as the channel on the railroad. He came through England on a bicycle. Arriving home, he recounted the principal events of the tour at the family centennial in Vermont. Meanwhile, however, he had been called to the Assistant-Professorship in Physics at Harvard, where he remained his customary period of two years. At the conclusion of these he was to be found at this college.

In his career the professor has accumulated a number of honors. He is a member of the American Institute of Electrical Engineers, and a fellow of the American Association for the Advancement of Science. He advances science five hours every day at the Polytechnic. Since he has been in this city he has become President of the Department of Physics, Brooklyn Institute.

If there is any department of labor which is especially hard to pursue, it is original investigation. Men consider it tolerably easy to be conventional. Therefore, it is his original work that has done more to distinguish Dr. Sheldon than all his other accomplishments combined. It does more than a fine ear for music. Among his writings revealing that which is new, we find the Neutralization of Induction, a contribution of which, however, he was only author in part. There are, furthermore, treatises upon Electrical Waves, Magneto-Optical Generation of Electricity, and upon Storage of Electricity. These have appeared at intervals in the Popular Science Monthly, the American Journal of Science, and other publications.

Dr. Sheldon has endeared himself to the rising generation. He has reached their hearts through the Youth's Companion. From the number of letters he has received, coming from within a territory that extends from Maine to Georgia, it is impossible to say how many deaths he may have occasioned among the young of the land, inciting them to construct, at their peril, ingenious dynamos and motors.

It may be thought that Dr. Sheldon, whose articles have extracted comment from English, German, and Italian journals, has always walked in the clouds with the goddess Science. To correct this error it is sufficient to state that, when graduating from Middlebury, he delivered an oration on the Substantiality of the Soul.

As the Institute appeared at the turn of the century.

The Poly became more focused on preparing students for admission to the Institute or other colleges.

DIVIDED WE STAND

The Institute's new building was completed in 1892. The architect, William B. Tubby, a former Poly student, crafted the building in a Romanesque style that was distinctly different from the original building, which now housed the Academic Department, or the Poly. This marked the first time the two schools were physically separated.[45]

The Institute quickly experienced money problems, which arose in large part because of the construction costs of the new building. The total cost of the project was approximately $300,000. To help balance the debt, annual tuition was raised from $100 to $180 for the Poly, and a flat fee of $200 for the Institute.[46]

William Augustus White, president of the board of trustees, addressed the faculty at the 21st Polytechnic Alumni Dinner on February 4, 1893. His speech summarized the division of the school, what it meant then, and what it would mean for the future:

Two years ago, you remember, this institution received a charter from the board of regents and is now a college. The cost of this wing of this building has been nearly $300,000. One half of that still on mortgage. At the present time it has a larger attendance than ever before. The receipts have increased to $120,000, but the increases in expenses reach nearly that figure. We hope some of these days to be entirely out of debt.[47]

Under the new charter, the Institute could receive gifts and bequests, while before it was required to turn down any endowments. With new rules came new gifts. The first came in the form of a scholarship, which was established in 1892 in memory of Henry Ginnel DeWitt, class of 1884. The following year the first bequests were received in the form of a parcel of land valued at approximately $10,000 from Samuel B. Duryea, a former Poly student. These were the first of many endowments that the Institute would receive. However, due to the charter, and the formation of The Corporation, the Poly was not entitled to any of these monies. This was not easily accepted by many faculty and administration members, considering the Poly had over five times the enrollment of the Institute.[48]

However, one benefit the Poly enjoyed was the use of the new gymnasium, which was in the new building that housed the Institute. In the following years, a pool, the largest in the city, would be constructed. The gym and the resulting athletic teams were the result of hard work and perseverance of students who wanted nothing more than a suitable building to conduct their athletic activities.[49]

This period put a strain on both departments, the faculty, and the administration, which was recounted in *The Story of Poly*, written by Miles Merwin Kastendieck, a Poly alumnus.

It was only natural, then, that during the same time period the school, its men, and its boys became self-conscious. Gradually and inevitably the two departments grew more and more apart. In aim, in scope, in outlook, they were fundamentally different.[50]

While this transition was taking place, the Institute had reasons to celebrate. In 1892, the board of regents authorized the conferral of degrees in civil engineering and electrical engineering, each of which required one year of postgraduate study. The same year, William A. White was named chairman of The Corporation.

During the next few years the division between the Institute and the Poly grew deeper. In 1894, the Poly Prep Athletic Association was formed, which was a clear signal that the boys of the Poly no longer wanted to associate with the men of the Institute. The first Poly football and baseball teams were also established that year. Other divisions between the two schools were equally apparent, such as the Poly Prep Debating Society, which was established in 1894.

Also in 1894, Cochran had a change of heart about athletics. A story passed through the generations describes "Old Davy" attending a baseball game in 1895 and handing the team's manager a five dollar bill in support as long as he promised not to tell "on penalty of death."[51]

While the Poly strove to become more independent, it was running out of room in the original building. One recollection of this period described the school as a "somewhat dark and dingy affair well filled and comparatively noisy with almost seven hundred boys moving about daily."[52]

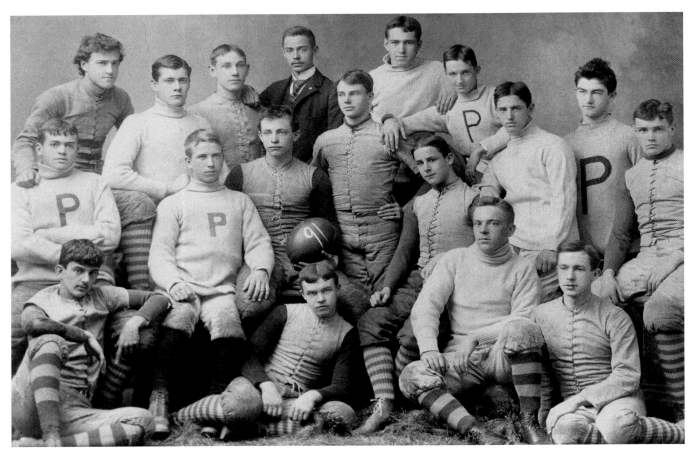

The Institute's 1891 football team.

On September 17, 1896, students of both the Institute and the Poly received devastating news: Dr. Edward C. Seymour had died. During his tenure he was estimated to have taught over 10,000 students many of whom regarded him a "true and loyal friend." Seymour was a general educator, teaching everything from mathematics to philosophy. In addition, he was an accomplished administrator. It was said that Dr. Seymour went about his work "with an unaffected simplicity and a resolute fearlessness that did inestimable good for the school." He received similar praise from his peers and faculty and the steadfast support of Dr. Cochran. Indeed, it was Dr. Seymour's early support that led to "Old Davy's" presidency.[53]

The day following his death, Dr. Cochran eulogized his friend and colleague in the pages of the *Brooklyn Daily Eagle*:

He was in large measure the cause of my connection to the Institute. I had twice declined an invitation to the school. Dr. Seymour visited me, represented what we might do, was so enthusiastic that I became fired and cast in my lot with him to see what we could accomplish ... I wish to say here that to no man does the Polytechnic owe more than to him. Teachers and students alike testify to the nobility and ability of the man. They love and respect the man whose purity of life has exemplified the purity of his teaching.[54]

Dr. Seymour was revered, and he approached every situation with "love and esteem." He was described as "a man with a boy's heart, sympathetic, loyal, and fair."[55] In his opinion, a teacher's ideal was threefold: "to inform the intellect, to develop the man, and to shape the soul of the boy so as to fit him for time and eternity."[56]

After his funeral, which was attended by thousands of students, faculty, parents, and residents, a plaque was erected in his memory and was placed on the right-hand wall of the entrance to the Poly, so all could remember his contributions.[57]

AN END OF AN ERA

Since the construction of the Brooklyn Bridge, New York City and Brooklyn became in many ways one city. However, it wasn't until 1898 that Brooklyn officially became a part of New York City. This was considered a huge development for not only Brooklynites, but for both the Institute and the Poly whose enrollment continued to rise after the marriage of the two cities.

Soon after Seymour's passing, Cochran's reign came to an end. In June of 1899 he submitted his resignation. His presence at the Institute and the Poly brought fame and recognition to the school. Cochran, known for his baronial sway, vision, academic prowess, and dictatorial procedures, was honored that same year as former students, and residents, presented him with a gold and silver loving cup and a $10,000 check.[58]

His resignation was a surprise to some. The *Brooklyn Daily Eagle* had been his consistent supporter. Its editorial team composed the following article after news broke of his departure.

The resignation of the Doctor is more than a Polytechnic event. It is of interest and of importance to the entire domain of higher education.

He has stayed in Brooklyn, stood by Brooklyn, wrought for Brooklyn, and made the influence of Brooklyn greater than it was, because of the success of the Brooklyn Polytechnic under his charge, and of the fame and of the force of that success, as an effect throughout the whole province of learning in the land.[59]

The next president, who had large shoes to fill, was Henry Sanger Snow. He performed as an interim president. During the previous academic year, Snow had become chairman of the board of trustees. From day one, President Snow was on a deliberate mission to make the Institute a full-fledged engineering college. While this caused an even further divide between the two schools, Snow pressed on. But he overextended the Institute and only held the office for five years. When he resigned, he left a debt of roughly $400,000.[60]

The Academy saw that this was a serious blunder. That same year the Collegiate Department asserted itself as it had done in 1889, when it took the initial steps to separate itself.

Although President Snow left the school in financial quicksand, he did push it to establish mechanical engineering courses, which further solidified the Institute as an engineering college that also featured strong programs in liberal arts and chemistry. The school had a well-rounded curriculum and was poised to play a prominent role educating Brooklynites and New Yorkers, along with students from other locales, in the years to come.

The Institute had separate libraries for each department. The Spicer Library, pictured here in 1918, was the Institute's main library.

CHAPTER THREE

PROGRESSIVE STEPS IN ENGINEERING

1900 – 1930

It is believed that a school of technology should be in or near a great city, where its students may study the actual processes of chemical manufacture, of electrical and chemical construction, of engineering, architecture and the fine arts—in the theory of which they are being instructed.

—*Brooklyn Daily Eagle*, May 2, 1902

WITH A NEW CENTURY UN-folding, the Institute, entering its 46th year, was in the process of change. This was due, in part, to a continued desire to separate the Academic Department from the Collegiate Department. Under the guidance of President Snow, the Institute developed a far-reaching educational program with more dedication to scientific courses, while continuing a solid liberal arts program. Under Snow's presidency, the curriculum was revised so as to place the course instruction "on par with those of any technical school in the country and the plans and equipment were modernized and improved," the trustees noted.[1]

The liberal arts course included language, literature, history, and philosophy, leading to a bachelor of arts degree; the electrical course included theoretical and applied electrical science, laboratory work, electrical measurements, and testing, leading to a degree in electrical engineering; the civil engineering course included mathematics, engineering, physics, mechanics, and field work, leading to a degree in civil engineering; the mechanical engineering course included mathematics, physics, mechanics, shop work, and machine design, leading to a degree in mechanical engineering; and the chemical course, which included physics, mathematics, chemical analysis, assaying, industrial, and commercial chemistry, leading to a bachelor of science degree.[2]

The expanded academic offerings were among expenditures that President Snow approved "in carrying out the objects of the school."[3] These advancements in technical education were shared not only by the Institute but by the community, which was covered in the *Brooklyn Daily Eagle*.

It is believed that a school of technology should be in or near a great city, where its students may study the actual processes of chemical manufacture, of electrical and chemical construction, of engineering, architecture and the fine arts—in the theory of which they are being instructed.[4]

In October of 1900, President Snow addressed The Corporation in his annual report, explaining the need for future growth.

Very substantial repairs and improvements were made, in the beginning of the year, upon the academic building. It has been felt that the requirements

Henry Sanger Snow was named acting president after Cochran retired, a position he would hold for nearly five years. Snow is credited with changing the school's charter and name to Polytechnic Institute of Brooklyn, and instituting alumni funding.

of the school for instruction in science should be substantially enlarged. Well appointed laboratories in physics and chemistry have, therefore, been installed.[5]

One of Snow's first actions was to appoint Professor Brainerd Kellogg, professor of English, as dean of the Institute. He was responsible for all administrative tasks.[6]

It was under President Snow's guidance that the Institute further developed its reputation as a technological college. At the same time technology was advancing across the nation and around the world, especially with new applications of steel and power. In the first four years of the century, for example, Guglielmo Marconi sent the first wireless transmission across the Atlantic; two automobiles made the first transcontinental trip; the Model T Ford was developed; and Orville Wright made the first successful flight in a mechanically powered aircraft.

ALUMNI MAKING THEIR MARK

Alumni were also making great strides. In 1900, Charles R. Flint, class of 1868, made his mark in the business and finance world, and was responsible for the United States Rubber Company (now Uniroyal) and what is now IBM.[7] He was also instrumental in

By the early 1920s, the Chemistry Department had physically expanded due to an increase in enrollment. In this photo, approximately 30 students are conducting various experiments in a recently improved chemistry laboratory.

the development of the American Woolen Company. He was an exporter, ship owner, arms dealer, and overall financial speculator. He served as secretary to the U.S. minister to Peru, consultant to the czar of Russia, and as New York consul for Chile. In 1907, he flew with the Wright brothers to discuss buying their flying machine.[8]

Flint was also the progenitor, through his unscrupulous business practices, of the Sherman Anti-Trust Act. Indeed, he was considered a primary nemesis of the U.S. labor movement in the early twentieth century. Flint deeply hated labor unions, as evidenced by this statement he made while defending trusts before an audience comprised almost exclusively of Boston bankers.

If the people employed in one factory are not satisfied with the terms fixed by the employers and strike, the trust can close that factory and let the employees starve while work goes on in other factories without loss to the manufacturer.[9]

Another Polytechnic alumnus who was making notable strides in life around this time was Spencer Trask, a legendary venture capitalist and financial investor who was active during the late nineteenth century and at the turn of the twentieth century.

Trask provided financial services to numerous entrepreneurs and companies that have helped shape history—dating back to 1879 when he financed Thomas Edison's discovery of the light bulb. Other milestones include financing the start-up of General Electric.

Trask was the banker and broker who on August 13, 1896, bought the *New York Times* for $75,000 on behalf of Adolf S. Ochs, owner of the *Chattanooga Times*. Ochs helped turn the *New York Times* into one of the world's great newspapers.

Trask was one of Polytechnic's earliest student graduates and alums. In 1857, he received a certificate of honor, with a first degree, from Polytechnic's Academic Department. (He went on from there to graduate from Princeton.) Later, he was active in Polytechnic's alumni association. It has been speculated that Dr. Cochran's steering of Polytechnic's curriculum toward scientific and technical subjects may have influenced Trask regarding his forward-thinking venture capital support for technology, including Thomas Edison's earth-shaking scientific pursuits. Thus, Polytechnic can be considered among the progenitors of high-tech venture capital in the United States during the advent of the Industrial Age.

The Institute's long research relationship with the nation's military forces began with Edward R. Knowles, class of 1870, who went on to develop searchlights for the navy. Knowles later designed the heat, light, and power installations for many New York City buildings.[10] Henry C. Goldmark, class of 1874, was a pioneer in the use of steel in bridge construction and went on to design the lock machinery on the Panama Canal.[11]

The Institute matched the growing enthusiasm for discovery, and in 1901, the New York State Board of Regents approved graduate programs leading to master of science and master of arts degrees.[12] Later that year, Magnus C. Ihlseng was named first professor of mechanical engineering, an area of study that would grow and flourish in the years that followed, ultimately becoming a defining aspect of the Institute. The Institute benefited from Professor Ihlseng's dynamic energy and inspiring intellect.

DIVERGENCE OF MISSIONS

The two arms of the School grew further apart with each passing year. It was felt among students and faculty of the Institute that a proper collegiate education could not be achieved by focusing on the boys of the Preparatory. Therefore, the "Institute assumed a more collegiate atmosphere as the preparatory-school procedures were concentrated in the old building and a more mature approach was possible in handling the college."[13]

In 1901, the alumni of the Preparatory school formed their own organization because the boys felt outnumbered and outclassed by the interests of the older men who made up the majority of the association.[14] Thus, the Brooklyn Polytechnic Alumni Association was reorganized.[15]

POLY'S ROLE IN BROOKLYN'S SOCIETY

While academics were continually improved and expanded, it was the diligent persistence of the students of the 19th century who paved the way for not only a growing athletic arm of the Institute, but for a gymnasium that doubled as a social center for

For years the Institute didn't have adequate athletic facilities, but the addition of the gymnasium (pictured in 1920), which was located in the basement of the main building, changed that. It was used by students and faculty for education and sporting events.

Brooklyn's elite, regardless of age. On one such occasion, the *Brooklyn Daily Eagle* recounted:

> *What gave the Polytechnic Ball of last night its distinction and its interest was readily to be seen. It is difficult to recount a dance of any size, within the last decade that has brought together a more complete representation of society of this borough. From each and every set, from uptown to downtown, from the Park Slope, the Eastern District and Flatbush, there were people of prominence. Nor was it a dance of extreme youth only. A feature of the [event] was the appearance of many from the older set. These gave the evening added distinction.[16]*

Athletics, perhaps to the dismay of past presidents like Cochran, were becoming more of a focal point. In 1902, the Institute's football team traveled to Chicago to compete against Hyde Park High School. While the score was not recorded, this trip demonstrated that the students were not only exercising their minds, but their bodies as well.[17]

The reputation of both divisions of the school was excellent during this time period, and as the

ALFRED P. SLOAN JR.

ALFRED P. SLOAN JR. WAS BORN IN NEW Haven, Connecticut, on May 23, 1875. In 1885, the family moved to Brooklyn. Alfred Jr. excelled as a student, both in public schools and at Brooklyn Polytechnic Institute, where he completed the college-preparatory course. After some delay in being admitted to the Massachusetts Institute of Technology (which considered him too young when he first applied), he matriculated in 1892 and earned a degree in electrical engineering in three years, becoming the youngest member of his graduating class.[1]

He began his career working as a draftsman at a small machine shop, the Hyatt Roller Bearing Company, of Newark, New Jersey. At his urging, Hyatt was soon producing new antifriction bearings for automobiles. At the age of 24, he became president of Hyatt, where he supervised all aspects of the company's business. Hyatt bearings became a standard in the auto-

mobile industry, and the company grew rapidly under Sloan's leadership. In 1916, the Hyatt Roller Bearing Company, together with a number of other manufacturers of automobile accessories, merged with the United Motors Corporation, and Sloan became president of the new entity. Two years later, that company became part of the General Motors Corporation, and Sloan was named vice president in charge of accessories and a member of the executive committee.[2]

He was elected president of General Motors in 1923, succeeding Pierre S. du Pont, who said of him on one occasion:

The greater part of the successful development of the corporation's operations and the building of a strong manufacturing and sales organization is due to Mr. Sloan. His election to the presidency is a natural and well-merited recognition

---

Institute expanded and grew, so did the Preparatory school. During this period a biweekly publication, *Poly Prep*, was established.[18]

In the spirit of school pride, two anthems were composed, which were often sung in unison by students at athletic outings and official ceremonies. The popular tune "The Blue and The Gray" celebrated not only the history of the nation, but also the importance of the school within the fabric of society.

Sing, comrades, sing, in praise of Poly's glory.
Sing of the victories that crown
The Blue and Gray.
Sing of the little toils and of the battles gory
That mould the man to face the fuller day.
Play, comrades, play, defending Poly's honor,
Toiling with the brain and
Brawn in contest on the field;
Play so that brightest wreaths of
Victory may crown her,
For the Blue and Gray
You wear mean "never yield."[19]

POLY ALUMNUS ELECTED MAYOR, AGAIN

Perhaps the true spirit of "The Blue and The Gray" was realized On November 26, 1901, when alumnus Seth Low was elected the second mayor of the Greater City of New York, which was established in 1898. At the turn of the century, the estimated population of the new city was 800,000. The city was rife with political divergence, and citizens desperately sought a third party candidate.[20]

Low stepped down as president of Columbia University to pursue the city's highest office. He was the first mayor to be elected on a fusion ticket with the backing of both the Republican and Citizens Union parties.[21]

Famed author and humorist Mark Twain was a devoted supporter of Low. During a campaign rally in lower Manhattan, Twain spoke on behalf of the future mayor:

In this campaign there is nothing very much simpler than to decide if we are to vote for the

of his untiring and able efforts and successful achievement. Mr. Sloan had developed by then his system of disciplined, professional management that provided for decentralized operations with coordinated centralized policy control. Applying it to General Motors, he set the corporation on its course of industrial leadership. The next 23 years, with Mr. Sloan as chief executive officer, were years of enormous expansion for the Corporation and of a steady increase in its share of the automobile market.[3]

In 1937, Sloan was elected chairman of the board of General Motors. He continued as chief executive officer until 1946. When he resigned from the chairmanship in 1956, the General Motors board said of him:

The Board of Directors has acceded to Mr. Sloan's wish to retire as chairman. He has served the corporation long and magnificently. His analysis and grasp of the problems of corporate management laid the solid foundation which has made possible the growth and progress of General Motors over the years.[4]

Sloan was then named honorary chairman of the board, a title he retained until his death on February 17, 1966. For many years he had devoted the largest share of his time and energy to philanthropic activities, both as a private donor to many causes and organizations and through the Alfred P. Sloan Foundation, which he established in 1934.[5]

A realist as well as a humanist and philanthropist, Sloan looked upon the foundation as an extension of his own life and work. Although he recognized the inevitability of change that might dictate a different course, he expected the foundation would "continue as an operating facility indefinitely into the future ... to represent my accomplishments in this life." His accomplishments during his lifetime were of the highest order, and in themselves provide the most dramatic and lasting tribute to his extraordinary talent. Through the foundation, his accomplishments have been extended and expanded.[6]

continuance of Crokerism and Tammany rule or whether we shall not. I think we have had enough of a system of American royalty residing in Europe. What we need is a doctor to handle the feeling within. I think I can introduce you to a very good doctor, too—Seth Low.[22]

Upon taking the oath of office, Low delivered a brief speech vowing to "consecrate myself to the welfare of the people."[23] In stark contrast to his predecessor, Robert A. Van Wyck (the man for whom the Van Wyck Expressway in the New York City area was named) Low's administration was perceived by the public as honest and competent.

Among his accomplishments while in office, Low is credited with introducing civil service and a merit system for hiring city employees, lowering taxes while streamlining government services, improving the public school system, and greatly reducing graft in the police department.[24]

In the 1880s, while mayor of Brooklyn, Seth Low was on the committee for the Brooklyn Bridge.

Less than twenty years later, Low would again invest his time and influence in connecting the boroughs by further developing the city's transit system.

To this end, Mayor Low hired noted bridge engineer Gustav Lindenthal to serve as commissioner of the Department of Bridges. Lindenthal developed and later proposed a number of bridges, including the Williamsburg Bridge, which was under construction when Low took office, and the Manhattan Bridge.[25]

WILLIAMSBURG BRIDGE OPENS

On December 19, 1903, the Williamsburg Bridge officially opened. It took seven years, $15 million, and 31 lives to create. According to historical records, Mayor Low stood at the entranceway to the Manhattan side of the bridge, and Edward Swanstrom, president of the borough of Brooklyn, stood at the opposite end. "At 2:30 P.M. the two men walked onto the bridge and a few minutes later, just east of the exact center, shook hands. It was a gesture which represented the manifestation of a dream termed, as Greg Ayres described it in his book, *An XXXcellent Bridge,* "The Greater New York Area—the greatest city in the world."[26]

Low would also be responsible for the Manhattan Bridge, which was started in early 1902. The bridge was completed in 1909 at a cost of $31 million.[27] While Low was defeated as mayor in 1903, he remained active in politics and labor issues. He died on September 17, 1916, at his upstate New York home. Among his honorary pallbearers were J. P. Morgan and Samuel Gompers.[28]

A REMARKABLE INVENTOR

As the Institute marveled at having an alumnus in the highest office in New York City, a fellow graduate, James J. Wood, class of 1879, was achieving greatness. In 1902, Wood received the patent for the first electric fan. This would be one of 240 patents held by Wood through the course of his life. Wood was responsible for the machinery that put up the cables of the Brooklyn Bridge, and he installed the first floodlight system at the Statue of Liberty in New York Harbor in 1885. Wood's accomplishments were far-reaching. He was also one of the first to recognize the business potential of the household refrigerator. His company, Fort Wayne, played a major role in the creation of General Electric's refrigerator business, a development whose success he was able to foresee before his death in 1928.[29]

The Institute, while known for scientific achievements, also produced a number of world-class artists. In 1903, Guy C. Wiggins, class of 1899, a renowned American impressionist painter and member of the historic Lyme Art Colony in Connecticut, became the youngest artist ever to have a painting accepted in Metropolitan Museum of Art's permanent collection. Today, Wiggins' paintings sell for more than $100,000 at auctions.[30] Fellow alumnus Wilford Conrow was also recognized as a great early twentieth-century American artist. Among his notable paintings is *The Viaduct, Marel,* completed in 1914.

While students of the Institute were serious and focused on their studies, they also enjoyed socializing. In this picture, students enjoy the 1916 Junior Promenade dance.

PRESIDENTIAL PLIGHT

The Brooklyn and Williamsburg Bridges supported the growth of New York City, and as changes occurred across the metropolis, the Institute, too, was in the process of a metamorphosis.

The year 1903 marked the first game in a long-standing rivalry between the Institute's basketball team and that of neighboring Pratt Institute. However, a far more serious division existed between President Snow and members of the Alumni Association. Snow's unwavering dedication to making the Institute solely an engineering school ruffled some feathers, especially those associated with the Preparatory Department. The political climate of the time forced his hand, and in 1904 Snow resigned "because of the exacting requirements of his outside interests."[31] His resignation was accepted with "regret from The Corporation." During his five-year presidency, Preparatory enrollment dipped, while the Collegiate Department gained students. The average deficit during President Snow's tenure was $20,000 per year, which was caused mainly by "expenditures which were necessary to place both the Preparatory school and the Institute on a footing to enable it to compete with other schools of the same class."[32]

While Snow was lauded by some colleagues for pushing the Institute toward higher educational standards and practices, his initiatives could not be supported by the Institute's coffers, and upon his resignation the Institute was in debt $400,000. This problem of outstanding debt had plagued the Institute since its inception and would continue throughout the rest of the century.

President Frederick Washington Atkinson succeeded Henry Snow in 1904. President Atkinson was a highly decorated educator before coming to the Institute, and his success continued throughout his tenure. Perhaps his best contribution to the Institute was establishing night school courses.

In the spirit of assiduousness, Professor William Henry Nichols, founder of the Nichols Chemical Company, was named chairman of The Corporation in 1904, while the search commenced for a new president.

Nichols would continue with the task of making the Institute a leading college, but he also made certain that the Preparatory Department was progressing. "He looked with special ... interest on the Preparatory school and gave a great deal of encouragement to its expanding student activity," a historian noted.[33] Later that year, the Institute tapped Professor Frederick Washington Atkinson to be the third president of the Institute, a position he would hold for nearly 20 years.[34]

However, President Atkinson initially had mixed feelings concerning the appointment. At the time, The Corporation believed that "a man of proven merit and outstanding ability ... should be chosen." The Alumni Association, however, "strongly urged that a technical man not be chosen but that the president selected be a man of liberal training and of tried administrative ability."[35]

President Atkinson, who was one of a few nominees, had returned the year before from the Philippines, where as general superintendent of education, he organized the school system following the Spanish American War.[36]

Atkinson, who knew of the Institute's financial troubles, accepted the job for a period of three years on the condition that the elimination of the annual deficit of $40,000 be guaranteed and that an endowment of $2 million be raised in that period. The Alumni Association was asked to guarantee a portion of the deficit and upon their agreement to underwrite one-quarter, The Corporation guaranteed the remaining three-quarters. With his terms and conditions met, Professor Atkinson took the helm in the fall of 1904.[37]

During this period, business and industry were booming. To keep things moving ahead, businesses required highly educated men and women to fill new positions that were being created every passing

POLY'S FAMOUS ARTIST

ALUMNUS CHARLES ROBERT KNIGHT IS internationally recognized as the preeminent artist of both prehistoric animals and contemporary wildlife, through his paintings, drawings and sculpture.

At the age of six, the Brooklyn-born artist was struck in the eye by a stone thrown by a playmate. The corneal damage left Knight visually impaired. While attending Polytechnic, at age 10, Knight was encouraged by Professor Constantine Hertzberg to complete his first drawing, *The Family Dog*. Knight later credited Professor Hertzberg with launching his career as an artist.

By 13, Knight graduated from Poly's Preparatory Department and began studying at the Metropolitan Art School, which at the time was located in the basement of the Metropolitan Museum of Art. As a result of his accident, Knight wore thick glasses all of his life, and was forced to paint with his face inches from the canvas; however, this only increased his desire to create groundbreaking art.

As Knight grew older, his artistic abilities landed him many high-profile jobs as a muralist for leading museums. During this time, he also became friendly with many notables of the early twentieth century including Arthur Conan Doyle, Charles Darwin, Rudyard Kipling, and J. P. Morgan, Knight's greatest patron. He also became a close friend of paleontologist Henry Fairfield Osborn.

A MAJOR INFLUENCE ON OTHERS

Knight's influence on the world of art and science is far-reaching. Filmmaker Steven Spielberg, animator Ray Harryhausen, and author Ray Bradbury are among many artists who cite Knight as a major influence on their respective careers. Knight's *Bushman, the Male Gorilla*, a pencil drawing completed in 1944, inspired Willis O'Brien's classic RKO film, *King Kong*. Knight also sculpted Princeton University's Palmer Square tiger.[1]

His technical approach to art was lauded by scientists, particularly paleontologists who created countless fossil exhibitions based on his paintings. Stephen Jay Gould, famed evolutionary biologist and former Harvard professor, paid

Left: Charles Robert Knight did this pencil drawing of himself as a young man. His drawings of prehistoric animals influenced movie portrayals of dinosaurs and other prehistoric beasts. Knight's work was highly regarded both for its artistic skill and scientific accuracy. It remains treasured to this day by scientists and paleoartists. *(Image copyright Rhoda Knight Kalt.)*

Opposite: Though classified as visually impaired as a boy, Knight went on to become one of the most celebrated artists depicting animals, both current and prehistoric. His paintings and drawings have become major influences on artists around the world. *(Image copyright Rhoda Knight Kalt.)*

tribute to Knight in his book, *Wonderful Life*, published in 1989:

> Not since the Lord himself showed his stuff to Ezekiel in the valley of dry bones had anyone shown such grace and skill in the reconstruction of animals from disarticulated skeletons. Charles R. Knight, the most celebrated of artists in the reanimation of fossils, painted all the canonical figures of dinosaurs that fire our fear and imagination to this day.[2]

Besides his many murals, paintings, and drawings, Knight was also an accomplished author. He published his first book in 1935, *Before the Dawn of History*, for which he wrote the text as well as provided the illustrations. He went on to publish articles in *National Geographic*. In 1946, he published his second book, *Life through the Ages*, again handling the text and illustrations. The following year, his third book, *Animal Drawing: Anatomy and Action for Artists*, was released to critical acclaim. His final book, *Prehistoric Man: The Great Adventure*, was published in 1949.

Knight's granddaughter, Rhoda Knight Kalt, who travels the world lecturing on behalf of her grandfather's art and influence, recalled in a recent interview that her grandfather would often talk fondly of his days at Polytechnic as the two would visit one of their favorite New York City treasures, the Bronx Zoo. It was during these countless field trips that Knight would explain his artistic process to Rhoda. "'To do the prehistoric creatures,'" he would always say, "'you have to study the anatomy of living creatures,'" said Rhoda. Knight's philosophy and approach to mastering his art form found him studying in taxidermy studios, in New England by the ocean, in California's Rancho La Brea "Tar Pits," and in Palm Beach, Florida.[3]

In 1951, Knight painted his final mural for Everhart Museum in Scranton, Pennsylvania. He died April 15, 1953, at the age of 79 in his favorite city, New York. While Knight died over fifty years ago, his spirit lives on in his paintings, many of which are featured in the American Museum of Natural History, the Field Museum of Natural History, and the Natural History Museum of Los Angeles County.[4]

day. However, money was an obstacle for many, so the Institute catered to the working class in 1904 by becoming one of the first colleges in the nation to inaugurate an evening program paralleling its daytime courses of study.[38]

The Institute's faculty was augmented as a result of the new program, and new instructors included practicing engineers and scientists from New York industry. This relationship between the school and local industries continues to this day.[39]

At his first meeting with The Corporation, President Atkinson spoke of the admirable spirit in the faculty. He stated that in spite of a decrease in registration, he was convinced that "we have

here a school of the first class both in technical and arts and that proper attention should be drawn to it."[40]

He immediately made plans to increase the technical literature in the library, which was less than adequate; improve the salary scale in the Preparatory School because many faculty members left for higher–paying public school jobs; and strengthen the technical areas he felt were weak, such as the civil engineering and mechanical drawing department. In addition, President Atkinson aimed to increase the number of students receiving the benefits of the college program.[41]

To this end, late afternoon classes, and then evening classes in arts, chemistry, and engineering were further developed for the "professional study to employed persons." The evening courses were offered by the Polytechnic and the Brooklyn Institute of Arts and Sciences.[42]

Students study electronics in the Thomas Potts Laboratory of Electricity in 1920. Thomas Potts, a benefactor of the Institute, also had the Laboratory of Physics named after him.

FINANCIAL WOES

Despite the best efforts, financial problems plagued the Institute, as well as the surrounding academic institutions, to the point where serious consideration was directed to consolidating the Institute, Adelphi College, and the Long Island Medical College. "All three colleges had been plagued by inadequate endowments and the union had been in the minds of many for a score of years," a reporter wrote in the *Globe*.[43]

The following February, the controller of New York City, Edwin G. Grout, adopted the project and expanded it by proposing the inclusion of additional facilities like the Brooklyn Public Library, the Brooklyn Institute of Arts and Sciences, Packer Collegiate Institute, and Pratt Institute. This supposed "mega-university," which would be maintained by the city, would be tuition free. The proposal was met with harsh criticism from Board of Education members and presidents and trustees of the respective schools. It was widely reported in the media, and general dismay was felt throughout the entire educational atmosphere.

However, the shifting population had caused overcrowding in the public schools in all five boroughs, but particularly in Brooklyn, which grew "in leaps and bounds especially after each bridge opened and transportation lines expanded." It was estimated that between 1,000 and 3,000 students were turned away from various institutions due to lack of space.[44] Therefore, the idea of a merger was welcomed by many residents.

Chairman of The Corporation William H. Nichols "referred to the serious crisis confronting the Institute at this time and emphasized the necessity of securing the interest and cooperation of all citizens of Brooklyn."[45] While there was great condemnation of the merger from universities and educators, "the first influential body to declare against 'Mr. Grout's University' was the Alumni Association of the Polytechnic."[46]

The legislation, presented in Albany in March of 1906, never left committee chambers and fell from the public radar soon thereafter.[47] However, a very serious problem still faced the Institute—a lack of sustainable finances. While the Institute was saved from a merger in 1906, nearly 70 years later, again reeling from financial problems, the Institute

Students study and read the classics in the English Department library. Among the books on its shelves was alumnus James Truslow Adams' *The Founding of New England*, which won the 1922 Pulitzer Prize in history.

decided to merge with New York University's School of Engineering and Science, a move that, it was hoped, would improve the financial picture.

Days after the bill failed in Albany, President Atkinson submitted a report to The Corporation outlining, according to Alice Woller, in her unpublished *History of Polytechnic 1890-1920*, "in considerable detail his ideas as to the future development of the Institute, and expressed the belief that the best engineering school in the country should be built here in Brooklyn; that the civil, mechanical, and electrical engineering courses should be fully developed; and that the arts course should be ultimately abandoned."[48]

He estimated that $2 million was needed to purchase land, buildings, and equipment. The drive for a "Greater Polytechnic" was announced to the public at the next commencement and "was hailed as the most important educational development in Brooklyn in many years."[49]

It was under this directive that separating the Preparatory from the Institute was revisited. Under Atkinson's watch, the Institute was making the necessary strides not only to survive but to flourish. "The best educators in America and Europe had been consulted in preparation of the plan, and the way was already being paved for the addition of chemical engineering and architecture and for the prosecution of scientific research and equipment," President Atkinson remarked.[50] This new direction was designed to turn the Institute into the " 'West Point' for captains of industry."[51]

To further the directive, William Nichols pledged $500,000, and another trustee pledged $250,000. Yet another trustee amended his will so that $500,000 would be left to the Institute after his demise.

Aside from his strained presidential duties, Atkinson, a Harvard graduate, managed to publish *The Philippines Islands* during his second year as president. At that time the Philippines was a United States colony. The book provided detailed information about the Philippines on general geography, history, climate, public health, commercial geography, Manila, superstitions and religion, government, and education.[52]

HOW TO BEST EDUCATE ENGINEERS?

Atkinson, a highly respected individual, was dedicated to developing all aspects of the Institute, and to this end, he and other trustees debated the necessary requirements for the education of the typical engineer.

In 1905, the Institute addressed this issue and offered an experimental six-year combined arts and engineering program; however this program was not destined to survive, and the Institute would decide in

the following years to devote all its energies to the engineering and science curricula because of the constant need to develop new courses to keep up with technological innovations and the application of new scientific discovery.[53]

It was for this reason that the Institute dropped its liberal arts program in 1908, committing to science and engineering as its areas of specialization. However, liberal arts remained an important element of the curriculum.[54]

In recognition of the Institute's pioneering work in evening classes, the Carnegie Foundation for the Advancement of Teaching included the Polytechnic as one of its beneficiaries in 1906, which was another feather in the Institute's cap.[55] This type of accolade from the Carnegie Foundation was a clear sign that the Institute was rapidly progressing as a leading academic college.

President Atkinson's initial three-year contract expired in 1907. During this short tenure, the freshman class had grown from 20 to 50, and graduate registration rose from 18 to 53. The freshmen predominately came from Brooklyn, but the other students hailed from upstate New York, New Jersey, Pennsylvania, Connecticut, Massachusetts, Cuba, the Philippines, and Russia.[56] The practice of accepting foreign students dates back to 1871 when the first Japanese students were enrolled at Poly.

President Atkinson further augmented the teaching staff, hiring Charles Steinmetz of General Electric to join the Chemistry and Engineering Department. However, educational achievements were overshadowed by acute financial problems. The Institute had a mortgage of $230,000 and outstanding loans of $150,000; the interest on these debts accounted for roughly two-thirds of the school's annual deficit.[57] In 1907, President Atkinson wrote:

Although we have not raised one-half of the two million dollar endowment required for our plans, I have consented to remain here another year. It seemed neither fair nor just, in view of the increase

Pictured here in 1920 is the Institute's Materials Testing Laboratory. Through the windows students and professors could view downtown Brooklyn. It was in laboratories like this one that the Institute conducted research, as well as instruction.

in the interest in the Institution, in the attendance and in the efficiency of the instruction, to leave without another attempt to solve the financial question.[58]

In order to keep the Institute afloat, trustees and members of The Corporation guaranteed to pay $22,500 each year, for a period of three years. This represented over two-thirds of the approximate $30,000 in new debts the school was absorbing each year.

Donations continued to play a vital part in keeping the Institute operating. They came largely from influential Brooklyn residents, and also from alumnus Seth Low.[59]

ALUMNI MAKING THEIR MARK

As the Institute rebuilt itself, alumni continued to make their mark on history. In 1905, Reverend Henry J. Van Dyke, class of 1869, became editor of the *Presbyterian Book of Common Worship.* He was pastor of Brooklyn's Second Presbyterian Church and authored more than 50 published sermons and hymns, including the popular, "Joyful, Joyful, We Adore Thee," which was first published in 1907. Van Dyke also served as American ambassador to the Netherlands and Luxembourg.[60]

Dr. Van Dyke was appointed minister to The Hague in 1913, retaining the position until 1917, when he resigned to resume literary work. He authored a handful of books including *Little Rivers, Fisherman's Luck, The Blue Flower,* and *The Story of the Other Wise Man.*[61] Among his famous sayings, was: "Time is too slow for those who wait, too swift for those who fear, too long for those who grieve, too short for those who rejoice, but for those who love, time is eternity."[62]

ANNA ERDMAN—
FIRST WOMAN GRADUATE

While both the Institute and the Preparatory were known for educating and rearing young men, a momentous event took place during the commencement ceremonies of 1907 when Anna Erdman became the first woman to receive a bachelor of arts degree from the Institute.

As the years unfolded, the Institute was continually defining and redefining its approach to the

Pictured here is the cover of the 1920 booklet *The Polytechnic Institute of Brooklyn — For City, State, and Nation.* This publication was a milestone. It illustrated the Institute's growth and its facilities, and depicted the method of training for chemists and engineers, all of whom were intended for public service.

art of education. In 1909, Polytechnic began hosting meetings of the American Society of Mechanical Engineers (ASME). Founded in 1880, ASME is a professional organization focused on technical, educational, and research issues of the engineering and technology community.[63]

As the Institute expanded and concentrated on its future, so did the Preparatory. However, as each year passed, it became clear that an official break between the two divisions of the Institute was imminent. This discussion of not only separating the schools but also of the direction in

POLY PREP

WHILE THERE WAS MUCH DISCUS-sion concerning the separation of the Institute and the Academic Department throughout the years, The Corporation and the Alumni Association valued the Preparatory division and concluded that while there would be a physical separation of the schools, the merit and history of "Poly Prep" would not be diminished. As early as the late 1890s, this idea was considered, as it was nearly every year thereafter. At a Poly Prep Alumni Association dinner in 1908, President Atkinson "suggested the desirability of the further separation of the Collegiate and Preparatory Departments of the Institution."[1]

This thought of separating the schools was shared by past presidents, including Snow; however it wasn't until an alumni dinner in 1915 that William H. Nichols, chairman of The Corporation, announced:

The board had long realized the wisdom of separating the school and the college and moving the school to a site more suitable for its purposes; that officially some such plan was under consideration; and the Alumni Association could not better justify its existence than by supporting and by furthering the idea.[2]

This transition was anticipated for years by students and faculty alike. However, certain parents and teachers had reservations when serious discussion ensued. "At first a great deal of doubt and trepidation was felt by many of the patrons of the school as to the wisdom of the change, but so strong was the faith of enough Brooklyn men and women in the change that they subscribed in full the sum of $500,000 to meet the necessary expenses," a historian noted.[3]

The headmaster at the time, Professor Francis Lane, supported the students and encouraged attention to physical activity as a critical part of the students' education and development. In 1905, the school purchased a plot of land between Ocean Parkway and Gravesend Avenue to use as athletic fields. The students traveled there by elevated train.[4]

Professor Lane believed that the inclusion of physical education had broad benefits. Of the new program, he wrote, "In addition to the sounder bodies and surer morals that naturally attend properly regulated athletics, the school has been able to secure a more consistent scholarship and a finer *esprit de corps*, and to give wider opportunity for development

---

which the Institute was headed became more pronounced because many members of the Alumni Association thought that abandoning the "classical" aspect of the curriculum was against the interest and traditions of the Institute.[64]

In April 1909, an editorial ran in the *Brooklyn Daily Eagle* on this topic:

The hope will be widespread and earnest that the Polytechnic may emerge from its financial difficulties and the trustees may be harmonized in a way which will secure to the Polytechnic the cordial support and interest in the community, so that it may enter upon that higher sphere of usefulness which has seemed to be about to open before it. But whatever course is

decided upon, the Brooklyn Polytechnic Institute should have the hearty support of all Brooklyn. It has already done much for the citizenship of our town and it should continue to be a powerful force for the up building of the better life of Brooklyn.[65]

To keep the Institute running, President Atkinson, with the approval of The Corporation and the trustees, fixed the needed endowment at $800,000 in 1909. While this goal was not reached, enough funds were raised to satisfy "the minimum needed to meet current expenses and provide a slight margin for development." After a visit from the General Education Board, a trustee noted that he was "very much impressed by the high and unusual character in leadership and in practical experience." In keeping with the mission of the school's founders, Lane argued that the school could best provide for its students by offering a full program of academics, arts, and athletics in a campus setting.[5]

In 1916, a 25-acre parcel of land, formerly the Dyker Meadow Golf Course, was offered to the trustees. On July 1 of that year, the Polytechnic Preparatory Country Day School was incorporated.[6]

Construction at the new site was still underway as 350 students arrived on September, 18, 1917. According to the Internet Web site www.polyprep.org, "A crowd of 325 excited boys put in an appearance. They came to an unfinished building where there were … rooms without windows, classrooms without desks, camp stools for seats, no blackboards except for portable ones, and meager plumbing facilities."[7] The students welcomed this change and quickly became accustomed to staying on after school, engaged in the wide range of activities that continue to make up the Country Day School experience today.

Joseph Dana Allen, headmaster from 1917 to 1949, said of the new school, "The school aims to develop mentality, physique, and character; but because the first two of these are menaces without the last, the greatest of these are character."[8]

After 53 years, the boys of the Preparatory, and the men of the Polytechnic Institute of Brooklyn, would forever be separated, linked only by a lineage that created two distinct and well-respected institutions.[9]

Under the leadership of Headmaster William M. Williams, Poly Prep began the transition to coeducation in the mid-1970s, graduating its first class of girls and boys in 1979. The headmaster and trustees believed that young people must be educated in an environment that would reflect the world around them. Admitting girls was just the first step in creating the diverse student body that is Poly Prep today.[10]

Poly Prep expanded dramatically in 1995 with the acquisition of the historic Woodward Park School (or, as it's sometimes known, "The Castle") on Prospect Park West in Park Slope. Renamed Poly Prep Lower School, this second campus provides an intimate, nurturing, and academically stimulating early childhood experience for nursery through grade four students.[11]

The Poly Prep family today is as diverse and rich in experience and tradition as New York City itself. Poly Prep described it this way:

After 150 years, we continue to honor the mission of the school's founders, providing an outstanding academic program and a strong, supportive community for the city's brightest and most promising young men and women.[12]

of the educational service which the evening work represented and complimented the Institute on its excellent system of accounting and on its high standard of admission requirements."[66]

In the two years that followed, members of The Corporation pledged $520,000, allowing the Institute to balance its outstanding debts while increasing its academic offerings.[67] At this time, 11 professors, four assistant professors, three consulting professors, two lecturers, 13 instructors, and eight assistants comprised the faculty that taught the roughly 160 students.[68]

President Atkinson was not pleased that the full endowment goal wasn't met, but he valued the hard work put forth to keep the Institute alive and running. He even had a sense of humor about the predicament. "The endowment will not enable the Institute to advance much, but will make it sure of keeping what it now has. The money paid out for interest has educated no one, unless it has been the president who has already adopted as an eleventh commandment: Thou shalt keep the Institute out of debt."[69]

In 1911, the first issue of the college newspaper, the *Reporter*, was published. The same year, the borough welcomed the Brooklyn Botanic Gardens, a scientific marvel of the times, which still exists today. The year 1911 also marked the release of alumnus Charles Benedict Davenport's *Heredity in Relation to Eugenics*, which was met with distinct acclaim in the scientific world. Davenport graduated from the Institute with a civil engineering degree in the mid-1880s.

As the Institute's financial woes lessened over the following years, there was a great demand to establish a college or university within Brooklyn. This pressure fell on the Institute, which was in the process of transforming itself into an engineering school. In 1913, President Atkinson announced the largest enrollment in the history of the Institute. The same month, a new site was proposed in Flatbush for the relocation of the Preparatory. These talks would grow more serious in 1915 and come to fruition in 1917.[70]

Under the direction of principal Alvin E. Duerr, the Preparatory was divided into two general groups: required work and elective work. The school offered limited opportunity for technical training along commercial lines. This decision was made, as Miles Merwin Kastendieck, wrote in his book *The Story of Poly*, "because of the firm belief that the boy who was planning to enter active business life without the advantage of a college background needed not so much specific knowledge of commercial subjects as thorough mental training which would teach him how to work, how to overcome difficulties, and how to make the best of his opportunities."[71]

Mr. Duerr stated specifically "that the boy who is not going to college needs a better education, not a poorer one, than the boy who intends to add four years' training to his secondary course."[72]

In order to help the underprivileged who sought higher education, faculty scholarships were created in 1913 to "assist those of limited means to earn their way through college." The benefactors were alumni. Included were the Henry Ginnell Dewit Scholarship, which was founded in memory of his graduating class of 1884; and the Walter E. Duryea Scholarship. Each of these scholarships was for $275 which was $25 less than tuition.[73]

THE WORLD AT WAR; POLY DIVIDES

The Institute continued to meet its objective by producing engineers and scientists needed by all areas of industry in the metropolitan area. However, nations would divide in 1914, leading to World War I.

The war had devastating effects on the Institute, as it did to so many families and communities in the United States. One historian recounted, "The war called away some of the older boys, two of the teachers, and as many as five hundred of the alumni, 22 of whom would lose their lives."[74]

It was common for students and teachers to witness training sessions at the Fort Hamilton military base, which is now home to the North Atlantic Division, U.S. Army Corps of Engineers. Kastendieck's book, *The Story of Poly*, described it this way:

Fort Hamilton was feverish with the rush of troops training for active service. The rat-tat-tat of machine guns broke the stillness; the whir of airplanes brought excitement; great transports decked out in strange futuristic zig-zag designs of camouflage caused wonder; and the sight of dummy bayonet practice going on daily just beyond the fence around the playing fields struck horror into the hearts of Poly boys.[75]

The events of the war were covered in many student publications, including the *Poly Prep* magazine, the *Reporter*, and the *Polygon*. Among the many brave men who served their country during the war was Reverend Henry J. Van Dyke, who acted as American minister to the Netherlands from 1913 to 1916, and then naval chaplain, for which he was awarded the Legion of Honor. In 1917, 78 men from the Institute were in service.[76]

In remembrance of alumni, students, and faculty who lost their lives defending the United States, a war memorial wall stands today at Polytechnic and lists those lost in the Civil War, World War I, World War II, the Korean War, Vietnam, and as a result of terrorist attacks of September 11. The etching reads:

We Dedicate This Memorial to the Polytechnic Family Whose Valor and Sacrifice in Service of our Country We Honor. We Pledge Never to Forget Them.[77]

As the war continued, the final steps for officially separating the two schools neared completion. After years of contemplation, the two divisions of the Institute officially divided, ending a longstanding history, which harkened back to 1854—the year the Institute was founded. Polytechnic Preparatory Country Day School was chartered by the Board of Education as a separate institution and moved in 1917 to Dyker Heights, Brooklyn, where it remains today.

The Institute wasted no time in quickly taking over the 99 Livingston Street location. Major changes in the building included moving the stairwells and installing fireproof stairs. The luxury of a new elevator was ruled out due to expenses; instead a six-inch steam line and new water and gas connections were approved for laboratories, which allowed for great discovery in the years ahead.[78]

THE WAR ENDS; A NEW ORDER

Toward the end of 1918, diplomatic talks between heads of state gave way to peace, and in 1919, the war officially ended.

During 1917 and 1918, evening and graduate registration dipped, but day enrollment continued to thrive. The same year, the Institute was among the first colleges in the nation to establish, in full working order, a unit of the Students' Army Training Corps. The Institute's program was operational in October. Two hundred and sixty-seven enlisted men in the Students' Army Training Corps were housed in the Old Prep School Chapel for months before Armistice Day, swelling day registration to 468.[79]

THE EDWIN F. CHURCH MEDAL

In 1918, the Institute welcomed Professor Edwin F. Church, who was named head of the Mechanical Engineering Department, a position he would hold for 32 years. In 1972, for his contribution to engineering, the American Society of Mechanical

Pictured here is an early coal tar laboratory, circa 1910. This picture illustrates a then state-of-the-art environment.

Engineers (ASME) established the Edwin F. Church Medal. This award is given to an individual who has rendered eminent service in increasing the value, importance, and attractiveness of mechanical engineering education.[80]

While the focus of the Institute remained on science and technology, great importance continued to be on developing well-balanced minds. *The Story of the Polytechnic and Its Service to the Public* described it this way:

The Institute believes in a liberal education for the chemist and engineer ... an education as broad as is consistent with thoroughness in the purely technical subjects.[81]

THE MAXWELL—AND MORE

In 1920, the Mechanical Engineering Department obtained a four-cylinder Maxwell car for testing purposes—the Maxwell was the car made famous by comedian Jack Benny; he used to say the only way he could get it to stop was to throw out an anchor—as part of the mechanical laboratory course.

The Mechanical Engineering Department later moved into its own building with $50,000 worth of new equipment and more than twice the space it had before. This was a clear indication of the direction in which the trustees of the Institute were heading, and with the Polytechnic Preparatory Country Day School

succeeding on its own merits, the future of the Institute was promising. The evening school continued to be a success, and enrollment for the 1919–1920 year was 845, well above the previous peak of 604 in 1916.[82]

As The Polytechnic Institute of Brooklyn entered 1920, there was much to celebrate. The Institute had rebounded from the financial pitfalls of a decade earlier. Enrollment had increased, especially after the war. At the end of the academic school year in 1920, total monies earned from tuition equaled $147,250, compared to $65,965 in 1915 and $19,156 in 1905.[83] In 1905, the student body consisted of 95, in 1920 approximately 1,245 students were enrolled. During that period the square footage of the floor space grew from 51,000 to 108,933.[84]

In 1917, the Institute began expanding and updating its equipment for a total of 33 shops and laboratories. There were 13 shops and laboratories devoted to chemistry and chemical engineering, including laboratories for coal tar dyes and water analysis. Also, there was a chemical engineering laboratory. The latter was equipped with small working units identical to chemical factories of the time. There was also the addition of the metallographic laboratory to the mechanical engineering laboratory

Above: Pictured on the left playing a woman is rising actor Edward Everett Horton, class of 1910. Since the Institute was an all-male school, male actors often had to dress as women, as was the case in this play. Horton's name was synonymous with the long-running stage comedy *Springtime for Henry*. Horton went on to appear in more than 150 motion pictures.

Right: Alumnus Walter Hampden, class of 1900, was one of the Institute's most famous actors. He is perhaps best known for his portrayal of Cyrano de Bergerac.

WALTER HAMPDEN AND EDWARD EVERETT HORTON

WALTER HAMPDEN DOUGHERTY was born in Brooklyn in 1879. At age 16, while studying at Brooklyn Polytechnic Institute, he played Shylock in a student production of *The Merchant of Venice*. He graduated from the Institute in 1900 and went to France to study music, but the lure of the stage soon brought him to England, where he joined the Frank Benson Stock Company, touring Great Britain and becoming known for what has been called his "orotund voice."[1]

He returned to the United States in 1907. In 1919, he formed his own company with a predominantly Shakespearean repertory. In the 1920s, he opened his own theater in New York, playing *Hamlet* alongside Ethel Barrymore in the premier production.[2]

In 1923, he performed Cyrano de Bergerac to critical acclaim, and he revived the play several times during his career. While he acted throughout the majority of his life, his last Broadway performance was in Arthur Miller's *The Crucible* in 1953. He later turned to film, often playing "distinguished old blowhards," as one critic put it. His film roles included the archbishop in *The Hunchback of Notre Dame* (1939), an American Indian in Cecil B. DeMille's *Unconquered* (1947), a pompous actor in *All About Eve* (1950), the British ambassador in *Five Fingers* (1952), and the father in *Sabrina* (1954). He died of a cerebral hemorrhage while in Hollywood playing a leading role in the film *Diana*, with Lana Turner. His wife, the actress Mabel Moore, and son Paul were at his side when he died. He was 75 years old.[3]

Edward Everett Horton, often mistaken for an Englishman, was actually born in Brooklyn, the son of a newspaper print machine operator.

Horton left Oberlin College in his junior year to pursue his dreams of becoming a stage actor, receiving his training at Brooklyn's Polytechnic Institute and then at Columbia University, where he made his first stage appearance in a variety show. Starting out as a chorus boy and stage manager, Horton was given his first leading role as a Japanese prince in the venerable stage melodrama, *The Typhoon*. Thereafter, despite a few forays into heavy drama, Horton specialized in comedy. His film debut was in 1921's *Too Much Business*. By the end of the 1920s, Horton was managing the Majestic Theatre in Los Angeles, casting his fellow character actors in the meaty, demanding roles often denied them by the movies.[4]

Horton also helped train several silent film leading men to use their voices properly in stage work, in a way that prepared them for talking pictures. Horton was pretty much locked into second lead and supporting roles in the 1930s and 1940s, most notably in Fred Astaire and Ginger Rogers musicals at RKO. During this period he also established himself as a reliable radio actor, frequently enlivening second-rate scripts with his own amusing elaboration. After a decade-long concentration on theater, usually touring as star of the reliable stage vehicle *Springtime for Henry*, Horton resumed his film career in 1957.[5]

In the 1950s and 1960s, Horton suddenly found himself a favorite of the younger generation thanks to his narration of the *Fractured Fairy Tales* segment on the legendary TV cartoon series *Rocky and His Friends* and his semiregular appearances as medicine man Roaring Chicken on the western situation comedy *F Troop*. Horton died on September 29, 1970, at the age of 84.[6]

and a new hydraulic laboratory, each of which was "unexcelled by any of its kind."[85]

Manufacturers took notice of the advances at the Institute and began employing more technically trained men. Among businesses that sought Institute graduates were New York and New Jersey Telephone Company, Brooklyn Edison Company, Pennsylvania Railroad, United States Rubber Company, Curtis Engineering Company, Standard Oil Company, General Chemical Company, and Westinghouse, to name a few.[86] "The employer recognizes the superior ability of the men trained at the Institute and encourages other employees to attend," a historian noted.[87]

In 1921, the first issue of the alumni magazine, *Poly Men*, was published. The publication would see a few incarnations and from 1973 became known as *Cable*, named after the cables on the Brooklyn Bridge.

NEW PRESIDENTS; GREAT ACHIEVEMENTS

The leadership provided to The Corporation for 18 years by William H. Nichols ended in 1922. His successor was Charles E. Potts, a graduate of the Institute and chairman for 30 years. He was considered a wise counselor and staunch supporter through this period, when vision and sympathetic counsel were essential.[88] Potts would also serve as interim president as the Institute bade a fond farewell to Professor Atkinson, a man who kept the Institute alive during a dark time.

This photo of the Institute's steam laboratory was taken after the turn of the century. The steam laboratory was one of approximately eight laboratories in operation on the grounds of the campus. In the far right of this publicity photograph (circa 1920), an African-American student conducts an experiment in the refrigeration laboratory. Including an African-American in a publicity photo was very progressive for this time period and underscores the administration's policy of supporting the rights of all students to receive an education, despite ethnicity.

While there is often a fine line between science and art, the Institute produced grand minds from each set. One was James Truslow Adams, class of 1898, biographer, historian, and editor. He won the 1922 Pulitzer Prize in history for *The Founding of New England*. Adams went on to author a number of notable books, including *Provincial Society* and *The Epic of America*.[89] Among Adams' famous quotes was, "We cannot advance without new experiments in living, but no wise man tries every day what he has proved wrong the day before."[90] Adams also coined the phrase "The American Dream," which Poly borrowed in the late 1990s when launching its $275 million capital campaign: Fulfilling the American Dream.

Among graduates who went on to become successful actors were Walter Hampden, class of 1900, famous for his Cyrano de Bergerac, and Edward Everett Horton, class of 1910, a name synonymous with the long-running stage comedy *Springtime For Henry*. Horton appeared in more than 150 motion pictures.

Professor Parke E. Kolbe succeeded Potts in 1925 as the Institute's fourth president. President Kolbe came to the Institute from the University of Akron, where, according to historical records, he balanced the financial and academic needs of the university equally; these traits ultimately would benefit the Institute. "Kolbe added a new element to the president's role, the political leadership required of an institution that is dependent on public tax money. He is regarded as a founder of the University of Akron, due to his leadership in transforming the private college into a municipal university."[91]

Under the guidance of President Kolbe, the graduate program was extended to the evening session so that by 1928, master's degrees were offered in chemistry and in chemical, civil, electrical, and mechanical engineering. The first degrees awarded were to Joseph A. Lambertine, Harold J. Mahoney, Robert V. Muscarell, and Herman J. P. Schubert. Soon after, the South Building of the Institute,

located across the street, was acquired. That same year, the first summer session was established. The Institute was growing and expanding, meeting the needs of the day.

As the school and student body grew, so did the Alumni Association. In 1927, John R. Brierley, class of 1910, the man who penned Poly's alumni song, "Alma Mater," was appointed the first executive secretary; and an alumni office was officially established. Under this office, the Institute established the college's first placement service. The alumni magazine *Poly Men* became the official publication of the Association in 1928. That same year, the Living Endowment Fund was established as a means of united support of the alumni of the Institute.[92]

The events of the following year included the establishment of the master of science degree in mechanical engineering and the creation of the divisions of industrial engineering and materials engineering. These advancements would prepare the Institute for astonishing discoveries by professors and students in the years and decades that followed. This was truly an exciting time for the Institute.

With the country approaching the devastating grip of the Great Depression, the next decade would be a trying time; however, the Institute would survive. Perhaps the spirit of the Institute was best reflected in song, a practice that went back generations in its history. The following song was featured in the graduating class of 1929's yearbook:

We are here to give a cheer for Poly,
With a happy song let us begin
Lift your voices high, cheer them to the sky
Ready, may the best team win.
Poly men we're here to shout your valor!
Fight as only Poly men can fight.
We stand back of you, we know
you are true blue.
Strive to win with your might.[93]

In 1930 the Institute celebrated its 75th anniversary. Pictured here is an exhibit in Namm's store window located in downtown Brooklyn. For one week in June of that year, spectators marveled at the display that included a model of a six-cylinder engine with a device to measure vibrations, a 15-watt audio frequency amplifier, and the Polytechnic mercury-vapor sign lamp.

CHAPTER FOUR

THE DEPRESSION YEARS
1930 –1939

Industry has only just recently attained its functional needs of materials, power, manufacturing processes and distribution processes. In looking forward for something constructive in recovery and in the future, it will be necessary to have a very definite picture of industry and engineering.

—President Harry Rogers, 1933

AS THE GREAT DEPRESSION swelled and millions of families struggled to make ends meet, the faculty and students of the Institute breathed a collective sigh of relief because the economic status of the school was not in jeopardy. President Kolbe wrote the following in his 1930 annual report:

Fortunately the position of the Institute is satisfactory and in common with other engineering colleges, particularly in large cities, the attendance has not been adversely affected by the long continued depression.[1]

While it was clear that New York City and the nation were reeling from an economic drought, the Institute was in a beneficial position due to the need for scientific minds in various industries. However, the Institute would suffer a significant loss when the news spread that William H. Nichols had died on February 2, 1930. He was 78.

Nichols, who served as a member of The Corporation, as chairman of the board, and as vice chairman of the board, graduated from the Institute in 1868. He was an industrial chemist, copper refiner, and smelter who went on to found the Nichols Chemical Company, originally named the G. H. Nichols and Company after his father.

Nichols was revered nationally for his contributions to science, which yielded a handful of honorary degrees. Lafayette College and New York University made him a doctor of laws; and Columbia, the University of Pittsburgh, and Tufts conferred upon him the honorary degree of doctor of science. He was one of the founders and a former president of the American Chemical Society, and a former president of the Society of the Chemical Industry. Nichols was a philanthropist with one such effort resulting in the "William H. Nichols Scholarship for Chemistry."[2]

Shortly before his death, Nichols was quoted as saying:

Even as a youth I realized that I had only one life to live and I was determined to make it count. Any fellow who has a chance to acquire a proper education and neglects the opportunity is foolish.[3]

Nichols bequeathed $250,000 to the Institute when he died. Endowments like these kept the Institution afloat and would continue to do so into the future.

President Harry Rogers approximately five years after he came to the Institute in 1933. Rogers was often called "Prexy."

Upon receiving the endowment, President Kolbe remarked:

Dr. Nichols was never anxious to see Polytechnic an institute of large numbers, but he always strove for the highest standards of teaching and curriculum. I am sure that this indicates the uses for which he would desire his generous bequest to be used.[4]

THE INSTITUTE GROWS

As the first academic year of the 1930s came to a close, the total enrollment, including day, evening, and graduate courses, was 2,597, roughly 300 less than 1929.[5] However, as a result of Nichols' endowment, substantial salary increases were realized; and in order to support the increased course load, The Corporation authorized alumnus William F. Jacob, class of 1916, librarian of the General Electric Company, and Wharton Miller, dean of the Syracuse Library School, to survey the existing Spicer Library.[6] Their recommendations eventually resulted in additional space and a more efficient way of processing material needed to further develop course offerings.

The overflow of books came because of new departments. The Chemistry Department was divided into two parts: chemistry and chemical engineering. The Civil Engineering Department was also expanded to include the establishment of the Materials Testing Laboratory.

Among new pieces of equipment was a 200,000-pound testing machine, a concrete mixer, and a Deval abrasion machine for testing stone.[7] New offerings such as these increased the Institute's profile in the business world, as did the fact that graduates easily found work. Some were even offered employment before graduation.

The Institute also developed new criteria for entering freshmen. Starting in 1930, all students were required to take a psychological exam. The test was designed to show to what degree the applicant was fitted for technical studies. That year 56 students were enrolled out of the 86 who applied. At this time, graduates were earning $140 per month, which was a comfortable salary, especially during the Depression that left thousands of men and woman waiting in long lines for free soup and bread.[8] The students, who passed these soup lines on their way to class, applied their energies in hopes of attaining a specific degree that would land them a job upon graduation.

HONORARY DEGREES

Furthering the Institute's reputation worldwide, the first two honorary degrees in engineering were granted to Karyl Taylor Compton and Charles Franklin Kettering in 1930. Kettering co-invented the first electrical ignition system or electric starter motor for cars while working at General Motors. The self-starting ignition was first installed in a Cadillac on February 17, 1911, and eliminated the need for hand cranking. He later founded Delco (Dayton Engineering Laboratories Company).

Kettering kept busy and went on to invent improved automotive lighting and ignition systems, lacquer finishes for cars, antilock fuels, leaded gasoline, and an electric cash register. Kettering also co-developed freon. He was known for the saying: "The world hates change, but it is the only thing that has brought progress."[9]

The following year, Laurence McKinley Gould and Admiral Richard Evelyn Byrd were granted the first honorary degrees of Doctor of Science.[10] This tradition of making awards to men and women of scientific achievement continues to this day and enhances, as it did then, the Institute's reputation. Admiral Byrd, a graduate of the United States Naval Academy, was awarded this honor for his explorations in Antarctica. In 1925 he was a member of the MacMillan Polar Expedition and a year later flew over the North Pole from King's Bay, Spitsbergen, Norway, in one of the most sensational flights ever attempted at that time. The following year, his transatlantic flight was hailed as "brilliant evidence of the engineering mind overcoming [the] almost unconquerable elements of nature."[11]

The admiral could not attend the commencement ceremony and instead accepted the degree in the following radiogram from Little America, Antarctica transmitted through the *New York Times* to General Robert L. Rees, chairman of the committee on honorary degrees of the Institute.[12]

It gave me great pleasure to hear that Polytechnic Institute of Brooklyn desires to confer upon me the honorary degree of Doctor of Science and that this is the first in the long history of the Institution.[13]

While Admiral Byrd reveled in his award, a student at the Institute would also have cause for celebration. Jules Podnossoff, class of 1931, won the Charles T. Main Award, which is the highest student award given by the American Society of Mechanical Engineers. The subject of his essay was "The Value of the Safety Movement in Industry." Along with his award, he received $150, which was equivalent to one month's salary, or about half of the annual tuition at the time ($360).[14]

ACCOMPLISHED PROFESSORS

For many years the Institute worked with universities around the world by exchanging professors for various lengths of time; some would teach one class a week, while others taught a handful of courses; thus they became ingrained in the "Poly" way.

This practice occurred with schools as close as New York University and colleges located in lands as far away as Scotland. In 1930, a young man from the Technical University, Charlottenburg, in Berlin, Germany, arrived. His name was Professor Ernst Weber. Weber's name would become synonymous with the Institute over the next three decades. In his autobiography, *The Evolution of Electrical Engineering, A Personal Perspective*, Professor Weber recalled his first years at the Institute:

Classes at Polytechnic went better than I expected, even though I was not very fluent in English at the onset. The students were very polite and showed a great deal of interest, and they asked many more questions than was common in German classrooms. I found teaching very much to my liking, so I was delighted when, in February 1931, I was offered a permanent position at Polytechnic—as research professor of electrical engineering with an annual salary of $6,000. The appealing title and the higher salary made this attractive; also, the prospect of staying permanently in the United States appealed to me.[15]

Two years later, the Institute welcomed another visiting professor who eventually would equal Professor Weber's contributions to the Institute; his name was Donald F. Othmer.

While the Institute had long established extracurricular clubs and athletic teams, a more adventurous society, the Glider Club, was established in 1929 and slowly grew as more students and professors took aerodynamics. In the early 1930s, the club established a primary training port at the (then) Brentwood Airport on Long Island where they had access to a hangar, which housed two gliders that were purchased by the Institute. Fred C. Krummel, class of 1922, was in charge of the program. He described it this way:

We are getting some wonderful aeronautical experience from our activities even though they are somewhat curtailed. Our program this winter is very interesting and our club will doubtlessly furnish the aviation industry with valuable men.[16]

The Glider Club was an extension of a new course that was added that same year, Aerodynamics and Airplane Structures, which was part of the expanding mechanical engineering curriculum. Krummel was correct in his estimation because in the years and decades that followed, the Institute would aid the military and NASA in aerodynamic research at the Aerodynamic Laboratories in Farmingdale, New York.

HISTORICAL ACHIEVEMENTS

The Institute was perhaps best known for its science and engineering contributions, but great accomplishments were also realized in the Philosophy and English Departments. Professors William

Pictured above is Jules Podnossoff, class of 1931. Before graduating, Podnossoff won the Charles T. Main Award, the highest student award given by the American Society of Mechanical Engineers, for his essay, "The Value of the Safety Movement in Industry."

Richards and Leo E. Saidla made history in 1930 when they translated from Danish Harold Hoffding's *Jean Jacques Rousseau and His Philosophy*. Originally published in 1896, the book was later revised in 1912. However, it was only available in French, German, and Danish until Richards and Saidla made this world-respected publication available in English. The Radio Book Club said of the effort:

> *The genius of the translators [is apparent] who have not only the perfect mechanism of translating*

from one language to another, but a knowledge and appreciation of the subject matter which enables them to bring over into English their feel, as well as the words of the original author.[17]

DEPRESSION YEARS

By 1932, U.S. manufacturing output had fallen to 54 percent of its 1929 level, and unemployment had risen to between 12 and 15 million workers, or 25 to 30 percent of the workforce. This year was the worst of the Great Depression.[18]

Despite shrinking enrollment numbers, the Institute answered the demand for higher education by further developing the Living Endowment Fund, which provided scholarships to outstanding students and equipment and supplies for different departments. In 1932 a total of $3,500 was raised, which resulted in the Electrical Engineering Department receiving an oscillograph

With the establishment of the Aeronautical Engineering Department, an increasing number of students joined the program. Pictured here, in 1939, is Professor R. Paul Harrington (on right) instructing students at the Floyd Bennett Field in Brooklyn, New York.

and the Mechanical Engineering Department receiving funds that went toward the construction of a wind tunnel.[19] These funds were generated and supported mainly by alumni, although it was common for manufacturers to donate equipment.[20]

President Kolbe said of the Alumni Association and the Living Endowment Fund:

We have one of the best small college alumni associations in the country insofar as organization and loyalty are concerned. The Living Endowment Fund, while it has naturally suffered with the Depression, is an excellent achievement. It has done a great deal of good at Polytechnic and its greatest results and possibilities lie before it.[21]

DEPARTMENTS AND COURSES

The Institute was flush with leading professors that headed its various departments. And in the 15 years since the Preparatory officially incorporated and separated, new courses and departments were established, including the Department of Electrical Engineering; the Department of Chemical Engineering; the Department of Chemistry; the Department of Mechanical Engineering; the Department of Physics; the Department of English; the Department of History and Economics; the Department of Mathematics; and the Department of Physical Education.[22]

With each passing year, every department had cause for celebration. During the summer of 1932, Professor John L. Knudson of the Department of History and Economics was among researchers who attended a special meeting of International Law at Geneva, Switzerland, and subsequent meetings at The Hague. While at Geneva, he attended the World Disarmament Conference, the Congress of the International Society of Comparative Legislation, and the Academy of International Law. He was later elected as a member of the latter's council, representing the United States.

His work and resulting findings were later published in the book *Rules of Procedures in International Conferences.*[23] Two years later, the French government conferred upon him the *Chevalier de la Legion d'Honneur* for his contributions to international understanding and amity. This award, the

Parke E. Kolbe became president in 1925 but resigned in 1933 to become president at Drexel Institute.

"Legion of Honor," is France's most prestigious honor bestowed on a civilian.[24]

During this period, the Institute was physically expanding as well. In 1930, the Institute acquired 94 Livingston Street from the Brooklyn Eye and Ear Hospital, and renamed it the South Building. The property was a gift from the family of William Augustus White, who graduated in 1859. After construction work and renovation, the South Building housed new laboratories, including a laboratory dedicated to the testing of highway materials, several new classrooms, drawing and instrument rooms, a trophy room; offices for the school newspaper, the *Reporter*, and the alumni office suite.[25]

RESEARCH EFFORTS

Professors and their students were actively involved on a regular basis with various research projects that aided the advancement of science and technology, the progress of the engineering and scientific professions, and the improvement of technical education in many diverse ways. This was a vocation, a

The Institute's enrollment numbers steadily increased during the 1930s. Evening course enrollment was at an all-time high by the end of the decade. Pictured here is the entrance to 99 Livingston Street, which was perhaps the most common view of the school for most students.

creed of scientific exploration. In 1932, 22 scientific publications, 12 presentations before scientific societies, 76 research projects, and 10 patents were achieved.[26]

At that time, there were two principal fields of research directly supported by the Institute. One was electrical engineering, where Professor Weber concentrated his attention and skills upon electron flow and distribution in large conductors, and the other was chemical engineering where Professor William H. Gardner concentrated on the study of shellac and its uses.

The latter research was also supported by the United States Shellac Importers Association, which signed a three-year research contract with the Institute. As a result of his research, Professor Gardner became a leading authority throughout the world, and his work would eventually open the door for more industry-related research programs.[27]

Faculty were habitually on the cutting edge of technology, always striving to advance science.

For example, Professor Otto H. Henry pushed the Department of Mechanical Engineering to grasp the importance of alloys. "The possibilities of the alloy field have not been scratched," he wrote. "The strengths obtainable at the present time are much greater than those of ten years ago but the apparent inherent strength of the alloys has not been approached."[28]

Professor Henry was correct, as there was a greater need for metal metallurgists than for ore metallurgists. At the time, metals were abundantly available and were being used because of their high strength and light weight, which allowed for higher pressure machines and longer bridge spans.[29] The Institute answered this call by expanding its metallurgy course offerings.

While the scope of research was vast at that time, a few highlights are worth mentioning. In chemistry and chemical engineering, research efforts were focused on the decomposition of photographic film, preparation of metals by electrolysis, studies on fractionating columns, and driers in paints, emulsifying agents, and cutting oils.

In the Civil Engineering Department, research was conducted in cement and concrete, flooring compounds, physical properties of bituminous materials, and soils in reference to highway upgrades. In electrical engineering, under the direction of Professor Weber, research was conducted in vacuum tubes, associated circuits, phonographic transcribers, sound reproducers and loudspeakers, and cathode-ray oscillographs.

In the Mechanical Engineering Department, research was conducted on automotive equipment, combustion fuels, the making of alloys in air, vacuo or controlled atmospheres, heat treatments, thermal analyses, and metallographic investigations. The flow of fluids through pipes and fittings, viscosity, aerodynamics in a 42-inch wind tunnel, streamline

effects, and wind resistance and forces also were studied. The Physics Department was busy researching the absorption and emission of spectra in the ultraviolet and near infrared ranges with low resolution; crystal structure and chemical reactions of substances that are optically active; thermoelectric effects with dissimilar metals; standardization and calibration of electrical instruments; and the permeability of ferro-magnetic materials.[30]

All these studies and findings aided the scientific community at large, and industry leaders took note of the Institute's pioneering advances by supporting their employees in furthering their education. The Institute's evening course enrollment increased, as did its summer session enrollment.

FACULTY ACHIEVEMENTS

In December of 1932, Bancroft Gherardi, class of 1891, was awarded the Edison Medal for his contributions to the art of telephoning, mechanical engineering, and the development of electrical communications. At the time, Gherardi was a vice president at AT&T.[31] The American Institute of Electrical Engineers, a predecessor of today's Institute of Electrical and Electronics Engineers (IEEE), first conceived the award four years after Thomas Edison created the first electric light bulb in 1879.[32] At the commencement ceremony Gherardi was awarded the honorary Doctor of Engineering degree.

That same year, alumnus James Truslow Adams published another book, this one entitled *The March of Democracy. Time* magazine said of his effort: "No one who has read his books would accuse James Truslow Adams of being a merely theoretical historian, in spite of his recent best-selling thesis, *The Epic of America.*"[33]

That summer, a handful of students were fortunate to make a historic cross-country trip funded by the Thorne-Loomis Foundation. A special, and for the time, state-of-the-art vehicle was built that was a combined bus, tent, dining car, and sleeper. The

Professor Ernst Weber. Weber came to the Institute in 1930 as a visiting professor from the Technical University, Charlottenburg, Berlin.

trip, organized by Professor Edwin F. Church Jr., head of the Mechanical Engineering Department, allowed nine students and Assistant Professor George H. Neugebauer to visit famous laboratories and industrial sites.

During their trip they witnessed the applications required to make automobiles, steel, glass, and airplanes. Stops along the way included Carborundum Company in Niagara Falls, the Hammermill Bond Paper Company in Erie, Pennsylvania, the Goodyear Tire and Rubber Company and the Guggenheim Airship Institute, both located in Akron, Ohio. One student recalled, "The Guggenheim Airship Institute has the largest vertical wind tunnel in the world and is capable of developing an air velocity of 175 miles per hour." The tunnel, he said, "was used for the design of Zeppelins."[34]

During an interview conducted in 2003, Charles D. Strang, class of 1943, and current member on the advisory board of trustees, recalled his memories of Professor Church:

I was particularly impressed by the fellow who was head of the Mechanical Engineering Department. His name was Church, Professor Church. He was fascinating ... In addition to being a great teacher of thermodynamics, this, that, and the other thing, he had apparently in his youth, when he first got out of school, worked for Thomas Alva Edison from New Jersey.

He would tell great stories about working for Thomas Edison. Very impressive stuff. Edison was basically unschooled. He [Church] was doing a calculus computation on something and he said Edison came along, leaned over his shoulder, and said, "What are you doing?" He said that he explained to Edison what he was doing. Edison said, "Oh, you're sort of taking an average."[35]

HELPING HANDS

With the Institute's long history of aiding the development of not only Brooklyn, but also of New York City, it was no surprise to students and faculty that upon addressing the commencement assembly in June of 1933, honorary alumnus George A. McAneny delivered a speech entitled "Engineers as Good Citizens." At the time, McAneny was the com-

In 1933, Charles E. Potts, chairman of The Corporation, also assumed the role of acting president after President Kolbe resigned. He held office until President Harry Rogers was chosen as the Institute's next president. Chairman Potts served twice as interim president. He also was acting president before President Kolbe was selected in 1925.

missioner of sanitation of New York City. He pointed out the vital need for engineers to "take a more active interest in the problems of government as well as those of his profession in order that professional accomplishments could be a value to the public as a whole."[36] Despite tough economic times, many graduates of the Institute went into the private sector, which was the reason governmental representatives, like McAneny, eagerly sought the service of Institute alumni. Visits like these confirmed the increasing role engineering was playing in all aspects of society.

Also in attendance during the commencement was Edward R. Knowles, class of 1871. His association with the school was legendary, and he was granted the honorary degree of Bachelor of Science in Civil Engineering. Upon receiving this accolade, Knowles said, "It is the climax of my professional career and coming as it does from 'old Poly' will always be held in remembrance as one of the brightest achievements of my life."[37] In 1887, Knowles began to associate himself with inventor William A. Sawyer, Thomas Edison's rival in the electrical world.[38]

ROGERS NAMED PRESIDENT

As the academic year 1932 came to a close, the Institute bade a fond farewell to President Kolbe, who accepted the position of president at Drexel Institute. President Kolbe was a well-respected administrator, teacher, and facilitator of all issues that faced the Institute during his tenure, especially during the perils of the Depression. Since taking office in 1925, Kolbe had enhanced and developed evening and graduate programs so that doctoral degrees were attainable. He, along, with The Corporation, made the first, and subsequent, honorary degrees a reality. It was with great pride that President Kolbe passed the baton. Charles E. Potts, who was acting president for three years in the 1920s before Kolbe was chosen, again stepped into the role of acting president, while also being chairman of The Corporation.

Acting President Potts assumed the great responsibility of managing all arms of the Institute with a sense of simple ease, which was part and parcel of his overall character. The faculty, students, and alumni alike often referred to him as "good old Charley." At the commencement ceremony that year, which was before the formal announcement of the new president, Potts said, "I am very glad to know that the Polytechnic Institute of Brooklyn is under the control of its graduates. Whether they are from the North Pole, the South Pole, or other parts of the earth, I know the Institute is close to the hearts of the graduates."[39]

After many months of searching, The Corporation nominated Harry Stanley Rogers as president. Kolbe remarked on the nomination:

The members of The Corporation have faced a change of administration in a year of panic and financial crisis with courage and with confidence. In the nearly eighty years of its existence there have been but four presidents and each has contributed mightily toward some stage of development; each has ... been supported throughout his administration by a devoted faculty and a loyal alumni. The fifth president, Harry Rogers, having practiced as an engineer and having had long and successful experience in administration, being well-known to the engineering societies, and having youth, health, and personality in his favor, has been chosen by unanimous vote of The Corporation. The future of Polytechnic is in safe hands.[40]

In 1933, President Rogers assumed his role with dedication and certainty. He had many plans

HARRY STANLEY ROGERS

PRESIDENT HARRY STANley Rogers had a distinguished career in engineering before accepting his position at the Institute. He was appointed professor of hydraulic engineering at Oregon State in 1920 and later became dean of the college in 1927. He served as dean until 1933, when he resigned to become the Institute's fifth president, a position he held for 24 years. Throughout his career, President Rogers was active in professional societies, particularly the Society for the Promotion of Engineering Education and the American Society for Engineering Education. He was president of the latter in 1945 and 1946.[1]

A well-respected engineer, Rogers is credited with securing research contracts with business and industry, as well as hiring distinguished Professors Weber, Othmer, and Mark, and supporting their research efforts. It was Rogers' excellent leadership skills and brilliant intellect that led the Institute through the 1930s into a period of prosperity.

Today, Rogers Hall stands as a tribute to one of Poly's greatest administrators. It is interesting to note that there is another Rogers Hall at Oregon State University, this one also named after Harry Rogers.

for the Institute, but at his first meeting as president, he stressed the importance of building stronger relationships with industry in order to better facilitate the overall operation of the Institute:

We now have the Shellac Institute which has been operating at Polytechnic for the past five years. The Institute has carried on research under Dr. Gardner for the United States Shellac Importers Association. Similar contacts are possible with other industries and the alumni are the men who have the knowledge of these possibilities. Industry has only just recently attained its functional needs of materials, power, manufacturing processes, and distribution processes. In looking forward for something constructive in recovery and in the future, it will be necessary to have a very definite picture of industry and engineering.[41]

ACADEMIC ADVANCES

President Rogers immediately began to reassess the Institute's academic offerings. The following year, the Institute announced a new liberal science curriculum for students of both day and evening sessions. The new program was designed to meet the needs and desires of students who wished to pursue a broad education in the fundamentals of science or technology. The program offered the opportunity to pursue a particular field of interest while providing a broad preparation for a career in modern social organizations. Students were required to choose one major and one minor from the following five subjects: administration, chemistry, applied mechanics, mathematics, and physics.[42]

Although these pursuits aided many students who sought the benefits of a more generalized education, the Depression was still wreaking havoc. In 1934 and 1935, the Living Endowment Fund dipped to just over $1,000, which eliminated the opportunity for many students to benefit from financial aid. Enrollment numbers dropped, and this too resulted in fewer funds available for improvements at the Institute.[43]

THE LOSS OF NOTED ALUMNI

The deaths of alumni and professors from Polytechnic seemed prevalent in the 1930s. Many of the "Poly" men, those who graced the Institute for 30 years or more and gave their lives to the pursuit of higher education, reached their senior years during this time. Professor George Stuart Collins, formerly the head of the Modern Language Department and professor emeritus passed in November of 1935, and Professor Irving Wetherbee Fay, formerly head of the Chemistry Department and professor emeritus, died the following February.[44]

Professor Collins began teaching at the Institute in 1892. His career was highly decorated, and after his passing, the following statements were made at a faculty meeting: "Professor Collins belonged to the older generation of college teachers, the counterparts of whom are not to be found today. Those that knew him and loved him know there is no more fitting description than the immortal lines of Horace: *Integer vitae scelerisque purus.*"[45] Translation: Blameless of life and free from crime.

Professor Fay, a Harvard graduate, began teaching at the Institute in 1897. He was the executive head of the Chemistry Department until 1932 when he became professor emeritus. He guided the Polytechnic Chemical Society and was a member of the American Association for the Advancement of Science, the American Chemical Society, and the *Gesellschaft Deutscher Chemiker e.V. (GDCh)*, that is, the German Chemical Society. He published numerous pioneering papers on coal tar dyes.[46] In remembrance, the faculty noted:

Let us, as teachers, always have before us the thought that guided Dr. Fay in his long career and made him the successful teacher he was, namely, that it is our duty to create out of youthful and largely unformed men, men rounded in intellect, in judgment, and in morals, and fit for life.[47]

TURNING THE CORNER

It was the lineage of professors like Collins and Fay that made the Institute a legend in its own time. While the Institute remained academically strong throughout the beginning of the decade, it wasn't until 1935 that the tide began to turn financially. With industry rebuilding, engineers fared well on the job front. Nationwide, freshmen enrollment in engineering courses rose over 20 percent compared to the prior year.[48]

The Institute's graduates, most of whom had attended evening classes, experienced an employment rate of 80 percent or better in the second part of the decade. This was due in large part to the fact that chemical industries experienced little effect from the Depression and that public works projects absorbed the graduates of the Civil Engineering Department.[49] In President Rogers' opinion, unemployment was lower in professional groups and was increasingly more pronounced in business groups, and in skilled, semi-skilled, and unskilled trade groups.[50]

In 1935, President Rogers wrote in his annual report:

We seem to have forgotten that the new scientific developments and new industries have lifted us out of past depressions and have given men re-employment in new fields and we seem oblivious of the facts that these new fields universally have called for better preparation and better understanding of engineering and science. The catch words and phrases with which scientific fields and industry have been disparaged may result in drying up at the source the support for engineering and scientific study which has brought us not only new standards of living, but has multiplied industrial and business employment many-fold.[51]

Great emphasis was put on redefining the undergraduate course offerings. Each year, with the changing times, the Institute developed new courses that equipped graduates with the tools and skills necessary for success in the working world. "We may look forward to the future with the conviction, it seems, that developments in engineering courses at the undergraduate level will take the nature of intensifying the fundamentals rather than expanding the applications," President Rogers said.[52]

This process occurred in the graduate program as well. By 1936, the graduate program was growing so rapidly that the Institute had to turn away qualified candidates. This was truly the mark of changing times. The Depression, which rendered most of the working class immobile for the better half of the decade, began to dissipate almost as quickly as it came. This was best reflected in enrollment numbers. In 1935, the total number of students reached 2,193; in 1936 it rose to 2,352.

Research efforts were increasing as well. Over 20 professors and their students were conducting experiments. Among them were Professor Roland Ward, who studied the mechanism of reactions between fused substances; Professor Weber, who had ongoing experiments in electron flow, mapping of electric fields, and sinusoidal waves on transmission lines; and Professor Othmer who was busy researching the utilization of waste wood and the recovery of acids and solvents.[53] President Rogers supported the research of the professors and all related programs;

On September 20, 1939, the George Collins Memorial Organ was presented to President Rogers (standing, right) and the Polytechnic Institute by alumni secretary John R. Brierley (standing, left). Charles O. Banks, the Institute's Glee Club director, is playing the organ. Professor Collins taught modern languages from 1862 until he died in 1935. He was also an accomplished organist and performed at countless chapel ceremonies at the Institute.

Since the establishment of the aerodynamics program at the Institute in the early 1930s, many students became interested in flying. Pictured here are four students preparing for flight at the Floyd Bennett Field in Brooklyn.

however, the Department of Chemistry was leading the way in research related endeavors. "The programs of instruction and research, both essential to a vigorous educational institution, have shown continuous and sound growth the current year," President Rogers commented.[54]

The following year, in 1936, PhD programs were authorized in chemical and electrical engineering. These programs, offered in both day and evening sessions, allowed many engineers from the metropolitan area who were working day jobs the opportunity to advance their education while continuing to work. This trend toward night education came about before the Depression, and continued afterwards. These offerings truly made the Institute shine and further developed its status as a top-notch commuter engineering college.

PROFESSOR OTHMER PROMOTED; RESEARCH EFFORTS CONTINUE

Since coming to the Institute in 1932, Professor Othmer held the position of assistant professor of chemistry. However, in 1937, he was promoted to head the department and given the title of professor of chemistry. Despite being at the Institute for only five years, he had an enviable record in the field of chemical engineering as a teacher, researcher, and professional consultant. Among his accomplishments that year, he developed a process for refining petroleum products which was utilized in the construction of a petroleum plant in India. Later that year, he received an invitation from the Farm Chemurgic Council to develop new processes for utilizing farm products.[55] It was strides like these that elevated the Institute in the eyes of industry leaders worldwide, as well as commanding the respect of competing technical schools like Massachusetts Institute of Technology.

While the Chemistry Department was being recognized for its accomplishments, the Electrical Engineering Department celebrated a milestone, conferring its first doctorates in the spring of that year.

In the following months, the United Gas Improvement Company of Philadelphia partnered with the Institute to study the chlorination of piperlyne, a substance used for adhesive applications. The following year the Novocol Chemical Manufacturing Company of Brooklyn established a research fellowship in cooperation with the Department of Chemistry for the study of the catalytic hydrogenation of organic compounds.[56] These were truly exciting times at Polytechnic and professors and students were eager to contribute their talents in the name of science.

Across the board, the Institute was furthering its research efforts. The research committee prepared a volume of papers written by members of the faculty and research staff and previously published in numerous technical presses between September 1, 1937, and September 1, 1938, under the title *Research Publications of the Polytechnic Institute of Brooklyn*. The first volume contained 17 papers and was distributed to schools, libraries, and a special mailing list of leading industrial and manufacturing companies. In the years that followed, volumes such as this one would become commonplace.[57]

A TURN FOR THE WORSE

As the national economy began finally to improve, the Institute was succeeding at every turn. At the beginning of 1938, it was housed in three main buildings: the administration and Institute buildings on the north side of Livingston Street, and the South Building on the opposite corner. There were approximately 550 day students, 1,700 night students, and 450 graduate students. The total teaching staff reached its highest level of 130 professors and assistant professors. Aside from the guidance offered by President Rogers, two deans, Ernest Streubel and Erich Hausman, oversaw general matters of instruction for the growing Institute.[58]

Despite the Institute's good fortune, a devastating blow was delivered in the spring of 1938 when a fire ravished the Institute's main building. On the morning of March 4, two freshmen students,

A SPECIAL MILESTONE FOR THE DEPARTMENT OF CHEMISTRY

AN IMPORTANT MILESTONE WAS reached in 1935 when Samuel David Goldberg became the first recipient of a Doctor of Philosophy degree in the Department of Chemistry. Dr. Goldberg went on to become chief chemist and vice president of the Novocol Chemical Manufacturing Company, where he studied local anesthetics and developed patented substances related to this research.[1]

Goldberg revolutionized the practice of dentistry, inventing new local anesthetics, developing the first buffered solutions to relieve the pain of injections, and made the use of novocaine commercially feasible.[2]

POLY FIRE

ON THAT FATEFUL MORNING IN MARCH, 1938, at approximately 9:30 A.M., 16 fire trucks were called to the Institute. In little over two hours, the fire was extinguished, but not before rendering the building all but useless. While the flames roared mainly throughout the library wing, located on the fifth floor of the Institute, the general chemistry laboratory, the Shaw Laboratory, and the chemical engineering laboratory were completely ruined. The heat from the burning attic and roof and the falling embers destroyed most of the furniture and equipment. The water which was poured into the building to quench the fire flowed down through the classrooms, laboratories, and offices to the basement, where it destroyed plaster, wiring, fixtures, furniture, and various pieces of equipment.[1] The water damage was so severe that the floor of the gymnasium, located in the basement, buckled.

The overall replacements included a new roof, new plastering throughout the building, new flooring in the upper stories and in the gymnasium, a completely new electrical system, reconditioning of the elevator, replacement of much

Bruce Eytinge and Chester Mayforth, were making their way to class when they noticed smoke billowing from under the eaves of the Institute building, which housed the qualitative laboratory on the fifth floor. As the students ran up the stairs, they were met by flames licking the walls. They quickly sounded the building's fire alarms while trying to extinguish the flames, but the smoke and heat forced them out of the building. Within minutes fire trucks surrounded the building. After a few hours the firemen were able to drown the flames, as students stood in the streets cheering.[59]

President Rogers, a member of the Oregon Fire Chief Association, provided coffee and sandwiches from a local restaurant. Since the fire was caused by an overheated chimney, the majority of the damages were covered by the Institute's insurance policy. That same day, President Rogers, along with members of the faculty and The Corporation, developed reorganization plans.[60]

As good fortune would have it, no one was hurt by the fire, which caused over $150,000 in damage.[61] However, the fire seriously hampered the Institute's educational progress for the next three years. It destroyed the majority of classrooms

Opposite: Pictured here is the Institute's main building engulfed in flames. The fire caused $150,000 in damage.

Right: After the fire in 1938, the main building needed more than a year's worth of construction, which included a new roof, flooring, wiring, laboratory equipment, and plumbing improvements.

of the plumbing and water systems, new laboratory desks and equipment, and painting throughout.[2]

Construction would last for more than a year, and the Institute would have to reevaluate and adjust all course offerings. While the fire was devastating, the spirit of the Institute matched the challenge. President Rogers reflected the following sentiments:

The problems seemed perplexing and the burdens heavy at times, but the loyalty and devotion of the faculty, of the maintenance staff, and of the students were at all times splendid and encouraging. In fact it seems that our difficulty brought a better spirit to the Institute than had been recognized previously.[3]

and laboratories in the main building and halted the progress of research along with instruction in certain areas.

The Department of Chemistry was moved to available space at Long Island University, which was located a few blocks away. The Supreme Laboratory in Jersey City and the Childs Pulp Color Company also made space available to the Institute. While the insurance covered most of the reconstruction costs, the Alumni Association also made considerable donations to resurrect the Institute.[62] President Rogers was so consumed with the construction and reevaluation of the Institute's offerings that for the first time in the Institute's history the annual report was suspended. In 1939, he released an annual report covering two years, 1937 and 1938.[63]

While ideas for new course offerings were tabled during this period, the fire provided the Institute with an opportunity to enhance its laboratories and classrooms. After a year of construction, the building was not only completed but also improved. The chemical laboratories acquired more locker space; lighting was improved; DC and AC power distribution systems were updated; and new dispensing rooms, new furniture, and new equipment were added. After a tumultuous year of dealing with the fallout from the fire, President Rogers commented, "The year 1938–39 became one of very substantial growth and development."[64]

A NEW DAY

With construction completed on the main building, the Institute's annual Open House Day in February became a highly visible event and a cause for real celebration. Despite a brutal snow storm, over 3,000 people attended. Professors and students alike were surprised that over 20 percent of attendees were women. This called for a change in educational assumptions, and officials at the Institute understood that it would soon be accepting women in larger numbers than ever before. The event was so popular that for the first time the *Reporter* published a special section with various advertisements, including one that featured the Institute's modern wind tunnel.[65]

The professors on hand showcased their education services, along with all of the Institute's technical equipment, to the eager onlookers. The Department of Chemistry demonstrated a

micromethod of producing indigo from coal tar, which was an experiment taught in one of the classes at the Institute. A Ford V-8 engine running on specially manufactured gas was demonstrated, together with a Fairbanks-Morse Diesel and an International Harvester Diesel engine.[66] Gasoline and steam engines, a stroboscope, and dynamoter equipment for automobiles were also viewed with awe by visitors.

The electrical engineering department dazzled guests with a high-voltage transformer which caused the electric current to jump the gap between two parallel wires three feet apart. A participant recalled, "The display in fluorescence and the two stroboscopes proved, for some reason, to be particularly fascinating for the female spectators."[67]

The Open House Day program was used each year as a recruitment tool—and the Institute was overwhelmed annually by the responses.[68]

POLY TAKES FLIGHT

As the decade came to a close, the Institute reached the highest enrollment in its 86-year history. Including the summer session, enrollment for 1939–40 was 3,818.[69] As new regulations were developed and put in place by organizations like the Engineers' Council for Professional Development, the National Council of State Boards of Engineering, and the Committee on Aims and Objectives of the Society for the Promotion of Engineering Education, the Institute reevaluated its course offerings in various departments.[70]

As one result, the aeronautical and metallurgical engineering courses were separated from the Mechanical Engineering Department.[71] This resulted in bachelor of science degrees in aeronautical engineering and metallurgical engineering. The changing of course descriptions and development of new degree programs was a common practice for the Institute as it continually evaluated each department, its respective enrollment, and the increasing demands of the industrial world.

Thirteen new courses in the graduate division were also offered, including electro-chemistry, chemistry of non-aqueous solutions, chemistry of coordination compounds, chemistry of petroleum, chemistry of resins and plastics, metallurgical thermodynamics, and fundamentals of radiation.[72]

At the beginning of 1939, a cooperative program was established among Westinghouse Electric, New York University, Stevens Institute, and Polytechnic Institute.[73] This initiative was a continuation of the research and development efforts pioneered by the Institute through the preceding decade. Later that year, the Institute welcomed Professor Paul Bruins, who co-invented the basis for improved plastic composites and taught the world's first graduate course in plastics at Polytechnic.[74]

While the Institute had bounced back from the Depression and a devastating fire, it would soon face a major crisis with the rest of the nation: World War II. The scientific discoveries and contributions made by alumni, professors, and students would greatly aid the U.S. military in winning the war and ridding the world of Adolf Hitler.

Pictured above is the building on Schermerhorn Street that housed the Mechanical Engineering Department in the 1940s. To its immediate right sits the Quonset hut, which was used as a research facility. Nobel Prize winner Professor Rudolph Marcus conducted groundbreaking research on electron transfer theory in the Quonset hut.

CHAPTER FIVE

POLYTECHNIC'S GOLDEN YEARS

1940 –1952

Before the fateful December 7, 1941, Polytechnic's facilities, both experimental and pedagogical, have been directed toward the swift execution of the task at hand—the destruction of the Axis and all it stands for.

—*Polywog*, 1943

AS THE NATION EMERGED from the depths of the Great Depression of the 1930s, Polytechnic experienced its highest enrollment numbers to date. Between 1940 and 1941, approximately 3,900 students attended the day, evening, and summer sessions.[1] Tuition at this time was $180 per semester.

The foresight and guidance provided by President Kolbe in the late 1920s and early 1930s, and the Institute's president, Harry Rogers, enabled Polytechnic to realize such success. However, in order to meet increasing demands, the Institute was forced to continually acquire more space, which was rented from neighboring businesses.

The technological advances experienced in the 1930s, despite the economic crisis, came to be characterized as the "American Way of Life." Another catch phrase of this time was the image of America as a "nation on wheels." In many ways the United States had reached a pinnacle of technological advancement with the various innovative applications of steel, power, and electricity.[2] Polytechnic was instrumental in many of the technological advances experienced during this time.

By 1941, the Aeronautical Engineering (A.E.) Department had been established and was headed by Professor R. Paul Harrington. The first Bachelor of Science degrees in A.E. were awarded to William S.

Holmes and Aaron Krushner. The following year, Masters of Science in A.E. degrees were offered.

As it did in the 1930s, the Institute increased its research efforts. In the early 1940s, research in science and civil engineering was conducted in three ways: in specific assignments of staff with direct budgetary support; in investigations undertaken for graduate or undergraduate theses; and in individual studies carried out by members of the faculty.[3] Research included methods for refining lubricants in cooperation with the Sherwood Refining Company; studies in the field of polymer chemistry with the Monsanto Chemical Company and the Jay Novelty Company; the derivation and application of citric acid with Charles Pfizer and Company; and studies in the field of high molecular weight chemistry with Colgate-Palmolive-Peet Company, among others.[4]

With enrollment numbers increasing, the Institute was well-known academically for two reasons:

Following the untimely death of alumnus Dr. Joseph J. Mattiello, class of 1925, the New York Paint and Varnish Club presented this plaque to the Institute in recognition of Mattiello's contribution to scientific developments and human relations within the surface coating industry.

providing an excellent education for first generation Americans and for continuing education towards masters and doctorate degrees.

While the campus itself was less than appealing, it was the educational excellence that brought students and professors to Brooklyn. Harry Wechsler, president of Borden Chemical Company, received his doctorate from Polytechnic in 1948, and is a current trustee. He recently recalled his first memories of Polytechnic.

I looked at [Polytechnic] mostly as a fountainhead of very thorough and scholarly research being done in several fields, chemistry being one of them. Polytechnic was a school where you went for a solid education, no frills. Polytechnic represents an opportunity for first generation students and for immigrant families to send their children on to higher education. So Polytechnic had these two important identities. One was in its undergraduate school to attract the immigrant population of New York primarily. It was a subway school in one way. At the same time, however, in parallel, you had some very high class work being done in the graduate school.[5]

WORLD WAR II

United States involvement in World War II became inevitable on December 7, 1941, when the Japanese attacked Pearl Harbor. Until September 11, 2001, this was the deadliest attack on American soil. The following day the United States declared war on Japan. Three days later Hitler declared war on the United States.[6] The magnitude of this conflict would test the minds, souls, and hearts of all Americans and its allies around the world.

As did other colleges and universities, Polytechnic contributed significantly to the war effort. Aside from students and faculty called to serve, the Institute developed courses to aid the military. In April 1941, a new defense course was established, designed to function as part of a nationwide plan to prepare 1,500 men as inspectors of powder and explosives under the engineering defense training program. The course, offered in both day and evening sessions, was taught by Professor Vincent F. Eckstein of the Chemistry Department. He was designated as one of 20 experts to direct such courses at technical schools nationwide.[7]

The following month, President Rogers joined the war effort in Washington and was appointed chairman of a government effort entitled "General Priorities." Since all materials were at a premium, he was appointed to develop and organize the distribution and usage of rubber, rubber synthetics, polyvinylchloride, and cork. Rogers was later called to serve as chief of the rubber and rubber products branch of the War Production Board.[8]

President Rogers was also an officer on the Engineers Defense Board, which included leaders representing the American Society of Civil Engineers, the American Institute of Mining and Metallurgical Engineers, the American Society of Mechanical Engineers, the American Institute of Electrical Engineers, the Society of Automotive Engineers, and the American Institute of Chemical Engineers.[9]

Due to the United States' rapid military expansion program, engineering and aviation officers were in great demand. In 1941, the Institute was designated as a college whose graduates were eligible for commissions as ensigns in the United States Naval Reserve, and the U.S. Army was also actively recruiting students.[10]

Students of the Institute took out their aggressions against the tyrants of the time, as evidenced in the pages of the *Polywog*.

The spirit of belligerency within the Polytechnic extended to the local bowling alleys. A favorite innovation was pretending the ten-pins were miniature Mussolinis and Hitlers, and then blasting them from the alleys with well-directed throws.[11]

WOMEN AT POLY

Historically known as a "men's" institution, Polytechnic began receiving applications from women during this era. This was due in part to many men being called to service. However, the interest and aptitude of the women students confirmed the notion that men would not only have to accept women in the field of science, but also realize that their accomplishments would be equal within the scientific community.

On October 12, 1941, the *Brooklyn Eagle* ran a story about Marjorie Wilson, who at the age of 18 was the only woman studying during the day session out of 752 students. She enrolled as an engineering student with a concentration on drafting. The reporter wrote of her first day on campus: "Marjorie has introduced a bit of silk-stocking glamour into the citadel of machinery, compasses and blackboards." The article noted that her professors had to assign her to sit in the rear of the classroom because her presence resulted in "wandering" eyes.

One of her professors, Frederick W. Minge, encouraged the idea of women seeking higher education. "It is common in wartime to have girl tracers."

Above right: Professor of Chemistry Sophie Kahn explains the history of plastics to two army trainees, Charles H. Stevens of Chicago, and Ralph P. Weiss Jr. of Dubuque, Iowa. In 1943, Kahn became the Institute's first female instructor.

Below: Alice Weltman and Elise C. Stahl set up laboratory equipment for an experiment in advanced chemistry in 1941. As World War II became a reality and men were called to serve, the Institute began enrolling more female students.

Professor Minge continued, "Not only because they free men for the armed forces, but also because they have the patience and neatness so necessary for drafting."[12]

Steps taken by students like Marjorie Wilson would eventually result in the Institute becoming a full-fledged coeducational college. However, in many ways, it was an uphill battle for women to be accepted into the scientific community. Among women enrolled at Polytechnic in the early 1940s was Gertrude Elion, who never completed her doctoral degree at Polytechnic because of financial constraints, but went on to receive the Nobel Prize in Medicine in 1988. The Institute awarded her an honorary degree the following year. A chapter in the 1998 book by Tom Brokaw, *The Greatest Generation*, was devoted to her.

In 1943, another important milestone was reached at Polytechnic regarding coeducation when Sophie Kahn became the first female science instructor in the Institute's history.

A LEADING FACULTY

As the war pushed into 1942, the Institute continued to progress by offering the first Bachelor of Science in Metallurgical Engineering. The first degree was awarded to James G. Farmer. The same year, the first Master of Science in A.E. degrees were awarded to Edwin F. Miller and

Sebastian V. Nardo. The accelerated speed with which the A.E. Department flourished was later supported by aeronautical research the Institute conducted in conjunction with the military and the National Advisory Committee for Aeronautics (NACA), now the National Aeronautics and Space Administration (NASA).

It was during this period that the Institute would reinforce its teaching program, attracting leading scholars to mold the minds of its high caliber students. The notion of recruiting world-renowned professors began in the early 1930s with the additions of Professor Weber and Professor Othmer.

Students and faculty enjoy a good laugh during a seminar at the Institute conducted by Professor John Charles Olsen (seated on stage closest to the audience) in 1946. While Olsen retired in 1944, he continued teaching a handful of subjects. Among those in the front row are John Brierley, President Rogers, and Professor Othmer.

Professor Othmer drove the Chemical Engineering Department to even greater heights than his predecessor, Professor John C. Olsen, who was instrumental in establishing chemical engineering as a separate discipline. Professor Olsen was also a secretary and the third president of the American Institute of Chemical Engineers.

Another leading scientist who joined the faculty in 1942 was Professor Isidor Fankuchen. Professor Fankuchen would become known as a renowned crystallographer. Like many other notable scientists before him, Professor Fankuchen would use the Institute's laboratories as his canvas. He was most interested in biological structures, and his early research focused on steroids, chymotrypsin and hemoglobin, and plant virus preparations. His later interests included crystal structure determination, small-angle scattering, X-ray instrumentation, powder diffraction, low temperature studies, and optics of visible light and X-rays.[13]

Fankuchen later founded, and for a period of time operated on a non-profit basis, the Polycrystal

Book Service, and was the first American editor of *Acta Crystallographica*. He was the first president of the American Crystallographic Association (ACA) in 1950. He was best known as a superb teacher, and for building an outstanding center for crystallography at Polytechnic. In his honor, ACA established the Isidor Fankuchen Award in 1971.

Fankuchen was aided during this time by Professor Benjamin Post, who along with other Poly scientists, made the Institute one of the world's leading research institutions in X-ray crystallography. Post went on to develop a three-beam experimental technique for determining certain features (phases) of the interactions between X-ray beams and atomic structure from an analysis of the intensity of the reflected X-ray beam. For this work, he received the ACA's Bertram E. Warren Award in 1982, an award given every three years for distinguished contributions to the physics of solids or liquids using X-ray, neutron, or electron diffraction techniques.

POLY WELCOMES HERMAN MARK

In 1942, Poly also welcomed to its faculty the renowned scientist Herman F. Mark, who joined the faculty as professor of chemistry. Professor Mark led an eminent industrial research team in creating many commercial polymers and later established the Polymer Research Institute in 1946. His principal research concentrated on X-rays and electrons for the study of the structure of matter, and on the synthesis, characterization, reactions, and properties of natural and synthetic polymers.

His career was legendary before he arrived at the Institute, but the heights to which his career would rise while at the Institute was nothing short of amazing.

Professor Mark's son, Hans Mark, former chancellor of the University of Texas, has been a trustee of the Institute since 1985. In a recent interview, Hans Mark, who was born in Mannheim, Germany in 1929, explained how important the immigrant experience has been to the Institute since its inception, and today.

If you look at our student bodies, they have not reflected the demographics of the whole city, but the demographics of the most recent cohort of immigrants. You know, when I was a kid, I'd say

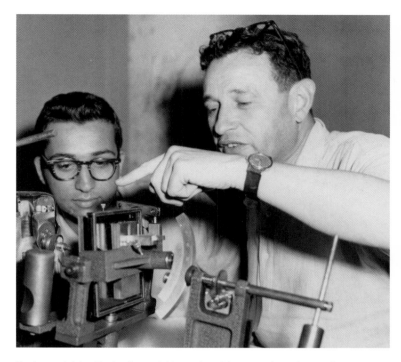

Professor Isidor Fankuchen, right, works with research assistants in his laboratory. Fankuchen's research in crystallography would make him world-famous, and in 1950, he became the first president of the American Crystallographic Association (ACA). In his honor, ACA established the Isidor Fankuchen Award in 1971.

80 percent of the students at Poly were Jews, and many of them were immigrants.

It has been literally true, that engineering has been the loophole through which the immigrants climb into the middle class ... our function was to create an elite of the new immigrant, and by and large, we succeeded if you look at our alumni.[14]

In addition to teaching an introductory course in polymer chemistry, Professor Mark organized a Saturday morning symposium series at which leading scientists spoke. These included Linus Pauling, the only person to receive two unshared Nobel Prizes: for Chemistry in 1954, and for Peace in 1962.

These symposia were widely attended and allowed students to observe first-hand the latest in polymer research. Over the years these weekly meetings would become legendary and achieved international recognition in the field of polymer

POLY GRADUATE INVENTS FIRST "GISMO"

TELEVISION PRODUCTION WAS IN MANY ways uncharted territory in the late 1940s and 1950s. Television programs, particularly fantasy shows, were very popular, but very limited technologically. While faced with a restricted budget, George Gould, class of 1946, the director of the once popular television program, *Tom Corbett, Space Cadet*, designed a piece of equipment that he called the "gismo," in 1951.[1] This phrase would later become a part of the American lexicon, meaning a piece of equipment that saves time or money.

The gismo, which was developed with ABC engineers Ralph Drucker and David Fee, was the size of a record player. It was an electronic device which synchronized two television cameras, permitting one picture to be superimposed on the other.[2]

From a technical perspective, the gismo removed the electrons at a point in one picture so that electrons from the other picture could come through the resulting space. The pictures were then automatically coordinated by a television synch-generator.

In one episode of the series, space cadets crossed boiling mud on a faraway planet. The men jumped from rock to rock in what seemed to be a realistic setting. However, the boiling mud was actually a pot of hot cereal, and the rocks were papier-mâché pieces, about an inch and a half in diameter. The space cadets were actually jumping around in a room painted black. The gismo superimposed their actions on to the fabricated cereal and papier-mâché.[3]

This invention revolutionized the art of special effects. In the months and years that followed, directors, producers, and advertising agencies sought Gould's permission to use the gismo.

In addition to the term "gismo," another widely used term, "transistor," also has a Poly connection. It was originated by John Pierce, who received an honorary doctorate from Polytechnic.

The revolutionary new switch, invented in Bell Labs in Murray Hill, New Jersey, in 1947, soon would replace vacuum tubes, thus turning the world of electronics—and the world itself—upside down and into a world of miniaturized circuits. Pierce, who was an engineer at Bell Labs at the time, was asked by a colleague to come up with a name for the new device. Combining some of the qualities and features of the new device, Pierce suggested "transistor."

Pierce was proud of his contribution to the evolving vocabulary of science. "It's the most significant thing that ever happened to me," he once said.[4] Pierce is also the originator of the Echo and Telstar communication satellite programs.

science. Professor Mark also organized intensive summer courses for the study of macromolecular science to which he invited outside university scholars and industrial researchers.[15]

During a recent interview, Professor Herbert Morawetz recalled his reasons for attending Polytechnic. In 1947, while working during the day, he, like many others, took advantage of the evening courses offered at the Institute. In 1951 he earned a doctoral degree and began teaching at the Institute as an assistant professor. In the years that followed he became a full professor. In 1971, he was named director of the Polymer Research Institute, a position he held until 1981. Professor Morawetz, currently the associate editor of *Macromolecules*, said a primary reason for attending the Institute was the opportunity to study under Professor Mark.

I was employed in industry. I was thirty-two years old. I was married. I had a child, and I

Left: Herbert Morawetz received his Doctorate in Chemistry from Polytechnic in 1950. He taught chemistry at Polytechnic from 1951 to 1981. During that time, he guided 57 students to their doctorates. He served from 1971 to 1981 as the director of the Polymer Research Institute. He published over 200 research papers, wrote the books *Macromolecules in Solution* and *Polymers: The Origins and Growth of a Science*, and received an ACS award in polymer chemistry in 1986. He retired from Polytechnic in 1986 with the title of university professor emeritus.

Right: Professor Herman F. Mark, known worldwide as the "Father of Polymer Science," conducts an experiment.

applied science and engineering, were in progress.[17] For example, in 1941, Joseph J. Jacobs, class of 1937, developed a system that could manufacture soap in 15 minutes compared to the traditional process that required between three and seven days.[18]

Jacobs continued as an assistant professor of chemical engineering at the Institute for approximately six years, while studying for both his master and doctorate degrees, and then headed west to San Francisco to take a position assisting in the engineering of liquid fertilizers. After doing consultant work for two years at Kaiser Aluminum and Chemical Company, in which he helped develop caustic soda, Jacobs started his own business. Today, Jacobs Engineering Group Inc. employs approximately 30,000 and yields $5 billion in revenues.[19]

could not afford to go to school in the daytime, but I heard that Professor Mark had joined Polytechnic. He was more or less one of the grandfathers of polymer chemistry, and he started the first polymer graduate work in America. There was no such thing at the time, and I heard I could take courses at night. Since I couldn't attend full-time, this was a wonderful opportunity to get an education. When I started, science was practically a religion, and people worked terribly hard.[16]

With Professors Weber, Othmer, Mark, and Fankuchen teaching the gifted scientific minds of the time, it was the beginning of the Institute's golden years.

RESEARCH ADVANCEMENTS

As the nation soldiered on during World War II, Polytechnic continued to grow. By 1941, the graduate division had increased enrollment by 60 percent from 1935. In this division, 87 separate projects, including original research in basic or

POLYMER RESEARCH INSTITUTE

PROFESSOR HERMAN F. MARK ARRIVED at Polytechnic Institute in 1942 after fleeing Europe and the tyranny of Adolf Hitler. He quickly began formulating a curriculum for the teaching of polymer chemistry. After six years, he created the world-renowned Polymer Research Institute (PRI), currently headed by Professor Richard Gross.

When Mark established the Institute, there were only a handful of chemists working with synthetic polymers at U.S. universities. Among them were such accomplished scientists as Carl Speed Marvel and Paul Flory. But none succeeded in creating a facility like the Polymer Research Institute.

Under Mark's active leadership, PRI quickly grew and attracted first-class scientists, students, and postdoctoral researchers from all over the world, including Great Britain, India, France, Israel, Italy, Japan, and the Soviet Union.

Among those who came to study, teach, or do postdoctoral work were Turner Alfrey, Herbert Morawetz, Eli Pearce, Charles Overberger, Gerald Oster, Murray Goodman, Paul Doty, Bruno Zimm, Frederick Eirich, Robert Simha, Arthur Tobolsky, and many others. The program was open to undergraduates and graduate students, awarding MS and PhD degrees in Polymer Chemistry.

PRI changed the way industry approached polymer science. Following PRI's lead, numerous companies began polymer programs, including Dow Chemical, Phillips Petroleum, Rohm and Haas, and Shell Oil. Many of these were started by scientists who had studied or taught at PRI. Without PRI's influence, polymer science would not have advanced at such an accelerated rate.

POLYMER CHEMISTRY

Polymers are substances made of giant molecules formed by uniting simple molecules, or monomers, by covalent bonds. The term "polymer" derives from the Greek and means "many parts." Polymers have high molecular weights, which give them useful characteristics such as high viscosity, elasticity, and great strength.

Today, the existence of polymers is readily accepted in the scientific world, and polymer

Professor Herman F. Mark developed the Institute of Polymer Research, which eventually became known as the Polymer Research Institute. The organization acted as a magnet for top-notch scientists and researchers from all around the world.

In an interview conducted months before his death on October 23, 2004, Jacobs, then 88, explained his initial interest in Polytechnic.

Well, I went to Brooklyn Tech High School because I was interested in engineering, and the natural extension for Brooklyn Tech High School was Polytechnic. It was in a section of Brooklyn that wasn't very desirable, but it was almost a logical step from Brooklyn Tech to Polytech. Also, I could commute, live at home, save money, and could have a job while I worked at Polytech.[20]

Jacobs, a first generation Lebanese-American, explained why he chose to start his own company.

That was a primal urge to start my own company. It was a natural thing for me wanting to do that. It comes from my family background and

science has become a vital branch of chemistry. But that acceptance has come fairly recently. As late as the early 20th century, many of the world's most prominent chemists resisted the concept of macromolecules. Professor Mark, along with Herman Staudinger, another giant in the field of polymer chemistry, helped to change that. Another important influence came from the work of Wallace Carothers, whose investigations at DuPont demonstrated that polymers, made up of hundreds of covalently-joined monomers, could be synthesized. This work led to the introduction of the first synthetic fiber, nylon, in the 1930s.

MARK'S EARLY DAYS

Herman Mark was born in Vienna, Austria, in 1895. After receiving his education at the University of Vienna, Mark joined the newly organized Institute for Fiber Research at the Kaiser Wilhelm Institute in Germany. Mark worked on the molecular structure of fibers using the new tools of X-ray diffraction and ultramicroscopy.

In 1926, Mark took a position at I.G. Farben, which had begun to focus on the manufacture of cellulose acetate and viscose, and was investigating the production of synthetic fibers. In 1932, the plant's managing director informed Mark that since Hitler would soon take power in Germany, his exposure as a foreigner and the son of a Jewish man made him politically vulnerable. Mark sought employment outside Germany, and eventually accepted a position as professor of physical chemistry at the University of Vienna, where he designed a curriculum in polymer chemistry. His years in Vienna proved to be an important prelude for the later Polymer Research Institute.

Austria proved to be only a temporary haven from the Nazis, however, and by early 1938, Mark began preparing to leave Europe for good. He covertly began buying platinum wire, which he bent into coat hangers to smuggle out of Austria. The value of the platinum was roughly $50,000, a considerable amount of money in the 1930s, and enough to pay for Mark and his wife to flee Europe. Mark initially lived in Canada before accepting an offer to become an adjunct professor at the Polytechnic Institute.

A brilliant orator and professor, Mark was Viennese to the core, genteel and urbane. Professor Murray Goodman, who taught at PRI, describes Mark as "a combination of a European and Viennese gentleman, with the openness to people, places, and ideas which are really typically American." According to another colleague, Professor Eli Pearce, former director of the Polymer Research Institute, Mark was "formal in an informal way."

Editor's Note: Text in this feature is adapted, in part, from a historical brochure entitled Polymer Research Institute, *published by the American Chemical Society (ACS), in recognition of PRI being designated a National Historic Chemical Landmark on September 3, 2003. The brochure was written by ACS's Judah Ginsberg. Dr. Eli Pearce of Polytechnic also furnished information for this feature. He is a past president and current board member of ACS, and a former director of PRI.*

my cultural background of being the son of immigrants for whom the main objective was to be in business for yourself.[21]

The American dream of gold-paved streets was shared by a number of Jacobs' peers, many of whose parents hailed from Europe, as did Professors Mark and Weber. While Jacobs' early achievements in chemical engineering were lauded by faculty and students, pressing concerns resulting from the war drove the Institute's agenda, which was enunciated in the pages of the 1943 *Polywog*.

Since even before the fateful December 7, 1941, the Polytechnic's facilities, both experimental and pedagogical, have been directed toward the swift execution of the task at hand—the destruction of the Axis and all it stands for.[22]

WAR EFFORTS

Prior to the declaration of war, the United States Office of Education sponsored engineering, science, and management defense training courses at Polytechnic. These courses were renamed *war-training courses* after the attack on Pearl Harbor.

The Polytechnic research program applied itself to the war effort by offering courses studying phenomena under ultra-high frequency conditions, the performance of various dielectrics under the influence of ultra-high frequencies, and investigations into the field of radar. Within the chemical engineering department, research was being conducted in the fields of polystyrene and sucrose acetate plastics, butadiene production for synthetic rubber manufacturing, high-octane gasoline production by polymerization, and solvent recovery by absorption.[23]

One direct contact between Polytechnic and the war was made when 500 U.S. Army Specialized Training Program students moved into barracks at the Fort Greene housing project, located a few blocks from the Institute. Two thirds of the group were enrolled as freshmen, the others as upper classmen.[24]

In the midst of war, President Rogers underscored the nation's need for bright engineers.

Engineers are needed to plan, design, and produce the innumerable items by which we will be enabled to defend ourselves against a brutal, ruthless, and arrogant totalitarianism, to support democracies, and to preserve the freedoms in which these democracies believe.[25]

FRATERNITIES

The Institute was home to a handful of fraternities in the 1940s. Some of these chapters had been in existence since the 19th century. Students and alumni enjoyed, and benefited from, these organizations as an outlet during their school years and again when they entered the workforce.

Among active chapters was Alpha Chi Rho, which was established in April 1896. Their faculty advisor was John Brierley, secretary of the alumni association. Other active chapters included Alpha Kappa Pi, founded in 1926; Alpha Phi Delta and Lambda Chi Alpha, both founded in 1920; Eta Kappa Nu, founded in 1936; Tau Beta Pi, of which

President Rogers was a member, founded in 1931; and Phi Lambda Upsilon, the honorary chemical society, founded in 1932.[26]

In 1939, Lambda Chi Alpha bought a house on Sydney Place, which is still in use at Polytechnic.

In March 1943, a chapter of the Society of The Sigma Xi was also established. The fundamental purpose of Sigma Xi was to encourage original investigation in pure and applied science. Students invited to join Sigma Xi were required to have demonstrated an aptitude for scientific research.[27]

Like the rest of the country, the Institute continued to contribute to the development of a stronger America during the war. With more governmental

As early as 1896, fraternities were an important part of the Institute, and by the 1940s, there were a growing number of active chapters on campus. President Rogers, standing, presided over the National Interfraternity Conference in New York City on November, 19, 1941. Next to Rogers is Wendell Willkie, a principal speaker at the event. Willkie unsuccessfully campaigned against Franklin D. Roosevelt for president in 1940.

National Interfraternity Conference

Harry Rogers presides at N. I. C. banquet in New York Nov. 29. Almost sixty Alpha Taus attend program featuring Wendell Willkie, Lowell Thomas, Dixon Ryan Fox, and Henry M. Wriston. John MacGregor on conference executive committee.

HARRY S. ROGERS (right), who presided at the National Interfraternity Conference banquet, chats with Wendell Willkie, principal speaker.

HANS J. REISSNER

BORN ON JANUARY 18, 1874, IN BERLIN, Germany, Hans Jacob Reissner earned a degree in civil engineering from Berlin's Technische Hochschule in 1897. He then spent a year in the United States working as a structural draftsman. Reissner returned to Germany to study physics with the world-renowned Max Planck at Berlin University. In 1900, Reissner returned to the Technische Hochschule, where he studied under Heinrich Mueller-Breslau and completed his engineering doctorate in 1902. His dissertation was on the vibrations of framed structures.

Reissner then joined the faculty at Berlin's Technische Hochschule, but he also worked on side projects, including structural analysis for Count Zeppelin. In 1904, he was awarded a fellowship to study the use of iron in construction in the United States.[1]

In 1906, Reissner returned to Germany and was appointed professor of mechanics at the Technische Hochschule in Aachen. Until this time, his research had dealt with topics at the intersections of mechanics and physics. But he decided to turn his attention to the field of aviation, which was an uncharted field at the time. By 1908, Reissner had become familiar enough with aircraft stability, control, and propulsion to deliver a seminal paper on the topic. His research led to the first successful all-metal airplane.[2]

After seven years in Aachen, Reissner was invited to return to Berlin's Technische Hochschule in 1913 as professor of mathematics in the Civil Engineering Department. During World War I, he was responsible for the structural engineering of the Staaken four-engine bomber; and he designed the first controllable-pitch propellers for this aircraft. He was awarded the Iron Cross for civilians for his effort.[3]

In 1938, Reissner, like Professor Herman Mark, escaped the odious rule of Nazi Germany and immigrated to the United States. He began teaching at the Illinois Institute of Technology, where he stayed until 1944. Later that year, he joined the A.E. Department at Polytechnic where he taught until 1954. For his 75th birthday in 1949, he was honored with the presentation of the *Reissner Anniversary Volume* at a dinner in New York City. Professor Reissner retired from professional life in 1954 and died in 1967.[4] His contribution to aviation and to the students and faculty of the Institute is legendary.

Inset: Throughout his career, Hans Jacob Reissner, shown here at age 81, revolutionized the field of aerodynamics. He imparted his expertise and knowledge to students of the Institute from 1944 to 1954.

Below is the experimental airplane of 1913, built by Hans Reissner in Aachen, Germany. Professor Reissner was one of the first scientists to investigate the problems of flight with scientific methods. In this all-metal plane, the fuselage and controls are located in front of the wing, which for the first time was manufactured out of corrugated sheet by the Junkers Company.

funding, research programs were initiated at technical schools across the nation. As a result, new courses were offered at the Institute. In 1943, the Mechanical Engineering Department established Polytechnic's first courses in air pollution control. Later that year, doctorates in aerospace engineering were offered for the first time.

AERODYNAMICS ON THE RISE

The A.E. Department received a renowned professor in 1944, Hans Jacob Reissner. Professor Reissner, a civil engineer, taught at the Illinois Institute of Technology for six years before arriving at Polytechnic. Earlier in his career, he held the position of professor of mathematics at the Technische Hochschule in Aachen, Germany. During this time his research dealt with the intersections of mechanics and physics. However, his attention gradually turned to aviation. In 1908, he began working on what would become the first successful all-metal airplane, the *Ente*, which was completed in 1913.[28]

With his vast knowledge and experience, Professor Reissner proved to be a catalyst in advancing the A.E. Department. Students, who referred to him as "Big Doc," wrote of him: "Although here but a relatively short time, the students of the Aero Department have come deeply to admire and respect him."[29]

MASS PRODUCING PENICILLIN DURING WORLD WAR II

ONE OF THE INSTITUTE'S FAVORITE sons, Jasper H. Kane, was a chemist working for Charles Pfizer and Company in Brooklyn during World War II. One day, as the war continued and casualties mounted, he had a vision that would ultimately change the world.

In 1942, he offered a bold proposal to executives at Pfizer. Kane was convinced that he could develop a process to make penicillin in large quantities with equipment Pfizer used to make citric acid, an ingredient manufactured by deep-tank fermentation. Kane's idea was radical. In order to put his concept in motion, Pfizer would have to cease its most profitable business, the making of citric acid, and retool its equipment to attempt making penicillin in mass quantities. While Kane was confident, many executives at Pfizer had trepidations.[1] A senior executive at Pfizer wrote his opinion of Kane's idea.

This mold is as temperamental as an opera singer. The yields are low ... the isolation is difficult ... the extraction is murder ... and the purification process itself invites disaster. I implore all of you to think of the risks.[2]

While the risks were clear from a corporate standpoint, Allied soldiers were dying by the hundreds from infections resulting from wounds, and a remedy was desperately needed. After considerable deliberation, Pfizer's board approved Kane's idea. To achieve its goal, Pfizer bought an old ice-making plant in Brooklyn. In order to complete construction, Kane turned to another Institute graduate, John E. McKeen, class of 1925, who earned an electrical engineering degree before joining Pfizer, to oversee development.[3]

With everything from scrap metal to gasoline rationed, Kane handed McKeen the challenge of a lifetime: to build a plant in six months in the middle of a war. McKeen met the challenge and scrambled for every rivet and bolt. Piece by piece, working 24 hours a day, seven days a week, McKeen and his team built the plant in four months. A driving force behind working at this rate was best illustrated by a sign posted

Recently, alumnus Professor Martin Bloom, who went on to become dean of engineering, and later director of the Aerodynamics Laboratory, recalled his first memories of Professor Reissner. "The man who was my thesis advisor for my undergraduate work was a very famous person in aeronautics. His name was Hans Reissner."[30]

I was once doing mathematics exercises. I had a professor who gave us a lot of math exercises to do, and I was sitting there and doing them hour after hour. [Professor] Reissner came over. He spoke with a deep German accent. "Mr. Bloom," he said, "what have you been doing there all this time?" I said, "Well, Professor Whitford gave us fifty problems in mathe-matics to do for homework." He said, "I didn't know there were fifty problems in mathematics."[31]

OVER 2,000 POLY VETS DURING WORLD WAR II

As the war continued into 1944, America and its Allies steadily gained ground, and edged closer to victory. However, casualty rates were increasing at alarming rates. While all materials were at a premium, medical supplies, specifically penicillin, were in steep demand. The lack of such medical supplies unfortunately resulted in the deaths of many soldiers suffering from wounds that could have been treated with the proper medicine.

by the then chairman of Pfizer, John Smith, which read, "The faster you build this plant, the more soldiers we will save."[4]

On March 1, 1943, Jasper Kane and John McKeen made history when they flipped the switches on fourteen 7,500-gallon tanks to begin production. By the end of 1943, Pfizer was making 45 million units of penicillin a month. While Pfizer's team was the most proficient at mass producing penicillin, they shared the deep-tank process with roughly twenty other major companies to meet the needs presented by war.[5]

This "Race Against Death" poster was used to motivate construction workers to quickly build a new facility so penicillin could be immediately manufactured and made available during World War II. Originally planned to be constructed in six months, the building was completed in four months.

Kane went on to become vice president and director of Pfizer Inc., and was leader of the team that developed Terramycin, an antibiotic effective against more than 100 diseases. He also helped developed a new fermentation process for organic acids and vitamins. His generous support of Polytechnic allowed the creation of two new laboratories in 1999: the Jasper H. Kane Organic Chemistry Laboratory and the Jasper H. Kane Crystallography Laboratory. Research in these laboratories is expected to produce more pure pharmaceuticals and other materials.[6]

Kane was an honorary Doctorate of Science recipient in 1995. He died November 16, 2004, in Delray Beach, Florida, at the age of 101.

During a commencement speech in May of 2004, Henry A. McKinnell Jr., chairman of the board and chief executive officer of Pfizer Inc., implored the graduating class that achievements made by their fellow alumni should not only be cherished but also should serve as inspiration. He said, "The genius of Jasper Kane and John McKeen soon made Pfizer the world's largest producer of penicillin. Did that achievement turn the tide of the Second World War? No—brave men and women did that. But cheap and readily available penicillin did save hundreds of thousands of lives during the war ... and tens of millions of lives after it."[7]

Left: In 1945, President Rogers, left, and Secretary John Brierley commissioned a plaque in remembrance of the 2,088 Poly men who served during World War II. The Institute lost 36 alumni during the war.

Below: President Rogers (right) and Professor Weber enjoy a conversation over a cup of coffee at a luncheon in the late 1940s. Together, these two men led the Institute to new heights.

The groundbreaking work in this area conducted by Jasper H. Kane, class of 1928, would ultimately save thousands of soldiers' lives, and later millions of other lives around the world. Alexander Fleming developed penicillin, the first true antibiotic, in 1928; however, it was difficult to produce. Before, and during the first years of the war, penicillin had to be made flask by flask, a process resulting in scant supplies.[32]

Kane was the leader of the research team at Charles Pfizer and Company, which included Dr. Peter P. Regna, class of 1932, '35, '37, '42, H'94, that developed the processes for the mass production of penicillin, streptomycin, Terramycin, and other antibiotics.

Despite Kane's best efforts, however, the war would take the lives of 36 alumni. In the end, 2,088 Poly men served their country during World War II. In 1945, a World War II memorial plaque was presented to the school. It reads:

In honor of the 2,088 Polytechnic men who have studied the arts of peace in this institution, went forth at the call of their country to fight for the establishment of a world in which they might be freely practiced, and in memory of those who gave their lives as the price of victory.[33]

Among the brave and dedicated alumni who served during World War II was Charles E. Anderson, class of 1948. Anderson was a captain in the Air Force and also served as the weather officer for the Tuskegee Airmen Regiment. Twelve years after graduating from Poly, Anderson became one of the first African-Americans to earn a PhD in Meteorology from MIT.[34]

THE MICROWAVE RESEARCH INSTITUTE

As World War II came to a close, the Institute was expanding at an astonishing rate. In 1946, the Microwave Research Institute (MRI) was established under Professor Ernst Weber, who was instrumental in developing radar systems employed by the military.

During the early days of World War II, Professor Weber organized a microwave research group to

THE FIRST ENCYCLOPEDIA OF CHEMICAL ENGINEERING

AFTER YEARS OF WORK, WHICH SOME called a "Herculean effort," Professors Raymond E. Kirk and Donald F. Othmer released the first edition of the *Kirk-Othmer Encyclopedia of Chemical Technology* in December 1947.[1]

This volume, which was edited by Anthony Standen and Janet D. Scott, was planned to be the first of 10 volumes. One reviewer called the encyclopedia a "veritable library of information for the chemical industry."[2]

The first volume was an excellent research tool. The articles included graphs, charts, and tables. Topics included air conditioning, distilled alcohol beverages, and abrasives. All the contributors were affiliated with well known companies such as Charles Pfizer and Company, Dow Chemical Company, and academic institutions like The College of the City of New York, Oklahoma Agricultural and Mechanical College, and of course, Polytechnic.[3] It was initiatives like this that further developed research partnerships with leading companies, and made the Institute a household name in the scientific community.

The fourth edition of the now 27-volume encyclopedia is used worldwide. It is built on the solid foundation of the previous editions, while reflecting the advances of the 21st century.

On December 10, 1947, Professor Donald F. Othmer (left) and Professor Raymond Kirk, dean of the Graduate Department, celebrated the release of the *Kirk-Othmer Encyclopedia of Chemical Technology* at the Hotel Bossert in Brooklyn, New York.

develop, among other things, the precision microwave attenuator, sorely needed for the accurate calibration of radar. In his autobiography, *The Evolution of Electrical Engineering, A Personal Perspective,* Professor Weber recalled his contributions to the war effort, and the resulting technology.

I decided the most pressing need was for a practical and accurate means of measuring the power output of a radar transmitter and the sensitivity of

a radar receiver. For this purpose, my colleagues and I at Polytechnic designed and built an accurately calibrated power attenuator. We knew the attenuator would be of great use to the military—for the calibration of radar sets in the field—only if it were extremely rugged, and we worked to achieve this quality.[35]

In recognition of these contributions, Weber was awarded the Presidential Certificate of Merit. From this wartime research grew MRI, the research arm of the Department of Electrical Engineering and the forerunner of the Department of Electrophysics, which existed from 1962 to 1975 when it merged into the Electrical Engineering Department. In 1945, Professor Weber was appointed head of the Department of Electrical Engineering and director of MRI. Under Professor Weber's direction, enrollment in electrical engineering grew and the graduate program became one of the largest in the country.[36]

Since attenuators were in high demand, Weber approached President Rogers and members of The Corporation proposing to start a related business. After that meeting, Rogers and two trustees offered $10,000 each to establish the Polytechnic Institute of Brooklyn Products Company, which was renamed a year later to Polytechnic Research and Development Company (PRD). The company's product line grew to include wave meters and other kinds of measuring equipment.[37] Professor Nathan Marcuvitz, an internationally renowned scientist in electromagnetic theory and systems, would later become head of the Electrophysics Department, head of the Microwave Research Institute, and vice president of research at Poly.

POST-WAR PROGRESS

Accomplishments abounded after the war, furthering the Institute's reputation. While MRI was succeeding, the Institute awarded the first undergraduate engineering degree to a woman, Sylvia Lepow Walker. Later that year, Professor Edwin F. Church retired after 28 years as head of the M.E. Department. Former director of research and design for American Engineering Company, Professor Ernst L. Midgette, was named the new department head. At the age of 36, he was the youngest head of a department in the Institute's history.[38] Another milestone was reached that year when Jorge G. Veiga was awarded the first MS in Metallurgy and Materials.

In 1947, the Institute was still expanding its course offerings. A PhD degree of Philosophy in Applied Mechanics was established. President Rogers explained that this new degree was created to keep up with the rapid pace of creative engineering. During the war, new problems arose and had to be solved in the design and calculation of heavy tanks, undersea pipelines, jet motors, guided bombs,

and atom bombs. This course was one of many being offered at the Institute aimed at preparing students for the ever changing field of technology. "The war demonstrated that the men who had a mastery of fundamentals ... were responsible for many revolutionary designs emerging from World War II," said President Rogers.[39]

In the fall of 1947, over five thousand students were enrolled at the Institute. Two-thirds were afforded privileges by the G.I. Bill. In the day school there were 1,492 students enrolled. Aside from scholarships and The Living Endowment Fund, the Institute established the World War II Memorial Scholarship, which provided many students with financial aid.

Due to space constraints resulting from increased enrollment, the Institute moved some of its operations to 69 Schermerhorn Street in 1947. The building, formerly the Brooklyn Bureau of Charities, was acquired by an allocation of $69,000 from the State of New York Department of Public Works. The building housed the Mechanical Engineering Department, laboratories, classrooms and offices for machine shops, power plant engineering, metallurgy, and drafting.[40]

By this time, the Institute was operating in roughly 20 locations, half of which were rented. "With the rental of space at a half of dozen locations, downtown Brooklyn has practically become our campus," President Rogers commented.[41]

The increased presence of women continued the following year, when Edythe Crescenzo De Gaeta became the first woman to receive a BS degree in M.E. Ann Elizabeth Gunsolus became the first woman to receive a BS degree in A.E. To further expand the Institute's association with the military, an engineers unit of the Army Reserve Officers Training Corps (ROTC) was organized at the Institute. The ROTC remained an important element of the Institute through the Vietnam War.

PASSAGE OF TIME

On May, 16, 1948, Dr. Joseph Mattiello, class of 1925, a chemist, died suddenly of a heart attack at the age of 48. Dr. Mattiello was the vice president and technical director of the Hilo Varnish Company located in Brooklyn. He was known worldwide for his contributions in the field of surface coating, and

Students in the ROTC program established after World War II catch up on their studies.

was awarded the Legion of Honor by the French government after a speech he gave the year before his death at the Federation of Paint and Varnish Productions Clubs in Paris, France.

A few years before his death, Dr. Mattiello spoke about the importance of surface coatings.

The manufacture of protective organic solutions is becoming an industrial science. The term "organic coatings" in its present meaning includes such materials as varnishes, paints, enamels, lacquers, clear and pigmented textile coatings and plastics. The impetus due to the war effort has given the chemists and the chemical engineers and the other technically trained men of the industry their first real opportunity to emphasize the chemical and engineering aspects of the protective coating industry.[42]

The Institute's connection with scientific societies was a long part of its tradition. In 1948, Dean Raymond E. Kirk was elected vice president of the American Institute of Chemists.[43]

The following year, Professor Reissner was honored at a party at the Fifth Avenue Hotel in Manhattan celebrating his 75th birthday. Among those in attendance were some of the nation's leading scientists, including Dr. J. Den Hartlog, Massachusetts Institute of Technology; Dr. Bruce Johnston, director of the Fritz Engineering Laboratory, Lehigh University; George Van Schliestett, chief of the Fluids Mechanics Branch, Office of Naval Research; and Charles E. Potts and President Rogers.[44]

In 1949, the Institute bade a fond farewell to Dean Ernest J. Streubel, class of 1905. Dean Streubel was associated with Polytechnic for 48 years. He became director of the evening program in 1921, and was dean of the college from 1924 to 1944, at which time he became dean of students. He was credited with making the evening program the largest on the

MEMORIES OF THE *GEHEIMRAT*

Editor's Note: The following material is excerpted from the memoirs of Harry C. Wechsler, who received his PhD in chemistry and chemical engineering from Polytechnic University. Dr. Wechsler was president of Borden Chemical Company, senior vice president of Beatrice Foods, and the former owner and president of Farboil, a producer of high-performance encapsulating compounds. He has been a trustee of Polytechnic University since 1980.

BY THE TIME I ARRIVED at Brooklyn Polytechnic, its Bureau of Polymer Science was already a beehive of research activity and a crossroads for international scientific exchange, although it had only recently been founded. An enthusiastic group of young scientists, drawn by Herman Mark and by the then still-new world of macromolecules, gave it a sense of excitement and adventure. There were no weekdays in the week, it seemed—every day was a festival. The year was 1946.

Morale was always riding high. Everyday classes, lab work, seminars, and even tests and examinations, were stimulating events. If the subject was polymers, you could get an audience for a new idea by the wave of a hand, or the wink of an eye. All of these important times, however, were only background accompaniment, serving to enhance the substantive part of the bureau's charter—conducting research at the cutting edge of high-polymer chemistry.

A bevy of talented scientists of varying stature were all a part of this exciting environment. So many names come to mind: Isidor Fankuchen, Kurt Stern, Turner Alfrey, Bruno Zimm, Paul Doty, Fritz Eirich, Charlie Overberger, Arthur Tobolsky, to name but a few. Also, joining the group as I was leaving the Institute were Gerry Oster, Herb Morawetz, and Murray Goodman.

Though weekdays were active enough, the greatest excitement was reserved for the Saturday morning symposia, usually organized around visiting senior scientists of renown from other universities. A loose but vibrant polymer community was being forged at Brooklyn Poly, a "family" of polymer scientists of diverse history and from many lands. At its head, or more

East Coast at that time. President Rogers said at the ceremony, "Your council and advice have helped many a young man in his quest for an education."[45] Dean Streubel was awarded a silver tray engraved with the names of notable faculty and alumni, which was a traditional gift at the time.

Among Streubel's last recommendations, along with the guidance of Kirk of the Graduate Department, was for the Institute to put an emphasis on other areas of education. This resulted in a departure from what was common in most engineering colleges. The Institute hired Dr. Charles Obermayer to join the faculty as a member of the English and Psychology Departments. He taught philosophy of education, which was developed to meet the needs of teachers of science and

accurately pulsing as its heart, was, of course, Herman Mark, the *Geheimrat*.

In time, as I got to know him better, Mark appeared to me as even more than that. He was also the consummate professorial populist. He would befriend not only the mighty names in science, but also many of us neophytes. When you graduated into Mark's orbit, you knew it. He would notice you a block away, would quicken his pace toward you, give you a tremendous "how-dee-do" greeting, calling you names like "*Herr Professor*" or "*Herr Doktor.*" You'd swear he had some great news to impart or great questions to ask, but no, nothing like that. He was just saying hello. With time, he would work you into seminar programs, lectures, or publications. He always wanted to make everyone feel good.

Mark's energy and power of concentration were legend. After a morning's full schedule, he would lock himself in his office at 99 Livingston Street and disappear for five to six hours. At the end of that time, he would emerge fresh and pert, announcing that he had just finished a couple of articles for publication and was ready for another full shift's work, consisting of evening classes, his trip home, dinner, and more scientific writing.

This seemingly inexhaustible energy and his great drive propelled Mark into a variety of endeavors that together weave a most extraordinary life pattern. World-renowned scientist, educator, prolific author, communicator, outstanding director of research, founder, the "Dean" of polymer chemistry—all of these achievements became *his* hallmarks and are well known.

When Mark crossed from Canada to the United States around 1940, he could probably have joined any of the prestigious Ivy League universities or the established American research institutes. What then attracted Mark to Poly? I believe it was not the reality of what was there, but the vision of what it could become. It was his chance to run his own show and to do his own thing. He enjoyed the stimulation of creating and putting his mark on a venture that did not exist before. Turning Brooklyn Poly into a world center of learning for macromolecular chemistry was to be his enterprise—and one that he achieved with spectacular success.

For many years I lost all contact with Mark and the school. But, three decades after leaving Poly, my bond to Mark became renewed. Following an initiative by Professors Ephraim Banks and Eli Pearce, I was asked in 1978 to organize a campaign for the establishment of a chair to be named for Dr. Mark. This was clearly a call I could not ignore. Mark was 83 at the time, and the school was in trouble. What better effort could combine memorializing Mark's historic contribution to polymers with helping to rejuvenate the ailing Polytechnic?

We set our goal at $1 million and proceeded to organize the drive. I found it relatively easy to attract participation in the "Herman F. Mark Chair" committee, drawing from among his alumni, his consulting contacts, and from Polytechnic's trustees.

Well, the money was raised and the Herman F. Mark Chair became a reality, the first endowed chair in polymer science in the United States. It was occupied for one year by Professor Ephraim Katzir, formerly president of the State of Israel, and is occupied today by Professor Richard Gross. Herman Mark derived a great deal of pride and pleasure from his named chair—it was his gift to Polytechnic and its students.

technology. Dr. Obermayer was internationally known for his expertise and his book, *Body, Soul and Society*, which was an introduction to modern psychology. Dean Kirk said of the appointment:

The scientist who teaches while carrying on research often finds that his background in educational procedures does not equal his scientific

background. This new course is offered to provide such a background.[46]

Women continued to excel as the decade of the 1940s came to a close. In 1949, Goldye Cohen Leeds became the first woman to receive a BS in Met. E. The same year, New York City Mayor William O'Dywer appointed William H. Byrne, class of 1923, to organize

Dr. Frederick Roland Eirich was associate professor of polymer chemistry at Polytechnic from 1947 to 1951. He also served as dean of the Graduate School. Eirich came to Polytechnic from Cambridge University in England, where he had been working on the peacetime aspects of certain explosive reactions under a special research grant awarded by the British Government. In chemistry, Professor Eirich was a noted authority on viscosity and colloid reactions. His appointment at Polytechnic marked an expansion of its work in the field of colloid chemistry. While at Polytechnic, Eirich collaborated with Dr. Herman Mark of the Polymer Research Institute. Eirich was associated with Mark at the beginning of his career in Vienna.

and direct the first Bureau of Smoke Control for the Department of Housing and Building. Byrne was called to this position because he had invented a powdered-fuel burner and methods to closely control temperature in combustion chambers.

POLY GRADUATE NAMED PFIZER'S CEO

Over the course of the 1930s and 1940s, the Institute had developed strong ties with leading manufacturers and businesses; among these relationships was its association with Charles Pfizer and Company, which was due in large part to alumni who propelled the company to great heights. Among alumni associated with Pfizer was John E. McKeen, class of 1925. McKeen began his career with Pfizer in 1926, earning $40 a week as a control chemist. Twenty-three years later, McKeen was named president and chief executive officer. Aside from his groundbreaking work in the mass production of penicillin during War World II with fellow alumnus and Pfizer associate Jasper Kane, McKeen managed a team of scientists that screened and tested thousands of soil samples from all over the world before finding the one from which the broad-range antibiotic Terramycin is derived.[47]

McKeen was a member of the American Chemical Society, the American Institute of Chemists, American Institute of Chemical Engineers, Sigma Xi, Newcomen Society, and the American Pharmaceutical Manufacturers Association, among others.[48] He was active in the alumni association and donated his time, money, and efforts to Polytechnic for many years. The same year he was appointed president of Pfizer, the Institute awarded McKeen an honorary Doctorate in Engineering. The following year while giving a speech, McKeen spoke modestly when characterizing his scientific achievements.

Mass-produced penicillin was brought to pass by the combined efforts of a group of American companies and their know-how in the techniques of fermentation chemistry. Thus, with the development of these fermentation processes, we in the industry were unwittingly forging a key link in a chain of events which culminated in [the development of] penicillin and the dramatic savings of millions of lives. Tonight's honor is therefore shared by the entire antibiotics industry.[49]

A NEW DECADE

As the Institute entered the 1950s, the accomplishments of the preceding decade elevated its international status. Research conducted by professors resulted in countless patents, and partnerships with leading manufacturers aided the Institute financially.

However, the United States would soon enter into another international conflict when the Korean War began in 1950. Members of the ROTC division of the Institute were called to service. Among alumni and students called to serve was Marine First Lieutenant Basile Lubka, class of 1949, who was presented with the Silver Star for gallantry in action against Communist forces in Korea in 1951.[50]

In 1950, Dr. Nicholas John Hoff, world-renowned aircraft structure analyst, was named head of the A.E. and A.M. Departments. Later that year the Brooklyn-Battery Tunnel was completed, providing yet another major transit artery from New York City to benefit commuters of the Institute. The Institute also offered the first doctoral degree in M.E in 1951, and the first computer course.

Later that year, the school newspaper, the *Polytechnic Reporter*, was awarded the highest honor given by the Associated Collegiate Press, the All-American Award. This was the first time the paper had received an award in over 10 years, and was in part due to the guidance offered by Professor Leo E. Saidla of the English Department.[51]

About this time, the aerodynamic laboratories began operating under the leadership of Professor Antonio Ferri in collaboration with a group which included Professor Martin H. Bloom.

Formerly a researcher at an Italian aeronautical laboratory at Guidonia, and also an Italian partisan in the war, Ferri had been involved in cutting-edge research in the field of aerodynamics. This involved obtaining airfoil force data through the supercritical range up to about Mach 0.94. When Ferri left Italy, he brought with him extensive airfoil data from the Italians' tests in a semi-open high-speed tunnel in the early forties.[52]

Professor Ferri rounded out the department organized by Professor Harrington, whose expertise lay in fluid aerodynamics, while Professor Hoff's focus was structural aerodynamics.[53] However, Professor Hoff would assume leadership the following year when Professor Harrington left to pursue other interests.

Bloom recently recalled his reaction to hearing the news that Professor Ferri was coming to the Institute.

Antonio Ferri was one of the pioneers of aerodynamics in Italy. At that time, he was a lieutenant in the Air Force and ran their wind tunnels. He was brought over to the United States because we were having problems during the war with testing our aircraft at what, at that time, was NACA. [National Advisory Committee for Aeronautics.] Now it's NASA.[54]

Later that year, the Institute regretfully accepted the resignation of Alumni Secretary, John R. Brierley, class of 1910, who served in this post for 25 years. From 1922 to 1925 he also served as president of the alumni association. His intention was to establish a strong alumni group as a major contributing factor to the development and success of Polytechnic. Among his countless duties, he also edited the monthly alumni magazine, *Poly Men*.

John E. McKeen, class of 1925, was named president and board chairman of Charles Pfizer and Company in 1949. Seven years earlier, while working at Pfizer, McKeen assisted Jasper H. Kane in developing the first system to mass produce penicillin, which saved the lives of thousands of soldiers during World War II.

As 1952 came to an end, women students continued to make their mark, typified by Edythe Crescenzo De Gaeta, the first woman to receive a Master's degree in M.E.

In the year that followed, the Institute would celebrate its centennial anniversary, an accomplishment that underscored its presence within the world of science and engineering. Soon, the Institute would welcome a new president, and achieve unparalleled success. For all things Poly, the future was bright.

The sphere at the Freeport Laboratory in Long Island enabled Poly professors to produce high-speed airflow, simulating conditions of supersonic aircraft while in flight. This research further fueled the U.S. space program.

CHAPTER SIX

MILESTONES
1953–1959

The search for knowledge means the systematic inquiry into our environment as well as into ourselves. Newton's discovery of the law of gravitation as such could have been made generations, nay, millennium before, if mankind had been ready for it.

—President Ernst Weber, 1958

BY 1953, POLYTECHNIC WAS the second-largest engineering school in the nation, and one of seven U.S. schools with accredited evening degree courses in undergraduate engineering. Its assets were valued at $8.35 million, which was up 130 percent from 1933 when President Rogers assumed office. However, like presidents before him, he put little emphasis on endowment. At the time the endowment stood at $1.7 million, which was up by roughly 29 percent from 1933, mainly by shifting from Institute assets into blue-chip securities, which had appreciated by 50 percent.[1]

Consequently, the Institute was in good financial standing as the centennial celebration approached. The ownership of Polytechnic Research and Development Company (PRD), a tax-paying manufacturer of electronic measuring devices, grossed $3 million annually, which supported many initiatives. The Institute's initial investment in PRD was minimal yet the school poured a great deal of its brainpower and managerial strengths into the business. The funds that resulted equaled an additional $1 million per year in endowment monies. Looking back on operating costs, in fiscal 1933, 75 percent of all revenues were derived from tuition. In 1953, with gross revenues more than seven times as large, only 47 percent were attributed to tuition. Almost exactly that much came from sponsored research, which contributed $1.76 million—a 27-fold increase from 1933.[2]

POLY'S BIG BOOM: RESEARCH

The United States government was investing billions of dollars each year for research with approximately $200 million allocated for colleges and universities; one percent went to Polytechnic. Since World War II, President Rogers had been working diligently at positioning the Institute into the federal research pool. Though he was successful in this effort, unless the research contributed directly to productive graduate engineering education, Rogers was not interested. Since many research assignments were commercial and often involved routine testing, they did not adequately challenge faculty or students.

The Institute conducted research in every department aside from the English, Psychology, History, and Economics Departments. Between 1952 and 1953, research was conducted in microwave electronics ($850,000); aeronautical engineering, including aerodynamics and aero-structures ($260,000);

Brigadier General Edgar T. Conley (left), commanding general of the New York Military District, presents the award of the Association of the Army to Cadet Master Sergeant Henry Martin Ziegler in 1956. Sergeant Ziegler, a junior, received this award at the eighth annual President's Review and Field Day of the ROTC engineer unit of the Polytechnic Institute of Brooklyn.

polymer chemistry (approximately $200,000); ion chemistry research (approximately $155,000); and physics, particularly X-ray diffraction and fluorescence (approximately $145,000).

In addition to this sponsored research, the Institute spent more than $250,000 of its own money annually on research.[3]

Professor Emeritus Leopold Felsen, class of 1948, PhD '52, worked in the MRI Department and was a research associate for Professors Ernst Weber and Nathan Marcuvitz. After years of related research, Professors Felsen and Marcuvitz coau-

thored *Radiation and Scattering of Waves*, published in 1973. The book, which was republished in 1994, has been used as an educational tool for decades. In 2004, Felsen recalled his time working alongside these distinguished scientists and the Institute's research program during the 1950s.

I got a fellowship with the Microwave Research Institute, which was then headed by Dr. Weber. My direct mentor there was Professor Marcuvitz. At that time, Brooklyn Poly was among the foremost institutions in the world that entered into the development of radar that had evolved during World War II, and people who were at the Radiation Laboratory of MIT, which brought together people from all different backgrounds—physicists, mathematicians, electrical engineers—to tackle that problem, and Marcuvitz was a member of that group. So when he came to Poly, a lot of that legacy was transferred.

He was always extremely kind in sharing whatever knowledge he had with faculty and students at

Students from the Civil Engineering Department spent two weeks of their summer during 1956 in Sloatsburg, New York, to get field practice in surveying. Shown are students Joseph McCarthy, holding a machete to clear the line of view; Benjamin Whang, taking notes; Joel H. Streich, with leveling rod; and Edmund Richardson using a dumpy level.

Left: Professor Nathan Marcuvitz was named head of the Microwave Research Institute in 1957. Professor Marcuvitz and Professor Emeritus Leopold Felsen co-authored *Radiation and Scattering of Waves*, published in 1973.

Below: After successfully developing and expanding the aerodynamics department, Professor Nicholas Hoff left Polytechnic in 1957 to join the faculty of Stanford University. He was succeeded at Polytechnic by Professor Joseph Kempner, as head of A.E. Structures Research. Hoff's published work comprised more than 200 papers and six books including the widely used text, *The Analysis of Structures*. Hoff was a consultant to both government and industry and was elected to the U.S. National Academy of Engineering, the Hungarian Academy of Science, the French Academy of Sciences, the French National Academy of Air and Space, and the International Academy of Astronautics. Professor Hoff died on August 4, 1997 at the age of 91.

special seminars. It was very good to work with him. It was a very high profile thing, and in fact, Marcuvitz and I published under the sponsorship of the Air Force Cambridge Research Laboratories a series of reports for the next 15 years.[4]

AFTER THE WAR

When the Korean War ended in July 1953, a significant portion of students enrolled in college were there thanks to the GI Bill. In addition, the Cold War resulted in a new wave of immigrant students. Alumnus Carmine Masucci, historian for the Alumni Association since 1996, was one of many students who benefited from the GI Bill.

I got my bachelor's degree at City College in 1944, and then I went into the Navy. After the Navy, I had the GI Bill, and I went to graduate school at Poly. [I] worked during the day and then went to Poly at night. I had some excellent teachers, and they did a good job. The school really was probably one of the first that took in a lot of the GIs coming home from World War II, as Tom Brokaw says in his book The Greatest Generation, *and I think the school contributed considerably to what happened afterwards.*[5]

It was the leadership provided by President Rogers that allowed Professors Weber, Mark, Hoff, and others to excel. Rogers was continually rewarded for both his academic and business prowess. In 1953 he received the Lamme Medal from the American Society for Engineering Education, one of the most prestigious awards in the field of engineering education.[6]

When a reporter asked him what his role was at Polytechnic, President Rogers responded in this fashion:

I run a hothouse, an institution where men and boys grow. It's my job to see that they have the conditions under which they can grow. In providing these conditions, I do everything from conferring degrees to janitorial work.[7]

Students were actively engaged in extracurricular activities, a long-time tradition at Polytechnic. Aside from fraternities, there was the math club, the radio club, the bridge club, the chess club, the

Above: One of the Institute's successful athletic teams in the 1950s was its fencing team. A couple of students enjoyed a practice duel on the streets of Brooklyn in the late-1950s.

Left: Fraternities have long been an integral part of the Polytechnic experience. Pictured here in the mid-1950s are three members of the Institute's Lambda Chi Alpha chapter. The map above their heads indicated the number of chapters nationwide. Membership in a fraternity often provided networking opportunities after graduation.

fine arts club, the music club, and the jazz club. In addition, athletic teams were growing, including fencing, basketball, rifle, swimming, and wrestling.

POLY BUILDS WORLD'S MOST ADVANCED HYPERSONIC WIND TUNNEL

In 1953, the Institute was in the process of developing one of the world's most advanced hypersonic wind tunnels. The department of aeronautical engineering and applied mathematics was charged with the task of analyzing, designing, and constructing the tunnel for the Air Force, which was located at the Aerodynamics Laboratory in Freeport, Long Island.[8] The Institute previously used a 16-year-old, 330-mile per hour wind tunnel in the basement of 94 Livingston Street.

It is interesting to note that a primary reason this research was moved to the relatively isolated location in Freeport was that it could often be quite noisy. Normally conducted at night, the research would create a large booming sound that would disturb the neighborhood. Ultimately, the local police discovered what was going on and forced Polytechnic to find a more remote location to conduct their experiments.

At that time, the Massachusetts Institute of Technology, Cal Tech, Princeton, and the Naval Ordinance Laboratory were operating wind tunnels at Mach 10 or less—that is 10 times or less the speed of sound in the air. The Institute's wind tunnel was distinguished from these other tunnels by the fact that the air within the tunnel was heated in the settling chamber in order to prevent component condensation in the tunnel's test section, and to simulate conditions encountered by aircraft and missiles in high-speed flight.[9] The wind tunnel was able to test wind blowing at a rate of 7,500 miles per hour at sea level. In comparison, natural wind at sea level seldom exceeds 130 miles per hour.[10]

Under the supervision of Professor Ferri, Polytechnic's wind tunnel was able to permit tests at above Mach 10. Ferri originally conceived this idea after World War II while engaged in pioneering research in Italy as a member of the Italian Air Force.[11]

Professors Nicholas Hoff (left) and Paul Libby inspect a piece of equipment that would be used for the world's most advanced hypersonic wind tunnel to be located within the Freeport, Long Island, laboratory. The 70-foot high, four-foot diameter steel stack with walls three and half inches thick was erected days after this picture was taken in 1953.

Dr. Theodore von Karman (left), the "dean of the aeronautical world," is welcomed by Chairman Preston R. Bassett, Professor Nicholas Hoff, and President Rogers during the High-Speed Aeronautics Conference, which was organized by Polytechnic in 1955.

In a veritable cloak-and-dagger operation, the U.S. War Department spirited him out of Italy and assigned him to the Langley Memorial Laboratory of the National Committee for Aeronautics in Virginia, where he remained until his appointment to the faculty of the Polytechnic in 1951.[12]

In the three years that followed, Professors Ferri, Hoff, Bloom, and Paul Libby, class of 1942, further developed the aeronautical laboratory. The construction included the development of a 70-foot tower which served as a chamber where the pre-heating took place. Compressed air stored outside in containers was discharged into the top of the tower which propelled a piston, which in turn compressed the air within the tunnel. Their work led to patents that aided NASA in its initial research into space flight. Dr. Theodore von Karman of Caltech, who was known as the "dean of the aeronautical world,"[13] was a mentor to the Institute's aeronautics professors. He became chairman of the U.S. Air Force Scientific Advisory Board.

In April 1955, von Karman, along with leading scientists from around the world, attended the High-Speed Aeronautics Conference organized by Polytechnic. During his speech at the conference,

he indicated his belief that military aircraft would be engaged in sustained supersonic flight at speeds up to Mach 3 within the next decade.

It was during this conference that von Karman outlined the greatest problem in the development of long-range missiles and, eventually, space vehicles: the accumulation of heat on aircraft surfaces due to friction. This obstacle became the focus of Polytechnic's aerodynamic research, eventually enhancing the United States missile program, and later its space program.[14] Following the conference, Professors Bloom, Libby, Hoff, and Ferri published a book entitled *Proceedings of the Conference on High-Speed Aeronautics.*

When interviewed, Bloom said this was an exciting time period for Polytechnic, and that advancements made there were groundbreaking.

High-speed aerodynamics was almost unknown in 1951. If you spoke to anybody in the United States, they didn't know what a missile was. So Tony [Ferri] asked a group of us if we would give up a couple of years of our lives to build a new type of laboratory with high-speed testing ... and a number of us did that. We worked with Tony until the laboratory was completed in 1954. At that time, there was a big conference on high-speed aerodynamics at Poly in honor of the opening of our laboratory. A who's who of both U.S. and foreign [scientists and engineers] came here to participate in this conference. It was a big thing.[15]

Professor Bloom went on to explain the functions of the laboratory.

It had two aspects. One was called supersonic aerodynamics. Today's fighter planes and missiles fly at Mach numbers of around maximum three or so. The Mach number is the multiple of the speed of sound. For a high Mach number flight, heating is extremely important. So we had to design a feature which was quite unique. It was a very high temperature, high pressure air heater system.[16]

Beside the hypersonic tunnel, the Freeport Laboratory eventually had three supersonic tunnels. Two of the tunnels belonged to the Institute, and the other was owned by the Grumman Aircraft

In 1953, Polytechnic welcomed a new dean, Dr. Warren L. McCabe. He replaced Dr. Erich Hausmann who retired after serving the Institute for over 45 years. Dr. McCabe was responsible for the undergraduate program and the evening program. He was a well-rounded educator, having held posts at MIT, the Worcester Institute of Technology, and the Carnegie Institute of Technology. In 1937 he received the William H. Walker Award from the American Institute of Chemical Engineers, and in 1950 he became president of the American Institute of Chemical Engineers.[27]

In 1953, the Institute's 2,052 graduate students—more than 1,700 of whom attended night classes—had unusual opportunities for significant work in the fields they wanted to explore. For example, the M.E. department began offering graduate programs in air pollution control under the direction of Professor Clifford A. Wojan, class of 1943. Later that year, Professor Charles T. Oergel was named head of the M.E. department.

In 1954, a journalist wrote an article in *Business Week* underscoring the reason for the growing enrollment at the Institute.

They're there—in spite of Poly's wretched physical plant—because they want to learn aerodynamics from Nicholas J. Hoff or Antonio Ferri, polymer chemistry from H. M. Mark, microwave electronics from Ernst Weber, or other specialties from any of a dozen others.[28]

POLY TURNS 100

The Polytechnic Institute of Brooklyn proudly celebrated its 100th year during the school year 1954-55. The Institute was noted as the second largest engineering school in the nation with 6,400 students, and ranked in the top 10 in the value of its research, which resulted in revenues of $2,100,000 on roughly 150 projects the preceding year. During the commencement ceremony, the 10,000th degree was conferred. To help celebrate, over 40 scientific, engineering, and educational symposia and meetings were conducted throughout the course of the academic year.[29]

This was a milestone event and hundreds of respected scholars from all over the world attended conferences held at the Institute. Topics ranged

President Harry S. Rogers (left) confers the 10,000th degree at the Institute's 100th annual commencement exercise to Thomas Lockwood. He earned his degree in mechanical engineering from the Institute's pioneering degree-granting evening session.

from high-speed aerodynamics and fluidization in practice to small gas turbines, advances in chelate chemistry, civil engineering in the Atomic Age, and the humanities in engineering education. The celebration climaxed on October 8, 1955, with a major convocation at the Brooklyn Academy of Music, where commencement ceremonies had been held as far back as the 1870s.[30]

The theme for this milestone event was "Science, Engineering, and Research for Human Well-Being." On reaching the 100-year mark, Brooklyn Poly, as it was commonly known, had become a leading scientific institution graduating students from 28 foreign countries, and enrolling students from 218 universities in its graduate programs.[31]

In the years following World War II, the Institute's research activity was impressive. Among research projects conducted by Professors Mark, Hoff, and Weber, the following programs received special note during the ceremony: design of radar domes for the Arctic; underwater ducted blade systems; communications between ships and aircraft; developing new techniques for testing color additives in food; separating metals from sea water through ionization; and the vibration characteristics of turbo-jet engines.[32]

Another exciting research program was spearheaded by Professor David Harker, a noted X-ray crystallographer, who embarked on a ten-year, $1,000,000 protein structure project, which was supported by several foundations as well as the Institute.[33]

Members of the alumni association and The Corporation extended their praise for Polytechnic's accomplishments over its first 100 years. Alumnus John E. McKeen, president of Charles Pfizer and Company, said of the occasion:

As a member of the Poly alumni, I am personally grateful for the opportunities received as a result of my studies in that Institute, and am, therefore, pleased to join with you and others paying tribute to a great educational center.[34]

The city of Brooklyn took notice of this grand event as well. Borough President John Cashmore proclaimed October 26th as Polytechnic Institute of Brooklyn Centennial Day. During the ceremony, 500 cadet engineers of Polytechnic's ROTC regiment and about 1,000 students, faculty, and friends were in attendance.[35]

During the Institute's centennial celebration at Borough Hall in 1955, Brooklyn Borough President John D. Cashmore (right, at podium) proclaimed that October 26th was Polytechnic Institute of Brooklyn Centennial Day. Members of the Institute's ROTC regiment (below) stand at parade rest while Poly President Rogers (at the podium) honors Polytechnic's service to New York City, and the world.

President Rogers praised the role of science in society in his centennial address.

It was not until the creative scientists and pioneer inventors, inspired by the living philosophy which taught that men were intellectually as well as morally free, began to pry loose the secrets of nature that the material lot of the human race began to be improved. To understand modern society, it is important to attain a perspective which reveals the untold, incalculable benefits that have been accrued to humankind through the disciplined and dedicated years spent by men of talent in the hidden laboratories of the world.

Such a perspective discloses that man has at his command the power to relieve human suffering throughout the world, to protect himself against the hazards of nature and to raise standards of living and prosperity, if he will utilize, in a spirit of high principle, the abilities and resources with which he has been endowed by his Creator.[36]

In the following weeks, many dinners and luncheons were held in further celebration of the centennial. Scores of alumni returned to Poly to participate and pay respect to their alma mater, including famed actor Edward Everett Horton, class of 1900, who entertained students and faculty at the Polytechnic Centennial Student Smoker in November of that year.[37]

The celebration also coincided with the Institute's largest freshman class. The 440 students starting classes in 1954 began coursework in nine different fields of science and engineering. This represented a 20 percent increase over 1953. The Aeronautical Engineering Department realized a 71 percent increase in students. Electrical and mechanical engineering realized a 30 percent increase. In several departments registration was cut off because of space limitations. The entering freshman class had 41 Korean War veterans, which added to the roughly 550 veterans of that war already attending. Albert D. Capuro, the director of admissions, made the following comment that autumn.

The many civilian, as well as military applications of the electronics [sector] continue to stimulate great interest in electrical engineering, while the attraction and opportunities of hypersonic and supersonic aircraft design have captured the imaginations of many engineering aspirants.[38]

The English Department continued to receive numerous accolades. In 1954, the poetry of Professor Louis Zukofsky appeared in national publications, including *Poetry*. Professor Zukofsky, one of the founders of the "Objective School" of poets, authored several books including *The First Half of A*, *55 Poems*, and *Anew*. His textbook, *A Test for Poetry*, was used in classrooms nationwide. His work was revered by the literary community, and he continued to publish books until his death in 1978. In 1991, *Complete Short Story*, an anthology of his writings, was published to critical acclaim.[39]

POLY'S NEW HOME

As the 1954-55 school year began, tuition was raised to $780 per year, a $50 increase from the previous year. President Rogers said the increase was made to cover personal services, equipment, and material costs. At the time, it cost the Institute $800 beyond tuition fees to educate one student for four years.[40]

It was becoming increasingly necessary for the Institute to acquire more classroom and laboratory space, especially due to the fact that the campus was spread across downtown Brooklyn. With over half of its buildings rented, nearly every conceivable space was utilized. A reporter for the *Polytechnite*, the student newspaper for evening students, wrote of the Institute's limitations.

For years the one outstanding shortcoming of our college has been its crowded and decrepit buildings, where hardly a broom closet has not been turned into a laboratory or a classroom.[41]

After a few years of searching for a new site to house the Institute, President Rogers announced that the school would purchase the American Safety Razor Company Building located on Jay Street between Johnson Street and Myrtle Avenue. The price tag for the eight-story building was $2 million. The building would enable the school to operate almost all of its services under one roof. The location was closer to subway lines and other public transportation, which benefited the commuter population.[42]

After careful study, it was determined that the building was already well-suited to meet the structural specifications of an up-to-date engineering, education, and research institution. With high ceilings, open areas, and fine lighting, it lent itself to efficient arrangements of classrooms and laboratories. Originally designed for heavy industrial loads, the floors would withstand the impact of machinery used

in the electrical workshops, and, at the same time provide a firm base for delicate research equipment.[43]

President Rogers, along with The Corporation, faculty, and students, considered the move to 333 Jay Street an important transition that would position the Institute for future success.

This step is another milestone in the 100-year history of a vigorous and dynamic scientific and engineering center, and a fuller realization of the dream of its founders. Consistently during its long career, Polytechnic has chosen to utilize its resources for the support of a renowned faculty and the acquisition of top-grade apparatus and equipment. The new building will provide the urgently required larger area for concentrating these resources on the task of rendering even greater service to science, engineering, and research.[44]

President Harry S. Rogers (right) hands a $2 million check to Milton Dammann, board chairman of the American Safety Razor Company, for its 320,000-square-foot industrial plant. Polytechnic converted the building into a modern science and engineering school.

A campaign was launched that year to raise $3.5 million to cover the cost of the building and the money necessary to remodel the facility to conform to building codes, purchase adjacent properties, and build a new student lounge and library. When the building was finished in 1958, the Institute gained 60 percent more space. However, the construction would continue for over three years, which placed a strain on the faculty, students, and President Rogers.

Along with daunting fundraising initiatives and construction, there was also an air of excitement in all things Poly. The Institute would not only have a centrally located university in the revitalized downtown Brooklyn area, but would also be positioned in what was deemed to be a better neighborhood. Along with its sterling academic reputation was the fact that the Institute had been located in somewhat questionable Brooklyn neighborhoods, and safety was a concern for both students and faculty.

Research and education remained the Institute's focus throughout this period. The golden years of Polytechnic, which began during World War II, continued into the 1950s. The major reason was funding supplied to the Institute from the government in Cold War research related efforts.

POLY ALUMNUS BECOMES FAMOUS PHOTOGRAPHER

It was during this time that alumnus O. Winston Link, class of 1937, became famous for his photographs. While he graduated with a civil engineering degree, Link is one of the most acclaimed photographers in the 20th century for his dramatic black and white photographs of trains and railroad towns. He photographed Norfolk and Western Railway's steam locomotives as they passed through the towns of Virginia, West Virginia, North Carolina, and Maryland from 1955 through 1960, when steam operations were terminated. Besides creating technically perfect images through the use of a complex synchronized flash system, Link's work captured the poignant conclusion of an American way of life.

Although a hearing disability precluded Link from fighting in World War II, he became a valuable asset as part of a Columbia University research project that developed equipment used by low altitude aircraft to locate submarines.[45]

O. Winston Link, class of 1937, became famous for his black and white photos of Norfolk and Western Railway's steam locomotives as they passed through Virginia, West Virginia, North Carolina, and Maryland. His photos have been displayed in museums worldwide, including the Museum of Modern Art. On January 10, 2004, the O. Winston Link Museum opened in Roanoke, Virginia. The museum is dedicated to collecting, preserving, and exhibiting Link's photographs and sound and video recordings.

In the early 1980s, Link's work was exhibited in several museums in the United States and England, including the Museum of Modern Art. The 1987 publication *Steam, Steel, and Stars* featured his railroad photographs and the subsequent 1995 book, *The Last Steam Railroad in America*, dramatically increased recognition of Link's photographs.

Link died in 2001 in South Salem, New York. On January 10, 2004, the O. Wilson Link Museum opened in Roanoke, Virginia. The museum is dedicated to collecting, preserving, and exhibiting Link's photographs and sound and video recordings.[46]

POLY PROFESSOR'S RESEARCH LEADS TO NOBEL PRIZE

After a chance meeting with Dean Kirk at an American Chemical Society meeting in Cleveland, Ohio, in 1951, Professor Rudolph A. Marcus was hired and began teaching at Polytechnic. He was well-respected by both his peers, and his students. He undertook an experimental research program on both gas phase and solution reaction rates.

His research in electron transfer reactions eventually led to the Nobel Prize in Chemistry in 1992. After publishing the Rice-Ramsperger-Kassel-Marcus (RRKM) papers, he wondered what he would do next in theoretical research. Ironically it was a student in his statistical mechanics class that brought to his attention a problem in polyelectrolytes. It was this question that ultimately led to the Nobel Prize.[47]

In 2004, Professors Marcus recalled that day, and how it changed science, and his life:

DISCOVERY AT POLY LEADS TO NOBEL PRIZE

PROFESSOR RUDOLPH A. Marcus, born in Montreal, Canada, in 1923, received his BS and PhD degrees from McGill University. His graduate research was on reactions in solution. After postdoctoral experimental research on free radical reactions at the National Research Council of Canada and theoretical research at the University of North Carolina, he joined the faculty of the

Polytechnic Institute of Brooklyn in 1951.[1]

Professor Marcus recalled the research that landed him a spot on Polytechnic's faculty.

I had worked in both postdoctorals on gas-based reaction rates. The first one at the Research Council, I did experimental work, and then I decided I wanted to learn about theory. So I went to Carolina and developed this theory that later became known as Rice-Ramsperger-Kassel-Marcus (RRKM) theory. It is still more than 50 years later a standard theory in texts and so on. My specialty was in rates of chemical reaction, both experimental and theoretical. It was on that basis that I was hired at Poly.[2]

It was during his time teaching at Polytechnic that Professor Rudolph Marcus conducted the initial research that led to his Nobel Prize in Chemistry, awarded in 1992.

This [Nobel] Prize arose because of a question that a student asked me in one of my classes at Poly. I named the student in the Nobel address. The student's name was Abe Kotliar, and he was a student of Herbert Morawetz. I think it was about 1954 or so. This was just several years after I arrived there, and he was in my statistical mechanics class. He asked me a question about whether something we were talking about at the time might apply to one of the problems in polymer chemistry that he was studying with Morawetz. I thought about it, and [agreed that] it would apply. So then I started to read a lot about polymers and electrostatic properties and then wrote some papers on electrostatic properties. In the process of doing that, I learned a lot [about] electrostatics so that a couple of years later when this problem in electron transfer arose, I heard about it, then I saw how I could apply that electrostatics in a much more extended form to this actual problem, but if that student had not asked me that question, I might not have known enough about electrostatics to know how to tackle this other problem.[48]

MODERN ART FOR POLY'S NEW HOME

To celebrate the scientific breakthroughs made by alumni and professors, like Professor Marcus, as well as the history of science itself, New York City artist Abraham Joel Tobias was hired to produce a three-part art project depicting science, engineering, and research, to be installed in the new quarters at 333 Jay Street.

Tobias is well-known for the murals he created for the Charles H. Silver Clinic at Beth Israel Hospital and for the Domestic Relations Court in Brooklyn. His work still stands today in Midwood High School in Brooklyn. His mural titled *The Student*, which was completed during World War II, is on display at Howard University in Washington, D.C.[49]

Part of Tobias' artwork for Polytechnic consisted of three translucent panels made to resemble

Professor Marcus left Polytechnic in 1964 and became professor of physical chemistry at the University of Illinois, and in 1978, professor of chemistry at the California Institute of Technology, where he teaches today.[3] While he visits the Institute on occasion, Marcus feels indebted to Polytechnic for giving him the opportunity to grow as a scientist, and conduct research that ultimately led to his Nobel Prize award in chemistry.

I just can't emphasize how much I enjoyed being at Poly and how much it meant to me and my late wife, Laura, to have an opportunity to get started in research, which Poly then offered to us.[4]

Through 1960-61 he was a temporary member of the Courant Institute of Mathematical Sciences at New York University. In 1975-76 he was a visiting professor of theoretical chemistry at the University of Oxford, where he was also a professional fellow. He also received the Alexander von Humboldt Award at the Technical University of Munich.[5]

A member of the National Academy of Sciences and the American Academy of Arts and Sciences, Marcus is known for his work in many areas of theoretical chemical kinetics, including theories of unimolecular reactions, electron transfer reactions, electrode reactions, various transfer reactions, the semiclassical theory of collisions and of bound states, and collision coordinates.

He has been the recipient of numerous other awards and honors: an Alfred P. Sloan Foundation fellowship (Sloan was an alumnus of the Institute), a National Science Foundation senior postdoctoral fellowship, a senior Fullbright-Hayes scholarship, the Anne Molson Prize in chemistry of McGill University, the Chandler Medal in chemistry of Columbia University, the Robinson Medal of the Faraday division, Royal Society of Chemistry, the Irving Langmuir Award in chemical physics of the American Chemical Society, and the 1984-85 Wolf Prize in chemistry. He has been awarded the honorary degrees of Doctor of Science by Polytechnic University and by the University of Chicago.[6]

stained glass. Approximately 3,500 pieces of Plexiglas, in 58 colors and shades, were used. Tobias explained that his art treatment represented something never tried before.

The murals open up new horizons in the field of architectural treatment. Because of the strength and light weight of the Plexiglas pieces, and the fact that they can be edge-cemented to each other, the traditional stained glass technique has been freed from the need for using lead around small individual sections, and the use of cross supports, thus providing greater scope of design for the artist and architect.[50]

The first two panels were both 10 feet tall and three feet wide. The third panel, which was never completed, was a 55-foot long, 12-foot high mural illustrating the history of science from the wheel to the atom. The Rohm and Haas Company, which pro-duced Plexiglas, sponsored the project.[51] President Rogers said of the art:

It seems especially fitting to adorn a new center of science and engineering education with an art form that was made possible by recent advances in science and chemistry.[52]

As Tobias was busy working on the mural of scientific history, changes were occurring within the Institute. In March 1957, President Rogers appointed Professor John G. Truxal to head the Electrical Engineering Department, and Professor Marcuvitz became the director of MRI. The same year, Professor Othmer was elected director of the American Institute of Chemical Engineers. With marked growth in research projects representing an annual expenditure of more than $2.5 million, the new position of vice president of research was established, which was filled by Professor Weber.[53]

ABRAHAM JOEL TOBIAS, POLY'S MOST FAMOUS ARTIST

COMMISSIONED IN THE EARLY 1950s, Abraham Joel Tobias' first two panels, which adorned the entrance at 333 Jay Street, were completed on schedule. However, a third mural, the *History of Science*, was another story altogether. Over the next three decades he labored over the mural, with sporadic breaks, but never completed it. In 1996 Tobias died at the age of 82 after a long bout with cancer. His wife, Caroline Tobias, recalled his passion for the project, and his art form.

He was extremely anxious to live, as an artist would be. His whole life, the most impor-

tant part of his life, was his work. His [family was] extremely important too, but it was all bound together, and when I first met him, I knew that creating work was the most important thing for him and especially murals. He wanted to do public work.[1]

While the administration, faculty, and students were initially enthused about the mural, Caroline Tobias said Professor Othmer showed the most interest.

He admired my husband so much, and I have letters from him. He was very involved. Whenever he would come across something that he thought would be of interest to my husband, he would send it. I mean he was extremely warm to my husband.[2]

Othmer was not alone, as other faculty members often spent time with Tobias as he slaved away at his masterpiece. They would often joke that his office was the biggest on campus. Tobias even received visits from celebrities like famed playwright, Arthur Miller, and from Isaac Asimov, the noted science fiction writer.

The center of the *History of Science* mural is dominated by the figure of Leonardo Da Vinci towering over other thinkers of the Renaissance.

This page and opposite: Abraham Joel Tobias' *History of Science* mural became his life's work. He began the mural in the 1950s and worked on it off and on for three decades but never completed it. Three days after his funeral in 1996, New York City's Art Commission presented his wife, Caroline Tobias, with a posthumous award for distinguished service to public art. Tobias' art is also on display at the Smithsonian Institution.

The equations visible in the mural include $E = mc^2$ and $E = hv$.

Portraits of the great scientists illustrate the tempo of scientific discovery, ranging from Galileo to Max Planck, and Isaac Newton to Sigmund Freud. Tobias studied the history of science for over a year before beginning the mural, and routinely called on the Institute's leading professors for advice.[3]

In the late 1950s, Tobias explained his thought process to the members of The Corporation.

The mural is built on an overall mathematically abstract design structure suitable to the space. The History of Science *is conceived as a continuous whole beginning at the dawn of history, continuing to the present and hinting at the challenges of the future.*[4]

Historically, Tobias was one of the first artists to paint on shaped canvas and to make the frame a part of the painting. In the 1930s, when he began, his technique went unrewarded, but in the 1980s, the techniques caused a stir among art critics. Among those interested in his early paintings was the Smithsonian Institution, which bought one painting shaped like a huge seashell. They called his work "astoundingly different."[5]

Throughout the decades of the 1960s, 1970s, and 1980s, Tobias worked on the mural, although there were significant lapses. In the early 1980s, he protested that the administration didn't support the completion of the mural, and went on a short-lived hunger strike on Jay Street. From that point forward, the ailing artist unsuccessfully tried to finish the mural.

Today, the mural is partially visible in the school's gymnasium. It is enclosed in glass. Three days after his funeral in 1996, New York City's Art Commission awarded Caroline Tobias a posthumous award in memory of her husband's contribution to the artistic community.[6]

Tobias' work of three decades—the unfinished mural,
History of Science.

In July of 1957, Professor Ines Kesler developed a new technique for a more efficient method of detecting harmful coloration of food. Her achievement highlighted the role of women at Polytechnic. Her discovery was used to safely detect any inconsistencies in 10 of the then 18 permitted American food color additives.[54]

At this time, teaching positions at Polytechnic were greatly sought after. George Schillinger, professor emeritus of management and founding editor of *Technology in Society: An International Journal,* said he was overjoyed when he was hired.

When I came to Brooklyn Poly in 1957, I thought that was the luckiest start in academia ... Let me tell you. You couldn't come in on Saturdays into the building unless you got yourself a pass. Everybody could get a pass. So I got a pass, and I showed up here at nine o'clock in my office, and I worked here, and I said to myself, How lucky can I get? They give me a pass to work on a Saturday, and that's how everybody felt in this place. People were proud, dedicated, committed. We were surrounded by great people who were accessible to us. That was Brooklyn Poly.[55]

PRESIDENT ROGERS' DEMISE

In the spring of 1957, the renovation of the new site had progressed far enough that plans were made for the transfer of almost one half the laboratory operations and all the lectures to the new location at 333 Jay Street. Then, President Rogers died suddenly on June 6, 1957, six days before the 102nd commencement ceremony. His death sent shock waves throughout the Institution as well as the scientific community, because his name had become synonymous with the Institute's success.

President Rogers had guided the school for 24 years. He had made great strides from 1940 to 1955, and later during the centennial year of Polytechnic as he helped the Institute welcome its largest student enrollment and expanded a vigorous research program.[56]

To ensure that President Rogers' vision of the new Polytechnic would be met, J. Stephen Ungar, the president of the Alumni Association, spoke for many in the pages of *Poly Men.*

We, the alumni, must carry on with his work to create a greater Polytechnic. We must persevere to reach the goal that Dr. Rogers did not live to see. The greater Polytechnic must be achieved not only for the enhancement of its graduates, but as a living monument to the leadership, the fidelity, and the visionary foresight of an outstanding leader, Dr. Harry S. Rogers.[57]

Professor Ernst Weber now became acting president. It was Weber's responsibility to facilitate the completion of the new campus and to continue the expansion of educational programs. As a first step, Professor Weber set a schedule for the renovation of the eight-story building on Jay Street as well as the five-story administrative building at the

corner of Jay and Johnson Streets. In early 1958, The Corporation approved his recommendations, and the faculty and staff rallied to meet the challenges of building a new Polytechnic.[58]

On April 19, 1958, Professor Weber was inaugurated as the sixth president of the Institute. This ceremony was accompanied by the dedication of the eight-story building, which still stands today, as Rogers Hall. The ceremony was attended by about 1,000 persons from all over the world. Among those in attendance was Rear Admiral Hyman G. Rickover, father of America's nuclear navy, who hailed Polytechnic as "an institution which has always been distinguished by single-minded concern with matters of the mind, and which can match its atmosphere of scholarly austerity with that of any of Europe's famous and remarkable centers of learning."[59]

President Weber, who held more than 50 American, Canadian, and British patents in the field of microwave techniques, began his first year with an ambitious program. His vision included increasing the ratio of doctoral-to-first degrees awarded. He further developed the teaching and research departments, and declared that Polytechnic would continue to be revered as a prominent technological university.[60] President Weber that year also was elected president of the world's second largest professional society, the Institute for Radio Engineers.[61]

In his Polytechnic inaugural address, Weber explained the importance of graduate education.

Search for knowledge means the systematic inquiry into our environment as well as into ourselves. Newton's discovery of the laws of gravitation as such could have been made generations, nay, millennium before, if mankind had been ready for it. Unless we can attract larger numbers of the outstanding engineering students to graduate schools, we shall not be able to supply the requisite number of scientific engineers of high caliber who will be our team leaders of tomorrow.[62]

Among Weber's first appointments was that of Professor Ferri as head of the Aerospace Engineering and Applied Mechanics Departments. This decision was rendered after Professor Hoff accepted a position at Stanford University. The same year, Louis N. Rowley Jr., class of 1931, was named chairman of The Corporation. Professor Ronald M. Foster, head of the mathematics department, became internationally recognized for his work in theoretical electrical engineering. His work in development of the Foster Reactance Theorem was a major breakthrough in the synthesis of electrical networks.[63]

Later that year, alumnus Bern Dibner donated $25,000 to establish the *Polytechnic Press*.[64] In 1936, he established the Burndy Library in Norwalk, Connecticut, partly to house a collection of original source materials embracing the major contributions to science in the book and pamphlet forms in which they were originally published. Designed to advance the history of science, this collection contained over 200 samples of the oldest typeset literature, including, some dating back to the 15th century.[65]

Toward the end of 1958, textbooks known as the *Brooklyn Polytechnic Series* were released. These textbooks, published by McGraw-Hill Book Company, were current with the electrical engineering advances of the times. While President Weber first conceived the idea for these textbooks eight years earlier when he was head of the department, the current department head, Professor Truxal, brought the project to fruition. Professor Mischa Schwartz authored *Information Transmission, Modulation, and Noise* in 1959, which became a best-seller and has been reissued four times since the first printing.[66] In 2004, Professor Schwartz, then retired, recalled how important the Polytechnic textbooks were to the field of electrical engineering.

> [Truxal] had the foresight to try to develop a series of books called the Brooklyn Polytechnic Series put out by McGraw-Hill. My book is part of that series. He had a very classic book in the control systems area, which is also part of that series. We were on the map in terms of teaching textbooks that were widely adopted, and research that was eminent in the field. The department really catapulted forward.[67]

POLY GOES COED

While women studied and taught at the Institute for a number of years, it wasn't until the fall semester of 1958 that the Institute became officially coeducational. The enrollment numbers for women were initially low, but the men of the Institute welcomed the female students with open arms. In 1959, the Institute held the first annual Polywog Queen Contest. The event was so popular that famed television personality Jack Paar was on hand to select Poly's first queen, Mary Ellen Barker.[68]

The Institute established the Women's Faculty Club, which also founded the annual scholarship fund that benefited members of the club. Dr. Sonya Weber, a member of the faculty of the School of Medicine of Columbia University, and wife of President Weber, was chair of the committee.[69]

The same year, Professor Rudolf F. Brill was appointed director of the Fritz Haber Institut der Max Planck Gesellschaft in Berlin. The Institute was among the largest centers of scientific research in the world. It was named in honor of Fritz Haber, the German chemist awarded the Nobel Prize in 1918 for his discovery of a method to synthesize ammonia. Professor Brill continued the research he initiated at Polytechnic in experimental physics, which

focused on crystal structures, and catalysis and solids at extremely low temperatures. He replaced Nobel Laureate Max von Laue who was awarded the Nobel Prize in Physics in 1914.[70]

As the Institute bade farewell to Professor Brill, Professor Ferri announced that the Institute would begin offering a new curriculum leading to a Master of Science degree in Astronautics and Space Technology. Dr. Ferri said, "To exploit, develop, and support activities in space technology requires engineers with sound fundamental and science-oriented graduate training."[71]

The educational principles expressed by Ferri were mirrored by advancements in Poly's Chemistry Department. In 1958 the department was nationally recognized as a leader in its field. This designation was achieved due to the success of the Polymer Research Institute and the accomplishments of Poly professors.

OPERATING IN THE RED

The lack of endowment funds became apparent once again in 1959. For the first time in the Institute's history, President Weber publicly released its financial statement, which showed an operational deficit of $37,500. The endowment funds amounted to just under $3 million, 42 percent of which was invested in Polytechnic Research and Development Corporation. "There is little question that the endowment funds of the Institute are woefully inadequate and that special attention must be paid to augment them in every feasible way," said President Weber.[72] In order to balance the budget, and provide new programs and to increase faculty salaries, tuition was raised to $1,100 per year. By comparison, tuition at MIT was $1,300 annually.[73]

President Weber also called for a new library which could house the scientific and engineering literature, and for athletic facilities to provide a more suitable athletic education. He called for new laboratories for graduate study and research, a nuclear reactor, and continued space research.[74]

At that time, the cost of the new campus headquarters on Jay Street reached $6 million, which included the initial cost of the factory. In 1959, almost $5 million was raised by alumni. Since new accelerated programs were on the horizon,

President Weber (in rear, third from left) and his wife, Sonya (seated to his left), took a break from one of his regular summer lecture tours to visit with the San Francisco Alumni Chapter of the Institute.

President Weber pushed for more funds to further expand the Institute. With the launch of *Sputnik* two years earlier by the Soviet Union, and the space race in full swing, he said:

> *Our enthusiasm for science and engineering must not be permitted to rise and fall with the* Sputniks. *American industry and American leaders must continually provide America's youth with encouragement and tangible support if we are to provide the creative scientists and engineers we desperately need.*[75]

As the Institute approached the 1960s, it was fully functioning in its new campus. President

Weber continued the legacy left by President Rogers and the four presidents who preceded him. With a world renowned faculty, increasing enrollment, and millions of dollars in research funds, Polytechnic was on the verge of groundbreaking discoveries, one of which would make man's first step on the moon a reality.

Students take a break from classes in the early 1970s at 333 Jay Street in Brooklyn, New York. While the Institute officially became coeducational in the later part of the 1950s, during this time, female enrollment was very small. Women students only began to come to Polytechnic in significant numbers after the 1973 arrival of President George Bugliarello, who actively recruited them.

CHAPTER SEVEN
TRIUMPH AND CHALLENGE
1960 –1972

The educational resources of the nation are enriched by the recent addition of the Long Island Graduate Center of the Polytechnic Institute of Brooklyn. In a society where the demand for a high degree of training in the sciences and engineering is constantly growing, a new center equipped to provide graduate education in these fields is a national asset.

—President John F. Kennedy, April 28, 1962

THE DOORS OF THE POLYtechnic at 85 Livingston Street were locked by President Weber in 1960, marking another milestone in the Institute's history. With the new campus at 333 Jay Street in full operation, the only remaining academic department that hadn't been moved was physical education, which was located at the Central Y.M.C.A., located in Brooklyn.[1]

Despite this forward motion there was a slight dip in enrollment. At this time there were 5,597 students registered, as compared with 5,732 in the preceding year.[2] But Polytechnic was not the only academic institution affected. Most engineering institutions across the country were experiencing a dip in enrollments at the time. One reason for this was considerable criticism by the American Civil Liberties Union (ACLU), which claimed that government-sponsored research—a mainstay at engineering colleges—was incompatible with academic freedom.[3]

While the ACLU agreed with the rationale for government-sponsored research during World War II, it and other concerned parties believed that these practices could represent a negative influence on the structure and function of universities.[4] And there was a great deal of such research being conducted at the time. In 1959, for example, $440,000,000 was given to academic institutions for research purposes by the federal government.

A total of 700 colleges were recipients, including Polytechnic.[5]

Businesses and industry also realized the great benefit of developing progressive relationships with universities—and with Polytechnic. In June of 1960, the Ford Foundation granted Polytechnic $750,000 to establish and support a Unified Honors Program for a period of five to seven years. This program was designed to provide in-depth studies, coupled with an early exposure to research, for a select group of outstanding students. That fall, the first 33 students in the program were enrolled.[6] Professor George Schillinger served as program director. He recently commented on the importance of enhancing and transferring knowledge from one generation to the next:

President Ernst Weber retired from Polytechnic in 1969 and spent the next decade working for the National Research Council. Weber was an innovator in the field of microwave engineering which encompasses advancements in everything from radar to microwave ovens. He held more than 30 patents in the field of microwave techniques, and published works on electromagnetic fields and linear and non-linear circuits in microwave measurements. In 1943, he founded the Microwave Research Institute at Polytechnic, which was renamed the Weber Research Institute in his honor in 1985 (and is now called the Weber Wireless Research Institute).

One of the main responsibilities of a university is to consolidate knowledge—to reorganize it, rethink it, refresh it, rephrase it, to inject it into the curriculum and text materials.[7]

A major reason the Unified Honors Program was developed was the dearth of engineering students who were working toward advanced degrees at the time. During the late '50s, most engineering graduates were being offered lucrative jobs upon graduation, leaving little desire for them to pursue further education. In 1959, for example, only 714 PhD degrees in engineering were awarded in all

Polytechnic's main campus located at 333 Jay Street, circa 1966. Since pioneering evening sessions in 1904, many of its students pursued graduate and doctoral degrees at night, while working for companies and businesses during the day. At the time, Poly was one of the few universities to offer night classes leading to an engineering degree.

accredited graduate schools across the country, yet the personnel requirements for just one of the nation's major companies alone amounted to 200 new engineering employees.[8]

SALARY INCREASES

In order to satisfy requests from the faculty, President Weber and members of The Corporation approved an additional $200,000 for salary increases in 1960. This allocation increased the minimum salary for an instructor to $4,500; assistant professor, $5,500; associate professor, $7,000; and professor, $9,000. These funds were covered by an increase in tuition. However, President Weber assured that financial assistance would continue to be available to students. At the time, 128 students held scholarships at Polytechnic, totaling $105,000. The three largest sources for these were the New York State Regents Scholarships, Polytechnic Corporation Scholarships, and New York State Engineering and Science Awards.[9]

IMMIGRANT STUDENTS

The majority of students at Polytechnic continued to come from immigrant families. Representative of this trend was Donald Weisstuch, current Poly trustee, and vice president of Sverdrup Corporation. Weisstuch received his undergraduate degree in 1957, and his Master's in Civil Engineering in 1962. He recently recalled his early memories of the Institute, and why he chose to attend Polytechnic:

Polytechnic, like so many urban, inner-city schools of technology, has historically served the sons and daughters of immigrants. A large proportion of the student body at Poly, over the last 75 years, have been first-generation Americans or even immigrants. That's why I chose Poly.[10]

A NEW HORIZON

The Institute received a substantial gift in 1960, a 25-acre parcel of land donated by the Long Island-based company, Republic Aviation Corporation. Construction of a new facility on the acreage began immediately—the Long Island Graduate Center, a new campus that initially consisted of two structures totaling more than 65,000 square-feet. The campus contained nine classrooms, a library, cafeteria, meeting rooms and administrative offices. Included in the main building were 12 laboratories for research in such areas as aerospace engineering and electrophysics. The second building, a 12,000-square-foot simple steel structure, housed the high-power microwave and plasma research centers as well as a shock tube, a device used to simulate high temperature and gas pressure effects.[11] From the 1960s to this time period, graduate courses were offered at night at Mineola High School.

In addition to the gift of land, the Institute also received a grant of $375,000 from the National Science Foundation. The funds were used to stimulate a closer relationship between Polytechnic's faculty and the industrial research laboratories near its Long Island campus.

Curricula at the campus included part-time and full-time day and evening programs leading to Master of Science and Doctoral degrees in Aerospace Engineering, Astronautics, Electrical Engineering, Electrophysics, Mathematics, Mechanical Engineering, and Physics.[12]

Mundy I. Pearle, president of Republic Aviation Corporation, said of Polytechnic's Graduate Center:

We are not giving anything away. We are making an investment, and a better and wiser one would be hard to find. It represents not only our best thinking but the ideas and recommendations of some of the nation's most knowledgeable men in the area of astronautics and aeronautics.[13]

ACCOLADES

The investment by business and industry on behalf of Polytechnic paid off handsomely in accomplishments by students, alumni, and faculty. For example, a team of Polytechnic mathematics students ranked first in the William Lowell Putnam Mathematics Competition of the Mathematical Association of America. This was the second time in a three-year period that the team placed first. A total of 633 contestants from 141 colleges and universities participated.[14]

Also, Professor Robert J. Ullman, class of 1946, associate professor of chemistry, and his group of graduate students, received a grant from the Office of Naval Research for a continuing study of polymers at liquid solid interfaces.[15]

Professor Mark, dean of the faculty, was presented by a committee of academic and industrial scientists with a bronze bust of his likeness on March 12, 1960, at a luncheon meeting at the Hotel St. Regis. Created by sculptress Jimilia Mason, the bust was the first of a series of internationally famous polymer scientists.[16] The following year, Mark received an honorary degree from Johannes Gutenberg University, in Mainz, Germany, the Distinguished Service Medal of Syracuse University, and the Gold Medal of the Indian Association For The Cultivation of Science.[17]

Also recognized for exceptional performance for forty years of teaching was Professor Otto H. Henry, a founder of the Metallurgical Department. Upon retirement, a dinner was held in his honor that was attended by 85 members of the faculty.[18]

BEQUEST FUELS FORWARD MOTION

As the Institute entered the 1961-62 academic year, it received a major bequest from the late

Students from the Institute competed in 1963 on NBC-TV's *College Bowl* television program. The Institute team beat Fairfield University during this match, which featured questions on engineering and science.

Colonel Willard T. Chevalier, class of 1910, member of The Corporation for 34 years, in the amount of $1,000,000.[19] This marked the largest single bequest so far in the history of the Institute. The money was used to further develop the academic programs at both the undergraduate and the graduate levels. Matched by private and governmental grants, the bequest provided a major "uplift" for the Institute, according to President Weber.[20]

Several years earlier, Chevalier had made a speech at the centennial celebration which underscored his strong feelings toward his alma mater.

As I contemplate my degree from Polytechnic ... I recognize that it has a far higher value today than it ever had before. I have had good profit in that degree and I'm trying this year to make some payment on a debt of honor.[21]

Two new programs were created during this academic year: the chemistry-oriented pre-medical program and the interdepartmental systems science curriculum. While the pre-medical program represented a marked departure from tradition, the Institute recognized its growing responsibility to assist in the education of research-oriented medical doctors. The Chemistry Department, under the direction of Professor Charles G. Overberger, received approval for the course of study from the American Medical Association.[22]

The growing benefit of interaction between physical scientists, engineers, and medical research groups was further solidified by the development of a medical engineering program within the Electrical and Mechanical Engineering Departments. This initiative was made possible through a partnership with the Long Island College of Medicine, whose physiology facilities were made available to the Institute under the direction of Dr. Jesse Crump, who later became a full-time member of the faculty.[23]

The Institute also began partnering with Rensselaer Polytechnic, Case Institute, Carnegie Institute of Technology, and the Illinois Institute of Technology regarding curriculum and program development issues. Also, it agreed to assist Oriente University in Venezuela in utilizing a Ford Foundation grant they received in the amount of $300,000.[24]

In 1961, after developing a chemistry-oriented pre-medical program, the Chemistry Department, under the direction of Professor Charles G. Overberger, was certified by the American Medical Association. Pictured here, Professor Overberger conducts an experiment in the chemistry laboratory.

DEDICATION DAY

After seven months of construction the Graduate Center was nearly complete, less a dormitory, which would eventually house 52 students from all over the world. Once built, it became the first dormitory in the Institute's 110 year history. On April 28, 1962, the Institute officially celebrated the opening of the new Graduate Center. In attendance was General Bernard A. Schriever, head of the United States Air Force Systems Command, who was instrumental in the development of our nation's missile and space programs; and Dr. Alan T. Waterman, director of the National Science Foundation. Governor Nelson Rockefeller, U.S. senators, and other leading governmental officials along with industry and educational leaders were also on hand for the ceremony.[25] The Graduate Center was furnished with research equipment valued at over $2 million.[26]

Perhaps the highest accolade came from President John F. Kennedy, who couldn't attend the ceremony but sent these thoughts via a telegram:

The Educational Resources of the nation are enriched by the recent addition of the Long Island Graduate Center of the Polytechnic Institute of Brooklyn. In a society where the demand for a high degree of training in the sciences and engineering is constantly growing, a new center equipped to provide graduate education in these fields is a national asset.[27]

Registration for the first semester at the Graduate Center was a resounding success. A total of 696 graduates from 97 colleges and universities registered in master's and doctoral classes. Students also came from 136 Long Island companies, including Grumman Aircraft Engineering Corporation, Sperry Gyroscope Company, Republic Aviation Corporation, and Airborne Instruments Labs.[28] Partnerships between these companies and the Institute resulted in additional research grants.

ACCOMPLISHMENTS

Polytechnic alumni continued to realize major successes in engineering. Alumnus Leopold H. Just, class of 1929, served as design engineer for the Throgs Neck Bridge, completed in 1961, which opened a new transit artery to New York City from Long Island. Dr. John G. Trump, class of 1929, was awarded the Lamme Award in 1961 for his X-ray related research while working as a professor at Massachusetts Institute of Technology. His work concerned the design of high voltage X-ray technology for medical research and for the treatment of malignant diseases.[29]

TWO MAJOR LOSSES

In February 1962, a distinguished former professor, Erich Hausmann, died. He had served on the faculty for over 45 years, retiring in 1953. He was internationally known for his texts in physics and electrical engineering and was the author of several books, including the textbooks *Physics, Telegraph Engineering, Dynamo Electric Machinery,* and *Physics Principles.*[30]

That same month Professor Emeritus S. Marion Tucker also died. Head of the Department of English and Psychology from 1911 to 1945, Tucker founded the Polytechnic Play Workshop, and was a member of the National Theatre Council and the Modern Language Association.[31]

RESEARCH CONCERNING RADIOACTIVE CONTAMINATION

During this period the Institute began research on the radioactive contamination of food supplies, especially milk. The focus of the research centered on ion-exchange resin membranes for three radioactive substances: iodine-131, cesium-137, and strontium-90. As a result, a decontamination process for milk using plastic sheets known as ion-exchange membranes was discovered. This technique was quickly employed across the nation and offset some of the dangerous effects of radioactive fallout.[32]

ADVANCES, ACCOMPLISHMENTS, ADDITIONAL GRANTS

In 1963, Professor Nathan Marcuvitz was named assistant director of defense research and engineering for the Department of Defense.[33] This appointment required Marcuvitz to take a one year sabbatical. President Weber said his appointment was "a great honor for the Polytechnic and indicative of the ever growing stature of the Institute."[34]

In 1963, the Institute spent what was then the largest amount in its history—$93,000—for 10,000 new books and periodicals. Under Library Director Leonard Cohan, the library also obtained the status of a U.S. Governmental Depository Library, joining a select group of only a few hundred other libraries across the nation. This designation permitted professors and students to obtain publications of the Government Printing Office in selected categories without charge. Included were many publications from NASA. This status was discontinued around 1984.[35]

The National Science Foundation granted $172,000 to support research in material sciences; a $216,000 fellowship grant was also received from NASA.[36]

Despite these and other research grants and increased enrollment, the Institute still faced financial hardships. At the end of 1963 an audit showed that available cash from the endowment fund was only a little more than $1,000.[37] Indeed, while the Institute's net worth from investments and

MODERN VISIONS

IN THE EARLY 1960s, GERALD OSTER, professor of chemistry, began researching the effects of moiré patterns in science, mathematics, engineering, art, and visual psychology. His work touched on various concepts concerning visual psychology, the hallucinatory possibilities of art, the intensification of perception due to the ingestion of certain drugs, and the shifting illusions of moiré, that is, a ripple or shimmering pattern.[1]

Oster discovered that when designs such as concentric circles, or any form made up of solid or open regions, are produced in a repetitious manner, a scientific explanation for the resulting moiré pattern can be precisely deduced. He quantified the moiré phenomena during chemistry research at Polytechnic, working with a graduate student from Japan, Yasunori Nishijima. Through a measurement of rates at which very small particles diffuse in liquids, they were able to invent a moiré microscope which had no lenses.[2]

Pursuing his interest in moiré research, Oster realized that its general principles could be applied to a wide range of scientific and engineering problems and issues, including a combination analog/digital computer; X-ray diffraction by a crystal lattice and related phenomena; computation of the electrical potential about a constellation of electric charges; and the microscopic examination of biological specimens without the use of magnifying lenses.[3]

Oster's seminal research resulted in over 130 scientific papers in the fields of molecular optics, including light scattering and fluorescence, photochemistry of dye solutions and high polymers, and the scientific aspects of photography. He authored a book entitled *The Science of Moiré Patterns*, and was awarded numerous patents in the graphical arts field.[4]

Indeed, it was Oster's amazing discovery that created a new dynamic of motion, space, and color for artists. World-famous artist Salvador Dali, who employed moiré concepts in many of his masterpieces, called Oster a "good friend and teacher."[5] Oster is also credited with the development of polymer photography, a process that revolutionized the printing industry and that is used widely today, including in the printing of this 150th anniversary history book about Polytechnic University.

In the early 1960s, Gerald Oster, professor of chemistry, began researching the effects of moiré patters in numerous areas, including the effects on the mind, as evidenced by his article "Moiré Patterns and Visual Hallucinations," published in 1966 in *Psychedelic Review*.

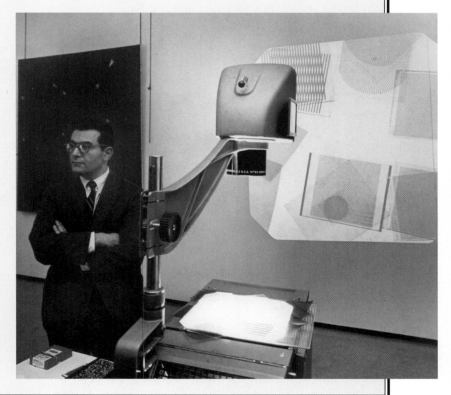

properties exceeded $5 million, the lack of endowment funds became an increasingly vexatious problem, one that grew worse each year.

ENROLLMENT ON THE RISE

By the 1963-64 school year the Institute's undergraduate enrollment was up, and the graduate enrollment was at the highest point in its history—1,439 full-time undergraduate students; 335 full-time graduate students; 1,230 part-time undergraduate students; and 2,661 part-time graduate students.[38] The following year, the Institute was forced to raise tuition—$1,700 annually for undergraduate students, and $1,900 annually for graduate students. This was on par with other leading institutions like MIT and Case Institute.[39]

As the Vietnam conflict began to heat up, important departmental changes took place at the Institute. Professor Charles G. Overberger left his post as head of the Chemistry Department and as associate director of the Polymer Research Institute to become dean of sciences. Professor F. Marshall Beringer was named head of the Chemistry Department. Professor John G. Truxal was appointed dean of engineering, and Professor Henry Q. Middendorf was appointed dean of humanities and social sciences.[40] (Professor Middendorf died on January 16, 2005, at the age of 98.)

NEW COMPUTER CENTER

In December 1963, Polytechnic's Computer Center opened on the second floor of Rogers Hall. An IBM 7074 was installed in the computer laboratory through a $200,000 National Science Foundation grant. This supported the expansion of computer education and research. The director of the Center was Professor Henry F. Soehngen. Computer courses were expanded in 1968 to eight undergraduate and 12 graduate courses as Professor Ed Smith in the Electrical Engineering Department led both the teaching and research effort. Professor Soehngen did specific application work in civil engineering. President Weber said of the new computer program: "It is obvious that the role of the computer in education and technology will be an ever-enlarging one."[41]

A major initiative in computer software was the development effort of a PL/I-like compiler,

Left: In 1963, Professor Henry Q. Middendorf was appointed dean of humanities and social sciences. He began teaching German at Polytechnic in 1934. During World War II, Professor Middendorf taught soldiers German before they were deployed. He retired as professor emeritus in the early 1970s.

Below: In support of the Institute's Aerodynamics Department, members of the Polytechnic faculty met with President John F. Kennedy in 1962. Pictured here, Professor Antonio Ferri shakes hands with President Kennedy. To President Kennedy's left is Dr. Theodore von Karman, director of the Air Force Scientific Advisory Board of the Air Force.

PLAGO (Poly Load and Go), led by Professor Harold W. "Bud" Lawson in electrical engineering, along with four students who all went on to senior positions in research and industry, with three of these individuals receiving PhDs in Ccomputer Science or Electrical Engineering.

THE TEN-YEAR PLAN

Under the leadership of President Weber, The Corporation accepted a 10-year plan that was proposed by an ad hoc committee organized to plan Polytechnic's future as a leading technological university. The plan was met with great enthusiasm by all involved. However, very lofty goals were set, along with increased expenses to reach them.[42]

This initiative complemented the Brooklyn Polytechnic Urban Renewal Project created by the city council to refurbish the decaying neighborhood surrounding Polytechnic. This project was ultimately abandoned, however, when a new city administration selected another area of Brooklyn for urban renewal.[43]

The Institute continued to develop its own 10-year plan, which included hiring new staff and expanding programs. A new partnership was born from the failed urban renewal effort. The Center for Urban Environmental Studies would study urban problems, including environmental studies, transportation, air pollution, urban information communication systems, and organization of city departments. Among those participating was Professor Charles E. Schaffner who was chairmen of the committee that revised New York City's building code.[44]

Following the building code revision, Polytechnic faculty members were encouraged to develop new educational programs that would assist in the building of advanced infrastructure. To this end, the Civil Engineering Department established the Division of Transportation Planning. Professor Louis Pignataro,

class of 1951, was named director. Pignataro and his team were involved in a number of research projects, including studying traffic congestion issues on Jay Street, which resulted in recommendations to city officials on ways traffic flow could be improved.[45]

DEFENDING THE NATION

In the winter of 1965, the Institute was awarded a $1,000,000, three-year contract by the Department of Defense to study electromagnetic phenomena associated with ballistic missile detection in the upper atmosphere, and to investigate the conditions encountered by space vehicles. President Weber said that this represented a "unique and farsighted commitment by the federal government's Advanced Research Projects Agency and the Office of Naval Research to aid in the developing within a university campus of a center of fundamental electromagnetic research [that was] responsive to both academic and Department of Defense needs."[46]

This partnership of course represented the government's continued strong confidence in the research capabilities of the Institute. The contract supported interdisciplinary studies in eight areas: communication theory, pattern recognition, information theory, scattering, radiation, plasma dynamics,

Professor Louis Pignataro was head of the Department of Transportation Planning and Engineering and director of the Transportation Training and Research Center, which he founded. Among a handful of books he wrote on transportation, his 1973 release, *Traffic Engineering: Theory and Practice*, has been used in over 65 colleges and universities across the nation.

POLY CHANGES NYC BUILDING CODE

ON FEBRUARY 25, 1960, AFTER YEARS of heated debate concerning the New York City Building Code bylaws, it was decided by the New York Building Congress to retain a local educational institution to outline a workable approach updating the antiquated building code, first written at the turn of the century and revised from 1928 to 1937.[1]

In February of 1962 the Polytechnic Institute of Brooklyn was hired for this work and began a three-year study of the code. Later that year, after successful preliminary results, a preliminary report was issued. New York City Mayor Robert Wagner then authorized the Institute to write the new building code.

The Institute created an executive board to oversee this project—the three Poly professionals who had written the original report: Professor R. B. B. Moorman, head of the Department of Civil Engineering, Professor Clifford A. Wojan, administrator officer for the Department of Mechanical Engineering, and

Charles E. Schaffner, vice president for administration and professor of civil engineering,

who served as project chairman. William Correale served as technical director.[2]

The work by Polytechnic, along with New York City officials, resulted in a new code that addressed numerous long overdue improvements, including: connected balconies replacing fire escapes; roofs without water tanks; apartments with effective soundproofing; less expensive plumbing materials to reduce work costs; double-flue incinerators in new apartment buildings to increase safety and reduce air pollution; setting performance requirements for heating systems, with minimum temperatures for each type of occupancy; the use of pre-tested and pre-cast concrete structural members for the first time; departures from the design requirements for large theaters, with sprinklers (water curtains) replacing the fire curtains, as well as high-capacity emergency ventilating systems; and new requirements for ramps or street-level entrances to all new buildings used by the public for the convenience of the handicapped, among others.[3]

The new code increased building productivity, reduced environmental hazards, and produced a safer New York City. President Weber was thrilled with this accomplishment:

The work of these men, their technical consultants and industry advisory committees, will have a direct impact on the safety, health, and welfare of our city for decades to come.[4]

The final report consisted of three volumes totaling 1,400 pages. The new building code was officially enacted into law in 1968. Mayor John V. Lindsay described the new regulations as a "truly modern, flexible building code that touches the life of every person in the city."[5]

The Institute created an executive board made up of three Poly academics for the New York City building code project: Professor R.B.B. Moorman, head of the Department of Civil Engineering, Professor Clifford A. Wojan (bottom photo), administrator officer for the Department of Mechanical Engineering, and Charles E. Schaffner (top photo).

chemical reactions in plasma, and applied mathematics.[47] The research was conducted at the Graduate Center in Farmingdale. To simulate the temperature conditions at altitudes ranging from 150,000 to 300,000 feet, the shock tunnel was operated at speeds of up to 20 times the speed of sound.[48]

At this time, about half of the Institute's annual research budget, $4,000,000, supported research concerning the understanding of electromagnetic phenomena. It resulted in furthering ballistic missile target identification, space communications and the nature of space environments, ultrahigh power radar, plasmas, and the technology of lasers. Professor Marcuvitz, dean of research, said that a major objective of the program was the training of doctoral level and postdoctoral level scientists, and "as a manpower resource for the sophisticated electromagnetic research ventures that must accompany man's penetration of the upper atmosphere and outer space."[49]

BRIDGING TECHNOLOGY

An historical event in the Institute's history occurred on November 21, 1964, with the opening of the Verrazano Narrows Bridge. Nomer Gray, class of 1939, partner at Ammann and Whitney, organized, administered, and coordinated the massive project,

Tobias' mural the *History of Science* was a work in progress, which spanned decades. In the early 1960s, Professor Ludwig Edelstein (third from left) of the Rockefeller Institute looks over a visual representation of the era of Greek science. Muralist Abraham Joel Tobias (right) shows the panel that will depict Socrates and his pupils. With them, are Professor Helmut Gruber (left) and Professor Frederick C. Kreiling.

which required 10,000 men and $325,000,000 to complete. It was then the longest and heaviest unsupported bridge span in the world—60 feet longer than San Francisco's Golden Gate Bridge.[50] The new bridge, which connected Bay Ridge, Brooklyn, to Staten Island, enabled cars to make the trip in six minutes.

Gray was also instrumental in the building of the Dulles International Airport in Washington, D.C., and the Throgs Neck Bridge. He benefited, as did many, from the Institute's highly respected evening program, and received his master's degree in civil engineering in 1943. After receiving praise for his signal accomplishment on the Verrazano Narrows Bridge project, he stated that Professor Edward Squire, head of the Civil Engineering Department at Polytechnic "had more effect on my thinking than anyone else I can think of."[51]

In 1963, a project center for undergraduate and graduate research was begun under the formal direction of the Mechanical Engineering Department. On May, 14, 1965, thanks to grants from Joseph W.

Wunsch, class of 1917, and from the National Science Foundation, the Wunsch Center for Project Engineering was opened. With the approval of a professor, students were permitted to select an open-ended research topic. The idea behind this program came from members of the faculty and The Corporation who decided that an atmosphere which would closely simulate the research and development laboratories within private industry would be beneficial to students.[52] Additionally, for the first time at Polytechnic, doctorate degrees in industrial engineering were offered.

Also, the Institute received $5 million from the National Science Foundation for Excellence. The money was invested in new faculty and research facilities. However, this hiring of new faculty and expenses would create an intense financial strain on the school after the grant ended in 1970.[53]

ALUMNI GIFTS

While tuition provided a vital revenue stream, it still didn't provide enough income to sustain all of the many ambitious developments and programs at Polytechnic. In 1966, two $250,000 gifts were received by Polytechnic: one from Mr. and Mrs. John E. McKeen, and the other from the Charles Pfizer Company which McKeen headed.[54] The gifts were made to enable Polytechnic to create a Molecular Biology Department as part of its overall life sciences program.

President Weber stated that the new department would be closely involved with the Chemistry Department's Polymer Research Institute; the Physics Department and its X-ray crystallography; programs in bioengineering and biomedicine;

Herbert Welch, class of 1882, unofficial patriarch of the Methodist Church, the oldest bishop of any church in the world and the oldest alumnus of any American college, died on Good Friday, April 4, 1969, at 106 years old. Pictured above, Welch blows out the candles on his 100th birthday in 1963. As a student at Polytechnic, he commuted to the Institute by way of horse car and ferry to study civil engineering. He later went on to become the president of Ohio Wesleyan University. In 1960, Bishop Welch received the Golden Jubilee Citation from the Institute.

MURRAY ROTHBARD

IN 1967, POLY WELCOMED MURRAY NEW-ton Rothbard to its staff as associate professor of economics. Throughout his 22-year career at Polytechnic, Rothbard authored numerous influential articles and books. He was a staunch supporter of the Libertarian Party, which he joined in 1974, and in which he remained active until 1989. He served several terms on the Libertarian National Committee, and helped write sections of the Party's platform. In 1995, Steve Dasbach, Libertarian Party national chair, said of Rothbard's influence, "His many works, particularly his classic book, *For a New Liberty*, have had a profound influence on the development of the modern libertarian movement."[1]

After leaving Polytechnic in 1985, Rothbard was the S. J. Hall Distinguished Professor of Economics at the University of Nevada, Las Vegas, and vice president for academic affairs at the Ludwig von Mises Institute at Auburn University.[2]

Among his 25 books, Rothbard authored *Man, Economy, and State* (1962), a treatise elucidating the full range of economics using logical methods he thought appropriate to the social sciences. *Power and Market* (1970), a policy-oriented elaboration, presented a taxonomy of political interventionism and a critique of all forms of regulation and taxation. Rothbard's *America's Great Depression* (1963), an empirical application of monetary theory to the business cycle, was also the first scholarly work to argue a non-market cause of the stock market crash and the subsequent Great Depression, as well as to reinterpret the presidency of Herbert Hoover as a "proto-New Deal."[3]

A year before his death in 1995, at the age of 69, Rothbard received the Ingersoll Foundation's Richard M. Weaver Prize for Scholarly Letters. The Foundation said Rothbard "almost defines the term *intellectual maverick*. A brilliant economic historian and philosopher, he has almost single-handedly revived the idealism of the old American Republic. He's an individualist to the core, but he has never for a moment lost sight of the social and moral dimensions of the marketplace."[4]

---

the Civil Engineering Department's work in sanitary engineering; and the Chemical Engineering Department's studies in industrial bacteriology, fermentation, and the production of drugs and biologicals.[55]

After his gift was made, McKeen delivered a speech that strongly underscored the Institute's importance to science and engineering:

With this gift, Charles Pfizer and Company salutes Polytechnic for its leadership as a scientific-technological college from which many of our key employees and leaders have graduated. Just as Polytechnic alumni have helped Pfizer in mass-producing penicillin, and in discovering and producing Terramycin, they are involved with Pfizer at virtually every level of employment, in research, development, and the production of a wide range of products for human well-being and comfort.[56]

In 1966, the American Council on Education issued its regular report entitled, *Assessment of*

Quality in Graduate Education. Of 2,200 colleges and universities in the nation, only 110 qualified to be ranked for the study. Numerous Polytechnic programs awarding doctoral degrees received top rankings vis-à-vis their competitors: electrical engineering (6th best); chemical engineering (16th), mechanical engineering (18th); chemistry (25th); plus, the physics department was rated in the top 50 programs in the United States.

The report also concluded that Polytechnic had the largest undergraduate engineering enrollment of any individual college in New York State, and the third largest in the nation for its various master's programs.[57]

LONG ISLAND RESEARCH LABORATORY

In April 1966, at the Long Island Graduate Center in Farmingdale, a new $1,000,000 research laboratory addition was officially dedicated. The research laboratory replaced facilities at Freeport, Long Island, thus allowing all Polytechnic activities to be consolidated in two locations rather than three.[58]

The $1,000,000 research laboratory addition at the Long Island Graduate Center in Farmingdale. It was constructed as a result of a major NASA grant.

The new laboratory, which was made possible by a $632,000 grant from NASA, was named in honor of Preston R. Bassett, the chairman of The Corporation. Part of the new facility included supersonic and hypersonic wind tunnels. It also included equipment for research in high-speed flight dynamics, interplanetary communications, and electrophysics.[59]

Since opening its doors in 1961, the Farmingdale campus had hosted over 20 symposia and seminars sponsored by the NASA Space Science program, plus the departments of aerospace, electrophysics, electrical engineering, and others. A symposium on Unconventional Inertial Sensors was conducted there by the Bureau of Naval Weapons, along with the Air Force Systems Command Research and Technical Division, and Republic Aviation. The Supersonic Tunnel Association held its 23rd semi-annual meeting there, and the Institute of Electrical and Electronics Engineers conducted two series of spring lectures in 1965 on Phased Arrays and Computer Programming for Scientists and Engineers.[60] During the dedication of the new laboratory, NASA director James Webb addressed the audience in attendance.

With substantial advances underway at the Long Island campus, The Corporation welcomed R. E. Lewis as the new chairman in 1966. That same year the Bioengineering Department was

pib 1966-67 pib
FALL
TELEPHONE APPEAL
ALUMNI FUND COUNCIL
NOV. 28 - 29, 1966
ANNUAL ALUMNI FUND

established, with Professor William B. Blesser named as its director.

FINANCIAL STRESS

By 1967, the Institute was facing highly challenging financial circumstances. As the Vietnam War became hotter, many students used education as a deferment. Nevertheless, the Institute realized shrinking enrollment numbers—in sharp contrast to the heavy funds spent on new faculty and research initiatives. Additionally, funds received from the Department of Defense shrunk from 61.5 percent of research grants in 1963 to 26.2 percent in 1967.[61]

To counter all of this, the alumni association quickly began various fund-raising campaigns involving phone-based initiatives. Tuition was also increased to $1,900 for undergraduate students, and $2,200 for graduate students. The total cost of educating one student in 1957 was $1,930. In 1967, that number had risen to $4,430. These tuition costs, however, did not cover the full expense of education, only representing roughly 75 percent of the overall cost.

In 1967, as research grants began dissipating, the Institute was forced to call on alumni for support. While bequests and gifts were received every year, the Institute was losing money. Pictured here, members of the alumni association participate in the Alumni Phone Appeal. This was one of the first serious fundraisers undertaken by the alumni association.

While the full-time undergraduate enrollment numbers were fairly steady, the evening degree program was markedly down in terms of enrollment. In 1957, part-time and evening students for that program totaled 2,034, but in 1967 that number had dropped to 700.[62] Conversely, the number of graduate students was steadily increasing. In 1957, there were 191 part-time graduate students, but by 1967 that number had risen to 537. Doctoral students increased as well with 84 enrolled in 1967 compared to only 32 in 1957.[63] Decreases in part-time undergraduate enrollment were driven by the growth of the low-cost public sector which made full-time study in the public sector readily affordable.

In President Weber's 1967 annual report, he made clear that Polytechnic could no longer sustain itself as a private institution in light of these various trends. He concluded that the Institute would need to realize $40 to $60 million in endowments to be able to continue its operations. This seemed highly unlikely, however, since the Institute had never put an emphasis on endowment funds, surviving largely by tuition and grants. Therefore he and The Corporation began preliminary talks with the State University of New York and Governor Nelson Rockefeller to discuss how New York State could assist in meeting Polytechnic's monetary requirements.[64]

President Weber wrote:

These considerations and earlier discussions concerning cooperation between the State University and Polytechnic ... evolved into [exploring] the feasibility of ... affiliation in a manner that would bring substantial support to Polytechnic and permit its

growth potential for service as a specialized science and engineering center for New York State.[65]

THE BEAT GOES ON

Financial problems aside, the Institute continued to achieve academic progress and to produce accomplished graduates inspired by brilliant professors. In 1967, Bachelor of Science degrees in Humanities and Social Sciences were established. During this time, Professor Edward Smith was the driving force behind the Poly computer science program. He was aided by Professor Bud Lawson. From their collective expertise and dedication, the program grew to great heights. The following year, the Metallurgical Engineering Department was established, headed by Professor Alan A. Johnson. Professor Joseph Kempner was named head of

TRIUMPHS AND TRANSITIONS

IN FEBRUARY OF 1964, THE OTTO H. HENRY Metallurgical Laboratory opened in memory of Henry's service to the Institute. The laboratory was partially funded by a grant from the National Science Foundation.

In early 1964, two appointments were made at the Long Island Graduate Center: Professor Anthony B. Giordano was named dean of graduate studies; and Professor Marcuvitz, returned from a one-year leave of absence, was named dean of research and dean of the Graduate Center. At the same time, at Polytechnic in Brooklyn, Professor James J. Conti was named head of the Chemical Engineering Department.[1]

After Professor Ferri announced that he was leaving the Institute for personal reasons, Professor Bloom was named head of the Department of Aerospace Engineering and Applied Mechanics. The year before Ferri left, he, along with a team of top engineers, and Dr. Theodore von Karman, director of the Scientific Advisory Board of the Air Force, met with President John F. Kennedy in Washington, D.C. Kennedy lauded their collective

efforts in helping to bring his dream to fruition— winning the space race.

In June 1964, Professor Fankuchen died. To honor him and his groundbreaking discoveries in X-ray crystallography, the Institute established the Isidor Fankuchen Memorial Fellowship, which was used to assist students in master's and doctoral programs.[2]

Faculty achievements were plentiful during this academic year. Professor Mark, at the request of the State Department, made an extensive lecture tour of six South American countries, giving addresses at 14 institutions. Professor Overberger toured and lectured in Japan after receiving an invitation from the Japanese Polymer Society. Before returning home, he also lectured at the Weitzman Institute in Israel, an institution which maintains a strong and active relationship with Polytechnic to the present day.[3]

Also, Professor Murray Goodman became founding editor of the journal *Biopolymers*, and Professor Harry Hochstadt, in the Mathematics Department, authored *Differential Equations—*

the Aerospace Engineering and Applied Mechanics Department. Professor John R. Curreri, class of 1944, was named head of the Mechanical Engineering Department. The Institute also developed the Operations Research (O.R.) and Industrial Engineering (I.E.) Departments, both headed by Professor Norbert Hauser.

In January of 1967, Captain Charles R. Dunn, class of 1959, made aviation history when he and his team made a non-stop flight from Eglin Air Force Base, Florida, to Le Bourget Airfield, Paris, in an army helicopter named *Jolly Green Giant*. The 30-hour record-breaking flight followed in the footsteps of Charles A. Lindbergh who flew the *Spirit of St. Louis* 40 years earlier, at the time the first non-stop intercontinental flight.[66]

A nine-year veteran in the United States Air Force, Dunn was stationed in Vietnam, where he flew helicopters as a member of the Air Rescue Mission team. He was awarded the Air medal for Airmanship and Courage during the war.[67] Dunn was one of many Vietnam veterans affiliated with the Institute.

STAYING CALM DURING STRESSFUL TIMES

The 1960s were a turbulent time, leading up to the Vietnam War. The assassinations of President John F. Kennedy, Martin Luther King Jr., and Robert F. Kennedy sent shock waves across the nation, which was bitterly divided on major issues, including not only the war, but also those issues regarding social and civil rights. However, the massive protests that sprang up at colleges and universities across the nation had little resonance with the student body at Polytechnic. It was a different situation, however, with the faculty. After the Kent State incident, the

Professors Herman Mark (left) and Murray Goodman discuss various applications in polymer science.

A Modern Approach, which was developed through the Unified Honors Program. The book was adopted by numerous universities across the nation for use as a standard textbook on the subject.[4]

The British Institution of Electrical Engineers awarded their highest honor to Professors Theodor Tamir and Arthur A. Oliner of the Electrophysics Department for the best paper published in their journal that year.[5]

Additionally, Professor Othmer was honored with a designation as one of the Master Builders of America on a television show broadcast on NBC. He also finished editing Volumes II, III, and IV of the second edition of the *Kirk-Othmer Encyclopedia of Chemical Technology*. In June of 1964, Othmer, as an honorary American delegate to the international chemical industry, flew to Frankfurt, Germany, and delivered the plenary lecture to the European Federation of Chemical Engineering. He also served with the United Nations at a Conference on Petrochemical Industries for developing nations, held in Tehran in November of that year.[6]

Other accomplishments included those of Professors Bernard Rechtschaffen and Conrad P. Homberger of the Modern Language Department, who authored a German phonetic dictionary in English-German and German-English that was distributed internationally.[7]

Also, in the early 1960s, Professor Leo Silber invented the "latching ferrite phase shifter," used for many years in the most advanced radar systems that employed phased array antennas.

faculty voted to close Polytechnic for a week in protest. No classes were held during this period.

While the Institute's students mourned the loss of friends and loved ones killed during the war, their focus largely was on improving engineering techniques, along with important research, that would benefit America in numerous ways, including its military operations. In this regard, the alumni association received a letter from Major Alvin Goldman, class of 1960, who was stationed in Vietnam.

*As a graduate of the Polytechnic and a career sol-
dier, I would like to say that the construction program
in Vietnam should be of keen interest to our engineering students, particularly in the civil and mechanical
fields. Due to local conditions, whole new approaches
must be taken in drainage, soil stabilization, concrete
and soil construction, quarry operations, and road
and air field construction.*[68]

At this time, the Institute successfully launched a high school course entitled *The Man-Made World*, which was developed in association with the Engineering Concepts Curriculum Project, sparked by Professor John. G. Truxal. In 1968, the program, which was sponsored at both the state and federal level, was used by over 4,000 students at more than 100 high schools throughout the nation, and at 20 liberal arts colleges. The resulting text books were published by McGraw-Hill.[69]

Supported by funds from the state legislature, the Institute also worked with neighboring high schools to afford inner-city students an exposure to higher education, Victor Wallach, who began working

The graduating class of 1966. The annual commencement, held at the Brooklyn Academy of Music, included undergraduates, graduates, and doctoral candidates.

When I first came, I felt [there was an attitude at Polytechnic that] going out and trying to raise huge sums of money was not dignified. We just won't go out and beg for it.[71]

In the final analysis, President Weber was not an administrative leader but instead a world-renowned scientist. His important research contributions—from military radar to microwave ovens—literally reshaped the world. It is interesting to note that the largest number of degrees in the Institute's history were awarded the year immediately following his retirement. The MS awards increased from 150 (in 1958) to 470 in 1970; for those same contrasting years, PhD awards increased from 36 to 108. Additionally, there were only seven graduate programs leading to a PhD degree in 1958. That number increased to 16 in 1970.[72]

at Polytechnic's Microwave Research Institute as a technician in 1956, recalled how the Institute assisted disadvantaged students:

We provide good service to the inner-city students. It is important to give them a good education and a start; and the way to be, in many cases, the first of their family to go to college or university and to graduate. So it was a very important mission that we were on and still continue to be. Of course we attract students from all over the world.[70]

PRESIDENT WEBER RETIRES

As the 1960s drew to a close, the Institute continued to face heady financial changes. President Weber had done an outstanding job during his 11-year tenure enhancing the reputation of the Institute, so it came as a surprise and disappointment when he announced his retirement shortly after the 1969 commencement activities.

President Weber was well respected as a scientists and professor, although some students and colleagues felt that he could have tried to re-orient the Institute's policies concerning endowments. Jim Jarman, then a librarian at the Institute, recalled his early memories of Weber's fiscal policy:

Left: A popular event in the 1960s was Homecoming Day, which included the annual tradition of picking a king and queen from the student body. Pictured here, holding a balloon is Christine Spejenkowski, Poly's 1968 Queen.

Below: An undergraduate civil engineer runs a compression test on a concrete cylinder for a group of high school students during Poly's annual Open House day. The Institute had a close relationship with surrounding high schools, which resulted in more students deciding to pursue degrees in engineering and science at Brooklyn Poly.

In President Weber's final year, it became obvious through independent studies conducted by Stanford University that the Institute would be best served by joining with the State University of New York educational system. The proposed new university would be called the Technological University of New York.[73] President Weber wrote in his final annual report:

Whatever the specific form of the long-range status of Polytechnic will be, private support from alumni, corporations and friends will be intensified. Private support is essential.... We must make certain that the growth potential of Polytechnic is maintained.[74]

POLY HELPS WINS THE SPACE RACE

In 1969, man took his first steps on the moon. Thomas Joseph Kelly, class of 1958, worked for more than a decade at NASA designing and engineering the lunar module program. It was Kelly's design of the lunar module that made the lunar landing a success, and that made the American space program the undeniable winner in the space race that began with the launch of *Sputnik* by the USSR in 1957. (It is interesting to note that Jay Greene, class of 1964, was a flight dynamics officer at Mission Control for *Apollo 8*, and is now the chief engineer at the Johnson Space Center.)

In the summer of 1969, The Corporation appointed Weber president emeritus and professor emeritus. During a search for the seventh president of the Institute, which included a review of over 100 educators and academics, Benjamin Adler, class of 1926, a trustee, was appointed acting president.[75] Adler participated in the first television transmission in Manhattan.

As the Institute prepared for an uncertain future, its alumni were continually being recognized for superior achievement. John Gilbert, class of 1953, '55 PhD, received the 1970 *Design News* Award for inventing a spiral gear to reduce friction. While chief engineer at the Bell and Howell Company, he also invented a mail-sorting machine. Additionally, he is well known for his recommendation to use Teflon in pots and pans.

Also in 1970, Uriel Domb, class of 1962, while working for Telsat Canada, the world's first domestic satellite communication company, designed the satellite tracking and mission control system that was used successfully to bring *Apollo 13* back to Earth after an oxygen tank explosion that rendered inoperative many of its key systems.

As the Vietnam War continued, the country became increasingly divided. On May 4, 1970, during a student protest at Kent State University, four students were killed by National Guard troops. Charles Hinkaty, class of 1970, Polytechnic student council president at the time, recalled the event and the era.

We had the tragic murders of those students on the Kent State campus. So universities around the country were in a state of upheaval, and there were demonstrations and sit-ins. But that didn't happen at Poly because Poly students were more conservative. They were people that were going to pursue careers in engineering, and they tended to be less political than students you might find at a liberal arts school.

The nation was in an uproar over this event. The Vietnam War had grown to be very unpopular. Students who were graduating were trying to figure out how they could avoid getting drafted into military service. This event at Kent State was monumental for students around the country.[76]

NEW PRESIDENT

In 1971, the Institute welcomed its seventh president, Arthur Grad. Before accepting the position, Dr. Grad was the dean of graduate studies at the Illinois Institute of Technology in Chicago. At Poly, Grad was faced with the same financial woes that had troubled President Weber. Plus, the number of engineering students continued to decrease. And the Institute experienced additional reductions in federal support for research and graduate training in engineering and science.

President Arthur Grad was instrumental in the negotiations to combine the Institute with New York University. However, he would only serve for 18 months.

As a result, Polytechnic was operating under a huge deficit while it endeavored to maintain its academic programs. Negotiations with both the State University of New York and the City University of New York were unsuccessful. To help Polytechnic over the hump, New York appropriated $3,000,000 for interim financial assistance.[77]

During the following 18 months, the New York State Legislature continued to toil over the merger of the Institute with New York University's School of Engineering and Science. If approved, the new entity would be known as the Polytechnic Institute of New York. While the specific details of the merger were being mediated, it was agreed that the primary location for the combined new university would be at the Brooklyn campus.

President Grad said of the decision:

The opportunities and challenges we will face in the near future, as our new institution begins to take form, are tremendous. I am confident, however, that the challenges will be squarely met and opportunities vigorously pursued as the Institute moves steadily forward into a fiscally sound and academically superior future.[78]

OTHER NOTABLE OCCURRENCES

During this period, the Electrical Engineering and Electrophysics Departments merged. In 1971, Professor Mark was invited by the Chinese Academy of Science to visit and lecture in mainland China—the first time an American scientist was officially invited by the Chinese government.[79] Later that year, Jack S. Howard, class of 1968, an IBM computer

In 1963, Professor Martin Bloom was named head of the Department of Aerospace Engineering and Applied Mechanics. In 1972, Bloom received the Outstanding Civilian Service Medal from the U.S. Army for work on the program. Later that year, Bloom founded *The International Journal of Computers and Fluids*.

engineer, served as the captain of America's first table tennis team which visited the People's Republic of China. The team's exploits were described in the press at the time as an example of "Ping-Pong Diplomacy" at its finest.

In 1972, Professors Martin H. Bloom and William B. Blesser received Outstanding Civilian Service Medals from the U.S. Army for their work on missile programs. Later that year, Professor Bloom founded *The International Journal of Computers and Fluids*.

As the Institute prepared to write another chapter in its rich history, it faced adversity. Aside from serious financial problems and a proposed merger, the Institute would also be charged with the task of finding a new president, necessitated as a result of Dr. Grad's questionable administrative practices—not supported by The Corporation—including denying tenure to deserving faculty.

While this was not an optimal situation, in the years that followed, Polytechnic would weather the financial storms of the 1970s to emerge even stronger.

Pictured above is a view of the school following its merger with the New York University of Science and Engineering. Starting in September of 1973, the new name was Polytechnic Institute of New York.

CHAPTER EIGHT
RECOVERY
1973–1977

We should challenge industry and Polytechnic alumni to support ideas that free men in a capitalistic society can recognize to be in their own self-interest. Support is not charity.

—Joseph J. Jacobs, 1976

BY THE END OF 1972, IT BECAME clear that the New York University School of Engineering and Science (NYU/SES) would be forced to close its campus in the Bronx and consolidate in Manhattan's Washington Square Park location. The following May, the Bronx campus was sold. This meant NYU/SES, which like Polytechnic had been founded in 1854, would be forced to close its doors permanently. The Bronx campus was sold for $60 million and incorporated into the City University system, later to become Bronx Community College.[1]

At this time, and after months of deliberations, New York State stepped forward and proposed a merger between NYU/SES and Polytechnic.[2] Ewald B. Nyquist, the New York State Commissioner of Education, guided the complex negotiations that led to the merger, beginning in November, 1972, and ending in late March of 1973.[3]

While many expected and supported the merger, others were surprised—and concerned—by the news. Nevertheless the Polytechnic Faculty Senate voted for the merger 110 to 38, and the faculty of NYU/SES also voted in the affirmative, 56 to 14.[4]

Current Vice President of Development and University Relations at Polytechnic, Richard Thorsen, served at the time on NYU's faculty. He played an instrumental role in the complex merger negotiations. He recalled that the idea to merge came after months of skittish deliberations.

The initial plan was to move the Engineering School to Washington Square. The Poly organization—Polytechnic Institution of Brooklyn, as it was called then—was not happy about that. They felt this would be a threatening move; two schools of comparable size, similar offerings, and just a couple of subway stops apart from each other. So the committee, searching hard for an alternative, eventually found one: thou shalt merge, which became a state decree.[5]

On April 23, 1973, therefore, in a ceremony at the University Club in Manhattan, the merger agreement was signed by NYU's president James H. Hester; Louis N. Rowley Jr., chairman of The Corporation; Professor Clifford Osborne, chairman of Polytechnic's faculty senate; and Richard Thorsen, secretary of NYU's engineering faculty.

NYU's Hester was very hopeful for the new union.

The long and complicated negotiations have resulted in a fair and viable agreement for the merger. Having established this measure of cooperation

---

In 1976, a year after donating $1 million to the Institute, alumnus Joseph J. Jacobs was elected chairman of The Corporation.

in engineering education, we look forward to a new relationship between New York University and [Polytechnic].[6]

The terms of the merger provided for the transfer of all research programs and specialized equipment from NYU to the new institution, with its primary location in Brooklyn.[7] Approximately 75

On April 23, 1973, the merger agreement between Polytechnic and New York University's School of Engineering and Science was signed. Pictured here, Professor Clifford Osborne of Polytechnic signs the agreement. Behind him, left to right, are Professor Richard Thorsen, then of NYU, NYU President James H. Hester, New York State Commissioner of Education, Ewald B. Nyquist, Acting President Norman Auburn, chairman of The Corporation, Louis N. Rowley Jr., and John Haines of the New York State Education Department.

members of the NYU faculty were offered positions at the new school, which at that time was referred to as the Merged Institute (MI), while a real name was contemplated. The effect of the merger was immediate. MI joined faculties and students, while the state provided financial assistance in the sum of $2 million for each year, until 1975.[8]

POLYTECHNIC INSTITUTE OF NEW YORK

While NYU enjoyed a sterling reputation academically around the world, it was decided that Polytechnic's name carried far more weight within the international scientific arena. Therefore it was decided that its name would be included in some fashion within the new title. Thus, it was agreed that the combined schools would be called Polytechnic Institute of New York. This name preserved Polytechnic, while signaling the broader base of operation authorized by the state—undergraduate

programs on Long Island and graduate programs at Westchester. This marked the second time in its history that the Institute had changed its name. Despite the official title, however, the majority of students and faculty continued to refer to the school as Brooklyn Poly. Thorsen said that the name chosen for the new entity represented a short-sighted, political decision.

The name Polytechnic Institute of New York was a politically correct choice. But after the merger, the identity as Brooklyn Poly was lost. We gave up something that was extremely important. It was hard at the time for the NYU faculty to understand this because they weren't part of it, but that name was a great asset, along with its strong tradition.[9]

The agreement also resulted in The Corporation's decision to release President Grad from his contract after serving only eighteen months. They then utilized the Academy for Educational Development who recommended Norman Auburn, a former president of the University of Akron, as interim president while the search for a permanent candidate continued. Meanwhile, student recruitment intensified, new research contracts were targeted, and costs and budgets were carefully planned and controlled. Additionally, Polytechnic Institute of New York began preparing the Farmingdale campus for the influx of undergraduates.[10]

A SEARCH FOR A NEW PRESIDENT

The Institute was also in search of a leader, a president who would guide the new institution to new heights, and perhaps most importantly, balance its budget and finally establish an endowment fund that would allow it to expand and grow. However, Polytechnic's first order of business was to calm the choppy waters resulting from the merger.

Acting President Norman Auburn, who assumed a small role in the merger process, announced the news to the alumni of the Institute in a letter:

The merger agreement is indeed a milestone. It marks the first time in history that two private engineering colleges have merged under the direct auspices of a state government. It is a positive step forward for your alma mater, although its true significance can only be measured in what transpires in the months and years to come.[11]

In the weeks and months that followed, certain faculty members continued to look askance at the new merger. Retired Professor Irving Cadoff, who taught for 25 years in NYU's Department of Metallurgy, and its College of Engineering, came to Polytechnic under the terms of the merger. He later became head of the Materials Science Department. During an interview last year, Cadoff recalled his initial feelings toward the move. "I was very unhappy," he commented. "It was a shotgun wedding."[12]

The fact that faculty members from both schools were familiar with each other and their respective work, however, made the assimilation process easier, according to Cadoff.

I don't remember any big problem. As far as I was concerned, my activities were restricted more or less to the department. We had known each other's groups because we worked for common programs in the city or were involved in the same professional organizations. Of course, the approach to the subject matter was different. The Poly program was more traditionally in metals, and we [NYU] had been going off in a new direction—materials science—which incorporated more than just metals.[13]

According to Thorsen, only some 60 percent (550) of the students from NYU chose to continue their education at Polytechnic Institute of New York after the merger. The Institute did not offer campus housing, while NYU's Bronx campus did. In those days, if students lived out of state, they rented rooms in the Bossert Hotel, or St. George Hotel. Certain floors of these hotels were transformed into makeshift dormitories to serve college students attending Polytechnic Institute of New York as well as St. John's University, and Brooklyn Law School.[14]

Tuition remained the same, approximately $2,700 per year for the first two years, and students were given the option to receive their diploma from New York University, Polytechnic Institute of Brooklyn, or Polytechnic Institute of New York.[15]

As the two schools prepared for their first shared academic year in September 1973, Polytechnic Institute of New York continued to search for a new president.

POLY WRITES NEW YORK CITY FIRE CODE

THANKS TO THE INSTITUTE'S GROUND-breaking work rewriting the city's building code, New York City again sought the guidance of Polytechnic's faculty in the summer of 1973 to revamp its fire safety code.[1]

The Institute's Center for Urban Environmental Studies (CUES), directed by Professor Paul DeCicco, studied the pressure in high-rise building staircases in New York when a fire breaks out. To do this, his research team deliberately set fires in buildings that were going to be demolished, the first time this type of planned test had ever been conducted in the United States.

One fire resulted in a roaring blaze that was started in the 22-story Hudson Terminal Building, which was the predecessor of the World Trade Center station on the Port Authority Trans-Hudson (PATH) system. The fire was permitted to burn for half an hour while research was conducted. DeCicco discovered that altering the air pressure slightly in stairwells could keep smoke from getting behind closed doors.[2]

The following summer, the New York Fire Department and CUES ran a unique two-week series of full-scale fire tests in the Bushwick section of Brooklyn. Set in a row of four abandoned tenements on Furman Avenue between Broadway and Bushwick Avenue, these blazes were among the most comprehensive fire tests ever conducted. In addition to elevators, cockloft fire barriers, detection and alarm systems, and sprinkler systems were evaluated. DeCicco explained the rationale for the groundbreaking tests.

Bushwick and communities like it all over this country are not going to be bulldozed tomorrow. They're going to house our people for many years to come. Fire protection is therefore a crucial need. What this is all about is to take a look at current codes, standards, and laws—

As a result of three years of research conducted by the Institute's Center for Urban Environmental Studies (CUES), directed by Professor Paul DeCicco, the New York City Fire Safety bill was passed in 1976. In this picture, DeCicco (kneeling) studies the air flow of smoke produced by a fire in a simulated high-rise building.

and then come up with not dozens of ideas but two or three good, solid, workable solutions.[3]

DeCicco and his team from Polytechnic Institute of New York, which included Professor Robert Cresci of the Aerospace Engineering and Applied Mechanics Department, concluded that a blanket of inexpensive, thick, felt-like material called Thermafiber, a mineral wool insulating material, could prevent fires from spreading. This was demonstrated when one row-house was set ablaze, but did not ignite neighboring houses.[4] Thanks to this research, a fire safety bill was enacted in 1976, which included countless recommendations from CUES, and ultimately saved thousands of lives.

HERE COMES GEORGE

On October 10, 1973, George Bugliarello was chosen as the first president of Polytechnic Institute of New York. He had a sterling academic reputation nationally, and had carved out a niche as a specialist in bioengineering concerned with the social implications and uses of technology, particularly in urban areas. He was former dean of engineering of the University of Illinois at Chicago Circle, and held doctorates from the University of Padua in Italy and from MIT. He served as chairman of the National Academy of Sciences Advisory Committee on Technical Innovation and Monitoring.[16]

Assuming the presidency of Polytechnic Institute of New York represented an enormous undertaking for Bugliarello. He recalled his first meeting with members of The Corporation, and his apprehension about accepting the position.

At the time, this [Brooklyn environs near Poly] was a terribly distressed area. I couldn't believe this was the famous Brooklyn Poly. So I turned it down. Three months later, however, they prevailed on me to assume the presidency. Here was the most important city in the United States, the most technological city, with all the infrastructure, and so on—but it didn't have [an institution like] MIT. I felt that was a very important challenge for Polytechnic. So I took the risk.[17]

Along with heady financial challenges, Polytechnic Institute of New York was facing another major problem: too many professors and not enough space as a result of the merger. President Bugliarello and The Corporation therefore began to look into establishing other campuses. Further illustrating the financial stress was the fact that Polytechnic's expenses exceeded income by 30 percent.[18]

However, Polytechnic Institute of New York enjoyed not only the highest engineering enrollment in New York City and in the state of New York, but also the highest engineering enrollment of any private, independent college in the nation, and the highest engineering graduate enrollment of any American university.[19]

Shown far right is George Bugliarello, accompanied by Joe Brown, a Polytechnic trustee, on the far left, and State Senator Jeremiah Bloom in the center.

Easing its financial burden, Polytechnic Institute of New York was awarded two generous grants after the first year of the merger. The Carnegie Corporation provided $360,000 for planning, while the A. W. Mellon Foundation gave $475,000 to assist in developing interfaces for engineering with the natural and physical sciences, and with the humanities and social sciences.

NEW PROGRAMS AND NEW PROFESSORS

Polytechnic Institute of New York used monies from the Carnegie Corporation grant to develop something called the "Program for Change," a major effort designed to fulfill the expectations of those who framed the merger—to build the foremost center for technological education and research in the metropolitan region, while reshaping the engineering and science curriculum to achieve greater social responsibility.[20] The Program for Change also doubled as a fundraising campaign for capital improvement projects.

Professor Rene Dubos was selected to participate in the new program. He also provided intellectual

BARCODE TECHNOLOGY

IN 1975, JEROME SWARTZ, CLASS OF 1963 and 1968 (doctorate), and Shelley A. Harrison, class of 1966 and 1971 (doctorate), founded Symbol Technologies Inc., the company responsible for creating barcode technology. These Poly graduates took consumerism to an exciting new level with their invention of the handheld barcode laser scanner. This innovation cut the waiting time in store lines globally, created more accurate and punctual package delivery and tracking, and met the efficiency needs of modern workers.

Swartz served as chairman of the board and chief scientist until July 2003, and held the title of chief executive officer through most of his 28 years with the company.

In the early 1960s, he served as a program manager on the NASA *Apollo* project. His independent consulting firm handled projects ranging from space shuttle experiments to specialty lens design, aircraft collision avoidance systems, electronic monitoring systems for medical patients, and the design of a computer-automated camera for manufacturing Universal Product Code (UPC) barcode film masters.[1]

He has taught electrical engineering at both Polytechnic and City University of New York. He is a member of the Foundation Board at Stony Brook University and a trustee at Polytechnic. In 1990, he was the recipient of Polytechnic's Distinguished Alumnus Award.[2]

In 1996, Swartz was named an Institute of Electrical and Electronic Engineers (IEEE) Fellow, that organization's highest technical honor. Two years later, he received the IEEE's prestigious Ernst Weber Leadership Award for career achievement, and in 2000 Swartz was honored with the IEEE's Third Millennium Medal for outstanding technical achievement. Also in 2000, Swartz was elected a member of the National Academy of Engineering for distinguished contributions to engineering.[3]

Harrison left Symbol Technologies in 1982. Since April 1996, he has served as the chief executive officer of Spacehab, Inc., the world's leading provider of commercial payload processing services for both astronaut-tended and unmanned payloads. Spacehab is the first company to commercially develop, own, and operate habitable modules that provide space-based laboratory facilities and logistics re-supply aboard the U.S. space shuttles to support people living and working in space.[4]

Harrison is a founder and managing general partner of PolyVentures I and II, organized in 1987 and 1991 respectively. These high-tech venture capital funds have financed and developed over 24 companies. He has also been a member of the technical staff at Bell Telephone Laboratories (now defunct), and a professor of electrical sciences at the State University of New York at Stony Brook.[5]

Today, Symbol Technologies provides the wireless network for Polytechnic University.

Polytechnic's Jerome Swartz revolutionized merchandising worldwide with his firm's development of barcode technology.

leadership for Polytechnic Institute of New York's Humanities and Science Interface Program. Dubos was a highly accomplished academic and author. His book, *So Human an Animal*, won the 1969 Pulitzer prize.[21]

Another result of the merger was the creation of new departments. The Nuclear Engineering (N.E.) Program, which was inherited from NYU, was established during the first year of Polytechnic Institute of New York. It was headed by Professor John R. Lamarsh.[22]

Later that year, Polytechnic Institute of New York served as one of the founders of the Independent Athletic Conference (IAC), which existed from 1973 to 1996. Of course, sporting events of all types had long helped develop well-rounded students at the Institute. Aside from the normal intercollegiate events, Poly alumni were also very active in sports, which served as a bridge between the various classes and generations. Indeed, each year, on the Saturday after Thanksgiving,

Among professors who came to the Institute from the NYU merger was John R. Lamarsh. He was named head of the nuclear engineering program in 1973, a position he held until his death in 1981. While at Polytechnic Institute of New York, he published *Introduction to Nuclear Engineering* (1975).

the alumni association would compete against the varsity fencing, cross country, swimming, and wrestling teams. Regardless of who won or lost, events like these helped foster a stronger sense of community at the commuter school. Perhaps the best example of Poly school spirit occurred a year after the merger when the alumni basketball team beat their longtime rival Pratt Institute by two points.[23]

EDUCATION OUTSHINES INFRASTRUCTURE

President Bugliarello was determined to improve and expand Polytechnic Institute of New York's academic offerings so they would match the exemplary faculty. University Archivist Heather Walters came to the Institute in 1964 and recently recalled her first impressions of the school.

It was shabby. I don't think anybody cared about the infrastructure. But we had an incredibly brilliant collection of faculty here at that time, mostly refugees from Europe, many Jewish or part-Jewish, and many from Vienna, who came to America to get away from the Nazis. They found a place for themselves at Poly and stayed for a very long time. As a result, the students got a very good education here.[24]

Indeed they did. In 1974, Polytechnic Institute of New York was ranked eighth in the nation by the Carter Report for the quality of its graduate programs in electrical engineering. Its Aerospace Engineering Department was ranked in the top 10 nationally by the Academy for Educational Development. The chemical engineering faculty placed among the top 16 by the American Council on Higher Education, which also rated Polytechnic Institute of New York's graduate program in mechanical engineering among the country's top 20.[25]

Individual professors and alumni also continued to distinguish themselves. Donald Othmer, professor of chemical engineering, designed a new system for heating Arctic oil pipelines by an electric "skin effect" that removed the need for insulation. In 1974, the *New York Times* featured Othmer in its regular section entitled "Patent of the Week." The following year, Othmer discussed his patent with Canadian authorities regarding Arctic installations, and also with authorities from Egypt and other Arab countries as a means of moving high-viscosity African oils.[26]

That same year, alumnus Bern Dibner, class of 1921, H'59, donated an extraordinary collection of 10,000 books and manuscripts to the Smithsonian Institution, establishing the Dibner Library of the History of Science and Technology. Two years later, he was awarded the Sarton Medal, given by the History of Science Society, and also the Smithson Gold Medal, awarded by the Smithsonian Institution.[27]

POLYTECHNIC INSTITUTE OF NEW YORK ESTABLISHES UNDERGRADUATE PROGRAMS AT FARMINGDALE

In September 1973, the New York State Board of Regents authorized Polytechnic Institute of New York and Long Island's Hofstra University to coordinate their undergraduate engineering programs. It was New York State's opinion that this innovative partnership would enable more undergraduate students in the tri-state area to pursue a technical education.[28] Under the agreement, both the Hofstra campus, located in Hempstead, and the Long Island

Center campus, located in Farmingdale, would be used jointly, which was a considerable change for Polytechnic students and professors who had to rearrange their respective schedules. Each institution, however, retained its own separate identity, and each exercised academic and administrative control over its own respective programs.[29]

At the time, Long Island was a booming technology center. One condition required by the State of New York for the Poly/NYU merger was that Polytechnic Institute of New York should coordinate its educational programs with other engineering schools located nearby. Bugliarello discussed this requirement during a recent interview.

When I first came here, it was clear that we had to build up our Long Island activities. New York State required that we first had to work more closely with all the Long Island universities that offered engineering. So, we came to terms with Hofstra University. The students there were given the opportunity to get a Poly degree or a Hofstra degree. Most of them wanted a Poly degree in engineering because we were better known.[30]

WOMEN AT POLYTECHNIC INSTITUTE OF NEW YORK

Helen Warren, along with a handful of other women, started an organization which has since become the Long Island Center for Business and Professional Women. In 2004, it celebrated its 26th anniversary.[31]

During Polytechnic Institute of New York's 1974 commencement ceremony, two distinguished women made history. The first woman ever to receive an honorary degree from the Institute, Marian S. Heiskell, was presented her Doctor of Laws degree. Heiskell eventually became the first woman to be appointed a member of the board at Polytechnic.

Heiskell was a noted civic leader and environmental conservationist. At this time, she was an advisor to the United States Department of the

Helen Warren, retired director of academic operations, was instrumental in furthering the women's movement at Poly in the early 1970s.

like Professors Mark and Morawetz by visiting the People's Republic of China to study different engineering practices. While visiting one of the nation's leading research institutes, he was shown a complete set of Donald Othmer and Raymond Kirk's notable *Kirk-Othmer Encyclopedia of Chemical Technology.*

Unlike his predecessors, Bugliarello understood the importance of reaching out to alumni to increase the endowment. During this trip he did just that. He began a new international university relations initiative, an effort that commenced with simple handshakes. Before visiting alumni in China, he met with alumni in Bombay (now Mumbai), India. He said of the experience, "There are Polytechnic people in virtually every part of the world. We're trying to weld this family into a network of people informed about and committed to Polytechnic."[35]

Interior, and a trustee of both Consolidated Edison and Rockefeller University. She had numerous ties to the New York Times Company as the daughter of the second publisher, Arthur Hays Sulzberger, the widow of the third publisher, Orvil E. Dryfoos, and the sister of the then current publisher, Arthur Ochs Sulzberger.[32]

Heiskell received her Doctor of Laws degree from Professor Dorothy Prohaska, who was head of the Humanities Department. Prohaska was the first woman appointed to head an academic department at Polytechnic.[33]

Polytechnic Institute of New York's women students also were making headlines. Since 1959, the selection of the Polytechnic Queen was an annual event. In 1974, Patrice Henderson, a 22-year-old Exxon chemical engineer completing her master's degree, was crowned Miss Jamaica. Fellow classmate, sophomore Irene Wajs, an electrical engineering student, was crowned Miss Polonia, which included being featured in the Pulaski Day Parade on Manhattan's Fifth Avenue.[34]

ACCOMPLISHMENTS AND ACCOLADES

During the summer of 1974, Bugliarello followed in the footsteps of other Poly academics

Left: In 1974, Professor Dorothy Prohaska was appointed to direct the Humanities Department. No woman ever headed up an academic department at Poly prior to her appointment.

Below left: Miss Jamaica, Patrice Henderson, a Poly graduate student. She was crowned in 1974.

Below right: In 1976, the first woman was elected to be president of the student council. Life Sciences major Anna-Maria Riccio, class of 1977, received the honor.

He continued this work when he returned to the United States by visiting alumni in Los Angeles, San Francisco, Chicago, Indianapolis, Washington, D.C., Boston, and Philadelphia.[36]

Back in Brooklyn, the student council honored French funambulist, Philippe Petit, for his remarkable feat of walking across a tightwire between the summits of the World Trade Center towers in August 1973. (Petit was arrested and sentenced for his death-defying act. His penalty: to perform in a free show in Central Park where he walked on a tightrope across Belvedere Lake.) For his World Trade Center feat, Petit received a Polytechnic Institute of New York tongue-in-cheek prize, the first Sir Isaac Newton Award for Defying Gravity.

The following year he visited Polytechnic Institute of New York to accept his award. While there, he disclosed how he had rigged a cable between the two 1,450-foot World Trade Center towers. This was accomplished with the help of his assistants, who dropped two ropes from the tops of both towers, tied them together at ground level, hauled in the slack, then used them to pull the heavy tightrope wire across the span.[37] He then gave a two-hour lecture on tightrope walking. He remarked:

High-wire walkers like me are engineers, but engineers can never be high-wire walkers. There's a difference between what's on paper and what's on earth.[38]

In 1974, Anthony Ameruso, class of 1969, was appointed New York City transportation commissioner under Mayor Koch, while a fellow alumnus, Herbert J. Simins, class of 1950, was appointed public works commissioner. Before Ameruso's nomination, he worked for Carnegie-Mellon University, researching mass transit systems in Paris, Hamburg, London, and Montreal. Among Simins' accomplishments was his work on the Nassau Coliseum. In 1974, Ameruso and Simins began tackling two

POLY'S BEER MAN

IN STORES ACROSS AMERICA, AND around the world, both men and women reach for light beer because the taste is satisfying, without all the unnecessary calories. The light beer phenomenon was first introduced in 1967 by alumnus Joseph L. Owades, class of 1950, while working at Rheingold Breweries in Brooklyn.

Owades pioneering ale was called Gablinger's Diet Beer, but it was not a hit. Owades went back to the drawing board, and developed a new formula that was sold to Meister Brau which was purchased by the Miller Brewing Company. In 1975, Miller tweaked Owades' formula and produced the first successful light beer to hit the shelves, Miller Lite, which remains a best-seller to this day.[1]

Owades, a biochemist, worked in the past for Carling Brewing Company in Boston, and Anheuser-Busch in St. Louis. For the past 25 years, he has been a much in-demand brewing consultant to breweries large and small, both in the United States and abroad. Among his clients are Samuel Adams and Foggy Bottom. In 1994, he was honored with the Award of Merit of the Master Brewers Association of the Americas. Owades commented on his popular alchemy.

When I got into the beer business, I used to ask people why they did not drink beer. The answer I got was twofold: "One, I don't like the way beer tastes. Two, I'm afraid it will make me fat."

It was a common belief then that drinking beer made you fat. People weren't jogging and everybody believed beer drinkers got big, fat beer bellies. I couldn't do anything about the taste of beer, but I could do something about the calories.[2]

major projects: development of the new Manhattan Civic Center and the renovation of Yankee Stadium.[39]

POLYTECHNIC INSTITUTE OF NEW YORK, AN EARLY SUCCESS

As the 1974 academic year came to a close, a 64 percent increase in freshman enrollment was realized at Polytechnic Institute of New York. This was the largest such enrollment increase in the state, and also one of the largest such increases in the nation.[40]

The fall enrollment was 446, in contrast to 273 in 1973.[41] The increase was due in part to the new undergraduate program at the Long Island campus. That same year, Richard Thorsen was named head of the M.E. Department.

In 1975, to answer the energy crisis plaguing the nation, Polytechnic Institute of New York announced the Energy Engineering & Policy Program. Eighty graduate students enrolled in this program in the first year. Thorsen was named director of the program.[42]

BUGLIARELLO INAUGURATED

While he had assumed the presidency in 1973, Bugliarello was officially inaugurated as Polytechnic Institute of New York's first president on March, 13, 1975, at Carnegie Hall in Manhattan. Among those in attendance were New York Governor Hugh L. Carey, President Ephraim Katzir of Israel, Dr. Fazollah Reza, class of 1950, the Iranian Ambassador to Canada, and Professor Arnaldo M. Angelini, president of the Italian National Board of Electric Power (Ente Nazionale Energia Elettrica). Carey and Katzir received honorary degrees.[43]

This event marked President Katzir's first visit to the United States as Israel's chief of state. He had been a post-doctoral fellow in Polytechnic's Polymer Research Institute from 1948 to 1949, working on synthetic polypeptides, a field in which he later became famous. His old friend, Herman Mark, presented him with his honorary degree. The following morning, Katzir gave his first lecture as honorary professor at Polytechnic Institute of New York, which was his first professional appearance as a scientist since assuming the Israeli presidency.[44]

The event also featured a symposium entitled, "Assessing Social Implications of Technology—What Lessons for the Future?" Dr. Gerard Piel, the publisher of *Scientific American*, chaired the symposium. Among those who addressed the crowd were H. Guyford Stever, director of the National Science Foundation, and Dr. Eugene P. Wigner of Princeton University, 1963 winner of the Nobel Prize for Physics.[45]

As Bugliarello stayed busy improving alumni relations, expanding academic offerings, and preparing for new city-based initiatives at the Brooklyn campus, Poly alumni continued to distinguish themselves.

Harold L. Brownman, class of 1944, was appointed Assistant Secretary of the Army in 1975. Brownman served with the Central Intelligence Agency (CIA) from 1970 to 1974 and was the head of its Office of Special Projects.[46]

MILLION-DOLLAR GIFT

In its first two years, Polytechnic Institute of New York was able to meet successfully the challenges that arose as a result of the merger. However, for Bugliarello's designs to further expand Polytechnic Institute of New York, substantial funds would be required. Historically, donations from alumni represented the core of Polytechnic's endowment. In 1975, alumnus Joseph J. Jacobs offered a challenge gift of $1,000,000 to Polytechnic Institute of New York. A stipulation of his gift was that it needed to be matched on a dollar-for-dollar basis. Due to the efforts of Bugliarello and the alumni association, $700,000 was raised in matching funds.[47] By the end of the year, over $2.2 million had been secured. In making the gift to Polytechnic, Jacobs said:

I am obviously proud of the formal training I received at Polytechnic. Its ideals have also been an inspiration. Poly was very important to me as a student. It was relatively small in those years, with an unusually close student-faculty identification. My professors contributed much more than knowledge to our development. Poly produced humanist-engineers and it still does, rather than cold, scientific professionals. I have always deeply valued the Poly experience.[48]

In March of 1975, President Ephraim Katzir of Israel received an honorary degree from the Institute. He was a post-doctoral fellow at Polytechnic's Polymer Research Institute from 1948 to 1949. President Katzir (left) is pictured above with Professor Harold G. Kaufman of the Management Department.

Following Jacobs' speech, Bugliarello announced that a $25 million fund-raising campaign for Polytechnic Institute of New York would be launched. This was an extension of the Program for Change. The goal of the first phase of the program was to secure $6 million by December 1976. The second phase was aimed at an additional $19 million by 1979, which would mark the 125th anniversary of both the Polytechnic Institute of Brooklyn and the New York University School of Engineering and Science.

Bugliarello expressed sincere appreciation on behalf of the students, faculty, and alumni for the gift from Jacobs. He also outlined his vision for Polytechnic Institute of New York's future:

This is no bricks-and-mortar effort. The emphasis will be on increasing our strength in instruction

and research. The Institute's leadership in aerospace engineering and electrophysics, microwave research, transportation planning and engineering, and polymer chemistry is widely recognized. Our main goal is to strengthen our curriculum and teaching staff, and to develop new programs.[49]

It was during this year that Bugliarello and members of The Corporation began discussing the idea of establishing an industrial research park in downtown Brooklyn. While Brooklyn city officials were intrigued by the idea, it would take a few years to get New York City to provide the needed funds for this, approximately $400 million.

RESEARCH GRANTS

An industrial research park made eminent good sense: after all, government and private industry continually engaged in important research contracts with Polytechnic Institute of New York, which in 1974-75 totaled $3.5 million. In addition, the Institute received a $350,000 grant from the Alfred P. Sloan Foundation to develop a School of Technology Management and Policy Studies.

Additionally, the following May, Poly received a $390,000 grant from the Urban Mass Transit Administration of the United States Department of Transportation for a three-year study of public transportation issues and problems in the metropolitan New York region.[50]

Polytechnic Institute of New York's Division of Transportation Planning and Engineering, led by Professor Louis Pignataro, used this grant to conduct interviews and to analyze the traveling behavior of people using mass transit.[51] Pignataro's efforts eventually led to the formation of the Transportation Training and Research Center. This entity was hired that year by the city of Rochester, New York, to perform an environmental impact study for a proposed highway.[52]

In 1975, the United States Golf Association (USGA) awarded Polytechnic Institute of New York a $90,000 grant to develop more accurate ways of testing the performance of golf balls and golf clubs as well as to monitor existing standards and research new standards concerning golf rules. This grant allowed Professor Phillip A. Abrami and his associates to continue working with USGA's

Mechanical Golfer, also known as the "Monster," which was a one-armed robot able to hold a golf club and simulate the swing of a human golfer. (It was modeled after Byron Nelson's swing.) Impressively, the Monster could drive a ball through 330 pages of a Manhattan telephone directory from a distance of 10 feet.[53]

WESTCHESTER CAMPUS OPENS

In the fall of 1975, Polytechnic Institute of New York, in conjunction with Pace University, began to offer classes in New York's Westchester County. As a joint effort, the two institutions began to offer Master of Science degrees in Management

Science at Pace's White Plains campus. In addition, Polytechnic Institute of New York began graduate programs with offerings in computer science, electrical engineering, industrial engineering, and operations research. The courses paralleled those

Edith Pignataro (right), class of 1954, shows her daughter Thea, class of 1978, X-ray crystallography equipment similar to the type she used while she was a graduate student at Polytechnic. When Edith Pignataro (wife of Professor Pignataro of the Transportation Department) attended the Institute there were only three other women in her program. In 1977, Thea was among 25 women in her graduating class.

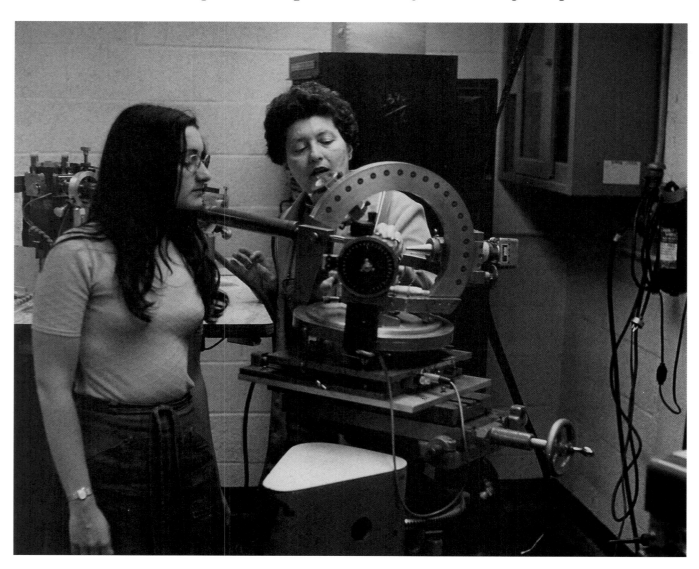

that Polytechnic Institute of New York was offering at its Brooklyn and Farmingdale campuses.[54]

The expansion into Westchester was also mandated by the 1973 merger agreement. This was to fulfill the function that had been provided earlier by the Bronx presence of the New York University School of Engineering and Science. The enrollment for the first year totaled only 65 men and women. But word quickly spread regarding the new academic offerings, and by the second year, 260 students were enrolled.

In 1975, Professor Irving Cadoff, coordinator of the program, discussed the Westchester program in the *Patent Trader* newspaper.

In a sense, the Polytechnic program in Westchester represents the reestablishment of engineering education service to the northern suburbs of New York City, which was previously provided by the New York University School of Engineering and Science. Commerce and industry are increasingly moving to Westchester, and our program should help them immeasurably.[55]

CHINA DELEGATION VISITS FARMINGDALE

Thanks to the brilliant diplomatic maneuvering by President Richard Nixon with the People's Republic of China (PRC) in 1972, and as a result of Mark and Bugliarello's visits to China, an historic moment occurred on October 1, 1975. A seven-member delegation from the PRC visited Polytechnic's Farmingdale campus and toured the aerospace, electrical engineering, and electrophysics research facilities. Dr. Chou Pei-Yuan, vice chairman of the Scientific and Technical Association of the PRC and vice chairman of the Revolutionary Committee of Peking University, delivered a special lecture at Polytechnic on the theory of homogeneous, isotropic turbulence for Polytechnic's faculty during the day-long visit.[56] Dr. Chou Pei-Yuan reflected: "We are especially honored to be here, and we are particularly impressed that there are so many distinguished professors here to meet us."[57] Professor Martin Bloom, Professor Samuel Lederman, Dean of Engineering Leopold Felsen, and Provost James Conti welcomed the delegation.

In a recent interview, Bloom recalled the groundbreaking research conducted at the center,

which resulted in numerous visits there by various delegations:

Since we had a fairly large amount of funding, I was able to offer funds for Sam Lederman to do some of his exploratory work in a corner of the laboratory. I knew what he was doing, but we didn't advertise it around until he really started doing work that was useful.

A colonel from the Air Force came through who worked at what's called the Defense Advanced Research Projects Agency in Washington. They're the ones who started the Internet. They were heavily involved in missile technology and so forth.

So we explained to him what was going on here and there in the lab, but when he came to this setup that Sam Lederman had, he said, "What's this?" Sam explained to him that we were trying to diagnose high temperature flows. He said, "Wow, you know the people at Livermore Lab have been trying to do this for a couple of years now, and they haven't been getting very far. Can I have a group of them come so you can show them what you're doing?"[58]

POLYTECHNIC INSTITUTE OF NEW YORK EXPANDS COURSE OFFERINGS

With its large number of distinguished professors, new departments were continually being created at Polytechnic Institute of New York. One example was the Division of Management, established by Professor Schillinger, who became its first dean.

Another new venture was a graduate program in ocean engineering, part of the C.E. Department. Program emphasis was on coastal offshore structures, coastal engineering, applied coastal oceanography, marine pollution, underwater acoustics, and instrumentation. Professor Henry R. Frey was named director. Frey was widely known for his work in underwater photographic and diving technology.[59] In 1996, he was named director of the National Oceanographic Data Center.

POLYTECHNIC INSTITUTE OF NEW YORK WINS NATIONAL CHAMPIONSHIP

On April 23, 1977, Polytechnic's Company H of the Eighth ROTC Regiment took first place in the John J. Pershing Memorial Drill Meet at Ohio

State, becoming national champions. The university team, comprised of 16 undergraduates, triumphed over two dozen schools from across the country. It practiced eight months out of the year at the Fort Hamilton military base, located a few miles from the Brooklyn campus.[60]

LONG ISLAND PROGRAM GROWS

With the addition of undergraduate classes, it became necessary to physically expand the Long Island Graduate Center in Farmingdale. On December 23, 1976, Grumman Hall, the first major structure to be added to the Long Island Graduate Center, was dedicated. Participating in the ceremonies were President Bugliarello, and Grumman Corporation President Joseph G. Gavin Jr., who at that time was a member of The Corporation.[61] The new addition to the campus provided 6,000 square feet of space to meet the needs of the rapidly growing full-time population of undergraduates participating in the engineering program.

Professor Benjamin Senitsky, now retired, began teaching at the Brooklyn campus in 1966 and

In October 1975, a seven-member delegation from the People's Republic of China visited the Institute's Farmingdale campus and toured the aerospace, electrical engineering, and electrophysics laboratory. Pictured here, Professors Martin Bloom, right, and Samuel Lederman, second from right, point out laboratory features during the historic visit.

became director of the Long Island Graduate Center undergraduate program in 1976. Senitsky recalled initiatives that were employed to increase the student population:

My main goal at that time was to develop a four-year undergraduate engineering program. That was a pretty interesting endeavor. We didn't have undergraduate students there before, but the faculty enthusiastically pitched in and we developed a nice program.

We started the program entirely from scratch by going around to all the high schools within a fifty-mile radius of our Long Island campus. We gave talks. As a matter of fact, we even went as

WHAT, ME WORRY?

NOT EVERY STUDENT WHO ATTENDED Poly graduated. Some even flunked out. In one case, a student flunked out, came back later, tried hard … and flunked out again. This would normally shake anyone's confidence, but it didn't for the student, William Gaines, who went on to create *Mad* Magazine.[1]

In April of 1977, Gaines once again returned to Poly to accept an honorary membership in the Student Council. The council praised him for "the perverse pleasure he has given thousands of his fellow Polytechnic students, past and present."[2]

That spring day, Gaines spoke to nearly 200 students and faculty, recalling the Poly of his era— the 1930s and 1940s—and the reasons for his poor academic performance.

The worst thing that ever happened to me was getting a 100 percent on the chemistry regents exam. That convinced me that I should be a chemist. But I didn't have the brains. In addition, I remember that Professor Kirk said at orientation, "Behind the nylon stocking, look for a chemist." I never forgot that.[3]

During his speech, Gaines told anecdotes about Polytechnic, which kept those in attendance roaring with laughter. During a question-and-answer segment, a student asked the *MAD* genius what he considered to be the most important lesson learned while at Poly. Gaines responded:

Physical chemistry lab was very tough in those days. They'd give you the beginning of the problem and the answer, and we'd have to work out everything in between. One person would work the problem halfway through from the end, and someone else would work it halfway through from the beginning. What you had left were two numbers which were never the same.

In April of 1977, *MAD* magazine publisher William Gaines, who held the rare distinction of flunking out of Polytechnic twice, entertained Polytechnic students and staff. Gaines returned to the Institute for the third time to accept an honorary Student Council membership.

So we introduced the Boogerean constant— the number by which we multiplied this to get that. And the lab report then became a test for the instructor—if he couldn't find the Boogerean constant, you passed. This method was so successful that to this day I use the same system in business. I sold MAD 17 years ago, although I still run it, and it's now owned by Warner Communications. They want all kinds of financial information, which I'm too lazy to provide. To this day I fudge all reports, using the Boogerean constant I learned at Poly.[4]

far out as Shelter Island, and we got some interest. The program really took off.[62]

POLYTECHNIC INSTITUTE OF NEW YORK CELEBRATES AMERICA'S BICENTENNIAL

Polytechnic made its own academic contribution to America's bicentennial in 1976 in the form of specialized courses that focused on the American Revolution.[63] Students launched their own program of bicentennial activities as well by hosting an arts and craft fair, held in the auditorium of Rogers Hall. The fair was officially opened with a talk by Dr. Joseph Palisi, Brooklyn's official historian, on the role Brooklyn played during the American Revolution. Among the facts he reported was that the Battle of Long Island, the largest battle in New York State, was fought on Brooklyn soil. "Had the British been able to claim victory," said Palisi, "the American Revolution could have dragged on an extra two years."[64]

The bicentennial year also marked the first time a woman was elected president of the student council. Life Sciences major Anna-Maria Riccio received this honor. Another first took place when the Institute welcomed a bona fide sheik, chemical engineering student, Khalifa Sagr, whose uncle was the ruler of Abu Dhabi. His interest in chemical engineering naturally followed from his country's main industry: a 15,000 barrel-a-day oil refinery. Sagr was originally enrolled at NYU, but as a result of the merger completed his studies at Polytechnic.

During the bicentennial year, the Institute hosted numerous events. In this picture, Allan Kwartler, the Poly fencing coach (left), crosses swords with a continental army soldier at the student Bicentennial Arts and Crafts Fair, December 1976.

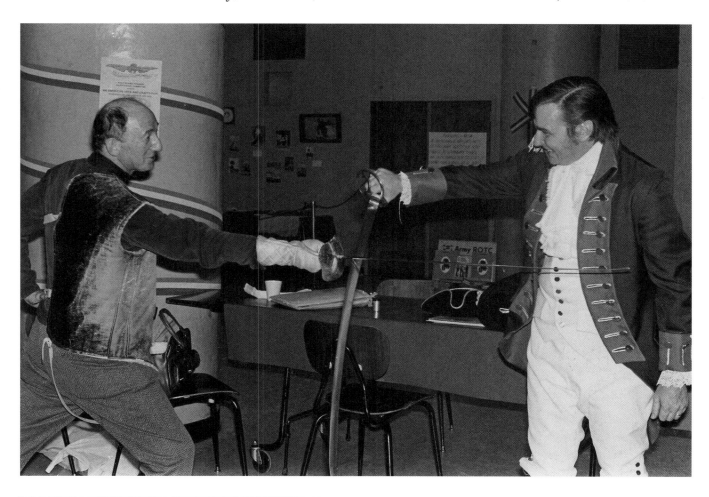

THE PASSAGE OF TIME

While the Institute joyfully celebrated the bicentennial, it would also lose two distinguished men. William Bennett Kouwehoven died that year at the age of 89. While at Polytechnic as a student, he majored in mechanical engineering in 1906 and electrical engineering in 1907. He was dean of Johns Hopkins School of Engineering from 1938 to 1954 and then became professor emeritus.

Kouwehoven is best known for creating the cardiac defibrillator and cardiopulmonary resuscitation (CPR), developments that have saved countless lives of patients suffering from heart disease. Kouwehoven did his first experiments concerning the defibrillator and CPR on dogs while at Johns Hopkins. That prestigious university awarded him an honorary Doctorate of Medicine degree, the first it ever awarded.

The same year, Professor Antonio Ferri, former head of the Aerospace Engineering, Department died at the age of 63.[65]

When Professor Bloom received news of Ferri's death, he responded with the following thoughts.

Professor Ferri stimulated the development of modern aerodynamics education and pioneered research. A warm human being, he has continued to be an inspiring engineer whose significant contributions are much valued.[66]

LARGEST NUMBER OF DEGREES CONFERRED

In recognition of its importance to the entire city of New York, the 121st commencement ceremony was held at Carnegie Hall in Manhattan in 1976. During this ceremony, a record 999 degrees were awarded by Polytechnic Institute of New York. This exceeded the previous year by 100.[67] President Bugliarello made the following comments at the ceremony:

Our freshman enrollment has more than doubled since the fall of 1972. Our graduate enrollment in engineering has become the largest in the United States. We have in these three years established actively growing programs at our Long Island campus and in Westchester. We have indeed become

the center of technological education in the metropolitan area.[68]

Following the commencement ceremony, Joseph Jacobs succeeded Lou Rowley as chairman of The Corporation. At the time, he was chief executive officer of Jacobs Engineering Group Inc., of Pasadena, California, which he founded. President Bugliarello said of the appointment:

We were extremely fortunate to have had Lou Rowley as chairman for nearly a decade. We are equally fortunate now to have Joe Jacobs take over the helm. Dr. Jacobs has shown immense dedication to his alma mater, Polytechnic, and to engineering education. His talents and energies, and his broad knowledge of the engineering field, will be a determining force in the future of the Institute.[69]

As Jacobs accepted the nomination, he outlined his philosophy by saying: "We should challenge industry and Polytechnic alumni to support ideas that free men in a capitalistic society can recognize in their own self-interest."[70]

FINANCIAL SOUND PRACTICES

During the mid 1970s, Polytechnic Institute of New York required at least $2,000,000 annually in private funding to be able to operate without state aid. Thanks to the Program for Change, $6 million was raised in three years.[71] The Corporation also launched a new campaign, Polytechnic Now! The exclamation point at the end of the slogan underscored the importance of raising adequate funds to not only maintain current operations but allow for the opportunity to expand in future years.

To help raise and manage these funds, the Institute hired Daniel Ross, former director of development at Boston University Medical Center, as vice president for development and public affairs, and Dr. Seymour Scher, former first deputy comptroller of New York City, as vice president for finance and administration.

As 1977 commenced, the Institute was providing over $600,000 annually in financial aid, which, coupled with the long-standing deficit woes, required significant alumni support. The alumni class that contributed the most money each year received the

Rowley Award at the annual alumni association's dinner dance. The award was named in honor of Louis Rowley Jr. The first award went to the class of 1922. By February of that year, roughly 60 percent of that sum was pledged by alumni. The Corporations and Foundations Program, an offshoot of the Polytechnic Now! campaign, helped to recruit bequests, gifts, and grants from city business leaders.

In four years, the Institute had completed a successful merger and expanded the academic offerings at its main campus, as well as at its satellite campuses. Also, Polytechnic was finally approaching financial stability, which would be realized before the end of the decade.

These achievements resulted from President Bugliarello's vision, along with the diligent guidance of The Corporation, the alumni association, and the faculty.

Indeed, whether it was referred to as Polytechnic Institute of New York, Brooklyn Poly, or the Polytechnic Institute of Brooklyn, two aspects of the Institute's reputation remained constant as the seventies drew to a close: perseverance matched by brilliance.

The development of MetroTech represents the vision, brought to life in concrete, steel, and stone, of George Bugliarello for a better Polytechnic University and a renewed downtown Brooklyn. This picture shows early work on the MetroTech construction site.

CHAPTER NINE

POLYTECHNIC: THE ENGINE FOR THE REBIRTH OF BROOKLYN
1977–1993

I think we have shown what a private university can do if it perseveres in its dream.

—President George Bugliarello, Dedication Day, Opening of
Bern Dibner Library of Science and Technology and the New York
State Center for Advanced Technology in Telecommunications
(CATT), 1992

BY THE END OF FISCAL YEAR 1976, Polytechnic had accumulated an operating deficit of $3.4 million, despite receipt of some $18 million in extraordinary state appropriations during the period 1968-1976. Actually, the financial picture at Polytechnic had been bleak for some time. The operating budget had not been balanced in 14 years, leaving the long-term financial viability of the Institute in serious question. Additionally, the merger created a number of other financial challenges.[1]

Facing these difficulties, President George Bugliarello, the Alumni Association, The Corporation, and Seymour Scher, vice president for finance, worked long and hard to help Polytechnic achieve financial stability. To this end, the Institute began to call on successful alumni to lend their talent and expertise to help rebuild Polytechnic. This was a key reason Paul Soros, class of 1950, was elected as a trustee to The Corporation in 1977.

Soros was a quintessential example of a successful alumnus. A native of Hungary, he escaped from the Nazis in World War II, and the Russians after they occupied his country at the end of the war. In 1948, Soros came to the United States alone and earned a master's degree in mechanical engineering from Polytechnic. He is the founder and former president of Soros Associates, an international engineering firm, which he sold in 1990.

Holding numerous engineering patents, Soros is renowned for his pioneering work conceiving and designing major improvements in offshore terminals around the world, and in improving materials handling procedures at bulk ports.[2]

As a way of giving back to a country that afforded him so much opportunity, in 1997 Soros along with his wife, Daisy, co-founded the Paul and Daisy Soros Fellowships for New Americans. To date, there are 62 fellows at 23 universities undertaking graduate study in 17 different fields. In 2002, Polytechnic President David Chang spoke of Soros' accomplishments and generosity.

Paul Soros' career is an inspiration to our students and a source of pride for the University. He is a successful entrepreneur and philanthropist who has never forgotten his roots.[3]

The Institute's efforts to reach out to famous alumni, along with all of the other hard work, paid off in 1978 when President Bugliarello announced

---

In 1978, Poly's Physics Department established the Microparticle Photo Physics Lab under the direction of Professor Stephen Arnold, who is pictured here working in the laboratory with a student.

that the Institute had finally balanced its budget for fiscal year 1977. This marked the first year since 1963 that the Institute reported numbers in the black. While the positive balance was only $625,000, Bugliarello said this event signaled a positive future.

Faced with chronic deficits, the emphasis previously was on sheer survival. In one year we have gained a new stability without cutting back on our faculty or academic staffing. We have introduced a businesslike management, reduced expenses, and increased outside funding. At the same time our tuition levels are below many comparable institutions, most of our students receive financial aid of some type, and over 95 percent of our graduates get jobs. We feel that, despite our small endowment, we have one of the most cost-effective universities in the nation.[4]

With the budget finally in the black, Polytechnic's leaders began discussing plans for the future, which not only included expanding academic offerings, but physical expansion as well. Meanwhile, the Department of Management was granted autonomous divisional status, joining Engineering and Arts and Sciences as the third division at the Institute. Professor George Schillinger was named dean of the new division.

Professor Leopold Felsen, dean of engineering, was appointed Institute Professor, the second such appointment in Polytechnic's history. The first appointee was Institute Professor Martin Bloom, director of the aerodynamics laboratories at the Long Island campus in Farmingdale.[5]

The Institute's satellite campuses were also undergoing change. The Westchester arm of Polytechnic moved into its new facilities at 456 North Street in White Plains during the summer of 1978 under the direction of Irving Cadoff, professor of physical metallurgy. Information Systems was among the new programs offered at that campus. The Westchester campus was also home to the Center for Regional Technology, which worked with Consolidated Edison to execute a three-year, $470,000 solar energy project.

Professor Cadoff, and Richard Thorsen, head of the Department of Mechanical Engineering and Aerospace Engineering, conducted research on solar

In March 1980, Poly, in association with the *New York Times'* Science Times section, produced the TV-series *The Scientific Minute*. The host of the program was Professor Richard Thorsen (pictured here).

energy systems that were installed in 19 residential sites and retirement homes.[6]

PLANNING FOR METROTECH

The idea for creating an industrial research park in conjunction with Polytechnic started to become a reality in the summer of 1979, when a feasibility study for the project was conducted by the Downtown Brooklyn Development Association (DBDA). The study was designed to determine possible uses for sites within the area bounded by Jay, Tillary, and Willoughby Streets, and the Flatbush Avenue Extension. In addition, the study was set up to determine alternative strategies for redevelopment, with special emphasis on attracting new high technology industries that could benefit from a close relationship with Polytechnic Institute of New York.[7]

The idea for revitalizing downtown Brooklyn was first discussed in 1963, when New York City designated the area for urban renewal. It was President Bugliarello's persistence that sparked the urban renewal process. At the time, Polytechnic was the main economic force in the area, with approximately

800 employees and 4,000 students in both day and evening classes.[8]

The development of MetroTech represented a long, complex process, with many twists and turns. The project was complicated by the demands of an environmental impact statement, along with opposition from numerous Brooklyn residents and business owners who would be displaced.

But in April 1982, after receiving the approval of Brooklyn Borough President Howard Golden, who conceded that the plan was far from perfect, the first official step was taken to make MetroTech and Polytechnic the new centerpiece of downtown Brooklyn.

The $770 million high-technology Metropolitan Technology Center, or MetroTech, called for a 16-acre complex of academic and commercial buildings, including a hotel. At the time, Polytechnic occupied roughly only two and a half acres. It was hoped and planned for that the complex would generate over 3,000 new jobs for the borough and thrust New York City into the front ranks of high technology centers, along with places like California's famed Silicon Valley.[9]

Once completed, the 10-year construction project would result in approximately 130,000 square feet of space for Polytechnic, and nearly seven million square feet for all else. Under the agreed-upon letter of intent, Polytechnic would be the exclusive developer of the site for the first four years. Plans were for the Institute to invest $45 million to build a technology library, a telecommunications and technology center, a student faculty residence hall, and to renovate existing buildings.

The agreement, signed at the offices of the New York City Public Development Corporation, obligated the city to provide funds to acquire privately owned land for the project. At the time, the projected investments from the city and Polytechnic were expected to exceed $120 million. The money was earmarked to build four major facilities for firms engaged in research and development, and would also be used to develop a 400-room hotel with banquet and conference facilities for 2,000 people.[10]

As the plans for MetroTech unfolded, Polytechnic experienced tremendous growth. This included development of the Center for Digital Systems, which was established on the Long Island Campus with a grant from the Fairchild Republic Corporation.

HIGHEST ENROLLMENT TO DATE

By the fall of 1982, the Institute's undergraduate enrollment exceeded 5,000, the highest number in its history. That year, 97 percent of Poly graduates received at least one job offer. There was no question that with the 10th anniversary of the merger in its sights, Polytechnic Institute of New York was positioned for continued success.

Although the budget was balanced, Polytechnic continued to need additional outside support to accomplish all of its heady objectives. As 1979 came to a close, therefore, the Institute had kicked off an ambitious fundraising campaign, with a goal of generating $850,000. The funds were earmarked for general operating needs, and to help provide aid for the more than 90 percent of students who required some

Dean Bernard J. Bulkin, Arts and Sciences Department, was awarded the 1978 New York Society for Applied Spectroscopy Medal for Excellence in Research.

form of financial assistance. Historically, the majority of funds came from alumni, corporations, and friends of Polytechnic. Additionally, every fall, a phone fund drive was launched by the alumni association to help meet the financial goals of the Institute.[11]

During this same period, in conjunction with the reconstruction of downtown Brooklyn, Polytechnic dedicated its new student center, located at 311 Bridge Street. The building, constructed in 1846, served as the Bridge Street African Wesleyan Methodist Episcopal Church from 1854 to 1938. The roots of the congregation dated back to 1776, and the church served as a way station for the Underground Railroad that helped slaves from the South escape to the North. The church eventually moved to 277 Stuyvesant Avenue in Brooklyn.

Prior to being acquired by Polytechnic in 1968, the church building was used as a warehouse and factory. After Poly bought it, the building featured classrooms and offices, primarily ROTC, until it was renovated into a student center in 1979.

At the dedication ceremony of the student center, the Bridge Street church's pastor, Reverend William P. Foley, said that the history of the church should not be forgotten, and that its spirit should provide "a sense of togetherness" for the downtown renewal project. President Bugliarello presented a memorial plaque at the ceremony that detailed the history of the building. The church building also had another owner prior to its becoming part of Poly.

Since Polytechnic was a commuter school, a student center was a welcome addition that afforded students the opportunity to relax and to develop relations and interests outside the classroom.[12]

Polytechnic has always been on the cutting edge of technology. In 1951, it offered its first computer course. Over the years, the program grew substantially. In 1979, the first Doctorate in Computer Science was conferred. In this picture, students study various computer applications.

HERMAN MARK REMEMBERS ALBERT EINSTEIN

ON SEPTEMBER 4, 1979, HERMAN Mark, dean emeritus, spoke about his memories and relationship with Albert Einstein for an Einstein Symposium held in Washington, D.C.

While speaking to an inquisitive audience, Mark recalled his first meeting with Einstein in the spring of 1924:

At the time, I was working at the Kaiser Wilhelm Institute— now the Max Planck Institute— in Berlin. He wanted to know everything about what we were doing. Einstein also talked about the permanent doubt that every scientist feels about his work. He once asked me if I knew the difference between a theory and an experiment. A theory,

Einstein said, is something that no one believes except the man who made it, while an experiment is something that everyone believes except the man who made it.

We all called him our "gentle genius." Einstein was a warm and friendly man and a good joke-teller as well. We wrote many letters to each other, and while I had saved most of my correspondence to Einstein, the Gestapo came into my office in 1938, went through all my files, and removed all of Einstein's letters to me.[1]

In 1979, Herman Mark participated in a symposium held in Washington D.C., celebrating the life and scientific accomplishments of Albert Einstein.

HOUSEHOLD NAME

One way in which the Institute furthered its reputation, thus creating more excitement about a possible industrial research complex in downtown Brooklyn, was by attracting illustrious professors, and forging relationships with leaders of business and industry.

Along this line, in 1979, some 350 representatives from major U.S. chemical companies, along with Polytechnic faculty, gathered to pay tribute to Professor Ephraim Katchalski-Katzir, former president of Israel, who was also the first incumbent of the Herman F. Mark Chair in Polymer Science.

Among those in attendance were Dr. Hans M. Mark, son of Herman Mark and Secretary of the United States Air Force; Dr. Joshua Lederberg, a Nobel Prize winner and president of Rockefeller

University; New York State Senator Jeremiah B. Bloom; and many Fortune 500 company executives.[13]

POLY TURNS 125 YEARS OLD

On May 29, 1980, Poly celebrated its 125th year during its annual commencement ceremony at Carnegie Hall. This marked one of the largest graduating classes in the Institute's history. The Institute awarded 435 bachelor's degrees, 526 master of science degrees, and 10 engineer and 39 PhD degrees. Dr. Lewis M. Branscomb, vice president and chief scientist of IBM, delivered the commencement address and also received an honorary degree.

Furthering Polytechnic Institute of New York's connection to business and industry, Barry M. Bloom, president of Pfizer Central Research, and Harold L. Brownman, president of Lockheed

ACCOMPLISHMENTS AND ACHIEVEMENTS

AS PAUL SOROS TOOK HIS SEAT WITH The Corporation, another immigrant and alumnus, Toruum Alteraas, class of 1977, made her mark on science by developing nontoxic processes to create food colorings and to remove caffeine from coffee.

The following year, Dr. Gordon Gould, professor of physics from 1967 to 1974, was named "Inventor of the Year" by the Patent Office Society for his work with laser amplifiers. In 1957, Gould, while researching different applications of forced lights sources, awoke from a dream and wrote down the word LASER (Light Amplification by Stimulated Emission of Radiation), the first time this acronym was used. Unfortunately, poor legal advice prevented Gould from filing a patent for his idea until 1959, at which point other scientists had already submitted their own patents related to his basic research.

It wasn't until 1977 that the first of Gould's basic laser patents was finally issued. Gould and his assignee, Patlex Corporation, now hold the basic patents covering optically-pumped and discharge-excited laser amplifiers. These lasers are used in 80 percent of the industrial, commercial, and medical applications employed today. In 1994, Gould received an honorary degree from Polytechnic.[1]

Each year, important awards are given to Polytechnic alumni and faculty for their accomplishments and achievements in various fields of science and engineering. One that was awarded in 1978 to Professor Othmer by the Society of Chemical Engineers Industry's was their Perkin Medal, regarded as the highest American honor in recognition of outstanding achievements in chemistry. The winner of this award is chosen annually by the American Institute of Chemical Engineers, the Electrochemical Society, the American Institute of Chemists, and the American Chemical Society. Professor Othmer was the 72nd recipient of the medal. He was praised by the committee for his successful work in the genetic engineering of plants for the production of chemical materials which serve fundamental human needs. At that time, Othmer held 125 patents.[2]

Electronics Company Inc. and vice president of Lockheed Corporation, were among thirteen prominent business leaders named fellows of Polytechnic.[14] Perhaps the best example of Polytechnic's strong ties with industry was its longstanding association with the Grumman Corporation. In 1980, 791 alumni were employed at the company.

The year 1980 also marked the best fundraising year in the Institute's history. The gift total reached $2,568,000—an increase of 55 percent from the previous year.[15]

As the year drew to a close, Polytechnic launched one of the most ambitious fundraising campaigns in its history—Program for Change.

When this program was developed, it was estimated that over $40 million would be raised by the year 1989. Under the direction of The Corporation and President Bugliarello, the program was designed to enhance the Institute's leadership role in responding to the emerging technologies of the 1980s and 1990s.[16]

Through the years of red ink and black, of new campuses and major new partnerships with business and local government, one thing remained constant at Polytechnic—its goal of providing a world-class education for all of its students, both day and evening, graduate and undergraduate. Arthur Martinez, class of 1960, current trustee, former chairman of The Corporation, and former head of

Other giants included Nathan Marcuvitz and Leopold Felsen, both of whom were awarded honorary degrees by Poly for their pioneering work in microwaves.

Also in 1978, Dr. Ines Mandl, class of 1947, received the Carl Neuberg Medal. Mandl, a noted authority on protein chemistry, was one of the first women to receive a PhD degree (1949) from Polytechnic. This was not her first honor. In 1972, Mandl received the Polytechnic Distinguished Alumnus award for her contributions to biomedical research, particularly for her pioneering studies regarding collagen and elastin.[3]

Later in the year, Professor Dante C. Youla of the Department of Electrical Engineering was elected to the National Academy of Engineering (NAE). At the time, Youla was a professor of electrical engineering at Polytechnic. (He is now university professor emeritus.) He was cited by the NAE for "contributions to broadband matching in microwave networks and to optimal controllers for multivariable feedback systems."

In addition to his administrative and planning duties, President Bugliarello remained focused on his first passion: science. In 1979, he, and Professor Schillinger became co-editors of *Technology in Society, An International Journal.* The quarterly, which celebrated its 25th anniversary in 2004,

is a pioneer in addressing issues that arise from the impacts of science and technology on society. The same year, Polytechnic, which offered its first computer course in 1951, conferred its first Doctorate in Computer Science.

Aspiring young scientists had good reason to choose Polytechnic because each year alumni and faculty were profusely awarded for their individual accomplishments. In January 1988, *Chemical & Engineering News*, the flagship publication of the American Chemical Society, listed Professor Othmer as one of the 75 greatest chemical scientists ever in its 75th anniversary issue. In the months that followed, Professor Dante C. Youla received the IEEE Control System Field Award.

In 1989, for groundbreaking research in microwaves and electromagnetics, Professor Nathan Marcuvitz was awarded the first Heinrich Hertz Medal of the Institute of Electrical and Electronics Engineers. Two years later, Professor Leopold Felsen received the same honor.[4]

In 1978, Dr. Ines Mandl, class of 1947, received the Carl Neuberg Medal. In 1949, Mandl was one of the first women to receive a PhD degree from Polytechnic.

Sears Roebuck and Company, recently commented on Polytechnic's strengths:

I think the special place that Polytechnic occupies has allowed it to be successful over a long period of time. Its reach has never exceeded its grasp. It's a place that has seen its function as educating people who are first in their family to go to college. There is a strong sense of humility about the University. It's not arrogant in any sense of the word. It's a stepladder for people to move on in their lives as it was for me. I think being faithful to that tradition and that mission is the reason it's still around.[17]

THE FEDERAL CONNECTION

In 1981, former Professor Richard V. Rahn joined the Chamber of Commerce of the United States as its vice president and chief economist, serving as its national spokesman on economic and tax policy issues. Showcase appointments such as Rahn's furthered Polytechnic's relations with important local and national entities, not the least of which was the federal government. During the 1981 commencement ceremony, William J. Casey, then head of the Central Intelligence Agency, delivered the address while more than 1,000 graduates received their degrees.[18]

In February 1984, Professor James Conti, vice president for educational development, unveiled Polytechnic's Farmingdale campus' new gymnasium worth $1 million. This addition greatly aided Poly's sports program.

INSTITUTE OF IMAGING SCIENCES RECEIVES $1 MILLION

Established in 1979, the Institute of Imaging Sciences received over $1 million in 1981. Based on a proposal written by Professor Stephen Arnold, this seed grant was given by Gregory Halpern, a fellow of the Institute, an honorary member of The Corporation, and the founder of the Institute of Imaging Sciences.[19]

The Institute was the only one of its kind in the country devoted to the acquisition, processing, and presentation of image information from electromagnetic, nuclear, and acoustic radiations.

Historically associated with conventional photography, printing, graphic arts, and television, the field was extended to include new technologies in computer science and engineering. Research efforts at the Institute of Imaging Sciences were directed toward developing materials that would simplify and reduce the cost of preparing images from satellite transmission, for conducting images in the military realm, and toward improvements in medical technology.[20]

GOVERNOR CUOMO DESIGNATES POLY AS STATE TELECOMMUNICATIONS CENTER

The importance of the Institute was recognized at the state level in March 1983, when Governor Mario M. Cuomo announced the designation of Polytechnic Institute of New York as a New York State Center for Advanced Technology in Telecommunications (CATT). This appointment made Polytechnic Institute of New York one of four schools in the state to hold such an honor.[21] During a press conference, Governor Cuomo discussed the appointment:

If we are going to take advantage of the future, we must prepare for it. We must make a concerted effort to lead the nation in partnership among government, business, and academia in the search for the best methods of advanced technology. What we do today will shape tomorrow.[22]

Designating Polytechnic Institute of New York as a Center for Advanced Technology in Telecommunications (CATT) meant that state funds would be available to implement and support, on a continuing basis, important research in telecommunications. This support, plus that of private industry and the resources of Polytechnic, made possible the work of seven research laboratories on both the Brooklyn and Long Island campuses. President Bugliarello responded to the appointment in the following address:

Polytechnic's designation as the New York State Center for Advanced Technology in Telecommunications has many implications for MetroTech. Telecommunications is a central concept in MetroTech planning and development; and with the New York State designation in telecommunications, each brings strength to the other. This is truly a great period in the 129-year history of Polytechnic, and the Institute is grateful to the students, faculty, staff, trustees, alumni, and supporters who have made this possible.[23]

Current Professor of Computer Science, Richard Van Slyke, came to Polytechnic Institute of New York in 1983 as the first director of CATT, and was

CLASS OF 1983 MAKES MEDIA HISTORY

JUNE 9, 1983, WENT DOWN IN THE ANNALS of Polytechnic Institute of New York as one of the most memorable graduation ceremonies in its celebrated history. The commencement ceremony at Carnegie Hall began as usual. However a small fire broke out in the basement of the famous hall, moments after the ceremony began. The building was evacuated, leaving 3,000 people in the streets. This resulted in what some witnesses called a giant block party. Polytechnic's band played on as students, professors, and guests danced in the streets. This was captured by many news organizations, including the *Associated Press*, *Reuters*, the *New York Times*, the *Daily News*, and the *New York Post*. Polytechnic faculty traveling in Europe at the time mentioned that the story made headlines in London, Paris, and Rome.[1]

As the building was evacuated and inspected, Mayor Koch, who was attending the ceremony, credited President Bugliarello's quick thinking and calming influence with averting a near panic following the first cries of fire. Modest by nature, Bugliarello responded to an *NBC* reporter with the following comment: "The real hero of the fire was the Mayor of New York."

Nearly two hours after the building was evacuated, the crowds returned to their seats in Carnegie Hall to resume the commencement exercise. Mayor Koch, who received an honorary degree during the ceremony, told the graduates: "The fireworks begin today; each diploma is a lighted match and each one of you a fuse."[2]

Months later, when the lights went out in New York City during the 1983 summer blackout, power was restored by a computer code written by alumnus Zivan Zabar, who was working for Consolidated Edison. His computer program restarted the electronic network in record time; the program was used again after the devastating attacks on September 11, 2001, to restore power in lower Manhattan.

New York City's Mayor Ed Koch receives an honorary degree from President Bugliarello in 1983. Mayor Koch was a staunch supporter of MetroTech.

instrumental in developing its program. He recently commented on the importance of the program, especially in the early 1980s.

The main objective was the idea of being a catalyst for joint activities in the newer technologies of communication and the companies that sold the technology and/or used it. So our objectives were trying to bring together our researchers with economically based activities, especially in New York. One way we did that was through an educational program for executives. We had a forum, which had active participation by industrial people. The major thing I liked about Polytechnic was this dual commitment to serious research and also to teaching.[24]

POLY'S FOCUS ON LIBERAL ARTS

Initiated in the fall of 1983 with a $480,000 grant from the Mellon Foundation, Polytechnic developed a new contemporary liberal arts program that offered undergraduates a modern and practical core of requirements that combined liberal arts and technology.[25]

The new program was the brainchild of President Bugliarello and Donald Hockney, chairman of the Humanities Department. At the time, Polytechnic had an even split of undergraduates and graduate students in its total enrollment of approximately 5,000 students.

In later years, Hockney led the Department of Computer Science, building the department's faculty, redesigning the undergraduate program, and tripling the department's research funding. One of his most notable achievements was the creation, in 1991, of the Center for Applied Large-Scale Computing (CALC), which later became known as Advanced Software Kinetics (ASK). Under his leadership, CALC designed software for NASA's Consortium for International Earth Science Information Network (CIESIN), where he served as director of the division of information technology. A strong advocate of interdisciplinary learning, Hockney established the BS program in journalism and technical writing, and the MS program in specialized writing.[26]

The Institute's connection with industry was considerable in the mid-1980s. For example, 155 of Hazeltine Corporation's 602 engineers were alumni. So were approximately 370 at Sperry Company, and 170 at Airborne Instrument Laboratories. Also, the CEOs of at least 100 Long Island firms were alumni. Altogether, there were about 4,900 alumni working or living on Long Island. Perhaps the most impressive statistic from this period was that one in every 60 engineers in the United States had graduated from Polytechnic.[27]

NEW GYMNASIUM SPARKS POLY PROGRAMS

In February 1984, a new $1 million gymnasium was opened at Polytechnic's Farmingdale campus, with President George Bugliarello on hand for the ceremonies. This addition greatly enhanced Poly's sports program. The facility consisted of a ground floor that featured a regulation college basketball court, which provided Poly's Blue Jay team with a suitable venue to challenge its long-standing rival, Pratt Institute, as well as newer rivals such as MIT. Other features of the new facility included an Athletics Hall of Fame room, weight training

Poly has enjoyed a fruitful relationship with many Long Island-based technological corporations. In 1980, 791 Poly alumni were employed at the Grumman Corporation. This engine test run was planned and administered, in part, by Poly alumni.

room, and a wrestling room which was also used for judo and other self-defense sports, aerobics, dance, and CPR classes.[28]

Athletics at Polytechnic Institute of New York was important, but since the Institute was an educational institution first and foremost, a concerted effort was continually made to expand academic offerings to keep pace with budding technologies, an approach Poly employed since its earliest days. To this end, new Master of Science programs were launched in Telecommunications Management, Imaging Sciences, and Microwave Engineering. Capitalizing on the successes experienced by its satellite campuses, a Master of Science in Information Systems Engineering program was also established at Poly's Westchester campus.

The following spring, Athanasois Papoulis, professor in the Department of Electrical Engineering and Computer Science, won the Institute of Electrical and Electronic Engineers' (IEEE) Education Medal. IEEE's board of directors presented him with the following citation: "For inspirational leadership in teaching through thought-provoking lectures, research, and creative textbooks in signal analysis, stochastic processes and systems."[29]

Later that year, Papoulis published *Signal Processing* under McGraw-Hill's imprint. Authoring textbooks was a common practice for Poly professors. Retired Professor Leonard Shaw, who began teaching at the Institute in 1960, recently recalled that he first heard about Polytechnic when he came across textbooks written by Professor Mischa Schwartz while completing his graduate work at Stanford University. The textbooks written by Schwartz and other Poly professors led Shaw to a 43-year teaching career at Polytechnic. When Papoulis' textbook was released, Shaw said it was a continuation of a great legacy.

THE NATIONAL ACADEMIES

POLYTECHNIC UNIVERSITY IS PROUD of its many graduates and/or faculty members—more than forty to date—who have been honored by nomination and election to one or more of America's prestigious National Academies. Four organizations comprise the Academies: the National Academy of Sciences, the National Academy of Engineering, the Institute of Medicine, and the National Research Council.

These organizations act as advisers to the nation on science, engineering, and medicine. They perform an unparalleled public service by bringing together committees of experts in all areas of scientific and technological endeavor. These experts serve pro bono to address critical national issues and give advice to the federal government and the public.

The National Academy of Engineering (NAE) is the portal for all engineering activities at the National Academies. Dr. Ernst Weber, the former Polytechnic president, was a founding member of the NAE. Its mission is to promote the technological welfare of the nation by marshaling the knowledge and insights of eminent members of the engineering profession.

Membership in one of the National Academies is based on a formal nomination and review process that normally takes around a year to conclude.

In 2003, Dr. George Bugliarello was elected Foreign Secretary of the National Academy of Engineering and was also named Lifetime National Associate of the National Academies, having served repeatedly on their council. As of the date of this book's publication, he is currently serving on the National Research Council (NRC) Governing Board.

Additionally, as of the date of this printing, a Polytechnic trustee, William Friend, serves as treasurer of the National Academy of Engineering and is a member of its council, as well as of the Governing Board of the NRC.

Today, 65 Poly alumni and former and present faculty are members of the National Academy of Engineering.

STAR WARS

THE WEBER RESEARCH INSTITUTE (WRI), formerly the Microwave Research Institute, officially opened at Poly in 1986. The majority of WRI's initial research stemmed from the $3.5 million grant from President Ronald Reagan's administration to study the Strategic Defensive Initiative (SDI), otherwise known as the Star Wars program.

The SDI research accounted for 30 percent of WRI's research. Professor Erich Kunhardt, a leading electrophysicist, directed the program. He and his team conducted cutting-edge research in gaseous electronics, pulse power, lasers, solid-state devices, and integrated optics. Poly's research team was also responsible for answering the following questions: What will be the impact of SDI on the Earth; what type of defense manufacturing research should be conducted in space; what is the future of the manned and unmanned space program; and what will be the impact of space electronics on industry.[1]

President Bugliarello told a *Long Island Business* reporter that this Polytechnic program set a precedent in research and development efforts in the New York metropolitan area:

It creates a strong nucleus of advanced research in areas fundamental to technology on Long Island— space and defense activities, and civilian expectations, such as air traffic control. Experience shows that it is the centers of strong research that have fueled high-tech … like Route 128 in Massachusetts and Silicon Valley.[2]

In 1985, Professor Erich Kunhardt (shown above) joined the faculty of Polytechnic University as Director of the Weber Research Institute.

Papoulis' first book from McGraw-Hill was considered to be a classic. There were several editions of it. The most recent edition came out a couple of years ago. I taught from some of the notes that he was using here that developed into his first textbook. There was a lot of emphasis on textbook writing, which helped the school build its reputation.[30]

POLY AGAIN CHANGES ITS NAME

In 1985, the New York State Board of Regents approved a new name for the Institute: Polytechnic University. This came after President Bugliarello and Chairman Jacobs lobbied the state for a name change. The primary reason for the name change was that some confusion existed in the minds of New Yorkers in trying to differentiate Polytechnic Institute of New York, New York Institute of Technology, and New York City Technical College.

With a new name, and MetroTech plans in the final stages of approval, Polytechnic University was approaching significant milestones. "Polytechnic Institute has had a major impact on the theory and practice of technology for more than a century," said President Bugliarello. "I look forward to Polytechnic University having an even greater impact in the decades ahead."[31]

The newly named university began with a financial advantage. By the end of fiscal year 1984, the Institute had successfully balanced its operating budget for eight consecutive years, and entirely repaid its pre-1977 deficit in the fiscal years 1977-1982.[32]

GRANTS AND GREEN LIGHTS

The Institute's 130th commencement ceremony also marked Bugliarello's 10th anniversary as president. He took the opportunity to formally announce Polytechnic's plans for the next 10 years. These called for the Institute to fulfill a key role in the development of new technology in the metropolitan region. This would be realized through the completion of MetroTech, which he said would be co-developed by Forest City Ratner Properties. Plans were also progressing for the Bern Dibner Science and Technology Library as part of the MetroTech site.[33]

To further its agenda, the Institute continued to receive major grants, including a $1.4 million grant from the National Science Foundation to conduct multi-disciplinary research on materials, and a $250,000 five-year grant from AT&T for Poly's CATT program.

In addition to these grants, Polytechnic celebrated its 50th year of granting doctorate degrees in chemistry. That same year the Weber Research Institute (WRI), formerly the Microwave Research Institute, was dedicated, with its founder, Ernst Weber on hand. Professor Erich Kunhardt was named director of WRI.

In 1987, Weber would again be honored when he, along with 19 other scientists, received the National Medal of Science on June 25 during a White House Rose Garden ceremony hosted by President Ronald Reagan and Vice President George H. W. Bush.

Weber was awarded this honor for "his distinguished and pioneering contributions to the profession of electrical engineering and allied areas as

BERN DIBNER

ONE OF POLY'S OLDEST AND MOST influential alumnus, Bern Dibner, died January 6, 1989, at the age of 90. He was best known as the founder of Burndy Corporation, a leading manufacturer of electronic, electrical, fiber optic, and microcircuit connectors. After his death, his son, David, became chairman of the company.[1]

Dibner founded Burndy Corp. in 1924 after he realized the need for better connectors while working as an engineer on the electrification of Cuba. He later founded the Burndy Library in 1935 as an expression of his love and admiration for early scientists and engineers. In 1975 he made a gift of a major part of his collection—the Dibner Library of the History of Science and Technology—to the Smithsonian Institution in Washington, D.C. His personal collection of

artifacts also included a bronze bell cast by the great artist Leonardo da Vinci.[2]

A year before his death, as a fitting tribute to his contributions to science and technology, five academic institutions—Brandeis University, Harvard University, MIT, Boston University, and the American Academy of Arts and Science—formed a consortium to establish the Dibner Institute, whose mission is to stimulate scholarship in the history of science and technology. The institute is located on MIT's campus.[3]

In 1992, Polytechnic honored Dibner, who held 24 patents, by naming one of the new buildings on the MetroTech complex as the Bern Dibner Library of Science and Technology. At the ceremony, fellow alumnus Joseph J. Jacobs said:

Bern Dibner was my ideal, my role model. This library is the centerpiece of MetroTech. It was the spark for MetroTech. And Bern Dibner was the epitome of a humanist with an engineering degree. This library stands as a tribute to "giving back" both to society and to Polytechnic.[4]

Alumnus Bern Dibner, class of 1921, died January 6, 1989, at age 90. His legacy was recognized in 1992 when the Bern Dibner Library of Science and Technology was opened.

In 1987, Dr. Ernst Weber received the National Medal of Science from Vice President George H. W. Bush.

educator, academic leader, author, researcher, and entrepreneur, which have inspired several generations of students and colleagues around the world."[34] President Reagan said of the honor:

These are the dreamers, the builders, the men and women who are the heroes of the modern age. What will serve America most in the years ahead—our most precious possession—is the genius of our people.[35]

As the Institute entered 1986, the Mechanical Engineering Department established the Manu-

HISTORY OF THE NICHOLS BUILDING

IN THE MID-EIGHTIES, POLYTECHNIC SOLD the Nichols Building, which at the time was located on the corner of Bridge and Johnson Streets, the current site of the New York City Fire Department Headquarters Building. The building had a long and colorful history. It had been the home of the *Brooklyn Daily Eagle*, which published from 1841 to 1902. (At one point the *Eagle* was the nation's most widely read afternoon newspaper.) For a while, the building housed parts of the New York City Sanitation Department.

Polytechnic took over the Nichols Building after it was forced to move from the top three floors of the Con-Edison Building on the corner of Adams and Johnson Streets (now Tech Place), when the building was sold to New York Tech. While it was part of Poly, the Nichols Building was used to house the Physics Department and the ROTC unit. It also housed the Physical Education Department, the Brooklyn contingent of the ElectroPhysics Department, which later became part of the Electrical Engineering Department, and some classrooms.

After Poly took over the building, a large plastic bubble was installed on the roof to house a basketball court that was located there. One winter, a very heavy snow collapsed the bubble, ruining the support frames for the basketball hoops. This was the end of Polytechnic's only home court.

The Nichols Building was situated opposite a gas station that was located on the site of the E911 Building. The gas station was once the site of an attempted heist of an armored truck that was prevented by the police.

After a while it became clear that the Nichols Building represented an under-utilized asset that would be worth more to Polytechnic if sold. And so, it was eventually sold. This sale was part of the real estate deal that secured the Dibner Building for Polytechnic.

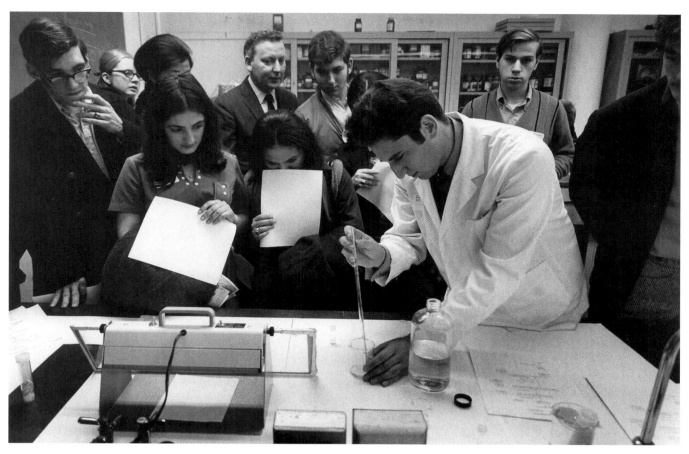

Over the course of the last 150 years, a large number of groundbreaking experiments have been conducted in Polytechnic classrooms.

facturing Engineering Program. This coincided with Polytechnic celebrating its 100th anniversary of offering a course of study in electrical engineering, and also coincided with Weber's 85th birthday, and the 50th anniversary of PhD programs in electrical engineering. The following year, Professor McShane was named head of the Mechanical Engineering Department and the Industrial Engineering Department, while Professor Pasquale Sforza remained the head of the Aerospace Engineering Department. North of Brooklyn, the Westchester Graduate Center moved from White Plains to Hawthorne, New York.

YES PROGRAM LAUNCHED

While Polytechnic University was in the process of raising money for the MetroTech project, it was also focused on providing assistance to its financially challenged students. This led to the establishment of the Youth in Engineering and Science Scholarships (YES) program.

The purpose of the program, which remains active today, is to identify and to reach out to local high schools and attract the most able students and assist their education through a broad program of financial aid. In the late 1980s, more than 90 percent of Poly's students received some sort of aid.

Beverly Johnson, the current executive director of the Youth in Engineering and Science Center and Summer Research Institute, explained in a recent interview the importance of the program.

The purpose of the YES Center was to try to get under-represented students interested and motivated concerning careers in math, science, and technology. When we refer to underrepresented students, we are referring to minorities—African-Americans and Latinos—as well as women.

We wanted to do a service for humanity, but in doing that service for humanity, we would get students interested in Poly as well. We do this in a variety of ways. We are running a research institute, the Summer Research Institute, where students spend six to seven weeks here on campus in our laboratories under the guidance of Polytechnic faculty members who are working on real research, whether it's *in engineering, math, science, chemical engineering, or other areas.[36]*

PROMISE FUND

In the late 1980s, the National Science Education Center projected a shortage of 70,000 American engineers by 2010. Further, women and minorities were greatly under represented in technological fields. These two factors became the catalyst for

POLY ALUMNA WINS NOBEL PRIZE

ON OCTOBER 17, 1988, GERTRUDE B. Elion received word from Stockholm that she, along with her long-time partner, George H. Hitchings, were named the recipients of the Nobel Prize in Medicine. Their research contributed to the development of drugs for treating AIDS (AZT), leukemia, gout, malaria, autoimmune disorders, and for the prevention of rejection of donated organs.[1]

The two scientists began working together in 1945, during the time that Elion was riding the subway two nights a week to Polytechnic in pursuit of her doctoral degree. In 1946, after two years of part-time study, Poly's administration told her that she had to choose between going to Polytechnic full-time or keeping her day job as a laboratory technician. Elion decided at that time that she couldn't afford to give up her job and parted ways with Polytechnic.[2]

More than 40 years later, while being interviewed by a *New York Times* reporter, Elion was humble when speaking about her award: "The Nobel Prize is fine, but the drugs I've developed are rewards in themselves." Elion, who received

an honorary doctor of science degree from Polytechnic the year following her award, joined another Nobel winner who studied at Polytechnic, Francis Crick, who won the prize for medicine in 1962. He was a post-doctorate student at the Institute.[3]

As the interview with the *Times* reporter concluded, it was clear that Elion bore no ill will toward the ultimatum she had been presented by Polytechnic's administration. Instead, she recalled her interactions with one of the Institute's famous professors: "At Polytechnic, one of my teachers was Dr. Herman Mark. He was down here for a lecture a couple of years ago—and he actually remembered me! I couldn't believe it."[4]

In 1988, Gertrude B. Elion and her long-time partner, George H. Hitchings, were named recipients of the Nobel Prize in Medicine. Their research led to the development of the AIDS drug AZT. In his book, *The Greatest Generation*, Tom Brokaw devotes a chapter to Dr. Elion.

MORE KUDOS

IN 1990, ALUMNUS CHARLES D. STRANG, class of 1943, received the American Vocation Success Award from President George H. W. Bush. The following year, in 1990, he retired as chairman and CEO and current director of Outboard Marine Corporation, which he joined in 1966. Strang went on to be the national commissioner to NASCAR. Previously, he was vice president of engineering and executive vice president at Kiekhaefer Corporation, the original manufacturer of Mercury Outboard motors, and a member of the Mechanical Engineering Staff at MIT. He has several dozen design patents for engine designs, and is credited with the design of the inboard-outboard engine drive system, the most successful design in the history of the marine industry.[1]

The same year, 1990, the Joseph J. Jacobs and Violet J. Jacobs Chair of Chemical Engineering was established at Polytechnic. Allan S. Myerson, head of the department, was named the first Jacobs Professor. The $2.5 million gift from Jacobs made him the largest individual donor in Polytechnic's history. At this time, Jacobs' gifts to the University totaled $7 million.[2]

Polytechnic's Promise Fund. Like the YES Program, the Promise Fund offers community outreach programs to encourage inner-city high school students to consider careers in science and engineering, with an emphasis on women and minorities. In the first five years of the program, the fund awarded $3.5 million in scholarships to hundreds of students, 75 percent of them women and minorities. The Promise Fund was founded by former trustee, Clifford H. Goldsmith, now retired from the Philip Morris Companies, and Henry J. Singer, a current trustee and retired vice president at General Electric.

Former Polytechnic trustee, R. William (Bill) Murray, retired chief executive officer of Philip Morris Corporation, became a trustee of The Corporation as the Promise Fund was established. In a recent interview, Murray explained that the Promise Fund required a tremendous amount of fundraising, which mostly came from corporations and companies in the metropolitan area. While the costs to attend Polytechnic were slightly higher than neighboring colleges, Murray said the tuition was more than worth the educational experience received at Polytechnic.

It's the major annual scholarship fundraising event for the college. The people that I solicited were contacts I had through business—advertising agencies, suppliers, and so on. I would suggest to them that they contribute and they did. We're known as a tena-cious school. We're not over-endowed with riches, but we provide a very good education at as low a cost as we can. I think the main argument that I try to use is that at Poly, you get your money's worth. We may not be the cheapest, but we give an exceptional scientific and engineering education for a reasonable fee.[37]

BIG BUSINESS SECURED FOR METROTECH

On September 15, 1988, after nearly a decade of planning, the Securities Industry Automation Corporation (SIAC) signed a lease to become MetroTech's first official tenant. SIAC, a subsidiary of the New York Stock Exchange, eventually moved approximately 1,000 employees from its Wall Street headquarters to a new 400,000-square-foot building constructed as part of the first phase of MetroTech. On the heels of this announcement came the news that KeySpan (then Brooklyn Union Gas Company) would be the second major company to relocate to the new facility.[38]

MetroTech tenants benefited from a variety of city-sponsored incentives, including a 22-year tax exemption program, a phased-in 30 percent reduction in commercial occupancy tax, and $10 million in municipal assistance funding reserved for development outside of Manhattan.[39]

Despite these extraordinary incentives, certain Manhattan-based corporations still hesitated. Alair

METROTECH–A VISIONARY DREAM MADE REAL

PIONEERED BY POLYTECHNIC PRESIdent George Bugliarello, the MetroTech Center was conceived as a means of revitalizing downtown Brooklyn by developing office space attractive to high-technology businesses and back-office operations, and integrating this activity with Polytechnic University. Due to its success, MetroTech has proven to be a primary case study in university, corporate, government, and private-developer cooperation, and has

The MetroTech Center surrounds Polytechnic's campus. The University's corporate neighbors are, by and large, well established, mature companies, some of which would have moved out of New York City if MetroTech had not become available. (This photo was taken prior to the construction of the Othmer Residence Hall.) *(Photo: Sara Krulwich/The New York Times.)*

resulted in renewing an area that once had been a site of urban decay.

The project, however, was not an easy one to get off the ground, and took 13 years from the time when Bugliarello first proposed the idea of a university-industry park to The Corporation in 1975 to the first groundbreaking ceremony for the Brooklyn Union Gas/Bear Stearns building in 1988, which was followed by the completion of the Dibner Library/ Center for Advanced Technology in Telecommunication, The Jacobs Building, and the Othmer Residence Hall.

OVER $1 BILLION IN NEW INVESTMENTS

In the past seventeen years, MetroTech, one of the largest urban university-corporate parks in the world and the largest in the United States,

Left: *Engineering News-Record*, a respected publication in the engineering industry, featured MetroTech on the cover of its February 10, 1992, edition. *(Cover photo © Matt Flynn.)*

Below: The following is taken from *Engineering News-Record's* editorial page. *(Reprinted from* Engineering News-Record, *copyright The Mcgraw-Hill Companies, Inc., Feb. 10, 1992. All rights reserved.)*

Something from Almost Nothing

The 4-million-square-foot MetroTech Center that is replacing a decrepit section of New York City's downtown Brooklyn with buildings that will soon provide a total of 16,000 permanent jobs would be a feather in any developer's cap. For sponsor Polytechnic University, a science and engineering school with no previous experience in real estate development, it's a major coup.

As intended, Polytechnic has no financial stake in the project. The school's president and MetroTech's mastermind, George Bugliarello, views the development basically as furnishing an academic achievement, not primarily as a real estate venture. Polytechnic is securing its future in Brooklyn by revitalizing its surroundings and putting itself on course as a center for advanced technology in telecommunications. Now on its doorstop are professionals with all the equipment to back it up. Joint research is already underway. For Polytechnic, MetroTech offers a ready source of teachers and students.

There's a lesson here for schools, planners, cities, and private developers: Don't try to reinvent the wheel, attempting to weave renewal in a vacuum. MetroTech stands as a prototype of what can be done by building a community around an existing focused institution.

has generated over $1 billion in new investments, and over 5 million square feet of new space.

Today, the 16-acre site is home to Polytechnic University and several technology-dependent companies, including Chase Manhattan Bank, KeySpan Energy, Empire Blue Cross/Blue Shield, Bear Stearns and Company, Securities Industries Automation Corporation, Brooklyn Union Gas Company, New York City Police Department's 911 Center, New York City Fire Department Headquarters, and the U.S. technology and operations functions of J.P. Morgan Chase.

Polytechnic has made a special effort to work closely with its MetroTech neighbors. This has included conducting research for at least one tenant, offering evening and weekend courses designed to appeal to the office park's thousands of workers. It even employed a vice president from Chase Manhattan Bank to teach classes on managing information technology.

In addition to MetroTech, the successful opening of Renaissance Plaza and the New York

Marriott Brooklyn Hotel has reinforced the vision of a vibrant downtown area for Brooklyn that will continue to thrive. The overall revitalization of downtown Brooklyn could not have been accomplished without Bugliarello's vision, guidance, and persistence. Always the optimist, Bugliarello believes that the MetroTech model is one that can be successfully employed by other urban educational institutions. "If you think big enough, you can probably pull it off," he says.[1]

Townsend, current publisher of *Crain's New York Business*, was at this time deputy mayor for finance and economic development in Mayor Ed Koch's administration. She recently recalled that Koch's administration fully supported the MetroTech project as a way of keeping firms from leaving New York City for cheaper rents in Westchester, Connecticut, and New Jersey.

Manhattan was too expensive for many of these operations. We couldn't offer reasonable incentives in Manhattan to keep firms. We would be giving away our tax base, but we thought that we could try to retain these operations by offering fairly deep incentives in the four boroughs.[40]

The major concern felt by all parties involved with MetroTech was persuading a huge corporation to relocate. Townsend said this goal was realized when Chase Bank expressed interest, although she said it wasn't an easy sell:

When I learned that Chase [bank] was just about ready to choose New Jersey, I told the mayor that we needed to reach out to Bill Butcher, the CEO, and ask him, if only as a courtesy, to let us talk with his people about city-based options in the boroughs.

Butcher was not interested in a lot of publicity about this meeting. He was very camera shy. So I met his car at the driveway into City Hall and took him into the mayor's office via the back door—totally private—directly into the mayor's office. The press couldn't see him. We just emerged into the mayor's office, and we kept our mouths shut about it.

Ed Koch was very persuasive. Butcher was reasonably convinced that we wouldn't be able to find anything that would meet their needs, but he was agreeable to asking his folks to exhaust all the possibilities with us before they roared ahead. I'll never forget going with Butcher to view the area around MetroTech. We were close to the area, and it wasn't looking all that nice, of course, and some truck either backfired or its tailgate fell down or something. There was this large bang that sounded almost like a shot. His security came out of that car in a heartbeat looking around. It was not an auspicious start.[41]

Left: There were countless professors at Polytechnic whose dedication and aptitude garnered the respect of both students and faculty. Perhaps the most beloved physics professor was John Dropkin (pictured here) who retired May 3, 1978, after teaching for 30 years at Poly. At a dinner held in his honor, Dropkin received a plaque acknowledging his unique gifts as a teacher, counselor, and good friend of the Polytechnic student body.

Opposite: Dedication Day: On May 28, 1992, the ribbon was cut to officially open the first Polytechnic building of the MetroTech complex. The $42-million structure houses the Bern Dibner Library of Science and Technology, New York State Center for Advanced Technology in Telecommunications, and the School of Electrical Engineering and Computer Science. Governor Mario Cuomo, center, delivered a speech underscoring the significance of Poly to Brooklyn and New York City. Shown, left to right, are Polytechnic President George Bugliarello; David Dibner, son of Bern Dibner; New York State Governor Mario Cuomo; Brooklyn Borough President Howard Golden; and Joe Jacobs, founder of Jacobs Engineering Group.

Townsend explained that last minute negotiations between the city and Chase resulted in a historic moment for Brooklyn.

I went into Ed's office that morning and said I might be ill I was so nervous. I think it's close, but I'm not sure we're there. He said, "What do you need?" I said if I could put $15-16 million on the table for infrastructure, I would feel we had done everything we could. He said, "You've got it!"[42]

With that multi-million dollar nod from Mayor Koch, Chase Manhattan Bank announced it would build a new $450 million financial services center and move 5,000 jobs to the new complex. This one transfer would ensure that 62 percent of the space in the 4.7-million-square foot complex would be committed. It was this historic decision that ensured MetroTech's success.

Unfortunately, as development of MetroTech progressed, it was necessary for both financial and safety reasons to close the student center in 1990. This had a negative effect on the quality of student life at Poly and caused poor relations with the student body. While the student center remained closed for six years, morale among students improved with the opening of a new student lounge in 1993.

MOVING AHEAD

This was a tricky time in the Institute's history. On the one hand, the Institute had to handle the difficult aspects of coaxing major corporations to MetroTech, while on the other hand it had to

GEORGE BUGLIARELLO – A LIFETIME OF ACCOMPLISHMENT

GEORGE BUGLIARELLO WAS THE visionary leader and guiding light that brought MetroTech to pass, one of the most significant accomplishments in the history of Polytechnic, and of Brooklyn. *Engineering News-Record* awarded Bugliarello an award of excellence for his leadership of the MetroTech project.

Dr. Bugliarello's life is filled with important achievements, accomplishments, and honors of all types. He was one of two academic members, along with John Sawhill, the president of NYU, of the Business-Labor Working Group established by David Rockefeller and Harry Van Arsdale in 1975 to develop a rescue plan for the City of New York, which at the time was in severe fiscal crisis. He chaired Mayor Koch's Commission on Science and Technology and

was the first recipient at Polytechnic of the Mayor's Award for Excellence in Science and Technology. (Later, Professor Othmer also would be a recipient of this prestigious award.) He also was appointed by the mayor to co-chair an investigation of a steam main explosion that covered several city blocks of the Gramercy Park area of Manhattan, forcing the evacuation of residents there for several weeks.

Bugliarello is the recipient of eight honorary degrees, the latest one from the University of Minnesota in May 2005. In 1987, he was elected ito the National Academy of Engineering and as its foreign secretary in 2003. He was for 14 years the U.S. member of NATO's Science for Stability Steering Committee, and was one of the reviewers for the Organization for Economic Cooperation

---

continue offering a world-class education to its 5,000-plus student population. During this period, many faculty were beginning to retire, and a concerted effort was made to hire new professors with strong reputations.

Also, Bugliarello was faced with various issues concerning the teaching staff who he said were put through the "wringer" as a result of the merger. In a recent interview, he explained his initial support of Poly's union, the American Association of University Professors (AAUP), that later turned sour.

I came here with a great deal of sympathy for the union. One of the first acts that I had to do after the merger was to balance the budget—we had a surplus of faculty. So I invited the department heads and the head of the union down to my office and said, "Look, we have to do something. Let's work together. We have to survive." The head of the union said, "We will help you. We'll work together."

So then I called a second meeting a few days later, and the head of the union got up and unfurled a piece of paper. It said the union would not "collaborate" with the administration. At that moment, I really lost my esteem for the union because they were playing games.[43]

As Bugliarello continued to rebuild Polytechnic's finances and overall reputation, the relationship between AAUP and Polytechnic worsened. Finally, after three years of Polytechnic fighting this issue in front of the National Labor Relations Board at great expense, the Supreme Court ruled in a similar case involving another New York private institution, Yeshiva University. The ruling decreed that faculty were, in effect, managers, and therefore were not entitled to the protection of a union.

After the Yeshiva ruling, the National Labor Relations Board supported Bugliarello and The Corporation's stance. However, by the late eighties, certain faculty members voiced their dissent in the only way they could—a vote of "no confi-

and Development's science policies for Greece, Portugal, Turkey, and Italy. He also chaired the Advisory Committee for Science Education of the National Science Foundation and the Board of Science and Technology for International Development of the National Academy of Sciences.

Dr. Bugliarello also was part of the first engineering delegation invited by China to visit it in 1974. This was during the height of the Cultural Revolution. Bugliarello and his colleagues were in China for a total of five weeks during this historic period.

George Bugliarello was the linchpin for the MetroTech project, one of the most notable accomplishments in Polytechnic's storied history. Portraits behind him, left to right, depict David Henry Cochran, Polytechnic president from 1864-1899; Henry R. Worthington, one of Polytechnic's original trustees; and John Charles Olsen, a professor emeritus at Polytechnic, former head of the Department of Chemical Engineering, and a founder of the American Institute of Chemical Engineers.

dence" against Bugliarello. This carried no official weight, but sent a clear message that certain members of the teaching faculty were angry, to say the least. "The faculty swore revenge on me," Bugliarello said.[44]

Despite the vote of no confidence, the faculty continued to provide the student body with an outstanding education. At the same time, a transition of leadership took place within the ranks of The Corporation. As SIAC signed its lease, Paul Hallingby Jr., a leading New York investment banker and strong proponent of technological development, assumed the chairmanship of The Corporation. He succeeded Clarence Silleck, class of 1932, who followed Jacobs as chairman when he retired in June 1986.[45]

The same year, Polytechnic honored one of its most distinguished alumni, benefactors, and supporters by dedicating the renovated administrative complex at 333 Jay Street, the old American Safety Razor Company headquarters, as the Joseph J. Jacobs Building.

POLY BREAKS GROUND

A celebration on the MetroTech Center Commons took place on April 19, 1990, complete with refreshments, banners, speakers, a robot, and a band, as ground was broken for the Dibner Library Center. Among those in attendance were President Bugliarello, David Dibner, son of the library's major benefactor and namesake, Bern Dibner, class of 1921, Ernst Weber, Brooklyn Borough President Howard Golden, and Corporation Chairman Paul Hallingby Jr.[46]

Over that summer, and on the heels of the momentum generated as a result of the groundbreaking ceremony, Professors Schillinger and Anthony J. Wiener were busy developing an executive format master's degree in Management of Technology (MOT). When Polytechnic launched the new program, it was one of the first in the nation.

Robert Maxwell succeeded Hallingby in 1991 and was named chairman of The Corporation. His first big announcement came when he declared a

$100 million capital campaign for Poly. However, the plan was aborted after Maxwell, the flamboyant *New York Daily News* publisher, who had earned his reputation as the "bouncing Czech," died mysteriously at sea. While the University was shocked at his death, it had to move ahead. It again turned to Joe Jacobs, naming him interim chairman. This was done the same year that Jacobs' released his autobiography, *The Anatomy of an Entrepreneur.*

As the Institute rebounded from the loss of Maxwell, Jacobs once again took the helm of The

Corporation. Computer Science, which had been a separate division within the Electrical Engineering Department, was given full departmental status. Together, the Electrical Engineering Department, headed by Henry Bertoni, and the Computer Science Department, headed by Donald Hockney, made up the School of Electrical Engineering and Computer Science under the direction of Leonard Shaw.

Later that year, Arthur A. Oliner, a professor of electrical engineering, was elected to the National Academy of Engineering. The previous year, Oliner received The Balthasar van der Pol Gold Medal Award from the Union Radio-Scientique Internationale, the highest honor in the field of radio science.[47]

The following year the worldwide scientific community mourned the loss of one of its brightest stars. On April 6, 1992, Herman Mark, the father of polymer science, died at the age of 96. A memorial symposium was held in his honor.

Ivan Frisch, retired provost and professor of electrical engineering and computer science at Polytechnic, was former Director of the New York State Center for Advanced Technology in Telecommunications (CATT). Here he is shown with a student during his teaching days.

DEDICATION DAY

On May 28, 1992, the entire University, joined by Governor Cuomo, New York City officials and MetroTech developers and tenants, dedicated the first new Polytechnic building at the MetroTech complex.

As the crowds cheered, a ribbon was cut to officially open the new $42-million structure, which houses the Bern Dibner Library of Science and Technology, the New York State Center for Advanced Technology in Telecommunications (CATT), and the School of Electrical Engineering and Computer Science.[48]

"I think we have shown what a private university can do if it perseveres in its dream," declared President Bugliarello. He went on to explain that the MetroTech development was the result of "an extraordinary collaboration of the public, private, and academic sectors."[49]

Governor Cuomo, and Albert B. Ratner, president and CEO of Forest City Enterprises Inc., were presented with honorary degrees during the ceremony. A beaming Cuomo spoke of the new generation of immigrants that would propel the country to great heights: "Today's new wave of immigrants are one of our secret sources of strength in New York. They are building a city that will be greater than the city Mama and Papa built."[50]

MetroTech not only dramatically changed Poly's campus but also the surrounding neighborhood. Ivan Frisch, retired provost and professor of electrical engineering and computer science at Polytechnic, and former deputy director of CATT, recalled the impact of the transformation.

I was there before MetroTech was initiated, and it was really a grim neighborhood. You had to watch where you walked. Derelicts [were] hanging around on the sidewalk. Then, 16 acres were devoted to Poly, a new library was built, and companies like Brooklyn Union Gas and Securities Industry Automation Corporation and many others came in.

So it changed it into one of the largest urban technology campuses in the country. That was just unbelievable. George, and his vice president for finance, Sy Scher, created that out of nothing in the sense that they started with nothing but a concept. It all came together, but basically, it was created out of whole cloth by George.[51]

As Polytechnic University proceeded through the early 1990s, it did so bolstered by the new MetroTech facilities—a remarkable accomplishment—that would enable it to rise to extraordinary heights into the future. And while it mourned the loss of notable faculty and alumni like Mark and Dibner, it continued to build upon the strengths of its founders, who first dedicated Polytechnic to the highest standards of educational excellence 140 years earlier.

Poly's CATT/Dibner Library building is located in the heart of MetroTech's beautiful two-acre commons, which features rotating art exhibitions, sidewalk dining, and cultural events.

CHAPTER TEN

New Beginnings

1994–1999

The reward to the educator lies in his pride in his students' accomplishments. The richness of that reward is the satisfaction in knowing that the frontiers of knowledge have been expanded.

—Donald Othmer

WITH THE METROTECH CENter officially launched, Polytechnic University entered a new period of growth and prosperity. The refurbished Brooklyn campus and surrounding neighborhoods greatly enhanced Polytechnic's profile. At long last its physical environment matched its celebrated history of providing academic excellence for its students.

For many Brooklynites, professors, and students, the transformation was astonishing. David Doucette, a current professor with the Computer and Information Science Department, received his BS, MS, and PhD (Electrical Engineering) from Polytechnic. He worked at the Brooklyn campus as an instructor (1968–1973) and as an assistant professor (1973–1974). From 1973 to 1994, he worked as an adjunct professor at the Long Island campus. In 1994, Doucette returned for the dedication of the Dibner/CATT building. During an interview that was conducted in 2004, he recalled his first impressions of the new campus.

I couldn't believe what it looked like. I was dumbstruck. I just stood there for a few minutes looking around. The street was still there, but it was nothing like I remembered. I don't know if Poly would have survived without the improvements because you could see clearly that the neighborhood was getting to be a very dangerous place to be. This totally transformed it.[1]

The physical renovation underscored Poly's superlative educational programs, that continued to become richer with each passing year. In the winter of 1994, President Bill Clinton's administration recognized Polytechnic's attributes by granting $3.3 million under its defense conversion program known as the Technology Reinvestment Project (TRP). The goal of the program was to improve the competitiveness of small and mid-size United States technological firms, as well as to promote employment opportunities for minorities and women. The federal grant, secured by Richard Thorsen, the vice president for research, resulted in Polytechnic's new graduate program in manufacturing. Professor Charles W. Hoover was tapped to head the new program.[2]

The grant for the TRP project furthered Poly's long history of catering to students and professionals who advanced their education while working.

The number of female students at Polytechnic University increased substantially during World War II when America's young men were away, fighting for their country. Female students now comprise approximately 25 percent of the student body.

This mirrored Poly's student body, historically comprised of immigrants and minorities. In 2004, Professor Robert Flynn of the computer and information science department, who began teaching at Poly in 1966 while taking graduate courses, commented on Polytechnic's support of minorities seeking education:

In 1994, Joseph J. Jacobs (left) and Henry Singer (right) pose for a picture during the tribute dinner to outgoing president, George Bugliarello.

> *In some sense, engineering and technology has, from a sociological point of view, usually been the immigrant's first step up because you don't require a lot of natural English skills. You require math skills.*
>
> *Over the years, Poly has educated an enormous number of kids from New York City whose parents are immigrants, who are first-generation Americans, first-generation high school graduates, first-generation college graduates, first-generation master's degree students. If it just requires raw talent and hard work, Poly is the place to come to.[3]*

While research grants were essential to Poly's success as an institution, the administration and alumni association realized that in order for its student body to thrive, private financial support would always be necessary. To this end, the 1994 Promise Fund Dinner, an annual black-tie gala established in 1989, raised more than $1 million for student scholarships.

Henry J. Singer, fund chairman, announced at the event that as a result of the money raised, Polytechnic was able to award over 200 undergraduate scholarships, primarily to women and minorities, as well as to continue to support the YES Center and its high school outreach program, the Summer Research Institute.[4] After the dinner, Singer commented on the benefits resulting from the program:

> *The Promise Fund is a lightning rod, for it shows what Polytechnic can do and how we can take a*

lead in the community in this area. In the future, Poly will always have at its core a commitment to those first-generation college students and the sons and daughters of immigrants to America. We are in a unique position by virtue of our students and faculty, but beyond that, Polytechnic is truly unique as a valuable asset to the city and State of New York.[5]

CHANGING OF THE GUARD

A few months after receiving the grant to establish the new manufacturing graduate program from the Defense Conversion Program of the Clinton Administration, Arthur C. Martinez, class of 1960, chairman and CEO of the Sears Merchandise Groups of Sears, Roebuck and Co., was elected chairman of The Corporation. He approached the new position with the same zeal as he did in his business career by saying, "We both face real challenges for our market share. There is a declining pool of qualified college-aged students. We are all in a market-share game. Those who build on their strengths will do well."

Martinez was first elected as a trustee in 1991, and now replaced Jacobs as chairman. Jacobs said of the appointment: "I am delighted to see Arthur Martinez succeed me at this moment of great opportunity for Polytechnic. He is the leader who can take us into the 21st century."[6]

As Jacobs stepped down from his second stint as chairman, he was elected to the National Academy of Engineering (NAE), one of the highest professional distinctions accorded an engineer. The NAE honored Jacobs as an engineer who "made important contributions to engineering theory and practice, including significant contributions to the literature of engineering theory and practice,"

Professor Isidor Fankuchen conducts an experiment while students watch on intently. A giant in his field, Fankuchen was part of the academic magic at Polytechnic during the late forties and early fifties. The Fankuchen Memorial Award, which is named after him, recognizes crystallographers for both research and effective teaching of crystallography.

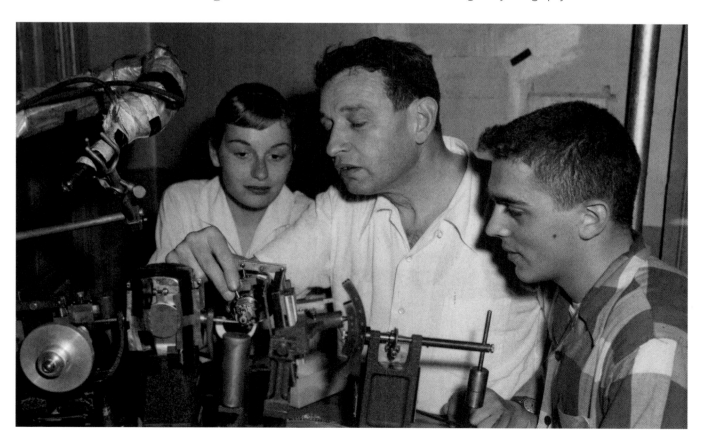

and for "unusual accomplishments in the pioneering of new and developing fields of technology."[7]

About this time, alumnus Joel A. Miele, class of 1955, highlighted the long-standing and close relationship between Polytechnic and New York City government when he was appointed New York City Commissioner of Buildings by Mayor Rudolph Giuliani.[8]

POLY WELCOMES NEW PRESIDENT

After 21 years of dutiful service to Polytechnic University, George Bugliarello stepped down as president. His tenure since 1973 had been eventful, including two name changes for the school. Among numerous academic pursuits, he established new departments, including the revolutionary freshman engineering program, and many new course offerings. Perhaps his greatest single accomplishment was the birth of MetroTech Center.

In July 1994, Bugliarello passed the baton to President David C. Chang, the ninth president of Polytechnic University, one of only two Asian American college/university presidents in the United States. Chang came to Polytechnic from Arizona State University where he served as dean of the College of Engineering and Applied Sciences and Motorola Professor of Electrical

Engineering since 1992. Before his tenure at Arizona State University, he was a member of the faculty of the University of Colorado in Boulder. He holds Master and Doctorate degrees in Applied Physics from Harvard University, and is a past president of the Society on Antennas and Propagation of the Institute of Electrical and Electronics Engineers (IEEE).[9]

Bugliarello, who currently serves as president emeritus and university professor, wrote the following lines in the summer, 1994 issue of the *Polytechnic Cable*:

As I pass the baton to David Chang and welcome him most heartily as the new president of Polytechnic, I would like to thank all members of the Polytechnic community for the privilege of steering Polytechnic through a most unique period in its long and glorious history. We can all take pride in having overcome together what, in 1973, seemed impossible odds and in now seeing Polytechnic poised for a new phase of growth and achievement.[10]

In a fitting tribute to Bugliarello's accomplishments, the Polytechnic community toasted him at a special dinner held under a tent on the MetroTech campus. Among those who spoke were David A. Andelman, Washington Correspondent for *CNBC*, and master of ceremonies; Brooklyn Borough

After the commencement ceremonies in 1994, Dr. David C. Chang was named the ninth president of Polytechnic University. In 2005, Chang was awarded an honorary professorship from the South China University of Technology by University President Li Yuanyuan. Chang announced that Polytechnic and South China University had signed a memorandum of understanding to collaborate on exchange programs, notably the 1-2-1 program, where students spend the freshman and senior years at their home university and the sophomore and junior years at the partnering school. South China University of Technology is the ninth national university in China that has entered a similar program with Polytechnic. Chang is shown in this picture with Board Vice Chairman Clifford H. Goldsmith, far left, and Chairman Arthur C. Martinez, '60, as he tries out the equipment in the fitness center at the dedication of the Wunsch Student Center in 1996.

DR. DAVID C. CHANG

DAVID C. CHANG SERVED AS POLY-technic's ninth president for 1994-2005. He was one of only two Asian American college/university presidents in the United States. During the period immediately preceding Chang's presidency, Dr. Ivan Frisch was appointed provost and served as chief executive. He brought stability to the university as the two-year search for the new president was conducted. During Chang's presidency, Frisch served for another nine years as provost and was the principal architect of the University's strategic plan "In Dreams Begin Responsibilities." At the core of the plan was the realization of new facilities and resources for enhanced student life.

GREATEST-EVER CAPITAL PROGRAM

During Chang's presidency, the University undertook its greatest-ever capital program consisting of two new buildings—the Donald and Mildred Topp Othmer Residence Hall and the Joseph J. and Violet J. Jacobs Academic Building and Athletic Facility—and two major renovations including the restoration/renovation of the Wunsch Student Center Building and Goldsmith Student Activities Union, along with major renovation of laboratories, classrooms, and student space in Rogers Hall, the University's flagship academic building since 1957.

Chang's presidency was characterized by a strong commitment to students. Beginning with a "paint-a-thon" in 1995 to clean and brighten up Rogers Hall and opening the Goldsmith Student Activities Union in 1996, the Chang years showed increasing focus on scholarship support and athletics. The Othmer Residence Hall was the cornerstone of a larger effort to create a vastly enhanced campus life for residential and commuting students alike. The National Survey of Student Engagement of freshmen and seniors showed dramatic improvement between 2001 and 2004 in student satisfaction regarding the quality of facilities and student life, attributable to the capital improvements made and the renewed focus on student needs and expectations.

Art depicting science was added to the campus. The Tobias murals were preserved and redisplayed in the new Jacobs building; the Gasner murals were added to the foyer outside the Dibner auditorium; *Balanced Cylinders*, the landmark display outside the new Jacobs Building, and the Alumni Wall in the entrance lobby of the new Jacobs Building are the most notable.

The strategic decision to relocate undergraduate programs, begun on Long Island in 1974, to the MetroTech campus was made and transitioned over three years to assure adequate opportunities to Long Island students to complete their degrees with minimum disruption. A new graduate center was opened, reaffirming the University's commitment to advanced education for the Long Island corporate community.

These advances were made possible by the extraordinary Othmer gifts and the energizing and successful Fulfilling the American Dream fund-raising campaign described on page 223.

President Howard Golden; Provost Ivan Frisch; and Professor George Schillinger. Before dinner, a special video entitled "Teacher, Engineer, and Visionary" was shown as a noticeably emotional Bugliarello watched.[11]

Before the celebration concluded, Joseph Jacobs presented Bugliarello with an engraved award for his service, while trustee Henry J. Singer unveiled the official portrait of Poly's eighth president. In addition, a book of tribute letters from corporate leaders and public dignitaries, including President George H. W. Bush and Governor George E. Pataki, was presented by trustee Robert D. Dalziel, class of 1956.[12] Bugliarello was later awarded the New York City Mayor's award for Excellence in Science and Technology.

In 2004, Jacobs described his friend, colleague, and fellow scientist. "I was taken with George and wanted to give my support, and so I became reattached to Poly."[13] In fact, this happened over and over. Were it not for Bugliarello's charisma and persuasiveness, notable, influential, and generous alumni like Jacobs might never have turned their attention back toward Polytechnic.

JACOBS COLLEGE OF ENGINEERING ESTABLISHED

In the summer of 1994, during the second annual dinner for Polytechnic's leading benefactors, the Poly 100 Society, Chairman Martinez announced that the Engineering and Science Departments at Polytechnic would be collectively renamed the Joseph J. and Violet J. Jacobs College of Engineering and Science. Preceding this news, the Jacobs family had made another donation to Polytechnic which brought their total pledge to the Institute to over $20 million since 1973. The Jacobs were praised for their extraordinary support of Polytechnic and for demonstrating the true meaning of alumni loyalty.[14]

During the dinner that featured a slide presentation of the Jacobs' countless contributions to Polytechnic, trustee Harry C. Wechsler made the following comments:

Joe is a man who is not afraid to risk failure, even as he pursues and attains success. He is a man who undergoes a repeated process of self-renewal, never losing sight, however, of his inner compass. He is a man eager to assume multiple noble tasks and committing his heart and soul to each and every one of them.[15]

Many alumni took Jacobs' lead in the 1990s by donating funds to Polytechnic. By 1994, the number of contributors spurred the creation of the Poly 1,000 Club. In September, alumni and friends of the Institute gathered in the foyer of the Dibner Library for the dedication of the Poly 1,000 Wall. The wall debuted with 161 inscribed names of alumni who donated $1,000 or more to the Institute.[16]

NEW PROGRAMS, MORE SOLUTIONS

Before Bugliarello stepped down as president, he spent his final year identifying the specific needs of industry and how Polytechnic could best respond to them. His efforts led to a $1,520,000 grant from the Sloan Foundation, enabling Polytechnic to establish the Center for Technology and Financial Services and hire two distinguished faculty members in the area of technology

Trustee R. William Murray, second from right, with members of staff and faculty as they ready their brushes during Paint-A-Thon to beautify the University's interior.

THE CHUDNOVSKY BROTHERS

IN 1997, THE INSTITUTE FOR MATHEMA-
tics and Advanced Supercomputing (IMAS)
was established with Professors David and
Gregory Chudnovsky named as department co-
directors, positions they hold today. The Russian-
born brothers are internationally celebrated mathematicians. Their work was first recognized when
the *New Yorker* ran an article "The Mountains of
Pi" in their March 2, 1992, edition, which highlighted David and Gregory's relentless tracking of
digits that march on to infinity.[1]

With their fundamental contributions to
number theory, computational mathematics,
and mathematical physics, Gregory and David
Chudnovsky previously worked at such renowned
institutions as the Ukrainian Academy of Science
in Kiev, the Ecole Polytechnique, the Institute
des Hautes Etudes Scientifiques in Paris, and
Columbia University in New York City. They
have been the recipients of countless awards
including the Prix Peccot, two Guggenheim
Fellowships, a MacArthur Award, and the 1994
Polya Prize.[2]

In announcing the Chudnovskys' appointment as Distinguished Industry Professors
charged with the responsibility of directing
IMAS, Vice President for Strategic Initiatives

Donald Hockney commented, "The combination
of breadth and depth in their work, and especially their ability to build connections between
pure mathematics and other areas of science and
engineering, is unmatched."[3]

Hockney went on to explain that a unique
aspect of IMAS is its focus on students learning
through participation in ongoing research activities that involve multimedia access to facilities
and seminars.[4]

Later that year, the brothers received another
distinction, but from an unlikely source. They were
listed among *Esquire* magazine's "The 100 Best
People in the World," a feature in which they were
referred to as the "pi guys."

World-renowned mathematicians, Professors David (left)
and Gregory (right) Chudnovsky, are co-directors at
Poly's Institute for Mathematics and Advanced
Supercomputers (IMAS). In the early 1990s, the
Chudnovsky brothers built a supercomputer called
"mzero" that cost an estimated $70,000. In March,
1996, they calculated over 8 billion digits of π on
mzero. The elapsed time on the supercomputer was
roughly one week for calculating and verifying.

and finance: Dr. Andrew Kalotay and Dr. John Marshall. The Center offers a master's of science program in financial engineering. The program was originally offered in Brooklyn, but later expanded to the Long Island campus.[17]

About this time, the Wireless Communications Systems Laboratory was established on the Long Island campus by Professor Frank A. Cassara of the Electrical Engineering Department. The program was made possible by a special grant from the National Science Foundation and with matching funds from Cellular One, Hewlett-Packard, Motorola, and the John Fluke Manufacturing Company. The leading reason for the program was the rapid development of technologies used for wireless information networks such as cellular phones, cordless phones, and pagers.[18]

Henry Bertoni, the former department head of Electrical and Computer Engineering, explained in a recent interview that in order for a student to become a successful engineer, he or she must be willing to embrace a certain style of thought and action.

Engineers are their own breed. They are willing to do things a step at a time; each step done right before going to the next. It's important to get each step right, and you've got to be prepared to accept it. There are only certain people who have the willingness to do this, to accept the hierarchical structure. Engineering also requires teamwork. Each engineer contributes their part to build a product. To create something as large as the cell phone network, many teams must collaborate, each treating a different part of the system.[19]

Although enrollment at the Long Island and Westchester campuses declined into the early nineties, new initiatives were launched. Under the direction of Vice President for Strategic Initiatives Donald Hockney, the Polytechnic Research Institute for Development and Enterprise (PRIDE) was established there in 1995. The program effectively applied cutting-edge technology and skills to real world needs through partnerships and research programs. Professor Ifay Chang, a former manager at the IBM T.J. Watson Research Center, was named executive director.[20]

In 1995, due to its excellent course offerings, Polytechnic University was ranked among the top ten private universities in the nation where 75 percent of the undergraduates commute and at least 40 percent of entering freshman graduate within six years. The annual survey included all private universities, not just those in science and technology fields.[21] This was yet another feather in Poly's cap.

President Chang put forth additional academic initiatives in his first year in office. He called for a new academic structure and merged ten separate departments to create four redesigned departments. Mechanical, Aerospace and Manufacturing Engineering became one department, headed by Professor Sunil Kumar. Chemical Engineering, Chemistry and Materials Science became one department; Applied Mathematics and Physics were combined; and finally, Humanities and Social Sciences united. In addition, a new Academy for Innovation in Education was established, and the Computer Science Department became the Computer and Information Science Department.[22] At the same time, 15 faculty opted for early retirement as the university charted a new academic course.

JOSEPH W. AND SAMUEL WUNSCH STUDENT CENTER BUILDING REOPENS

The 1996 fall semester represented a joyous time for the Polytechnic community—the famed Bridge Street African Wesleyan Methodist Church reopened and was renamed Wunsch Hall, in memory of two distinguished Polytechnic alumni brothers, Joseph Wunsch, class of 1917, and Samuel Wunsch, class of 1929.

The reopening of the student center was the fulfillment of a promise that President Chang had made to students upon arriving at Polytechnic. The building, which had been closed since 1990, had sat forlornly on the edge of the MetroTech Center Commons, surrounded by empty lots.

Through a $1 million bequest of the Wunsch family, including Martin Wunsch, son of Joseph Wunsch, and Elsie Wunsch, wife of Samuel Wunsch, the exterior of the building was renovated. In addition to funds received from the Wunsch family, Joseph Jacobs gave $500,000 toward interior renovations, while William Murray, deputy board chairman, announced that Philip Morris Companies would donate $250,000 to the cause

Elsie Wunsch, wife of Samuel Wunsch '29, center, and Martin Wunsch, the son of Joseph Wunsch '17, third from right, cut the ribbon officially opening the student center.

and creation of the Clifford H. Goldsmith Student Activities Union with the Wunsch Building.[23]

After renovation, the building's three floors housed offices for student clubs and organizations, including the student newspaper and yearbook, and space for students to study and relax. The first floor had a fully equipped fitness gym as well as offices for the athletic department. At a ceremony to celebrate its grand opening, a plaque was unveiled listing alumni and friends of Polytechnic who contributed $1,000 or more to the completion of the building.[24] Around the same time, the president of the student council, Philip Shpilberg, presented Chang with an award during a student awards banquet to thank him for fulfilling his promise.

While popular with a large portion of the student body, the student center was not conveniently located once Nichols Hall was demolished. And with the completion of the new gymnasium and fitness center, use of the building suffered further. In 2004, the building became the home of the Office of Admissions and of the YES Center.

(Since then, the building is slated to become Poly's Hall of Fame, and will be dedicated as such as part of the University's sesquicentennial celebration in the fall of 2005.)

As Polytechnic celebrated the opening of the Wunsch building, it mourned the passing of two of its greatest professors. On November 1, 1996, news spread that Donald F. Othmer had passed away at the age of 91. Othmer, who began teaching at Polytechnic in 1932, became a towering figure in the field of chemical engineering. The following month, a special memorial service was held for the famous educator, inventor, entrepreneur, and author. Chancellor Bugliarello said at the occasion:

How can we today, in a few minutes, even begin to recall all that was great and unique about Don Othmer—about a man greater than life, a man who with his research, his writing, his inventions, and his consulting indelibly impacted the engineering profession and the lives of virtually all of us?[25]

In an interview, Othmer had humorously recalled the beginning of his career at Polytechnic:

I came to work in September 1932, for $2,600 a year, and the Depression deepened that year. Spring of 1933 was a low-point; even professors and heads of departments were leaving involuntarily. I was given a $100 a year cut, but to show it was not meant, I was raised in rank from instructor to assistant professor![26]

Four years later, in 1936, Othmer was named head of the Chemical Engineering Department, a position he held for 24 years, when he became the first Distinguished Professor in Polytechnic's history. After his passing, the *New York Times* wrote of Othmer:

He joined the faculty in 1932, served for many years as department chairman and helped transform the obscure college in Brooklyn into one of the nations' leading technological centers.[27]

While he received countless medals, awards, and patents, Othmer regarded himself an educator first and foremost. Among his students were Dr. Joseph Jacobs, and Dr. Martin L. Perl, who won the 1995 Nobel Prize in Physics. "The reward to the educator lies in his pride in his students' accomplishments," said Othmer. "The richness of that reward is the satisfaction in knowing that the frontiers of knowledge have been expanded."[28]

The following February, President Emeritus Ernst Weber died at the age of 94. Weber, an immigrant from Vienna, began his career in 1930 when he accepted an invitation to become a visiting professor. This marked a long, celebrated career with Polytechnic, including the birth of the Microwave Research Institute, which he founded in 1943, and his appointment as Poly's sixth president, a position he held from 1957 to 1969.

He held over 30 patents in microwave technology and was the author of scores of scientific papers and two books, including *The Evolution of Electrical Engineering—A Personal Perspective*.[29]

ALUMNI MAKING THEIR MARK

The year 1996 proved to be one of great achievement for Polytechnic alumni. Alumnus S. Steve Greenfield, class of 1943, received the Distinguished Alumnus Award. Upon graduating from Polytechnic, Greenfield began a four-decade career at the world's largest engineering firm, Parsons Brinckerhoff. In the 1950s, Greenfield directed the development of the first state-of-the-art hardened underground defense facility at Fort Richie, Maryland. With achievements like these, he quickly rose in the company ranks, eventually serving as Parsons Brinckerhoff's chairman for 14 years.

Among his many accomplishments as an engineer, Greenfield worked diligently toward developing safe, comfortable, and efficient transportation solutions. A ventilation system he designed for San Francisco's Bay Area Rapid Transit (BART) became a model for public transportation systems across the country. Greenfield's transportation model is now the basis for a reference manual used industry-wide.[30]

POLY GRADUATE AWARDED 1995 NOBEL PRIZE IN PHYSICS

WHEN DR. MARTIN L. PERL, CLASS OF 1948, was contacted by an inquisitive *Associated Press* reporter asking him for his reactions to winning the 1995 Nobel Prize in Physics, he was shocked. "I thought that someone had made a mistake," Perl told the *Polytechnic Cable* in 1995. "I still can't believe it."[1]

It certainly wasn't a mistake. Rather, Perl was recognized for the discovery of one of the smallest constituents of the universe, a subatomic particle known as the tau lepton. The tau lepton is a super-heavy cousin of the electron, also a lepton and the

carrier of electrical current in household appliances, and everything else. The two particles are identical in all respects except that the tau lepton is more than 3,500 times heavier than the electron and survives for only a trillionth of a second, while the electron is stable. This was such a remarkable discovery that in 1982, Perl received the Wolf Prize in Physics.[2]

Dr. Martin L. Perl, class of 1948, H'96, was co-recipient of the 1995 Nobel Prize in Physics for discovering the tau lepton.

S. Steve Greenfield, class of 1943, received the Distinguished Alumnus Award in 1996.

In addition to alumni who distinguished themselves in the world of science and engineering, many of Polytechnic's 20th century graduates were achieving notable success in the world of business. This was the case when alumnus John M. Trani, class of 1966, and '69, was named chairman and CEO of Stanley Works Company Corporation. The previous year, Corporation Chairman Martinez was named *Financial World* magazine's CEO of the Year. The magazine said Martinez was "a role model for virtually every retailer in this country."[31]

That so many Poly alumni were able to achieve such remarkable success in life was due in part to the exceptional education they received at Polytechnic. The reshaping of the curriculum to meet the needs of the day was a practice that harkened back to the inception of the University. In 1996, this

A Brooklyn native, Perl was born to immigrant parents and was the first person in his family to attend college. After earning his undergraduate degree from Polytechnic, he received his PhD in Physics from Columbia University in 1955. He began teaching at the Stanford Linear Accelerator Center in 1963, a unit of Stanford University. He later was appointed chairman of that faculty. Perl has authored over 250 papers and four books. After receiving the Nobel Prize, Perl recalled the importance of his education at Polytechnic:

The skills and knowledge I acquired at the Polytechnic Institute have been crucial in all my experimental work: the use of strength of materials principles in equipment design, machine shop practice, engineering drawing, practical fluid mechanics, inorganic and organic chemistry, chemical laboratory techniques, manufacturing processes, metallurgy, basic concepts in mechanical engineering, basic concepts in electrical engineering, dimensional analysis, speed

and power in mental arithmetic, numerical estimation—crucial when depending on a slide rule for calculations—and much more.[3]

President Chang made the following comments after receiving the news of Perl's award. "The entire Polytechnic community takes great pride in knowing that one of its own has again achieved this world-renowned recognition. His story is such an inspiring one to our students, since so many share the same experience."[4]

When asked what possible benefits his discovery will have on science and society, Perl responded:

The use of the discovery of basic particles is indirect. We have found that everything of a complicated nature is made from three basic families of particles. Eventually, this will lead to an improved understanding of energy and time. From that we hope will come new ideas that lead to applications like a source of cheap energy which is truly safe.[5]

practice would be implemented in numerous new areas, including the establishment of the Institute for Technology and Enterprise.

Professor Mel Horwitch, currently on sabbatical, was instrumental in launching this new entity. In 2004, Horwitch explained the reason he, and the administration, championed this program.

Education is teaching people to ask the right questions. The actual substance may become obsolete, but if you ask the right questions, the half-life will be a lot longer. Poly is an incredible institute. It's urban. It's gritty. The faculty is outstanding and committed to their students. It's an asset for New York City, and Poly has educated generations of students in the area of technology, engineering in particular.

I think that it serves a market that is very different generally than MIT and Harvard. The market is comprised of people who feel the need to remain in New York City. Poly has served this market in superb fashion. Poly graduates have gone out and been very, very successful, starting their own companies and working for [professionally-oriented] companies.

Poly needs to continue to adapt to serve that market in my view. To do this, it's moving away from simple engineering and science to technology management and innovation management.

The notion of the Institute is to do things that are transformational in nature, that have a profound impact on the University, and that are going to improve the University. This is a faculty-driven activity.[32]

FULFILLING THE AMERICAN DREAM

In 1997 Polytechnic launched its most ambitious fundraising campaign to date: "Fulfilling the American Dream." This slogan was borrowed from alumnus and Pulitzer Prize-winning author

Board Chairman Arthur C. Martinez '60, addresses the audience during the launch of the Campaign for Polytechnic—Fulfilling the American Dream in 1997. The campaign successfully raised $275 million upon its completion in June 2001.

Every fall, faculty, alumni, and students join together for the annual phone drive, which dates back to the 1950s. The money raised benefits various programs, including the YES Center. In this picture, a group of Poly students take a break from the fundraiser to show their school spirit.

James Truslow Adams. The goal of the campaign was to raise $150 million. While Polytechnic benefited over the years from gifts, bequests, phone drives, and events like the Promise Fund, it never had an endowment that exceeded $15 million, which made the goal of this capital campaign truly a breathtaking one.

Money to be raised was earmarked for many bold initiatives. The first phase would include the modernization of the Brooklyn campus to include a dormitory tower to house 400 students. This marked the first time in Polytechnic's history that official campus housing would be offered in Brooklyn. The original tower plans also included space for a new cafeteria and a sports center. The next phase of development would focus on additions to Rogers Hall, including new classrooms and laboratories.[33]

The funds were allocated in four categories: $53 million for capital building and renovation projects; $70 million for endowments to support and sustain students, faculty, and infrastructure; $12 million to launch new learning initiatives and buy new equipment; and $15 million to fund innovative projects.

With the majority of the money funneled toward supporting students, Chairman Martinez said that many students would receive assistance to fulfill their educational dreams. This was important to Martinez since he was the first person in his family to receive a college degree. During a recent interview, he commented on the importance of this aid.

POLY GRADUATE SPACE BOUND

ADDING TO THE LONG LIST OF POLY firsts is alumnus Charles J. Camarda who in 1996 was one of 35 (out of 2,400 applicants) selected by NASA for astronaut training as a mission specialist.

In 1974, Camarda graduated from Polytechnic with a Bachelor of Science degree in Aerospace Engineering. Upon completing his degree, he began working at NASA's Langley Research Center, in Hampton, Virginia, where he conducted research in the Thermal Structures Branch of the Structures and Materials Division.

During an interview for the *Polytechnic Cable* in 1996, Camarda commented on the preparation he received while studying at Polytechnic Institute of New York. "Poly's structures and fluids programs were very good and they were a very helpful preparation for my graduate work."[1]

While at the Langley Research Center, Camarda's research responsibilities included demonstrating the feasibility of a heat-pipe-cooled leading edge for the space shuttle by analysis, laboratory experiments, and aerothermal testing in Langley's 8-foot High Temperature Tunnel. He also conducted analytical and experimental research concerning heat pipes, structural mechanics and dynamics, heat transfer, and numerical optimization for aircraft, spacecraft, and space launch vehicles.[2]

Aside from his research responsibilities at Langley, Camarda earned his Master's degree from George Washington University in Engineering Science with emphasis on mechanics of composite structures at elevated temperature. He received his PhD from Virginia Polytechnic Institute and State University with emphasis on the development of advanced modal methods for efficiently predicting transient thermal and structural performance. These additional degrees and experience furthered his chances for space exploration.[3]

In 1989, Camarda was selected to lead the Structures and Materials Technology Maturation Team for the National Aero-Space Plane (NASP) program, which was involved in the development of an airbreathing, hypersonic vehicle capable of horizontal take-off to orbit.

Camarda was then selected to head the Thermal Structures Branch (TSB) in 1994 with responsibility for a research engineering staff, two major focused programs (the high-speed research (HSR) and reusable launch vehicle (RLV) programs), and several structural test facilities including the Thermal Structures Laboratory.

Some of the primary responsibilities of the TSB are developing durable, lightweight metallic thermal protection systems, hypersonic vehicles using carbon material and heat pipes, reusable cryogenic tank systems, and graphite-composite primary structures for RLVs.

Since graduating from Poly, Camarda, who holds seven patents, has received over 21 NASA awards for technical innovations and accomplishments. He also received the Research and Development 100 Award from *Industrial Research* magazine for one of the top 100 technical innovations of 1983 entitled "Heat-Pipe-Cooled Sandwich Panel."

Camarda continued a long-standing relationship that has existed between Polytechnic, NASA, and the U.S. government. A year after Camarda was selected for space travel, Polytechnic announced that it joined the NASA/New York Space Consortium, which provides

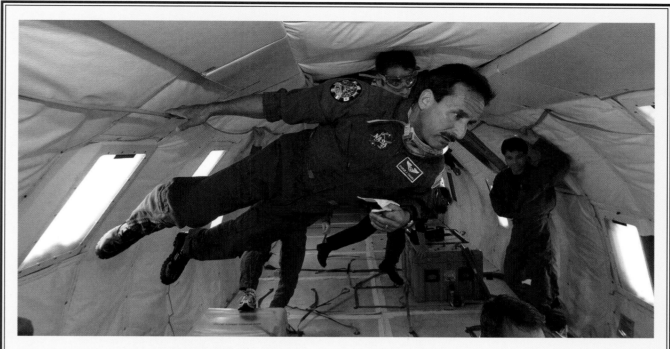

Poly graduate-turned-astronaut Mission Specialist Charles J. Camarda (opposite and above) participates in microgravity training aboard NASA's KC-135 aircraft, known as the "Vomit Comet." The aircraft flew a series of parabolic maneuvers, or steep ascents and descents, to simulate weightlessness for astronauts as they prepared for the space shuttle's return to space aboard *Discovery* (below) following the Columbia disaster. *(Photos this page and opposite courtesy of NASA.)*

grants to help students participate in research relevant to NASA missions.

Camarda was part of the space shuttle *Discovery*'s seven-person crew for Mission STS-114, which was successfully launched into space on July 26, 2005. This was the first launch since the *Columbia* disaster on February 1, 2003. He and his six crew members flew to the International Space Station to test new safety procedures and to service the orbital outpost on what was eventually a 14-day, 5.8-million-mile mission.

In a recent interview with journalist Nick Greene, Camarda reflected on the *Columbia* tragedy and his space shuttle mission:

> *I really do not believe I have changed since the* Columbia *tragedy. I have always been a dissenting opinion out there, asking questions, asking tough questions. I'm basically an engineer at heart, and so when I see a technical problem, I try to solve it. I think that's important. I've always been aware of the risks. I think every one of us understands that space flight is risky. We feel, and I feel, it's important that we take those risks for the future of space, and for the future of the development of technology to help us on the planet Earth.*[4]

THE KING OF PATENTS

PERHAPS ONE OF POLY'S most fertile minds was alumnus Jerome Lemelson who averaged more than one patent a month for more than 40 years—all of which he accomplished without support from established research institutions or corporate research and development departments. Covering a wide range of inventions, including the camcorder, VCR, magnetic tape drive mechanism used in Sony's Walkman, facsimile transmission, automatic warehousing, flexible manufacturing systems, and many popular toys, including the Hot Wheels car track, Lemelson's patent total exceeded 550, the fourth largest in American history.[1] Lemelson was awarded his first patent in 1953 for a toy cap, a variation of the propeller beanie.

However, invention often involves legal confrontation. Lemelson dealt with countless cases of patent infringement, which ultimately led to his crusade to defend the rights of independent inventors against corporate giants. After conceiving an idea for a cut-out face mask on the back of a cereal box,

---

A Poly degree means a lot to them, just as it did to me. And now we owe it to these students—and tomorrow's students—to guarantee that the Polytechnic University of the future assures them an education in science and engineering that is second to none anywhere in the world.[34]

William Murray, former chairman of the Philip Morris Company, and current Corporation trustee, was named the campaign chairman. In a recent interview, Murray, who is credited with the success of the campaign, recalled that while the amount of money to be raised was considerable, he felt secure with the guidance provided by Polytechnic's administration:

I think the main thing I had was good support from the staff. People like Richard Thorsen and David Chang were really exceptional. David is a very outgoing person. He's great at fundraising. He accepts it as the major part of his job. Richard was also very helpful to me in running the campaign. We did have a pretty clear plan to do it, and we identified the various sources of the money we hoped to raise. These were foundations, the

Board of Trustees itself, alumni, friends of the college, and corporate sources.[35]

As the administration and The Corporation continued to develop plans for Polytechnic's future, the University stayed with its "business as usual" approach to education. In June 1997, during the commencement ceremony held at Lincoln Center's Avery Fisher Hall, Polytechnic awarded degrees to 1,019 scientists and engineers—600 master of science degrees, 350 bachelor of science degrees, 67 doctoral degrees, and two degrees as engineer.[36]

At the 142nd commencement ceremony in 1998, Robert B. Catell, chairmen and CEO of Brooklyn Union Gas, Polytechnic's anchor partner at Metro-Tech, received an honorary doctor of engineering degree. During Catell's commencement speech, he encouraged the eager graduates to attain their dreams as they entered professional life.

To be an engineer, to me, is to be intimately connected to the modern world, the world of progress, the world in which things can be done that were not imaginable for all but the tiniest portion of human history.[37]

he filed for a patent and then took the concept to a major cereal manufacturer. The company rejected his idea. Roughly three years later the same company began packaging its cereal boxes with a mask on the back. Lemelson filed suit but the case was dismissed from court and dismissed again on an appeal. It was the first of nearly 20 courtroom battles he would face. He lost more than he had won.[2]

In his philanthropy, as in his professional work, Lemelson was devoted to invention. In the 1990s, he and his wife Dorothy established the Lemelson Foundation to fund new programs that promote invention and entrepreneurship. The Lemelson-MIT Prize Program at the Massachusetts Institute of Technology (MIT) was established. Each year the program gives out several awards, including the $500,000 Lemelson-MIT Prize, presented to an outstanding American inventor-innovator. Lemelson also donated money to create the Lemelson National

Program in Invention at Hampshire College in Massachusetts and at the University of Nevada, Reno. Another important legacy is the Lemelson Center for the Study of Invention and Innovation, created through a $10 million gift to the Smithsonian Institution's National Museum of American History.

In 1996, Lemelson was diagnosed with liver cancer, and not surprisingly he fought it the best way he knew how, by inventing improvements to medical devices and cancer treatment methodologies. He submitted nearly 40 patent applications during the last year of his life. He passed away on October 1, 1997, at the age of 74.

In 2000, his widow Dorothy established a $1 million Lemelson Scholarship Program at Polytechnic, where her husband received his undergraduate degree in 1947, his master's in 1949, and was the recipient of an honorary doctorate degree in 1995.

Within months of launching the Campaign for Polytechnic, $70 million had been committed by alumni and friends of Polytechnic. Among those who contributed was trustee Leonard Shustek, class of 1970, director of Network Associates Inc., who pledged $1.8 million. A $1 million gift was received from trustee David Dibner, retired chairman of Burndy Corporation. A $1 million fellowship gift was received from trustee Robert H. C. Tsao, who received an honorary degree in 1997, and was at that time chairman of United Microelectronics Corporation. In addition, a $1 million scholarship gift was given by Dorothy Lemelson, widow of the distinguished and prolific inventor and alumnus Jerome Lemelson. This was followed by a $785,000 donation by trustee Paul Soros, and unrestricted gifts in excess of $1.4 million were donated by Michael R. Corey.[38]

While this outpouring of support was overwhelming, no one could have imagined the news that appeared on the front page of the July 13, 1998, *New York Times*. The story announced that the Othmers had left a staggering estate of $750 million, and Polytechnic would receive the largest portion of their philanthropy, an estimated $175

million. This action marked the largest private cash gift ever given to a university in the United States.[39]

Due to the overwhelming Othmer gifts and the fact that Polytechnic was more than halfway to reaching its $150 million goal (which included $50 million from Donald Othmer) for "Fulfilling the American Dream," President Chang announced that the campaign would be enlarged to $275 million.

President Chang detailed his vision for Polytechnic's future in his 1998 President's Report:

The Othmers' gift and the campaign will make our aspirations a reality and provide the wherewithal to transform Poly. As part of the transformation, we intend to excel in selected disciplines that will be crucial for success in the 21st Century and that will be unique to Polytechnic and its special urban environment. Now, the challenge is to define our vision and implement it.[40]

Stewart Nagler, current chairman of The Corporation, class of 1963, and vice chairman and chief financial officer for MetLife, recalled in an interview last year that receiving the bequest was wonderful, but also represented a tremendous responsibility:

Pictured left to right: Casimir S. Skrzypczak, president, NYNEX Science and Technology Inc., and chairman of the Westchester Advisory Board; State Senator Suzie Oppenheimer; and President Chang. Working with the research and development division of NYNEX Science and Technology, Poly's CATT researchers developed a prototype, the Data Network Management and Optimization Tool (DATANMOT) which was used by NYNEX for its traffic planning. The prototype includes a generic model for the simulation and analysis of different network services and architectures. This system can be used for traffic planning for frame relay and asynchronous transfer mode-based services.

I would say certainly there was exhilaration in getting that kind of money, but at the same time, a real sense of responsibility to make sure that the money was used wisely. You get the money, but you know you have to preserve it for future generations and use it wisely.

We felt wonderful. There's no other way to say it, but it also highlighted the number of things that we needed to do. Of course, even with that amount of money, we couldn't do all the things that we needed to do.[41]

In order to make sure the money was well spent, Polytechnic launched a strategic planning program, known as "Strategic Planning 2000," to formulate the goals and objectives that would propel the school successfully into the 21st Century. The planning process was led by Professor Ivan Frisch. In addition, the Othmer Recognition Committee was launched to work in conjunction with Frisch's committee to aid in decision-making.[42]

The following year, IEEE selected Frisch as corecipient of its 1999 Eric E. Sumner Award for outstanding contributions to communication technology, specifically for innovative contributions to the modeling and design of communications networks.

In 1969, Frisch had co-founded the Network Analysis Corporation (NAC), which became the largest U.S. company devoted to telecommunications consulting before it was acquired by Contel in 1980. While at NAC, Frisch assisted in the design of ARPANET, the predecessor of the modern day Internet, and of the NASDAQ system, which automated the over-the-counter stock market.[43]

With millions of dollars on the table and Polytechnic's future full of new possibilities, President Chang announced in 1998 that Gregory Smith would become the new vice president of finance and administration.

Smith, a 35-year veteran as a planner and policy-maker in government and education, came to Poly from Manhattan's New School for Social Research, where he spent 14 years. He was instrumental in guiding the New School from a part-time non-credit and graduate student institution into a full-time undergraduate institution. Smith was excited about the new opportunity.

I see my challenge—really my opportunities—as helping President Chang, the board of trustees, the faculty—all constituents of Poly—devise strategies and tactics to take advantage of this opportune moment in Polytechnic's history, led by a relatively new president and inspired by a recently announced campaign.[44]

Smith and Frisch were in good company as the news came down the pike that Chairman Martinez was awarded the National Retailer Federation's 1998 Gold Medal Award for his masterful turnaround of the Sears Corporation. The award committee stated, "Federation officials bestowed this prestigious award on Martinez for his pioneering vision in the revitalization of Sears and his willingness to restore and reinvent business, pulling off what many consider to be the most stunning recovery in retail history."[45]

BROOKLYN AND POLY EXPAND

Thanks to MetroTech, more new corporations and businesses began to call the district home, and more people began moving to the area. The Brooklyn economy grew in proportion. Among new businesses created as result was the Marriott Hotel, built adjacent to MetroTech Center and completed in 1998.

The Marriott was the first hotel built in Brooklyn in more than 50 years. The 376-room hotel doubled as a convention center. This idea, originally conceived 20 years earlier by Bugliarello, finally came to fruition. Polytechnic now sat within the MetroTech Center, the largest urban university-corporate park in the United States and home to several technology-dependent companies, including KeySpan Energy, and Bear Stearns and Company. With dot.com startups driving the economy to new heights, Polytechnic, its alumni, and affiliated business partners were reaching new levels of success.

Also in 1998, the Department of Management and its Institute for Technology and Enterprise (ITE) relocated its executive master's programs to 55 Broad Street, in the heart of Manhattan's high-tech financial district, also known as "Silicon Alley." This name was based on California's famous Silicon Valley, which was developed, in part, by alumnus Eugene E. Kleiner, the brilliant high tech entrepreneur and venture capitalist. In the 1950s, Kleiner helped lay the groundwork for one of Silicon Valley's seminal companies, Fairchild Semiconductor, that revolutionized the computer industry.

As academic departments and programs grew, so did athletics at Poly. In 1998, Polytechnic established a track-and-field club, and for the first time in over 25 years, the Blue Jays participated

in an intercollegiate event at Ramapo College in New Jersey. Another athletic first for Poly occurred when the Blue Jays held the distinction of being the first team to play on the New Jersey Nets court, when they faced off against Savannah College. A few years later, MetroTech developer Bruce Ratner bought the New Jersey Nets with plans to move them to Brooklyn.

JACOBS GIVES $20 MILLION TO POLY

On the heels of the Othmer bequest, Joseph and Violet Jacobs announced they would give a $20 million dollar gift—including a $10 million challenge gift—to Polytechnic University. This gift and its matches were earmarked for capital projects and were counted toward the Campaign for Polytechnic, which in 1999 had raised $227 million toward its $275 million goal.[46] After making the bequest, Jacobs said:

The extraordinary gift to Polytechnic from my mentor and friend, Donald Othmer, and his wife,

Polytechnic University offers its students a superb educational experience that is comprised of demanding courses taught by some of America's most respected instructors. But success for students does not come cheap. It depends on long hours of focused and disciplined study.

EUGENE KLEINER

SILICON VALLEY PIONEER AND POLY-technic graduate Eugene Kleiner played a pivotal role in building Silicon Valley, first as a scientist, then as an entrepreneur and venture capitalist. Kleiner, who received his undergraduate degree from Poly in 1948, his master's in 1951, and an honorary degree in 1989, revolutionized the computer industry and helped the U.S. win the space race.

After receiving his master's from Poly, Kleiner, a native Austrian who fled Europe before World War II, settled in California. He and seven other East Coast scientists were recruited by Nobel Prize winner William Shockley to help build computer transistors. Shockley's recruits eventually rebelled and left their startup to form their own company. The men were tagged with the nickname "The Traitorous Eight."[1]

While considered traitors in Shockley's eyes, the men are hailed as Silicon Valley's founding fathers. Besides Kleiner, the group included Intel Corporation co-founders Robert Noyce and Gordon Moore (famous for Moore's Law concerning an exponential growth in the number of transistors per integrated circuit), along with Julius Blank, Victor Grinich, Jean Hoerni, Jay Last, and Sheldon Roberts.[2]

Using $3,500 of their own money, the eight entrepreneurs developed a way to manufacture multiple transistors on a single silicon wafer. The breakthrough enabled the men to raise $1.5 million from Fairchild Camera and Instrument Corp., and launch Fairchild Semiconductor in October 1957. Within six months, Fairchild Semiconductor was profitable.[3] The company revolutionized the chip industry and became the entrepreneurial breeding ground that hatched several other groundbreaking companies, including Silicon Valley bellwethers Intel Corp., National Semiconductor, and Advanced Micro Devices.[4]

Known as the father of venture capitalism, Kleiner, a man who shunned the limelight, was also known for coining what became some very well-traveled phrases, including "The time to

Opposite: "Father of venture capitalism," and Fairchild Semiconductor co-founder, alumnus Eugene Kleiner, far right, sits by a mock-up of a 33-cent stamp with three fellow Fairchild members. From left, Jay Last, C. Sheldon Roberts, and Julius Blank. Fairchild Semiconductor's accomplishments were recognized in 1999 when the U.S. Postal Service issued a commemorative stamp featuring the company's integrated circuits.

Left: Eugene Kleiner (1923-2003), class of 1948, '51, H'89.

eat the hors d'oeuvres is when they're being passed round." This was later adapted, by himself or others, to "When the hors d'oeuvres are passing, take two."

Kleiner later reconnected with Noyce and Moore to become an early investor in Santa Clara-based Intel, now one of the most world's most valuable companies with a market value of about $220 billion. In 1972, Kleiner joined forces with Tom Perkins to form their own venture capital firm, Kleiner, Perkins, Caufield and Byers, which has gone on to invest in more than 300 companies, including Amazon.com, America Online, Sun Microsystems, Tandem Computers, and Compaq Computer.[5]

Although he remained a partner emeritus at Kleiner, Perkins, Caufield and Byers until his death in 2003, Kleiner stepped down from a day-to-day role at the firm in the mid-1980s. After his death, his former company issued a short statement hailing its co-founder as a visionary who "virtually invented modern venture capital."[6]

In 1999, the U.S. Postal Service issued a commemorative stamp in honor of Fairchild Semiconductor. A trustee of Polytechnic, Kleiner received an Outstanding Alumnus of the Century Award in 1999, during the University's 100th anniversary celebration of mechanical engineering at Polytechnic.

Mildred, secures the financial future of the University and provides a seedbed for us to go forward, knowing that future gifts to Polytechnic will flourish.

Now, our greatest need is to complete the $275 million Campaign for Polytechnic, which will enable us to undertake essential building projects that will position Poly as a leader among U.S. technological universities. I want to lead that effort and encourage others to come forward with gifts for capital projects. There is no better time than now to invest in Poly.[47]

With bequests from two alumni totaling nearly $200 million, other alumni reached for their checkbooks. Among the many who pledged after Jacobs' matching gift was announced was Jasper H. Kane. While Kane initially gifted $1 million to the Campaign for Polytechnic in 1997, he again pledged $1 million in 1999 after hearing Jacobs' rallying call. "The Jacobs Challenge creates an especially opportune time to further support Poly," Kane, then retired, said from his Florida home. "Now, my gift can be so

Brooklyn's famed Bridge Street African Wesleyan Methodist Episcopal Church reopened and was renamed Wunsch Hall, in memory of two distinguished Polytechnic alumni brothers, Joseph Wunsch, class of 1917, and Samuel Wunsch, class of 1929. The Wunsch family donated $1 million to the restoration effort.

much more important, building upon the Othmer gift and being matched by Dr. Jacobs' exciting challenge. I'm thrilled to be part of the historic transformation now occurring at Poly."[48]

LOOKING TOWARD THE MILLENNIUM

With the new millennium approaching and Y2K hysteria reaching a fever pitch, Polytechnic continued on its path of excellence. In 1999, Polytechnic and the Technion-Israel Institute of Technology in Haifa, Israel, began a student exchange program. The two technological universities agreed to allow as many as 15 undergraduate and graduate students from each school to transfer to the other institution.

Polytechnic also received a $2.6 million federal grant in 1999 to develop a practical means for environmental bioagent detection. By agreeing to this research contract, Poly took a leadership role in fighting the threat of bio-terrorism in conjunction with the U.S. Defense Advanced Research Projects Agency (DARPA). The four-year grant was awarded to the Department of Chemical Engineering, Chemistry and Materials Science to develop special polymers and plastics that could help detect deadly microorganisms such as anthrax.

Professor Kalle Levon, director of the Polymer Research Institute and professor in the Department of Chemical and Biological Sciences and Engineering, said of the program:

Germ warfare is a major environmental and national threat. Poly is part of a high-level effort to detect deadly agents before they cause serious damage. This is a great honor for Polytechnic. Our research will contribute to national security and push the boundaries of materials science.[49]

In two short years, after the devastating events of September 11, results from this research would greatly aid federal law enforcement agencies in investigating the anthrax deaths and threats of 2001.

As the year 1999 drew to a close, The Center for Technology in Supply Chains and Merchandising was established under the leadership of Bugliarello

In 1999, the Center for Technology in Supply Chains and Merchandising was established under the leadership of Chancellor Bugliarello and Professor George Schillinger (pictured here).

and Professor George Schillinger. This was yet another signal that Polytechnic was not resting on the laurels of the Othmer bequest, or its acclaimed history, but rather was pushing the envelope, seeking new heights of technological success and achievement.

Since the launch of the Campaign for Polytechnic, over $240 million had been raised. This set the stage for new buildings, academic initiatives, and pioneering research activities. Seemingly with each passing month, Polytechnic received sizable bequests. This was the case in 1999 when Edward Nadro Jr., class of 1933, a retired senior research engineer with Mobil Oil Corporation, bequeathed his entire estate of $1.9 million to Polytechnic.

Actions like these, taken by the Othmers and the Jacobs, by Kane, by the Lemelsons, by Soros, by Nadro, by Corey, and by many others, not only laid the foundation for the future success of Polytechnic, but stood as a reminder that Poly alumni and professors never forgot Poly.

Indeed, as one generation of Poly graduates passed on, their accomplishments and generous financial gifts continued to set the stage for additional success as the University approached its 150th anniversary.

In 2001, Polytechnic University became one of the first universities in the New York metropolitan area to require freshmen to use notebook computers for their courses. Pictured here are two students on the Brooklyn Campus taking advantage of the advanced wireless capabilities at Polytechnic University.

CHAPTER ELEVEN

THE FUTURE IS BRIGHT
2000 – PRESENT

Today's celebration is the first physical manifestation of a transformation we have started at Poly—an emergence into a premier university that will educate and support the leaders of tomorrow in a world that is increasingly driven by technology.

—President David Chang, Groundbreaking Ceremony for the
Joseph J. and Violet J. Jacobs Building, May 18, 2000

AFTER EXPERIENCING A MOMENtous period of growth and prosperity in the 1990s, Polytechnic University entered the new millennium backed by an exemplary history of scientific and educational achievement. The Y2K threat, which gained significant steam worldwide in the years, months, and days approaching the millennium celebration, amounted to nothing more than a technological hiccup.

The year 2000 kicked off with Professor Yao Wang receiving the New York City Mayor's Award for Excellence in Science and Technology, and Provost and Executive Vice President Ivan Frisch being elected to the National Academy of Engineering. These honors were proof that Polytechnic's professors were carrying the scientific baton passed from Poly pioneers such as Herman Mark, Ernst Weber, Joseph Jacobs, Antonio Ferri, Gordon Gould, and Donald Othmer.

During this exciting and fruitful period, Poly benefited from the guidance of President Chang, who supported The Corporation's selection of Stewart G. Nagler as its chairman. A trustee since 1989 and former chairman of The Corporation's Finance Committee, Nagler, retired CFO and vice chairman of Metropolitan Life Insurance Company, succeeded Arthur Martinez in 2000.

As the 2000-2001 school year commenced, the current fundraising campaign for Polytechnic—Fulfilling the American Dream—was nearly complete with over $250 million of its stated goal of $275 million having been collected. Strategic Planning 2000, an offshoot of the campaign led by a group of professors, administrators, and benefactors charged with overseeing Poly's development, was also in full swing.

New initiatives established for the first five years of the millennium included investing $100 million for a new academic building, athletic facility, and construction of the downtown campus' first dormitory. An additional $25 million was earmarked for major renovations of Rogers Hall.[1]

In 2002, five murals by the late artist Mordi Gassner that interpret the sciences of physics, geology, astronomy, chemistry, and biology were donated by Gassner's only daughter, Judith Schlosser, and her husband, David. While Gassner, who died in 1995, was not an alumnus, he was Bern Dibner's close friend. The 6-foot by 9-foot murals, (one is pictured here), were painted between 1929 and 1931 in Italy with the assistance of two Guggenheim Foundation Fellowships. In the 1930s, the murals were exhibited at the Brooklyn Museum of Art. Today, the murals are permanently on display in the foyer of the Dibner/CATT building.

Above: Donald and Mildred Othmer's gift of $175 million to Polytechnic was the largest cash donation ever received from an individual donor, or in this case, donor couple, by any university. Shown here are the Othmers on their wedding day.

Right: In 2000, Trustee David Dibner (son of Bern Dibner) announced two gifts to Polytechnic: $375,000 to the University's Bern Dibner Library for Science and Technology, and $1,000,000 to the Campaign for Polytechnic—Fulfilling the American Dream. Later, the Dibner Family Chair in the History and Philosophy of Technology and Science was established.

When the Campaign for Polytechnic was launched in 1997, the university faced the old familiar challenge of raising significant funds to propel it into the future. Aside from the generous bequests received from the Othmer and Jacobs families, the challenge was also being met by countless alumni and benefactors who quickly came to Poly's aid, checkbooks in hand.

This pattern of supporting Poly continued in 2000 when alumnus Dr. Peter P. Regna bequeathed $1.5 million to establish a Laboratory for Biomacromolecular Engineering, the research arm of Polytechnic's Center for Biocatalysis and Biopro-

cessing of Macromolecules. A fellow alumnus and Corporation trustee, Jerome Swartz, co-founder and former chairman of Symbol Technologies Inc., also donated $2 million to fund a series of programs at Polytechnic, including biotechnology, wireless communication, manufacturing engineering, technology in merchandising, and computational electromagnetics.

Members of The Corporation also demonstrated their generosity. Trustee David Dibner donated $375,000 to the Bern Dibner Library for Science and Technology, continuing the tradition of his father's philanthropy. In a separate gift, Dibner gave $100,000 to the Campaign for Polytechnic, which was matched by Joseph Jacobs.[2]

ADVANCEMENTS IN EDUCATION

On January 18, 2001, Polytechnic and SUNY Downstate Medical Center signed an agreement fostering biotech research and education at Poly's Brooklyn campus. This expansion in course offerings was established to answer the call for educated professionals in the field of biotechnology. Today,

FULFILLING THE AMERICAN DREAM

IN THE EARLY 20TH CENTURY, JAMES Truslow Adams, a Poly alumnus from the class of 1898, coined the phrase, now universally recognized, "The American Dream." Throughout most of the 20th century and as we celebrate our 150th anniversary, Poly has encouraged and nurtured the dreams of tens of thousands. It has had as its informal mission, fulfilling the "American Dream."

This mission requires financial resources for student scholarships and fellowships, recruiting and retaining the best faculty and superior facilities. This was recognized by David Chang, and the board of trustees who appointed him as Poly's ninth president. The "Fulfilling the American Dream" campaign was conceived to provide the resources to enable Polytechnic to continue this noble mission. The campaign was the largest and first comprehensive campaign in Poly's history. Under the leadership of Trustee and Campaign Chairman R. William Murray, President David C. Chang and Vice President for Development and University Relations Richard S. Thorsen, the campaign goal was reached on time. The original goal of $150 million was raised to $275 million when it was learned that the Othmer gift would provide an unexpected additional $125 million.

Numerous other individuals were also instrumental in the success of the campaign, including Joseph J. Jacobs ('37, '39, '42), honorary campaign chairman and major benefactor; Arthur C. Martinez '60, chairman of the board until 2000 and Stewart G. Nagler, chairman of the board during the final year of the campaign.

LARGEST CASH GIFT EVER FOR A UNIVERSITY

The gift of $175 million from Professor Donald F. and Mildred Topp Othmer was the largest cash gift ever received from an individual or couple by any university. A few years later MIT announced a larger gift, but it is being paid over a twenty-year period with a value under $150 million at the time of the gift. RPI also announced a larger gift, but if the name of the donor or circumstances of the gift are revealed it can be revoked. Thus the Othmer gift remains the largest irrevocable cash gift ever received.

A total of 9,075 individual donors contributed to the campaign and the primary uses were for endowment, a new residence hall, a new academic building, scholarships, faculty development, new program development and laboratory renovations and additions. A memento of the campaign is permanently on display in the lobby of the Jacobs Academic Building. It has the names of the contributors and is in the likeness of the campaign symbol, Liberty's Torch.

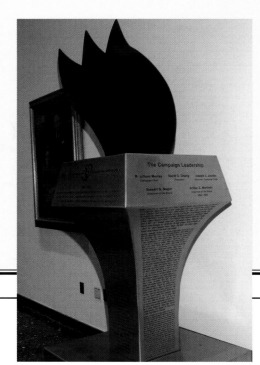

"Liberty's Torch" was the symbol for the highly successful "Fulfilling the American Dream" fundraising campaign.

President David Chang and then Brooklyn Borough President Howard Golden pose in front the Othmer Residence Hall while it was still under construction.

SUNY's School of Graduate Studies provides the biomedical component of Poly's successful and popular Master of Pcience program in Biomedical Engineering.[3]

The joint agreement between Polytechnic and SUNY Downstate was developed, in part, to encourage venture capitalists to create new businesses and jobs in Brooklyn. It was spearheaded by Bill McShane, vice president and dean of Applied Science and Engineering, and Richard Gross, Herman F. Mark Professor of Polymer Science. As a result, new research initiatives in the following fields were created: biomedical optics, neuro-robotics, computational neuroscience, tissue engineering, regulation of the immune system, and molecular drug targeting and delivery.[4]

Polytechnic University reached another important milestone when a doctorate program in biomedical engineering was approved by the state education department. This signaled yet another new chapter in Poly's long history of providing the latest in high-tech degree programs.

Around this same time, the Polytechnic Center for Advanced Technology in Telecommunications (CATT) was awarded a $1.5 million grant to expand its high-tech research and development activities. Poly was one of five centers awarded a total of $10 million through New York State's CATT Development Program. Under the leadership of CATT Director Shivendra Panwar and Project Director Phyllis Frankl, Polytechnic, in conjunction with Columbia University, began researching new technologies and tools that would help businesses and consumers maximize their use of the wireless Internet.[5]

The CATT project was also guided by David Goodman, head of electrical and computer engineering, and Mel Horwitch, chair of the department of management. Polytechnic researchers for the project included Henry Bertoni, professor of electrical and computer engineering, and Frank A. Cassara, professor of electrical and computer engineering.[6]

WEIZMANN INSTITUTE OF SCIENCE

In January 2001, more than 250 educators, entrepreneurs, business leaders, and government officials joined in an international conference to explore the key challenges of developing professional managers for Israel's high-tech industries.

The conference, held at the Weizmann Institute of Science in Rehovot, Israel, was sponsored by Poly's Institute for Technology and Enterprise, headed by Mel Horwitch, and the Poly-Israel Master of Science in Management (MSM) extension program, headed by Management Professor Harold Kaufman. The MSM program was established in 1997 by Polytechnic to fill a demand for managerial expertise in Israel. The conference also coincided with the MSM program's commencement of 130 students— the largest ever—at Rehovot's Yeda College.[7]

Back in Brooklyn, the Department of Introductory Design and Science was established in 2000 to instill in undergraduate students an understanding and appreciation of physical sciences and engineering design, providing a solid foundation for advanced courses.

At its Westchester campus in Hawthorne, Poly established the Graduate Center for Professional Studies. Historically, Polytechnic developed its course offerings to mirror the latest technologies of the day, thus matching higher education to scientific advancement.

To this end, Polytechnic took advantage of its advanced telecommunications structure at Metro-Tech Center, and in 2001 became the first university in New York City to require freshmen to use notebook computers for their courses. This is now a standard practice in colleges and universities around the world.

While construction was completed in 2000, the Donald F. and Mildred Topp Othmer Residence Hall (right) was dedicated in 2002. The opening of the 20-story, 400-bed facility is the University's first on-campus residence hall in Brooklyn. During the ceremony, a painting of Donald F. and Mildred Topp Othmer was unveiled (below). From left, Trustees Clifford H. Goldsmith and R. William Murray; Ellen F. Hartigan, vice president, student affairs; Stewart G. Nagler, corporation chairman; Amy Sabatelle, class of 2003, student council; President David Chang; Anthony Trotta, class of 2003, president, student government; and Dr. Gerhard J. Frohilch, class of 1957, a student of Othmer and family friend.

TUITION INCREASES

While Polytechnic's financial situation had dramatically improved in recent years, covering all of its expenses continued to be a challenge. The Corporation therefore announced a 5.5 percent tuition increase for undergraduate and graduate programs. This decision raised rates in the fall of 2001 to $11,140 per semester for full-time undergraduate students; plus it established rates of $708 per credit for undergraduates and $765 per unit for graduate students. President Chang discussed the increases in an open letter to the student body:

As I urge you to do each year, please remember that tuition covers only 75 percent of what it costs to educate an undergraduate student at Polytechnic University. Fundraising, such as our $275 million Campaign for Polytechnic, helps cover part of the balance. In addition, gifts to the campaign are used to continually upgrade our buildings, classrooms, laboratories, and other facilities, and to provide scholarship and other financial support for students.[8]

In addition, it was noted that this average was below national trends. It was President Chang's intention to carefully monitor the university's financial operations, and make sure Poly stayed in the black.

GROUNDBREAKING CEREMONY

The money raised by the Campaign for Polytechnic enabled the University to meet deadlines for needed construction and expansion. On May 18, 2000, more than 400 people gathered on the MetroTech campus to witness the groundbreaking ceremony for the $42-million Joseph J. and Violet J. Jacobs Building. The eight-story building stands today on Jay Street abutting Rogers Hall, and houses a full athletic facility and state-of-the-art classrooms, lecture halls, and laboratories.[9]

Among those in attendance were President Chang, Chairman Nagler, and outgoing Brooklyn

Above: In 2000, Professor Yao Wang received the New York City Mayor's Award for Excellence in Science and Technology.

Left: The Joseph J. and Violet J. Jacobs Academic Building houses advanced laboratories, state-of-the-art "smart" classrooms wired for the latest Internet and multimedia technologies, and a full, multi-purpose gymnasium.

Opposite: The Poly community, along with local and national dignitaries, gathers for the grand opening of the $26 million Joseph J. and Violet J. Jacobs Building.

Below: In 2002, the Alumni Wall was dedicated in the lobby of the Jacobs Academic Building during the 25th Annual President's Associates Reception. Designed by Susan Kaprov, the Alumni Wall (detail below) was created to honor those who gave their lives in our nation's wars, from the Civil War to the Iraq War, and also during 9/11; and also to honor those alumni who have been willing to give something back to their alma mater. *(S. L. Kaparov © 2000)*

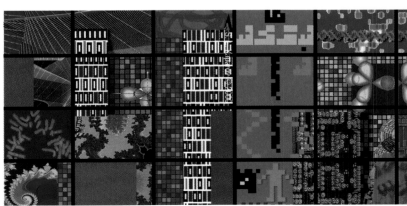

Borough President Howard Golden, who proclaimed May 18 "Polytechnic Groundbreaking Day." In the late 1970s, Golden had been one of the earliest supporters of MetroTech. At the ceremony, Golden said to the crowd, "On behalf of all Brooklynites, I salute the distinguished leadership, alumni, teaching professionals, and benefactors of Polytechnic University on this momentous occasion." Chairman Nagler then introduced Joseph Jacobs, calling him "one of Polytechnic's greatest alumni and its greatest living benefactor."[10]

The crowd rose in a standing ovation as a visibly emotional Jacobs, cane in hand, took center stage and recounted the dreams he had as a student and the lessons he learned since graduating from Polytechnic.

Today represents the accomplishment of my great dream, to see Polytechnic prosper and to give students a stepping stone to the American dream.[11]

After Jacobs' heartfelt speech, President Chang recognized another great benefactor, Donald F. Othmer, who along with his wife Mildred, had willed to Poly the largest gift ever made by an individual donor, or donor couple, to a private university, $175 million, ultimately providing for a number of significant capital improvements, including the Othmer Residence Hall. "You are joining us at an amazing time," President Chang told the audience. "Today's celebration is the first physical manifestation of a transformation we have started at Poly—an emergence into a premier university that will educate

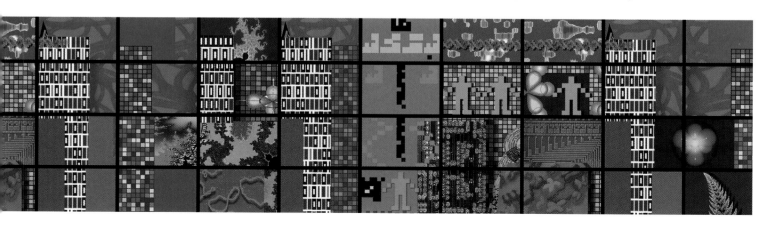

and support the leaders of tomorrow in a world that is increasingly driven by technology."[12]

Days after ground was broken, Polytechnic received a $1 million gift from the Kresge Foundation to assist with ancillary costs associated with the completion of the Joseph J. and Violet J. Jacobs Building.

OTHMER INSTITUTE FOR INTERDISCIPLINARY STUDIES

During this time, the Othmer Institute for Interdisciplinary Studies was officially established with $1.25 million annual funding from the Othmer endowment. Polytechnic named six distinguished scientists to serve on the board of overseers that included Dr. Arthur Bienenstock, class of 1957, professor, Stanford University; Dr. Paul Horn, senior vice president, research, IBM Corporation; Dr. Robert Langer, the Kenneth J. Germeshausen professor of chemical and biomedical engineering, Massachusetts Institute of Technology; Dr. Joshua Lederberg, president emeritus, Rockefeller University; Dr. Robert W. Lucky, corporate vice president for applied research, Bell Communications Research Inc.; and Dr. Arun Netravali, president, Bell Laboratories.[13]

Later, in 2001, eight professors were named fellows of the Othmer Institute for Interdisciplinary

PETER REGNA, DISTINGUISHED ALUMNUS AND BENEFACTOR

POLY ALUMNUS DR. PETER P. Regna played a key role in discovering, developing, and manufacturing many of the drugs that have revolutionized modern medical practice, including Terramycin, an antibiotic that is effective against more than 100 diseases. He also played a significant role in the production of penicillin, streptomycin and other antibiotics. Holding more than 35 patents, Regna was the recipient of the Perkin Medal from the American Section of the Society of the Chemical Industry.[1]

While known worldwide for his contributions to science, Regna, a son of a musician, was also a musician. He once said that if his career in science didn't pan out, he would aspire to become a professional musician. In his early days, he financed his Poly education by playing saxophone, clarinet, and violin in dance bands around the metropolitan area. He received his BS degree in 1932, his MS degree in Chemistry in 1937, and his PhD in Polymeric Materials in 1942. In 1996, Polytechnic awarded him an honorary doctorate and the Distinguished Alumnus Award.[2]

Among his generous contributions to Polytechnic was a $1.5 million gift to the Campaign for Polytechnic to endow the Laboratory for Biomacromolecular Engineering to research the production of environmentally friendly polymers. Regna's gift also allowed for the creation of a student lounge, to be named after him and his wife, Barbara.[3]

The Peter P. and Barbara L. Regna Student Lounge was dedicated on Tuesday, October 7, 2003. Those in attendance included Regna's sons, Robert, chief executive of U.S. Laser, and Peter, president and CEO of Aero Tech Laboratories. Regna died in 2001 at age 94.[4]

Studies. David Goodman, professor of electrical and computer science, was named the Weber-Othmer Senior Faculty Fellow, and Stephen Arnold, professor of physics, was named Poly's new Potts-Othmer Senior Faculty Fellow. Named as Othmer Senior Faculty Fellows were Mark Green, professor of chemistry; Lisa Hellerstein, associate professor of computer science; Professor Mel Horwitch, Sunil Kumar, associate professor of mechanical engineering; Erwin Lutwak, professor of mathematics and department head; and Yao Wang, professor of electrical and computer engineering.[14]

DEDICATION DAY

The physical transformation of the MetroTech Center was actively underway during this period. Jackhammers, cranes, dump trucks, and construction vehicles often made it challenging to both conduct and attend classes, and to adequately hear the lectures. While all of this construction made the lives of students, faculty, and surrounding business owners difficult, it was clear that Polytechnic's and Brooklyn's future were bright. Indeed, the last time Brooklyn's business community was this united and hopeful for the future was during construction of the Brooklyn Bridge.

As the long days of construction and planning turned into months, Polytechnic finally celebrated one of its most fateful days—June 13, 2002—as the university and its neighbors joined together to officially dedicate the Donald F. and Mildred Topp Othmer Residence Hall and the Joseph J. and Violet J. Jacobs Building on its MetroTech campus.

The unveiling fell on a beautiful spring day. In front of the Othmer Residence Hall, faculty, students, and onlookers gathered in joyous celebration. Speakers at the dedication included President Chang; Chairman Nagler; Ellen F. Hartigan, vice president of student affairs; and Bud Griffis, professor and department head of Civil Engineering who presented plaques of appreciation to members of the construction teams of Jacobs Facilities Inc. and J. A.

Above: Joseph J. Jacobs cuts the ceremonial ribbon during building dedication ceremonies on June 13, 2002. Looking on are, from left, daughters Linda, a Polytechnic Trustee; Margaret; Jacobs' wife Violet; and daughter Valerie.

Below: Poly's mascot—the Fighting Blue Jay.

Jones Construction. Griffis, who later became provost, oversaw the construction projects for Poly.

The event culminated in the unveiling of a portrait of Dr. and Mrs. Othmer, which today hangs in the residence hall. After the ceremony, a truly historic moment occurred when the first students moved into the 400-room dormitory. While Polytechnic had accepted students from all over the world since the 1870s, this was the first time in the commuter school's history that it offered housing on the Brooklyn campus, ultimately opening its doors to students from all corners of the world.[15]

The faculty, staff, students, alumni, and guests followed the festivities into the gymnasium in the new Jacobs Building where they were greeted by Poly's sports mascot, the Blue Jay, whose antic flapping and dancing added to the celebration.

Richard Thorsen hosted the event and paid tribute to the Jacobs family who flew in from their home state of California for the celebration. Among those

SEPTEMBER 11, 2001

AS BROOKLYNITES LOOKED ACROSS THE East River in horror at the burning World Trade Center Towers on September 11, 2001, Poly staff and faculty quickly mobilized and created an emergency information center in Rogers Hall. With thousands of pedestrians fleeing lower Manhattan via the Brooklyn Bridge, the Poly campus served as a safety zone for students, faculty, pedestrians, and emergency personnel.

As the early morning minutes of that fateful day passed, New Yorkers, along with millions of people around the world, watched in horror as the towers crumbled to the ground, creating a fiery dust cloud that enveloped lower Manhattan, and forever changed the world.

The nearly 3,000 that died that day included six Poly alumni: Alona Abraham, class of 2001; William Fallon Jr., class of 1987; Ye Wei Liang, class of 2001; Susan Miszkowicz, class of 1986; Nancy Yuen-Ngo, class of 1987; and James Ostrowski, class of 2001.[1]

Polytechnic's Institute for Technology and Enterprise (ITE), located at 55 Broad Street in lower Manhattan—a few blocks from Ground Zero-—lost all communication but experienced no casualties. Professor Mel Horwitch, director of ITE, was onsite when the towers were hit. After the events, he said: "We were fortunate. While we had to reconstruct student data and information files, we were able to shift classes to an uptown location."[2]

Polytechnic later decided that the ITE Department would remain in downtown Manhattan and thus contribute to the rebirth of the city.

In the days following the largest attack on American soil since Pearl Harbor, the Polytechnic community banded together and assisted the relief effort. Members of the faculty and student body donated blood and collected food and clothing for rescue workers. Poly's Web team, including Jim St. Lawrence, Webmaster, and Cynthia Feng, system administrator, developed

A Poly student took this picture of Ground Zero just a few days after the events of September 11, 2001. On that fateful day, six Polytechnic alumni perished. *(Photo: Alex Lis '02)*

a bulletin board, called "Helping Hands," for the New York City Department of Transportation's Web site.[3]

As the days turned into weeks, the rubble continued to burn, and questions concerning air quality and general safety became important issues. These questions, among others, were tackled in the book, *Beyond September 11th: An Account of Post-Disaster Research*. The nationwide cooperative publication includes the findings of research scientists from the Public Entity Risk Institute of Fairfax, Virginia, the Institute for Civil Infrastructure Systems at New York University's Robert F. Wagner Graduate School of Public Service (a partnership of New York University, Cornell University, Polytechnic University, the University of Southern California), and the Natural Hazards Information Center at the University of Colorado-Boulder.

Based on findings from these studies, the book includes numerous conclusions and recommendations for the improvement of public policy and disaster response.[4]

On September 19, 2001, President Chang led a standing-room only crowd in the Dibner Auditorium in a moment of silence for the victims and their families. Chang called on Poly students to remain strong, saying: "Your generation is mankind's best hope for a future of peace and prosperity."[5] Chang later announced that Poly had decided to establish a $1 million memorial scholarship fund for the dependents of fire and police personnel who died in the attack.[6]

Above: In 2002, Herbie Hancock, an Academy and Grammy Award-winning composer and musician, was awarded an honorary doctorate at the 14th annual Promise Fund Dinner. The black-tie gala was held in the Grand Ballroom of Manhattan's Waldorf-Astoria. The annual Promise Fund Dinner raises approximately $1 million for scholarships.

Right: In 2002, the Lynford Family Charitable Trust, headed by Trustee Jeffrey H. Lynford, donated a red-orange 28-foot high, 20,000-pound outdoor sculpture, entitled "Balanced Cylinders 5," by artist Paul Sisko to adorn the Jay Street plaza entrance. Pictured in front of the sculpture are, from left, Sisko, Tondra and Jeffrey Lynford, and Cecilia and David Chang. They are standing in front of the Jacobs Academic Building.

in attendance were Brooklyn's new borough president, Marty Markowitz; Charles Gargano, chairman of the Empire State Development; Andrew Alper, president of the New York City Economic Development Corporation; and MetroTech developer Bruce Ratner.

Markowitz presented a proclamation to the Jacobs' family naming June 13 "Jacobs Recognition Day in Brooklyn." While Mayor Michael Bloomberg was unable to attend the ceremony, Alper read from a note the mayor penned for the occasion. He saluted President Chang and The Corporation, noting, "Polytechnic continues to play a leading role in the economic and social renaissance of downtown Brooklyn."[16]

As the historic day came to a close, a portrait of Joseph and Violet Jacobs was unveiled that now graces the lobby of the building. This event coincided with Joseph Jacobs' 86th birthday, and the following day marked the Jacobs' 60th wedding anniversary.

After the unveiling, Jacobs talked off-the-cuff to the audience, saying, "The things in life that meant the most to me are friends. What we've done for Poly is only a continuation of what Poly and our friends have done for us." After a ceremonial ribbon-cutting on stage, the audience joined in a rousing happy birthday song to one of Poly's best friends, Joseph Jacobs.

As the new buildings were dedicated, the work to renovate Rogers Hall was also nearing completion. Aside from new classrooms and laboratories, the Jasper H. Kane Cafeteria, seating 300, was opened in Rogers Hall. Today, the cafeteria stands as a fitting tribute to Kane, a man who not only saved countless lives in World War II by developing a system to mass produce penicillin, but who was also a proud alumnus who donated $2 million to his alma mater before his death in 2004.

Henry Singer, a current vice president of The Corporation, explained in a recent interview his perception of Polytechnic's history:

We were able to get some of the most world-renowned people to be here at Poly. I know we can do more of that. We currently have some excellent professors. Yes, we've stumbled a little bit here and there, but I think we've got some outstanding potential.[17]

REDIRECTING ACADEMIC PROGRAMS

With the addition of the Othmer Residence Hall and the Joseph J. and Violet J. Jacobs Building to the MetroTech Center, Poly, traditionally a commuter school, now had more of a true collegiate setting. Deciding that it would be appropriate to focus

President David Chang (center) with student athletes in the gymnasium of the Joseph J. and Violet J. Jacobs Building, which opened in summer 2002 on the MetroTech campus. Clockwise from President Chang: Evelyn Adames, Joe Alifano, Henry Huang, Marianni Mejia, Jean Pierre Barthelemy, Farhan Mudasir, Kevin Power, Lauren Competello, Steven So, and Jeffrey Tse. Poly's sport teams experienced great success in 2003. The men's basketball team and volleyball team each won a Hudson Valley Conference championship—in men's basketball, the first such win in over 25 years; and the second consecutive year for volleyball. The women's basketball team defeated Bard College in the Hudson Valley Women's Athletic Conference inaugural basketball invitational. Top photo: The men's basketball team has the home court advantage playing in the University's gymnasium in the new Jacobs Building. *(Photo Credit: William Chin '04.)*

On April 25, 2002, Poly mourned the loss of Professor Emeritus Athanasios Papoulis. Papoulis (pictured here) joined the faculty in 1952 and retired in 1994. He published nine books, including the classic *Probability, Random Variables and Stochastic Processes*, which today is considered a standard in the field of electrical engineering and mathematics.

all of the university's undergraduate studies in Brooklyn, President Chang announced in 2002 that the University would redirect its educational programs, consolidating all undergraduate courses at MetroTech.

The decision resulted in the selling of the Farmingdale campus and the opening of the Long Island Graduate Center in Melville to serve Long Island's engineering community.

Several new degree programs were introduced which focused on the management of construction, on telecommunications technology, and on the impact of biology on the chemistry and chemical engineering professions. The new campus mirrored Poly's commitment to furthering technological enterprise on Long Island, an endeavor that started in the late 1950s and continues today.

POLYTECHNIC RECEIVES $3 MILLION SFS SCHOLARSHIP AWARD

As the year 2002 came to a close, Polytechnic received a $3 million, four-year Federal Cyber Service: Scholarship for Service (SFS) award, providing scholarships to students pursuing advanced studies in information assurance and security.

Not unlike the federal grants Polytechnic received during World War II and the Vietnam War to aid the nation in defense technology, the special scholarship program was created in response to the attacks on September 11, 2001, and the subsequent war on terrorism, which eventually led to the Iraq War.

President George W. Bush sponsored and fully supported the SFS program. He called on a number of academic institutions, including Polytechnic, to assist the federal government in addressing security challenges facing the nation. Currently, only 10 schools in the country are recipients of the scholarship awards, and Polytechnic is the only school in the state of New York to hold the designation.[18]

A stipulation of the SFS scholarship program requires that recipients work for the federal government for one year of service for each year of scholarship received.

To be eligible for this funding, Poly was one of the first universities designated as a Center of Academic Excellence in Information Assurance Education by the National Security Agency (NSA). Poly was recently re-designated with new criteria that only 19 universities have met, with Polytechnic being the only such institution in the New York City tri-state area. Total funding in this cyber-security area—with both education and research grants—has exceeded $8 million.

POLY'S TECHNOLOGICAL ADVANCES

The winter of 2003 was a confusing period for Poly. Through a $1.5 million grant from the New York State Office of Science, Technology, and Academic Research, an important new program was established—the Wireless Internet Center for Advanced Technology. Still, the university was again operating with a deficit, this time $12 million.

To many, it was difficult to understand how a private university that successfully raised $275 million dollars could in two short years be again experiencing financial troubles. At a special university-wide meeting on February 6, President Chang answered that question, among others, as he outlined his plans to reduce Polytechnic's $12 million deficit and balance the budget by June 2005.

Lowell W. Robinson, then interim chief financial officer, explained that of the $275 million raised,

$246 million was "cash in the bank," and $29 million represented unfulfilled pledges. From the money collected from the Campaign for Polytechnic, $135 million was put into the endowment; $46 million toward an unrestricted endowment to use as cash on hand; $23 million into new buildings, facility renovations and network upgrades; $13 million for annual funds; $12 million into academic programs; $9 million toward endowed chairs; and finally, $8 million for endowed scholarships.

In addition, Polytechnic was holding a $90 million bond debt for construction of two new facilities—the Kane Cafeteria and the Regna Student Lounge.[19]

Chang explained that with The Corporation's approval, a two-phase reduction plan had been set in motion. The first phase was completed in October 2002, saving $4.5 million in annual spending by combining several administrative offices, eliminating several senior-level staff positions, which reduced senior-management salaries by three percent, and by cutting budgets for materials, supplies, information technology, consulting services, and the financing of selected equipment.[20]

Later that year during an October meeting, which was opened to all Polytechnic faculty and students, Chang explained that Polytechnic's uncertain financial situation arose from numerous factors, including a bleak economic market that lowered the income from the University's invested endowment, an eight-percent decrease in new-student enrollment for fall 2002, a 25-percent vacancy rate in the Othmer Residence Hall, and an increase in financial aid for students. At the time, financial aid for students was running at approximately 42 percent of tuition.[21]

The second phase, launched in February 2003, focused on the remaining $7.5 million and affected operations, academic programs, and employee benefits. Cost-cutting efforts included canceling under-enrolled classes, not filling open positions, outsourcing Polytechnic's mailroom and print shop operations, temporarily halting annual merit raises, and reducing employee benefits. The Summer Research Institute, a pre-college internship program housed in the YES Center, also was reduced.[22]

Executive Vice President and Provost Ivan Frisch said the budget cuts and general housecleaning would correct "a structural problem that had been in place for the past 60 years," adding, "Our revenues cannot support the size of our overhead and administration."[23] The following summer, due to budget cuts, Frisch himself would lose his position as executive vice president.

President Chang said the reorganization placed priority on growing revenue for the University, particularly tuition, by improving recruiting and retention efforts. In 2003, for example, Polytechnic's retention

POLYTECHNIC AWARDED ITR GRANT BY NATIONAL SCIENCE FOUNDATION

POLYTECHNIC UNIVERSITY HAS BEEN awarded an ITR (Information Technology Research) Grant from the National Science Foundation to conduct research in the emerging area of peer-peer computing.

The proposed research work focuses on computer systems tasks such as file sharing, distributed storage, and utility computing. The principal investigator for the research program is Dr. Keith Ross, the Leonard J. Shustek Distinguished Professor in Computer Science. The total value of the National Science Foundation contract is $2.8 million.

University Research Professor Eli M. Pearce is the former head of the Polymer Research Institute, now headed by Professor Richard Gross. Professor Pearce is past president of the American Chemical Society (ACS) and a member of its board of directors since 1999.

The American Chemical Society has a program where three or four singular events in the history of chemistry are recognized. In this regard, we became a National Historic Chemical Landmark for the field of polymers in 2003.

This recognized not only our strong history and tradition, but also the fact that we were the first academic institution in the United States that had an institute to do graduate research in polymers in the United States.[25]

Continuing with Poly's long, celebrated history in the field of polymer research, Pearce explained that he and his colleagues recently received a special grant from the National Science Foundation. Focusing on the area of nanochemistry, research by Pearce and his colleagues will address mechanisms for reducing the flammability of polymers.

In the months that followed, a new undergraduate program in chemical and biological engineering was approved by the New York State Department of Education, and an undergraduate program in biomedical sciences was established.

Chancellor George Bugliarello, the man responsible for the success of MetroTech, was tapped for a four-year term as the Foreign Secretary of the National Academy of Engineering.

POLY-NYU MERGER AVERTED

Poly has made a number of milestone decisions in its 150-year history. The decision to separate the collegiate unit from the preparatory unit in 1917 was one and combining with the New York University School of Engineering and Science (NYU/SES) in 1973 was another. During our 150th year NYU sought a takeover of Poly. Though referred to as a merger, the proposal amounted to an acquisition and the loss of Poly's independence and its mission to prepare leaders for the broad areas of technology and technology dependent areas.

The prospect of joining NYU began in earnest in the winter of 2004 and accelerated in the fall of that year. At the same time, Board Chairman Stewart Nagler commissioned a committee of trustees, assisted by vice president Richard Thorsen, to develop a plan for Poly to go forward as an independent university. Known as the Futures Committee and chaired by Richard Foxen, a trustee, the committee

rate for first-year freshmen who return the following fall was 80 percent, but the six-year graduation rate was only 50 percent.[24]

Despite these financial challenges, which generated a certain amount of stress between faculty, students, and the administration, the University continued to be recognized for its numerous significant achievements.

In 2003, the Polymer Research Institute, founded by Herman Mark, was designated a National Historic Chemical Landmark by the American Chemical Society. University Research Professor Eli Pearce, who was the director of the Polymer Research Institute from 1981 to 1996, said in a recent interview that he and his esteemed colleagues at Poly were pleased to receive this distinct honor.

undertook the daunting task of developing in less than two months a realistic and optimistic plan for Poly's future.

At the core of the committee's recommendations was the University's strategic plan for 2004-2007: Securing the Future. Resources were identified to allow acceleration of key revenue-generating strategies in the plan. In addition, the proposal called for significant investment in faculty development. The successful capital campaign allowed investment in physical resources. Now, in the recommendation of the committee, was the time for investment in intellectual resources, particularly in emerging and strategically important areas of technology.

The faculty, along with alumni and student elected leaders, overwhelmingly voted to reject the NYU proposal, and on February 1, 2005, the board of trustees, in whom the ultimate decision-making authority was vested, voted overwhelmingly to go forward as an independent university and generously pledged their support to assuring Poly's bright future. On February 14, 2005 the board's executive committee adopted most of the recommendations of the futures committee. As this book goes to press these recommendations are being implemented. Although Poly faces challenges, the path to a bright future is clear and there is a collective will to position the University for future leadership. Future generations will reflect on the success of these actions and the collective foresight and optimism of the board of trustees, without which this 150-year history of Poly may have been an obituary for a proud institution whose contributions have become legend among technologists and society in general.

POLY'S PLAN TO SECURE ITS FUTURE

Polytechnic, known in academic circles as the "little engine that could," proactively decided in the winter of 2004 to deal with its financial problems, and to work to build faculty morale. The Corporation

Students enjoy socializing and studying with classmates in the Peter P. and Barbara Regna Student Lounge.

adopted a three-year strategic plan, "Securing the Future," to strengthen the university's long-term goals. This plan resulted from an intensive, 13-month planning process, involving over 50 trustees, faculty, staff, alumni, and students. "The plan is not grand or sweeping," said Richard Thorsen, who spearheaded the plan's development. "Rather, it is focused on those essential objectives that will position Poly to take its next great steps."[26]

Thorsen explained that the plan focuses on five key areas, known as R^4C: recruitment, retention, research, resources, and cultural change.

Another major area of focus included increasing annual research spending by $1 million each year (from $12 million in fiscal year 2004 to $16 million by the end of fiscal year 2007). In addition, President Chang planned to balance the operating budget by June 30, 2005, and to find additional sources of revenue. Thorsen also explained that it was the administration's overall mission to foster a sense of Polytechnic pride among staff, faculty, and students.[27]

As Polytechnic entered its 150th year, the plan to secure Poly's future was working. Enrollment numbers began increasing, faculty morale was on the rise, and the operating deficit was dropping. Once again, Polytechnic was beating the odds and succeeding in the face of adversity.

TWENTY YEARS OF CATT

After two decades of providing invaluable research and discovery in the field of telecommunications, Polytechnic's Center for Advanced Technology in Telecommunications (CATT) celebrated its 20th anniversary. In recognition of this milestone, New York State Governor George P. Pataki announced that the CATT Center, supported by the New York State Office of Science, Technology, and Academic Research (NYSTAR), will receive up to $1 million annually until 2014.

Graduates of the CATT program have contributed significantly to telecommunications improvements worldwide. Rajiv Mody, class of 1982, founded Sasken Ltd., a leading global provider of wireless communication software. One of Mody's recent innovations was providing emergency operators in New York City with the location of a person calling from a cell phone. Mody began in a garage in Silicon Valley with a tiny company, and

In 2004, Dr. Richard Gross, the Herman F. Mark Professor of Polymer Science, was appointed director of Polytechnic's Polymer Research Institute. In 2001, he established the nation's first Center for Biocatalysis and Bioprocessing of Macromolecules, funded by the National Science Foundation.

now owns one of India's most successful wireless technology firms.

Following the support the CATT program received from New York State, the U.S. Department of Defense announced a $1 million grant to Polytechnic, which was sponsored by U.S. Senators Charles E. Schumer and Hillary Rodham Clinton. The grant permits the Polymer Research Institute to continue to develop new field tests that can detect deadly microorganisms such as *B. anthracis*, the spore-forming bacteria that causes anthrax.

In addition, the Defense Advanced Research Projects Agency (DARPA), the central research and development organization for the Department of Defense, awarded Polytechnic $1.1 million to further develop a revolutionary new process by Professor Richard A. Gross to manufacture plastics that can be converted into liquid fuels.

In 2003, Professor Gross was honored with a Presidential Green Chemistry Challenge Award by the U.S. Environmental Protection Agency for his discovery. The plastics, which are made using an enzyme from yeast, can be built from all-natural materials such as sugars. The DARPA grant and resulting research would not have been possible without the groundbreaking research conducted in the field of polymers in the 1940s, 1950s, and 1960s by Herman Mark, the father of polymer science.

SESQUICENTENNIAL CELEBRATION

When Polytechnic was first established, its founding fathers, Isaac H. Frothingham, James S. T. Stranahan, and Josiah H. Low, among others, gambled, without an endowment or any security, that Polytechnic would establish itself as a leading institution of higher learning.

On November 4, 2004, Senator Hillary Rodham Clinton addressed a packed auditorium at the seventh annual Lynford Lecture. Clinton promoted federal investment in education and said it was an honor to be at Polytechnic because of its 150 years as a leader in science, education, and research. Clinton is pictured here (center) with Poly students.

POLYTECHNIC UNIVERSITY NAMES NEW PRESIDENT

PRESIDENT DAVID C. CHANG, THE NINTH president of Poly, announced early in 2004 that he would be stepping down as president on June 30, 2005, after serving the University for 11 years. As a result, a presidential search committee was organized by The Corporation to find a suitable replacement for Chang. After months of carefully reviewing numerous potential candidates, Poly announced that Jerry MacArthur Hultin, a former Under Secretary of the Navy, would be named the 10th president of Polytechnic University. Simultaneously, the board announced that Chang would be appointed chancellor.

Hultin, dean of the Wesley J. Howe School of Technology Management, Hoboken, New Jersey, and a professor of management at Stevens Institute of Technology, also in Hoboken, assumed the presidency of Polytechnic on July 1, 2005. Craig G. Matthews, chairman of Polytechnic's Board of Trustees, discussed the appointment.

Following an extensive national search for a new president, we are pleased that Jerry Hultin has agreed to join the University. He has the skill set, vision, and drive to expand Polytechnic's role as one of the nation's leading technological and research universities.

The trustees of Polytechnic University are excited by the opportunity to have Jerry Hultin join with Polytechnic's faculty and staff in meeting the scientific, engineering, and management challenges of the coming decades.[1]

As dean of the Howe School of Technology Management since 2000, Hultin was responsible for the leadership of Stevens' newest academic school dedicated to producing outstanding education and research that addresses the needs of companies, government, and individuals as they manage technology-dependent organizations. Hultin was influential in guiding research on homeland security at Stevens Institute.

From 1997 to 2000, Hultin served as Under Secretary of the Navy, the department's number two civilian leader. He was instrumental in fostering innovation in strategic vision, war fighting, and business operations to meet the evolving needs of the Navy and Marine Corps.

Hultin spent more than 25 years in the private sector. He also served as a member of the Chief of Naval Operations Executive Panel and as a board member of Freddie Mac, one of the nation's largest holders of housing mortgages.

A former commissioned officer in the U.S. Navy, Hultin is a 1964 graduate of Ohio State University and a 1972 graduate of Yale Law School. He is an honorary fellow of the Foreign Policy Association, a member of the NY Transatlantic Council, and a business adviser to various major firms.

On being named president, Hultin stated:

I am honored to be joining Polytechnic University. I believe the future belongs to those young women and men who are able to design, innovate, and manage with leading-edge science and technology. Here in the United States and around the world, the need is escalating for scientific innovation, engineering brilliance, and honest, entrepreneurial business leadership. Polytechnic, through its faculty, students, administrators, and graduates—and its location at the heart of the most vibrant urban culture in the world—is ready to take a key role in providing the education and research that results in real growth and development.[2]

Their faith was amply confirmed. On May 26, 2004, the University kicked off its Sesquicentennial Celebration at its 149th commencement ceremony. And when the ball dropped in Times Square across the East River on New Year's Day, 2005, Polytechnic University officially entered its 150th year, backed by a remarkably successful history of scientific and educational achievement.

As this book goes to press, a number of projects and activities are planned to recognize this important milestone. One such project is a documentary film entitled *Inspiration & Innovation: 150 Years of Discovery & Invention at Polytechnic University*, written and directed by Christopher Hayes, MS, MOT '01 (Management of Technology Program, for which he served as class representative for that year). Hayes also is the director of video and multimedia production in Polytechnic's World Wide Web Department.

In a recent interview, Hayes commented on the importance and significance of Polytechnic's contributions to science, and the value of alumni support:

In 2001, the University opened an 11,000-square-foot interdisciplinary laboratory for undergraduate students in mechanical, civil, and chemical engineering. Each discipline received its own studio classroom, featuring audiovisual equipment for instructors and student computer stations that can generate detailed 3-D images, complex simulations, and detailed analyses useful in student assignments.

The last 150 years represent probably the most condensed history in the evolution of mankind. And the technology portion of that is probably the most condensed bit of history within that history. Because people across the planet use technology for good or ill, it's important for them to know where it came from. Polytechnic has played a key role in that development.[28]

While working on the documentary, Hayes was aided by a number of Polytechnic's faculty and staff, including Therese Tillett, Poly's director of editorial services and special projects. Tillett also wrote a six-part series on the University's history for Poly's alumni magazine, *Cable*.

The 150th convocation is scheduled to take place on September 29, 2005, at the Brooklyn Academy of Music (BAM), the historic hall that hosted some of Poly's early commencement ceremonies, and was the site of the convocation celebrating Polytechnic's 100th anniversary. (It is interesting to note that Poly used to host BAM performances within the Institute's original chapel, which served, in effect, as BAM's first music hall. One such early concert, as reported in the now defunct *Brooklyn Eagle*, was entitled the "Ringing Bells" concert.) "This year, we are honoring ourselves," said Tillett. "It's a two-part celebration. The first part is a convocation during the day. The administration is going to cancel classes and do a formal dinner. It will be a very special occasion."[29]

THE NEXT CHAPTER:
150 YEARS AND BEYOND

Over the last 150 years, Polytechnic University has changed the course of scientific history. Its professors, students, and alumni have been responsible for numerous groundbreaking achievements and developments in the fields of microwave technology, aeronautics, barcode technology, polymer science, and telecommunications, to name just a few. They have helped to invent the VCR, the camcorder, the laser, and to put men on the moon. The discoveries and innovations of Polytechnic professors and

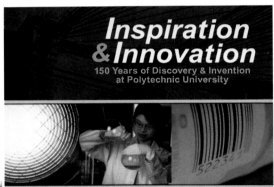

Left: Shown here is the cover of the documentary film *Inspiration & Innovation: 150 Years of Discovery & Invention at Polytechnic University*, written and directed by Christopher Hayes.

Below: Avery Fisher Hall at Lincoln Center was the setting for Polytechnic University's 149th commencement (and for many others).

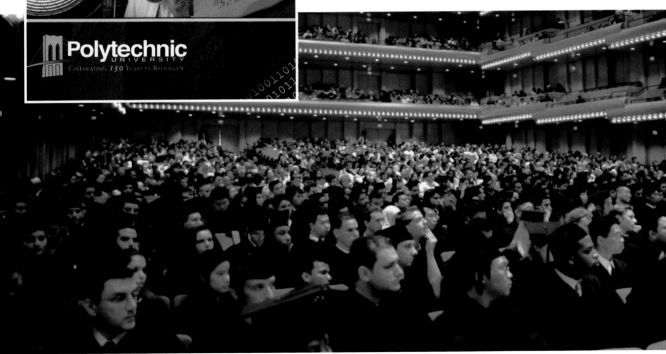

SAVE THE DATE • THURSDAY, SEPTEMBER 29, 2005

INAUGURATION
Celebrating 150 Years
CONVOCATION

The Power of PolyThinking ®...Our history, the world's future.

Poly's first 150 years will be celebrated at a convocation that will also set the stage for an equally glorious future as it inaugurates its tenth president, Jerry MacArthur Hultin.

---

alumni have been nothing less than astounding. They continue to add to this brilliant legacy of success with each passing day; and in doing so, tip their collective hat, as it were, to the fortitude and guidance of Poly's founding fathers.

Polytechnic's 40,000-plus alumni, many of whom come from humble beginnings, include business leaders, entrepreneurs, and inventors who collectively hold thousands of patents in numerous fields of science.

Top executives from AT&T, Bechtel, Consolidated Edison, General Electric, IBM, Ingersoll-Rand, KeySpan Energy, MetLife, Northrop Grumman Corporation, Parsons Brinkerhoff, Qwest, Lockheed Martin, Sears Roebuck, J. P. Morgan, Raytheon, Stanley Works, Symbol Technologies, UNISYS, Verizon Communications, and Xerox are proud of their roots at Polytechnic. Academic leaders, deans, and university presidents began their careers at Polytechnic, a school that has survived countless financial emergencies, a merger, and three different name changes.

Most important, the average Polytechnic graduate is both thankful and proud of the exceptional education that he or she has been able to receive while at the Institute.

"We would yet look forward to an early establishment upon a liberal foundation of a strictly Polytechnic Department inferior to no existing institution of the kind which our country can now boast," wrote Isaac H. Frothingham, Poly's first president, in 1854. Remarkably prescient, Frothingham aptly described the Poly of today.

Indeed, today, as on September 10, 1855, when Polytechnic first opened its doors to 265 students, the University is providing a new generation of aspiring scientists, engineers, and other students with the tools and educational support needed for them to continue to formulate groundbreaking discoveries and innovations, bravely and boldly, now and into the next century, and beyond.

There's no time like the future.

APPENDIX A

BOARD OF TRUSTEES

APPENDIX B

CHAIRMEN OF BOARD OF TRUSTEES

Isaac H. Frothingham 1854–1890

William A. White 1890–1899

Henry Sanger Snow 1899–1904

William H. Nichols 1904–1922

Charles Edwin Potts 1922–1952

Preston R. Bassett 1952–1961

Herbert H. Rogge 1961–1966

Robert E. Lewis 1966–1969

Louis N. Rowley Jr. 1969–1976

Joseph J. Jacobs 1976–1986

Clarence Silleck 1986–1987

Paul Hallingby Jr. 1988–1991

Robert Maxwell 1991

Joseph J. Jacobs 1991–1994

Arthur C. Martinez 1994–2000

Stewart G. Nagler 2000–2005

Craig G. Matthews 2005–

APPENDIX C

PRESIDENTS

John Howard Raymond 1855–1864

David Henry Cochran 1864–1899

Henry Sanger Snow (Interim President) . . 1899–1904

Frederick Washington Atkinson 1904–1925

Parke Rexford Kolbe 1925–1932

Charles Edwin Potts (Interim President) . . 1932–1933

Harry Stanley Rogers 1933–1957

Ernst Weber (Interim President) 1957–1958

Ernst Weber 1958–1969

Benjamin Adler (Acting President) 1969–1971

Arthur Grad 1971–1973

Norman Auburn (Acting President) 1973

George Bugliarello 1973–1994

David C. Chang 1994–2005

Jerry MacArthur Hultin 2005–

NOTES TO SOURCES

CHAPTER ONE

1. George Bugliarello, *Towards the Technological University: The Story of Polytechnic Institute of New York* (Princeton, NJ: Princeton University Press, 1975), 11.
2. Bugliarello, *Towards the Technological University: The Story of Polytechnic Institute of New York*, 11.
3. Ibid., 7.
4. Ibid.
5. Ibid.
6. John J. O'Connor, *Centennial: Polytechnic Institute of Brooklyn* (New York: Polytechnic Institute of Brooklyn, 1956), 3.
7. Bugliarello, *Towards the Technological University: The Story of Polytechnic Institute of New York*, 7.
8. Ibid., 12.
9. The City University of New York, "The History of Baruch Public Exhibit, Beginnings: From Free Academy to School of Business, 1847 to 1930," http://newman.baruch.cuny.edu/digital/2001/history/exhibit/chap_01/default.htm, date unknown.
10. Miles Merwin Kastendieck, *The Story of Poly*, (New York: Harvey Matthews and Company, 1940), 25, 15.
11. Staff Writer, "The New Academy," *Brooklyn Daily Eagle*, 20 March 1854, 2.
12. Bugliarello, *Towards the Technological University: The Story of Polytechnic Institute of New York*, 12.
13. Staff writer, *Brooklyn Daily Eagle*, September 6, 1855, 2.
14. Bugliarello, *Towards the Technological University: The Story of Polytechnic Institute of New York*, 12.
15. O'Connor, *Centennial: Polytechnic Institute of Brooklyn*, 6.
16. Ibid., 3.
17. Bugliarello, *Towards the Technological University: The Story of Polytechnic Institute of New York*, 10.
18. Ibid., 11.
19. Staff writer, "Brooklyn Collegiate and Polytechnic Institute," *New York Independent*, March 1855, 2.
20. O'Connor, *Centennial: Polytechnic Institute of Brooklyn*, 7.
21. Ibid.
22. Ibid.
23. Ibid., 8.
24. Ibid.
25. Ibid., 6
26. Staff writer, *Brooklyn Daily Eagle*, 1 February 1859, 3.
27. *Brooklyn Daily Eagle*, 6 September 1855, 2.
28. Staff writer, *Brooklyn Daily Eagle*, 6 September 1855, 2.
29. *Brooklyn Daily Eagle*, 22 October 1858, 2.
30. Kastendieck, *The Story of Poly*, 25.
31. *Brooklyn Daily Eagle*, 23 September 1859, 3.
32. Therese E. Tillet, Polytechnic University: 16th Annual Promise Fund Dinner (Brooklyn, NY: Polytechnic University Press, 2004), 2.
33. Therese E. Tillet, "Brooklyn Poly 1853-1904: A School of Higher Learning for Brooklyn's Future," *Cable* (Brooklyn, NY: Polytechnic University Press, Summer 2004, Volume 31, Issue 3), centerfold.
34. "1957 Alumni Roster," *Brief History of the Alumni Association* (Brooklyn, NY: Polytechnic University Press, 1957), 6.
35. Bugliarello, *Towards the Technological University: The Story of Polytechnic Institute of New York*, 14.
36. Ibid.

37. Kastendieck, *The Story of Poly*, 22.
38. Ibid., 35.
39. Ibid., 23.
40. Ibid., 48.
41. Ibid.
42. Bugliarello, *Towards the Technological University: The Story of Polytechnic Institute of New York*, 14.
43. O'Connor, *Centennial: Polytechnic Institute of Brooklyn*, 8
44. Bugliarello, *Towards the Technological University: The Story of Polytechnic Institute of New York*, 15.
45. Ibid.
46. William E. Golden, "An Historical Sketch: The Polytechnic Preparatory Country Day School," Polytechnic University Archives, 4.
47. Bugliarello, *Towards the Technological University: The Story of Polytechnic Institute of New York*, 15.
48. Ibid. 18.
49. Staff writer, *Brooklyn Daily Eagle*, 12 January 1876, Section: Sports, 2.

CHAPTER ONE SIDEBAR:
THE FIRST SETTLERS

1. James A. Jarman, "A Tribe, Early Settlers and a Church Once Stood on Poly's Site," Polytechnic University Archives.
2. Ibid.
3. Ibid.
4. Ibid.

CHAPTER ONE SIDEBAR:
THE NAMING OF BROOKLYN

1. Sonya Maven, *A Short Brooklyn History: History of Breuckelen, Kings County & Brooklyn* (Brooklyn, NY: Wynn Data Limited, copyright 1996-2002), http://www.brooklynonline.com/history/short.brooklyn.xhtml.

CHAPTER ONE SIDEBAR:
POLY'S CIVIL WAR HEROES

1. Therese E. Tillet, "Poly and the Civil War: Making their Mark," *Cable*, Fall 2004.
2. Department of the Navy, Naval Historical Center, "Rear Admiral George W. Melville, USN, (1841-1912)," http://www.history.navy.mil/photos/pers-us/uspers-m/g-melvil.htm.
3. Ibid.
4. Ibid.
5. Therese E. Tillet, "Poly and the Civil War: Making their Mark," *Cable*, Fall 2004.
6. Office of the Chief of Military History, *American Military History*, Army Historical Series, Chapter 10, "The Civil War: 1862," 209, http://www.army.mil/cmh-pg/books/amh/AMH-10.htm.
7. Ibid.

CHAPTER TWO

1. Kastendieck, *The Story of Poly*, 43.
2. Ibid., 44-45.
3. Ibid., 53.
4. University of Delaware, Special Collections Department, http://www.lib.udel.edu/ud/spec/exhibits/fairs/cent.htm.
5. Ibid.
6. NYCRoads.com, "Brooklyn Bridge, Historic Overview," http://www.nycroads.com/crossings/brooklyn/.
7. Ibid.
8. Ibid.
9. Ibid.
10. "Alumni Notes," *Polytechnic*, Vol. 5. No. 6, March 1895, 117.
11. NYCRoads.com, "Brooklyn Bridge, Historic Overview," http://www.nycroads.com/crossings/brooklyn/.
12. Ibid.
13. Ibid.
14. Ibid.
15. Ibid.
16. Ibid.
17. Ibid.
18. Ibid.
19. Ibid.
20. Ibid.
21. Ibid.
22. Kastendieck, *The Story of Poly*, 53.
23. Jay Mathews, *Washington Post*, 3 February 2002, Section C, 1.
24. Bugliarello, *Towards the Technological University: The Story of Polytechnic Institute of New York*, 20.
25. Ibid.,16.
26. Ibid.
27. Ibid.
28. Kastendieck, *The Story of Poly*, 38.
29. Ibid.
30. Ibid., 39.
31. Ibid., 68.
32. Staff writer, *Brooklyn Daily Eagle*, 19 September 1901, 1.
33. Kastendieck, *The Story of Poly*, 41.
34. Staff writer, *Brooklyn Daily Eagle*, 15 June 1887, 1.
35. Kastendieck, *The Story of Poly*, 42.
36. Ibid.
37. Ibid., 58.
38. Ibid.
39. Ibid., 59.
40. Ibid.
41. Ibid.
42. Ibid., 60.
43. Ibid.
44. Ibid., 61.
45. Ibid., 63.
46. Ibid., 65
47. Staff writer, *Brooklyn Daily Eagle*, 4 February 1893, 5.
48. Kastendieck, *The Story of Poly*, 65.
49. Ibid., 66.
50. Ibid., 65.
51. Ibid., 67.
52. Ibid., 68.
53. Ibid., 54.
54. Staff writer, *Brooklyn Daily Eagle*, 17 September 1896, 14.
55. Kastendieck, *The Story of Poly*, 54.
56. Ibid., 55.
57. Ibid., 56.
58. Ibid., 70.
59. Staff writer, *Brooklyn Daily Eagle*, 4 March 1899, 4.
60. Kastendieck, *The Story of Poly*, 70.

CHAPTER TWO SIDEBAR:
A SYMBOL OF
AMERICAN INGENUITY

1. NYCRoads.com, "Brooklyn Bridge, Historic Overview," http://www.nycroads.com/crossings/brooklyn/.
2. Ibid.

CHAPTER THREE

1. Alice Woller, *History of Polytechnic 1890-1920* (unpublished—manuscript copy at Polytechnic University Archives), 8.
2. *Brooklyn Daily Eagle*, 8 September 1900, 10.

3. *Brooklyn Daily Eagle*, 30 October 1900,17.
4. Staff Writer, *Brooklyn Daily Eagle*, 2 May 1900, 7.
5. *Brooklyn Daily Eagle*, 30 October 1900, 17.
6. Alice Woller, *History of Polytechnic 1890-1920* (unpublished—manuscript copy at Polytechnic University Archives), 7.
7. Polytechnic University, "The History of Polytechnic University," http://www.poly.edu/150/beginning.cfm.
8. Ibid.
9. http://staff.imsa.edu/socsci/jvictory/expansion00/1900/election_1900/1900_elect/trusts_dems.htm.
10. Polytechnic University, "History of Polytechnic University—Making their Mark; Alumni," http://www.poly.edu/150/beginning.cfm.
11. Polytechnic University, "The History of Polytechnic University," http://www.poly.edu/150/beginning.cfm.
12. Polytechnic University, "Important Dates in Polytechnic's History," http://www.poly.edu/glance2004/pages/page14.cfm.
13. Alice Woller, *History of Polytechnic 1890-1920* (unpublished—manuscript copy at Polytechnic University Archives), 8.
14. "1957 Alumni Roster," *Brief History of the Alumni Association* (Brooklyn, NY: Polytechnic University Press, 1957), 6.
15. Ibid.
16. *Brooklyn Daily Eagle*, 26 January 1901, 11.
17. Photographs from the *Chicago Daily News*, 1902-1933, http://memory.loc.gov/ammem/ndlpcoop/ichihtml/cdnsp4.html.
18. Kastendieck, *The Story of Poly*, 80.
19. Ibid., 81.
20. Greater New York Centennial Celebration, "Elected Mayors of New York City, 1898 to 1998," http://www.nyc.gov/html/nyc100/html/classroom/hist_info/mayors.html#low.
21. Ibid.
22 *New York Times*, 30 October 1901.
23. Greater New York Centennial Celebration, "Elected Mayors of New York City," 1898 to 1998, http://www.nyc.gov/html/nyc100/html/classroom/hist_info/mayors.html#low.
24. http://www.11211magazine.com/history/history3.html.
25. nycroads.com, Steve Anderson, "The Crossings Of Metro New York, Queensboro Bridge," http://www.nycroads.com/crossings/queensboro/.
26. *11211 Magazine*, Greg Ayres, "An XXXcelent Bridge," *11211 Magazine*, (Brooklyn, 2004) http://www.11211magazine.com/history/history3.html.
27. Ibid.
28. Greater New York Centennial Celebration, "Elected Mayors of New York City, 1898 to 1998," http://www.nyc.gov/html/nyc100/html/classroom/hist_info/mayors.html#low.
29. Biography: "James J. Wood," http://chem.ch.huji.ac.il/~eugeniik/history/wood.html.
30. Polytechnic University, "History of Polytechnic University—Making Their Mark; Alumni," http://www.poly.edu/150/beginning.cfm.
31. Kastendieck, *The Story of Poly*, 70.
32. Alice Woller, *History of Polytechnic 1890-1920* (unpublished—manuscript copy at Polytechnic University Archives), 10.
33. Kastendieck, *The Story of Poly*, 84.
34. Ibid.
35. Alice Woller, *History of Polytechnic 1890-1920* (unpublished—manuscript copy at Polytechnic University Archives), 10.
36. Ibid.
37. Ibid., 11.
38. Bugliarello, *Towards the Technological University: The Story of Polytechnic Institute of New York*, 22.
39. Ibid., 23.
40. Alice Woller, *History of Polytechnic 1890-1920* (unpublished—manuscript copy at Polytechnic University Archives), 12.
41. Ibid.
42. Ibid.
43. Ibid., 14.
44. Ibid., 15.
45. Ibid.
46. Ibid.
47. Ibid., 17.
48. Ibid.
49. Ibid.
50. Ibid.
51. Ibid.
52. Filipino Used and Rare Books, http://www.palhbooks.com/used_rare.html.
53. Bugliarello, *Towards the Technological University: The Story of Polytechnic Institute of New York*, 23.
54. Ibid., 24.
55. Ibid., 23.
56. Alice Woller, *History of Polytechnic 1890-1920* (unpublished—manuscript copy at Polytechnic University Archives), 19.
57. Ibid., 20.
58. Ibid.
59. Ibid., 22.
60. Polytechnic University, "History of Polytechnic University—Making Their Mark; Alumni," http://www.poly.edu/150/beginning.cfm.
61. Poetry Archive, Henry Van Dyke, http://www.poetry-archive.com/v/van_dyke_henry.html.
62. Polytechnic University, "History of Polytechnic University—Making Their Mark; Alumni," http://www.poly.edu/150/beginning.cfm.
63. American Society of Mechanical Engineers, "About ASME," http://www.asme.org/about/.
64. Alice Woller, *History of Polytechnic 1890-1920* (unpublished—manuscript copy at Polytechnic University Archives), 24.
65. Ibid.
66. Ibid., 25.
67. Ibid., 26.
68. Ibid., 27.
69. Ibid., 30.
70. Ibid., 31.
71. Kastendieck, *The Story of Poly*, 89, 90.
72. Ibid., 90.
73. Polytechnic Institute of Brooklyn, *Catalogue of the College of Engineering*, 1925, 20.
74. Kastendieck, *The Story of Poly*, 120.
75. Ibid.
76. Alice Woller, *History of Polytechnic 1890-1920* (unpublished—manuscript copy at Polytechnic University Archives), 32.
77. Polytechnic University, "History of Polytechnic University—

Making Their Mark; Alumni," http://www.poly.edu/150/beginning.cfm.

78. Alice Woller, *History of Polytechnic 1890-1920* (unpublished—manuscript copy at Polytechnic University Archives), 32.

79. Ibid.

80. The American Society of Engineers, "Edwin F. Church," http://www.asme.org/honors/ms71/gaa/church.html.

81. *The Story of the Polytechnic and Its Service to the Public*, (New York, 1920), 5.

82. Alice Woller, *History of Polytechnic 1890-1920* (unpublished—manuscript copy at Polytechnic University Archives), 32.

83. *The Story of the Polytechnic and Its Service to the Public*, (New York 1920), 31.

84. Ibid., 4.

85. Ibid., 15.

86. Ibid., 23.

87. Ibid., 27.

88. Bugliarello, *Towards the Technological University: The Story of Polytechnic Institute of New York*, 24.

89. Infoplease, "James Truslow Adams," http://www.infoplease.com/ce6/people/A0802434.html.

90. ThinkExist.com, James Truslow Adams, http://en.thinkexist.com/quotation/We_cannot_advance_without_new_experiments_in/256782.html.

91. The University of Akron Timeline, "President and Founder Parke R. Kolbe, 1913-1925," http://www.uakron.edu/resources/history/UAtimeline.php.

92. "1957 Alumni Roster," *Brief History of the Alumni Association* (Brooklyn, NY: Polytechnic University Press, 1957), 6.

93. "Poly Marching Song," *PolyWog*, (Polytechnic Institute of Brooklyn, 1929), 98.

CHAPTER THREE SIDEBAR: ALFRED P. SLOAN JR.

1. Dickinson State University, "Great Leaders," (North Dakota Higher Education Computing Network, 2000), http://www.dickinsonstate.com/TR_about_leaders.asp.

2. Ibid.

3. Ibid.

4. Ibid.

5. Ibid.

6. Ibid.

CHAPTER THREE SIDEBAR: POLY'S FAMOUS ARTIST

1. Welcome to the World of Charles R. Knight, http://www.charlesrknight.com/.

2. Ibid.

3. Ibid.

4. Ibid.

CHAPTER THREE SIDEBAR: POLY PREP

1. Kastendieck, *The Story of Poly*, 105.

2. Ibid., 106.

3. Ibid.

4. Poly Prep Country Day School, "Poly Prep Country Day School— Mission," http://www.polyprep.org/prospective/mission/default.asp?L3=2.

5. Ibid.

6. Ibid.

7. Kastendieck, *The Story of Poly*, 114.

8. Poly Prep Country Day School, "Poly Prep Country Day School— Mission," http://www.polyprep.org/prospective/mission/default.asp?L3=2.

9. Ibid.

10. Ibid.

11. Ibid.

12. Ibid.

CHAPTER THREE SIDEBAR: WALTER HAMPDEN AND EDWARD EVERETT HORTON

1. Hersam Acorn Newspapers, Acorn Online, http://www.acorn-online.com/G-L.htm.

2. Ibid.

3. MSN Movies, Hal Erickson, "All Movie Guide," http://entertainment.msn.com/celebs/celeb.aspx?mp=b&c=321780.

4. Ibid.

5. Ibid.

6. Ibid.

CHAPTER FOUR

1. *Annual Reports* (Brooklyn, NY: The Polytechnic Institute of Brooklyn, 1930-1935), 18.

2. *Poly Men, All the Alumni News of the Polytechnic Institute of Brooklyn*, Vol. 6, No. 2, 2.

3. Ibid.

4. Ibid.

5. *Annual Reports* (Brooklyn, NY: The Polytechnic Institute of Brooklyn, 1930 to 1935), 1.

6. Ibid., 15.

7. *Poly Men, All the Alumni News of the Polytechnic Institute of Brooklyn*, Vol. 6, No. 2, 8.

8. Ibid., 5.

9. About.com, "Inventors— "Charles Kettering (1876 to 1958)," http://inventors.about.com/library/inventors/blignition.htm.

10. The Polytechnic Institute of Brooklyn, *Catalogue of the Evening Session*, 1934 to 1935, 10.

11. *Poly Men, All the Alumni News of the Polytechnic Institute of Brooklyn*, Vol. 6, No. 3, 3.

12. Ibid.

13. Ibid.

14. *Poly Men, All the Alumni News of the Polytechnic Institute of Brooklyn*, Vol. 7, No. 1, 4.

15. Ernst Weber, *The Evolution of Electrical Engineering, A personal Perspective* (New York: IEEE Press, 1994) 153.

16. *Poly Men, All the Alumni News of the Polytechnic Institute of Brooklyn*, Vol. 6, No. 8, 8.

17. *Poly Men, All the Alumni News of the Polytechnic Institute of Brooklyn*, Vol. 7, No. 1, 7.

18. City University of New York, Gaurav Jain, "The Great Depression as a Transforming Force," http://academic.brooklyn.cuny.edu/history/dfg/core/jain.htm.

19. *Poly Men, All the Alumni News of the Polytechnic Institute of Brooklyn*, Vol. 6, No. 3, 1.

20. *Poly Men, All the Alumni News of the Polytechnic Institute of Brooklyn*, Vol. 7, No. 2, 19.

21. *Poly Men, All the Alumni News of the Polytechnic Institute of Brooklyn*, Vol. 10, No. 3, 1.

22. *Annual Reports* (Brooklyn, NY: The Polytechnic Institute of Brooklyn, 1931 to 1932), 12.

23. Ibid.

24. *Annual Reports* (Brooklyn, NY: The Polytechnic Institute of Brooklyn, 1933 to 1934), 11.

25. *Poly Men, All the Alumni News of the Polytechnic Institute of Brooklyn,* Vol. 6, No. 1, 3.
26. *Annual Reports* (Brooklyn, NY: The Polytechnic Institute of Brooklyn, 1932 to 1933), 10.
27. Ibid.
28. *Poly Men, All the Alumni News of the Polytechnic Institute of Brooklyn,* Vol. 6, No. 3, 9.
29. Ibid.
30. *Annual Reports* (Brooklyn, NY: The Polytechnic Institute of Brooklyn, 1932 to 1933), 14.
31. *Poly Men, All the Alumni News of the Polytechnic Institute of Brooklyn,* Vol. 6, No. 3, 12.
32. Institute of Electrical and Electronics Engineers, "IEEE Edison Medal," http://www.ieee.org/portal/site/mainsite/menuitem.818c0c39e85ef176fb2275875bac26c8/index.jsp?&pName=corp_level1&path=about/awards/sums&file=edisonsum.xml&xsl=generic.xsl.
33. *Poly Men, All the Alumni News of the Polytechnic Institute of Brooklyn,* Vol. 6, No. 2, 3.
34. Ibid., 5.
35. Charles D. Strang, interview by Jeffrey L. Rodengen, digital recording, 11 November 2004, Write Stuff Enterprises.
36. *Poly Men, All the Alumni News of the Polytechnic Institute of Brooklyn,* Vol. 6, No. 9, 3.
37. Ibid., 7.
38. Ibid.
39. Ibid., 1.
40. *Annual Reports* (Brooklyn, NY: The Polytechnic Institute of Brooklyn, 1932 to 1933), 24.
41. *Poly Men, All the Alumni News of the Polytechnic Institute of Brooklyn,* Vol. 6, No. 9, 2.
42. Ibid., 1.
43. Ibid., 3.
44. *Annual Reports* (Brooklyn, NY: The Polytechnic Institute of Brooklyn, 1935 to 1936), 15.
45. Ibid., 16.
46. Ibid.
47. Ibid., 17.
48. Ibid., 7.
49. *Annual Reports* (Brooklyn, NY: The Polytechnic Institute of Brooklyn, 1934 to 1935), 9.
50. Ibid., 10
51. Ibid.
52. Ibid., 5

53. Ibid., 27
54. Ibid., 12
55. Ibid., 24
56. Ibid., 15
57. Ibid., 21
58. William Fendrich, *The Polywog,* 1938, 1.
59. Ibid., 3.
60. Ibid., 4.
61. Ibid., 5.
62. *Annual Reports* (Brooklyn, NY: The Polytechnic Institute of Brooklyn, 1937 to 1939), 6.
63. Ibid., 5.
64. Ibid., 8.
65. Walter A. Dommers, *Polywog,* 1939, 4.
66. Ibid., 5.
67. Ibid.
68. Ibid., 4.
69. *Annual Reports* (Brooklyn, NY: The Polytechnic Institute of Brooklyn, 1939 to 1940), 11.
70. Ibid., 6.
71. Ibid., 8.
72. Ibid., 10.
73. Ibid.
74. Iowa State University, College of Engineering, News, Paul F. Bruins, http://www.eng.iastate.edu/news/storyarchive.asp?id=219.

CHAPTER FOUR SIDEBAR: HARRY STANLEY ROGERS

1. Oregon State University, College of Engineering, "Harry Rogers," http://engr.oregonstate.edu/oregonstater/fame/1998/ccee/harryrogers.html.

CHAPTER FOUR SIDEBAR: A SPECIAL MILESTONE FOR THE DEPARTMENT OF CHEMISTRY

1. *Annual Reports* (Brooklyn, NY: The Polytechnic Institute of Brooklyn, 1934 to 1935), 9.
2. Bugliarello, *Towards the Technological University: The Story of Polytechnic Institute of New York,* 25.

CHAPTER FOUR SIDEBAR: POLY FIRE

1. *Annual Reports* (Brooklyn, NY: The Polytechnic Institute of Brooklyn, 1937 to 1939), 5.
2. Ibid., 6.
3. Ibid., 7.

CHAPTER FIVE

1. Bugliarello, *Towards the Technological University: The Story of Polytechnic Institute of New York,* 25.
2. Ibid.
3. Polytechnic Institute of Brooklyn, "1942-1943 Evening Session" (Easton, PA: Polytechnic Institute of Brooklyn), 24.
4. Ibid., 25.
5. Harry Wechsler, interview by Jeffrey L. Rodengen, digital recording, 17 September 2004, Write Stuff Enterprises.
6. The History Place, World War Two in Europe, http://www.historyplace.com/worldwar2/timeline/ww2time.htm.
7. Staff writer, *Brooklyn Daily Eagle,* 23 March 1941, Section A 9.
8. *Polywog* (Brooklyn, NY: Polytechnic Institute of Brooklyn, 1942), Volume 48, Chapter One, 1.
9. Staff writer, *New York Times,* 30 September 1941.
10. *Polywog* (Brooklyn, NY: Polytechnic Institute of Brooklyn, 1942), Volume 48, Chapter One, 4.
11. Ibid.
12. Staff writer, *Brooklyn Daily Eagle,* 12 October 1941, 2.
13. ACA, American Crystallographic Association, Isidor Fankuchen Award, http://www.hwi.buffalo.edu/ACA/index.html.
14. Hans Mark, interview by Jeffrey L. Rodengen, digital recording, 9 September 2004, Write Stuff Enterprises.
15. City University of New York, "Herman Mark and the Polymer Research Institute," http://www.qcc.cuny.edu/NYACSReport2003/HistPolymer.htm.
16. Herbert Morawetz, interview by Jeffrey L. Rodengen, digital recording, 25 August 2004, Write Stuff Enterprises.
17. Staff Writer, *Brooklyn Eagle,* 2 February 1941.
18. Staff Writer, *Brooklyn Eagle,* 10 September 1941.
19. Joseph Jacobs, interview by Jeffrey L. Rodengen, digital recording, 25 August 2004, Write Stuff Enterprises.
20. Jacobs, interview.
21. Ibid.

22. *Polywog* (Brooklyn, NY: Polytechnic Institute of Brooklyn, 1943), 10.
23. Ibid.
24. Ibid.
25. Staff Writer, *New York Times*, 26 September 1941.
26. "Fraternities and Honor Societies," *PolyWog* (Brooklyn, NY: Polytechnic University, 1943) 90, 96.
27. *Polytechnic Institute of Brooklyn Bulletin*, 1945-46, Graduate Session, Vol. LXXXIX-XC, No. 3, 16.
28. University of California, San Diego, Mandeville Special Collections Library, Hans Reissner Papers—Background, http://orpeus.ucsd.edu/speccoll/html/mss0330d.html.
29. *Polywog* (Brooklyn, NY: Polytechnic University, 1945), 92.
30. Martin Bloom, interview by Jeffrey L. Rodengen, digital recording, 10 June 2004, Write Stuff Enterprises.
31. Bloom, interview.
32. Henry A. McKinnell Jr., "Commencement Address To the 2004 Graduates of Polytechnic University," New York City, 27 May 2004.
33. *Poly Men, All The Alumni News of the Polytechnic Institute of Brooklyn*, January 1948, Vol. XXIV, No. 2, 9.
34. James McQuirter, National Weather Service Forecast Office, "Black History Month," http://www.crh.noaa.gov/gld/diversity/africanamerican.htm.
35. Ernst Weber, *The Evolution of Electrical Engineering, A Personal Perspective* (New York: IEEE Press, 1994), 156-57.
36. Institute of Electrical and Electronics Engineers, Annual Banquet Brochure (IEEE, 1971), http://www.ieee.org/organizations/history_center/legacies/weber.html.
37. Ernst Weber, *The Evolution of Electrical Engineering, A Personal Perspective* (New York: IEEE Press, 1994), 157.

38. *Poly Men, All the Alumni News of the Polytechnic Institute of Brooklyn*, November 1946, 2.
39. *Poly Men, All the Alumni News of the Polytechnic Institute of Brooklyn*, November 1947, 2.
40. *Poly Men, All the Alumni News of the Polytechnic Institute of Brooklyn*, November 1946, 1.
41. *Poly Men, All the Alumni News of the Polytechnic Institute of Brooklyn*, January 1947, 1.
42. *Poly Men, All the Alumni News of the Polytechnic Institute of Brooklyn*, November 1946, 2.
43. *Poly Men, All the Alumni News of the Polytechnic Institute of Brooklyn*, July 1948, 7.
44. *Poly Men, All the Alumni News of the Polytechnic Institute of Brooklyn*, March 1949, 6.
45. *Poly Men, All the Alumni News of the Polytechnic Institute of Brooklyn*, November 1949, 1.
46. Ibid., 11.
47. *Poly Men, All the Alumni News of the Polytechnic Institute of Brooklyn*, January 1951, 8.
48. Ibid.
49. *Poly Men, All the Alumni News of the Polytechnic Institute of Brooklyn*, March 1952, 5.
50. *Poly Men, All the Alumni News of the Polytechnic Institute of Brooklyn*, November 1951, 5.
51. Ibid. 2.
52. National Aeronautics and Space Administration, http://www.hq.nasa.gov/office/pao/History/SP-445/ch2-4.htm.
53. Martin Bloom, interview by Jeffrey L. Rodengen, digital recording, 10 June 2004, Write Stuff Enterprises.
54. Bloom, interview.

CHAPTER FIVE SIDEBAR: POLY GRADUATE INVENTS THE FIRST "GISMO"

1. *Poly Men, All the News of the Polytechnic Institute of Brooklyn*, March 1952, 14.
2. Ibid.
3. Ibid.
4. Lucent Technologies, Bell Labs Innovations, http://www.bell-labs.com/new/features/pierce.html.

CHAPTER FIVE SIDEBAR: HANS J. REISSNER

1. University of California, San Diego, Mandeville Special Collections Library, Hans Reissner Papers—Background, http://orpheus.ucsd.edu/speccoll/testing/html/mss0030d.html.
2. Ibid.
3. Ibid.
4. Ibid.

CHAPTER FIVE SIDEBAR: MASS PRODUCING PENICILLIN DURING WORLD WAR II

1. Henry A. McKinnell Jr., "Commencement Address To the 2004 Graduates of Polytechnic University," New York City, 27 May 2004.
2. Ibid.
3. Ibid.
4. Ibid.
5. Ibid.
6. Polytechnic University, "The Power of PolyThinking—Jasper H. Kane," http://www.poly.edu/150/polythinkers.cfm#Kane.
7. Henry A. McKinnell Jr., "Commencement Address to the 2004 Graduates of Polytechnic University," New York City, 27 May 2004.

CHAPTER FIVE SIDEBAR: THE FIRST ENCYCLOPEDIA OF CHEMICAL ENGINEERING

1. *Poly Men, All the News of the Polytechnic Institute of Brooklyn*, January 1948, 6.
2. Ibid.
3. Ibid.

CHAPTER SIX

1. Staff Writer, *Business Week*, 24 April 1954, 58.
2. Ibid.
3. Ibid, 59.
4. Leopold Felsen, interview by Jeffrey L. Rodengen, digital recording, 24 August 2004, Write Stuff Enterprises.
5. Carmine Masucci, interview by Jeffrey L. Rodengen, digital recording, 24 August 2004, Write Stuff Enterprises.

6. Staff Writer, *Business Week*, 24 April 1954, 60.
7. Ibid.
8. *Poly Men*, March 1953, 7.
9. Ibid.
10. *Poly Men*, July 1954, 7.
11. *Poly Men*, March, 1953, 7.
12. Ibid.
13. Martin Bloom, interview by Jeffrey L. Rodengen, digital recording, 10 June 2004, Write Stuff Enterprises.
14. "High-Speed Aeronautics Conference—Major Event Marks Brooklyn Poly's Centennial Year," *Mechanical Engineering*, April 1955, 379.
15. Bloom, interview.
16. Ibid.
17. Staff Writer, *Aviation Week*, 21 October 1957.
18. *Polywog*, 1959, 138.
19. *Poly Men*, May 1953, 8.
20. *Poly Men*, March 1953, 6.
21. *Poly Men*, September 1954, 7.
22. *Poly Men*, May 1953, 6.
23. Ibid.
24. Ibid.
25. *Poly Men*, May 1954, 8.
26. Ibid.
27. *Poly Men*, May 1953, 2.
28. Staff Writer, *Business Week*, 24 April 1954, 59.
29. Staff Writer, "Brooklyn Poly Marks 100 Years of Service to Science" *Industrial Science and Engineering*, October 1955, 1.
30. Ibid.
31. Ibid.
32. Ibid.
33. Ibid.
34. "They Say of Us," Library Archives, Polytechnic Institute of Brooklyn, October 1955, 4.
35. *Poly Men*, September 1954, 3.
36. *Ibid.*
37. Staff Writer, *Polytechnic Reporter*, 2 December 1954, 1.
38. *Poly Men*, September 1954, 5.
39. *Polytechnite*, November 1954, 4.
40. Staff Writer, *Polytechnic Reporter*, 10 March, 1955, 1.
41. Ibid, 2.
42. *Poly Men*, May 1954, 2.
43. Ibid.
44. Ibid.
45. Obits.com—The Internet Obituary Network, "O. Wilson Link, 1914 -2001," http://obits.com/linkowinston.html.

46. Fenimore Art Museum, "Arrested Motion: 1950s Railroad Photographs by O. Winston Link," http://www.tfaoi.com/aa/4aa/4aa494a.htm.
47. Rudolph Marcus, interview by Jeffrey L. Rodengen, digital recording, 20 September 2004, Write Stuff Enterprises.
48. Marcus, interview.
49. Bill Bell, "Artist in Shadows Left Bright Legacy," *Daily News*, 5 February 1996.
50. News Release P-752, Harry V. Smith Inc.
51. Ibid.
52. Gene Currivan, *New York Times*, 21 April 1957.
53. *Poly Men*, March 1957, 5.
54. *Poly Men*, July 1956, 5.
55. George Schillinger, interview by Jeffrey L. Rodengen, digital recording, 6 June 2004, Write Stuff Enterprises.
56. Ernst Weber, *The Evolution of Electrical Engineering, A Personal Perspective* (New York: IEEE Press, 1994), 180.
57. *Poly Men*, July 1957, 1.
58. Ernst Weber, *The Evolution of Electrical Engineering, A Personal Perspective* (New York: IEEE Press, 1994), 180.
59. Ibid., 181.
60. Ibid.
61. Staff Writer, *Polytechnic Reporter*, 11 December 1958, 1.
62. *Poly Men*, May 1958, 9.
63. *Polytechnite*, May 1959, 6.
64. Ibid.
65. Ibid.
66. Mischa Schwartz, interview by Jeffrey L. Rodengen, digital recording, 5 November 2004, Write Stuff Enterprises.
67. Schwartz, interview.
68. Staff Writer, *Polytechnic Reporter*, 11 December 1959.
69. Public Relations Office, Polytechnic Institute of Brooklyn, 24 March 1958.
70. Staff Writer, *Polytechnic Reporter*, 16 October 1958, 1.
71. Staff Writer, *Polytechnic Reporter*, 9 October 1958, 1.
72. Staff Writer, *Polytechnic Reporter*, 19 March 1959, 1.
73. Staff Writer, *Polytechnic Reporter*, 13 November 1958, 1.
74. Staff Writer, *Polytechnic Reporter*, 19 March 1959, 1.

75. Staff Writer, *Polytechnic Reporter*, 25 September 1958, 1.

CHAPTER SIX SIDEBAR: DISCOVERY AT POLY LEADS TO NOBEL PRIZE

1. University of Pittsburgh, Phi Lambda Upsilon Xi Chapter, Francis Clifford Phillips Lecture Series, 1987, http://www.pitt.edu/~plu/PL/marcus.htm.
2. Rudolph Marcus, interview by Jeffrey L. Rodengen, digital recording, 20 September 2004, Write Stuff Enterprises.
3. University of Pittsburgh, Phi Lambda Upsilon Xi Chapter, Francis Clifford Phillips Lecture Series, 1987, http://www.pitt.edu/~plu/PL/marcus.htm.
4. Marcus interview.
5. University of Pittsburgh, Phi Lambda Upsilon Xi Chapter, Francis Clifford Phillips Lecture Series, 1987, http://www.pitt.edu/~plu/PL/marcus.htm.
6. Ibid.

CHAPTER SIX SIDEBAR: ABRAHAM JOEL TOBIAS, POLY'S MOST FAMOUS ARTIST

1. Caroline Tobias, interview by Jeffrey L. Rodengen, digital recording, 10 September 2004, Write Stuff Enterprises.
2. Tobias, interview.
3. "Science Mural Commissioned by Board of Trustees," *Polytechnic Newsletter*, 1957.
4. Ibid.
5. Bill Bell, "Artist in Shadows Left Bright Legacy," *Daily News*, 5 February 1996.
6. Ibid.

CHAPTER SEVEN

1. *Poly Men*, January 1960, 4.
2. *Report of the President*, Polytechnic Institute of Brooklyn, 1959-60, 30.
3. Ibid., 2.
4. Ibid., 3.
5. Ibid., 7.
6. Ibid., 1.
7. George Schillinger, interview by Jeffrey L. Rodengen, digital recording, 6 June 2004, Write Stuff Enterprises.

8. *Report of the President,* Polytechnic Institute of Brooklyn, 1959-60, 17.
9. *Poly Men,* September 1960, 2.
10. Donald Weisstuch, interview by Jeffrey L. Rodengen, digital recording, 15 September 2004, Write Stuff Enterprises.
11. *Report of the President,* Polytechnic Institute of Brooklyn, 1959-60, 14.
12. Ibid.
13. Ibid., 16.
14. *Poly Men,* April 1960, 13.
15. Ibid.
16. Ibid., 12.
17. *Report of the President,* Polytechnic Institute of Brooklyn, 1961-62, 20.
18. "A Special Report," *Poly Men,* May 1960, 8.
19. *Report of the President,* Polytechnic Institute of Brooklyn, 1961-62, 1.
20. Ibid.
21. *Poly Men,* November 1962, 6.
22. *Report of the President,* Polytechnic Institute of Brooklyn, 1961-62, 12.
23. Ibid.
24. Ibid., 13.
25. Ibid., 17.
26. Ibid., 7.
27. Ibid., 17.
28. *Poly Men,* January 1962, 8.
29. *Poly Men,* July 1961, 11.
30. *Poly Men,* April 1962, 2.
31. *Poly Men,* April 1962, 3.
32. *Poly Men,* November 1962, 2.
33. *Report of the President,* Polytechnic Institute of Brooklyn, 1962-63, 30.
34. *Poly Men,* April 1963, 1.
35. *Report of the President,* Polytechnic Institute of Brooklyn, 1962-63, 35.
36. Ibid.
37. *Report of the President,* Polytechnic Institute of Brooklyn, 1963-64, 46.
38. Ibid., 13.
39. *Poly Men,* Winter 1964-65, 7.
40. *Report of the President,* Polytechnic Institute of Brooklyn, 1963-64, 14.
41. Ibid., 34.
42. Ernst Weber, *The Evolution of Electrical Engineering, A Personal Perspective* (New York: IEEE Press, 1994), 184.
43. Ibid., 183.

44. Ibid.
45. *Poly Men,* February 1968, 18.
46. *Poly Men,* Winter 1964-65, 3.
47. Ibid., 4.
48. Ibid., 5.
49. Ibid., 4.
50. Ibid., 13.
51. Ibid., 14.
52. *Poly Men,* November 1965, 16.
53. Bugliarello, *Towards the Technological University: The Story of Polytechnic Institute of New York,* 30.
54. *Poly Men,* September 1966, 4.
55. Ibid., 5.
56. Ibid.
57. *Report of the President,* Polytechnic Institute of Brooklyn, 1969, 11.
58. *Report of the President,* Polytechnic Institute of Brooklyn, 1964-65, 36.
59. Ernst Weber, *The Evolution of Electrical Engineering, A Personal Perspective* (New York: IEEE Press, 1994), 184.
60. *Report of the President,* Polytechnic Institute of Brooklyn, 1964-65, 35.
61. *Report of the President,* Polytechnic Institute of Brooklyn, 1967, 9.
62. Ibid., 15.
63. Ibid., 16.
64. Ibid., 18.
65. Ibid.
66. *Poly Men,* September 1967, 17.
67. Ibid.
68. *Poly Men,* May 1968, 15.
69. *Report of the President,* Polytechnic Institute of Brooklyn, 1968, 16.
70. Victor Wallach, interview by Jeffrey L. Rodengen, digital recording, 10 June 2004, Write Stuff Enterprises.
71. Jim Jarman, interview by Jeffrey L. Rodengen, digital recording, 11 June 2004, Write Stuff Enterprises.
72. Ernst Weber, *The Evolution of Electrical Engineering, A Personal Perspective* (New York: IEEE Press, 1994) 181.
73. *Poly Men,* May 1969, 1.
74. Ibid., 5.
75. *Report of the President,* Polytechnic Institute of Brooklyn, 1968, 16.
76. Charles Hinkaty, interview by Jeffrey L. Rodengen, digital recording, 24 August 2004, Write Stuff Enterprises.
77. *Report of the President,* Polytechnic Institute of Brooklyn, 1971, 1.

78. *Report of the President,* Polytechnic Institute of Brooklyn, 1972, 1.
79. *Report of the President,* Polytechnic Institute of Brooklyn, 1972, 1.

CHAPTER SEVEN SIDEBAR:
MODERN VISIONS

1. *Poly Men,* September 1965, 11.
2. Ibid., 13.
3. Ibid., 14.
4. Ibid., 12.
5. Ibid., 11.

CHAPTER SEVEN SIDEBAR:
POLY CHANGES
NYC BUILDING CODE

1. *Poly Men,* September 1965, 2.
2. Ibid.
3. Ibid.
4. *Report of the President,* Polytechnic Institute of Brooklyn, 1963, 29.
5. *Poly Men,* May 1969, 8.

CHAPTER SEVEN SIDEBAR:
MURRAY ROTHBARD

1. LP News Archive, "Murray Rothbard, 1926-1995," February 1995, www.lp.org/lpn/ 9502-Rothbard.html.
2. Ibid.
3. Ibid.
4. Ibid.

CHAPTER SEVEN SIDEBAR:
TRIUMPHS AND TRANSITIONS

1. *Report of the President,* Polytechnic Institute of Brooklyn, 1963-64, 14.
2. *Poly Men,* September 1964, 20.
3. *Report of the President,* Polytechnic Institute of Brooklyn, 1963-64, 35.
4. Ibid.
5. Ibid., 36.
6. Ibid.
7. Ibid.

CHAPTER EIGHT

1. Bugliarello, *Towards the Technological University: The Story of Polytechnic Institute of New York,* 30.
2. Ibid.
3. Polytechnic University Office of Public Relations, "Merger Agreement Between NYU/SES and PIB," 23 April 1973, 4.
4. Ibid.

5. Richard Thorsen, interview by Jeffrey L. Rodengen, digital recording, 10 June 2004, Write Stuff Enterprises.
6. Office of Public Relations, Polytechnic University, "Merger Agreement Between NYU/SES and PIB," 23 April 1973, 2.
7. Ibid., 4.
8. Bugliarello, *Towards the Technological University: The Story of Polytechnic Institute of New York*, 31.
9. Richard Thorsen, interview by Jeffrey L. Rodengen, digital recording, 10 June 2004, Write Stuff Enterprises.
10. Bugliarello, *Towards the Technological University: The Story of Polytechnic Institute of New York*, 30.
11. Norman Auburn, "Acting President's Letter to the Alumni," 16 April 1973, 2.
12. Irving Kadoff, interview by Jeffrey L. Rodengen, digital recording, 26 August 2004, Write Stuff Enterprises.
13. Kadoff, interview.
14. Richard Thorsen, interview by Jeffrey L. Rodengen, digital recording, 10 June 2004, Write Stuff Enterprises.
15. Thorsen, interview.
16. "Curriculum Vitae of the Steering Committee," *Polytechnic Cable*, October 1974, 8.
17. George Bugliarello, interview by Jeffrey L. Rodengen, digital recording, 10 June 2004, Write Stuff Enterprises.
18. Bugliarello, *Towards the Technological University: The Story of Polytechnic Institute of New York*, 32.
19. Ibid.
20. Ibid.
21. Pace University Library, "Rene Jules Dubos," http://www.pace.edu/library/collection/Dubos.html.
22. New York University Archives, "Guide to the Papers of John R. Lamarsh, 1943-1981," http://dlib.nyu.edu:8083/archead/servlet/SaxonServlet?source=/lamarsh.xml&style=/saxon01a2002.xsl&part=body.
23. "Alumni Challenged by Poly Varsity Teams," *Polytechnic Cable*, Spring 1977, 10.

24. Heather Walters, interview by Jeffrey L. Rodengen, digital recording, 11 June 2004, Write Stuff Enterprises.
25. "PINY Prexy Speaks to Alumni," *Polygraphs*, Winter 1973-74, Vol. 4, No. 2, 1.
26. "New Process Heats Oil Lines," *Polytechnic Cable*, December 1974, 4.
27. Dibner Institute For the History of Science and Technology, "Bern Dibner, 1897-1988," http://dibinst.mit.edu/DIBNER/DIHistory/BernDibner/BernBio.htm.
28. *Polytechnic Cable*, January-February 1974, 1.
29. *Polytechnic Cable*, January-February 1974, 1.
30. George Bugliarello, interview by Jeffrey L. Rodengen, digital recording, 10 June 2004, Write Stuff Enterprises.
31. Helen Warren, interview by Jeffrey L. Rodengen, digital recording, 11 June 2004, Write Stuff Enterprises.
32. "Female Firsts: Honorary Degree and Deanship," *Polytechnic Cable*, October 1974, 2.
33. Ibid.
34. "Reigning Beauty Queens: Two for Polytechnic," *Polytechnic Cable*, December 1974, 2.
35. "Hands Around the World," *Polytechnic Cable*, December 1974, 3.
36. "President to Alumni Nationwide: Expect New Kind of University," *Polytechnic Cable*, October 1974, 2.
37. "In Defiance of Gravity," *Polytechnic Cable*, December 1974, 1.
38. Ibid., 3.
39. "Alumni Rule Highways and Public Works," *Polytechnic Cable*, October 1974, 3.
40. "Freshman Enrollment: The 64 Percent Increase," *Polytechnic Cable*, December 1974, 3.
41. Ibid.
42. "Energy Program Still Growing," *Polytechnic Cable*," April 1976, 4.
43. Bugliarello Inaugurated, *Polytechnic Cable*, March 1975, 1.
44. Ibid., 2.
45. Ibid., 1.

46. "Polytechnic Alumnus Appointed Assistant Secretary of the Army," *Polytechnic Cable*, March 1975, 5.
47. "Million Dollar Gift," *Polytechnic Cable*, April-May 1975, 1.
48. Ibid.
49. Ibid.
50. "Poly Receives $390,000 Grant," *Polytechnic Cable*, April-May 1975, 1.
51. Ibid.
52. "Polytechnic Transportation Center Announces Four Research Projects," *Polytechnic Cable*, November 1976, 9.
53. "Poly Receives $390,000 Grant," *Polytechnic Cable*, April-May 1975, 2.
54. "Polytechnic in Westchester," *Polytechnic Cable*, April-May 1975, 1.
55. Staff writer, "Polytechnic-Pace Affiliate to Bring Courses to County," *Patent Trader*, 4 September 1975.
56. "China Delegation Visits Farmingdale," *Polytechnic Cable*, November 1975, 1.
57. Ibid.
58. Martin Bloom, interview by Jeffrey L. Rodengen, digital recording, 10 June 2004, Write Stuff Enterprises.
59. "Ocean Engineering Set For Fall," *Polytechnic Cable*, April-May 1975, 2.
60. "Pershing Rifles March Off With National Championship," *Polytechnic Cable*, May 1977, 9.
61. "Grumman Hall Dedicated, *Polytechnic Cable*, February 1977, 1.
62. Benjamin Senitsky, interview by Jeffrey L. Rodengen, digital recording, 30 November 2004, Write Stuff Enterprises.
63. Marvin E. Gettleman, "Bicentennial Courses Focus on Revolution," *Polytechnic Cable*, January 1976, 5.
64. Ibid.
65. "Enrico Ferri, Founded Aero Labs," *Polytechnic Cable*, January 1976, 9.
66. Ibid.
67. "Polytechnic Awards 999 Degrees," *Polytechnic Cable*, July 1976, 1.
68. Ibid.
69. Ibid.

70. "Jacobs Elected Chairman as Rowley Retires," *Polytechnic Cable*, July 1976, 9.
71. "The Progress of Polytechnic Now," *Polytechnic Cable*, February 1977, 4.

CHAPTER EIGHT SIDEBAR: POLY WRITES NEW YORK CITY FIRE CODE

1. "Fighting Fire with Fire," *Polytechnic Cable*, October 1973, 3.
2. Ibid.
3. Ibid.
4. Ibid.

CHAPTER EIGHT SIDEBAR: BARCODE TECHNOLOGY

1. Symbol Technologies, "About Jerome Swartz," http://www.symbol.com/about/overview/overview_execleadership_jermom.html.
2. Ibid.
3. Ibid.
4. National Space Society, "Shelley A. Harrison," http://www.nss.org/about/bios/harrison.html.
5. Ibid.

CHAPTER EIGHT SIDEBAR: POLY'S BEER MAN

1. The Straight Dope, Cecil Adams, "Is Light Beer Made by Watering it Down?," 27 July 2000, http://www.straightdope.com/mailbag/mlitebeer.html.
2. Ibid.

CHAPTER EIGHT SIDEBAR: WHAT, ME WORRY?

1. "Mad's Mentor Returns to Poly," *Polytechnic Cable*, May 1977, 11.
2. Ibid.
3. Ibid.
4. Ibid.

CHAPTER NINE

1. *Report of the President*, Polytechnic University, 1986, 21.
2. "Polytechnic Trustee Paul Soros Named to CICU Alumni Hall of Distinction," *News at Poly*, 1 February 2002,

http://www.poly.edu/news2/view_story.cfm?id=750
3. Ibid.
4. "Polytechnic Achieves First Balanced Budget in Fourteen Years," *Polytechnic Cable*, February 1978, 3.
5. "Management Established as Third Academic Division at Polytechnic," *Polytechnic Cable*, February 1978, 2.
6. "Westchester Graduate Program Moves Into New Home," *Polytechnic Cable*, July 1978, 15.
7. "Plans Underway For Area Development," *Polytechnic Cable*, May 1979, 1.
8. Ibid.
9. "Metro-Tech: A Space-Age Idea For Big Apple," *Polytechnic Cable*, Summer 1982, 5.
10. Ibid.
11. "Poly Kicks Off $850,000 Annual Campaign," *Polytechnic Cable*, November 1979, 1.
12. "Polytechnic Dedicates New Student Center," *Polytechnic Cable*, November 1979, 2.
13. "Prof. Katzir Honored at Dinner," *Polytechnic Cable*, November 1979, 3.
14. "Poly Holds 125th Commencement," *Polytechnic Cable*, September 1980, 6.
15. "Poly Sets Fundraising Record," *Polytechnic Cable*, September 1980, 1.
16. Ibid.
17. Arthur Martinez, interview by Jeffrey L. Rodengen, digital recording, 8 August 2004, Write Stuff Enterprises.
18. "Polytechnic Graduates 1000," *Polytechnic Cable*, June 1981, 1.
19. "Imaging Institute Receives $1 Million," *Polytechnic Cable*, Winter 1982, 1.
20. Ibid.
21. "Governor Cuomo Names Poly as State Telecommunications Center," *Polytechnic Cable*, Winter-Spring 1983, 1.
22. Ibid.
23. Ibid.
24. Richard Van Slyke, interview by Jeffrey L. Rodengen, digital recording, 26 August 2004, Write Stuff Enterprises.
25. Gary Kimball, "Poly Enters the Liberal Arts," *The Brooklyn Paper*, 14 January 1984.

26. "People at Poly—Donald J. Hockney," *Polytechnic Cable*, http://media.poly.edu/alumni/cable/winter98/people_at_poly2.html.
27. Paul Schreiber, "The Poly Connection," *Newsday*, 11 February 1985.
28. "Physical Fitness and Weight Lifting Facilities," *Polytechnic Cable*, Spring 1984, 1.
29. "Papoulis Awarded IEEE '84 Medal," *Long-Islander*, 9 February, 1984.
30. Leonard Shaw, interview by Jeffrey L. Rodengen, digital recording, 25 August 2004, Write Stuff Enterprises.
31. "Regents Approve Name Change to Polytechnic University," *Polytechnic Cable*, Winter 1985, 1.
32. "The Year in Review," *Polytechnic Cable*, Fall 1984, 1.
33. Ibid.
34. Ernst Weber Awarded National Medal of Science, *Polytechnic Cable*, Summer 1987, 1.
35. "20 Receive U.S. Awards in Science, Technology," *Associated Press*, 26 June 1986.
36. Beverly Johnson, interview by Jeffrey L. Rodengen, digital recording, 8 November 2004, Write Stuff Enterprises.
37. Bill Murray, interview by Jeffrey L. Rodengen, digital recording, 15 September 2004, Write Stuff Enterprises.
38. Timothy McDarrah, *The Newspaper*, 18 April 1988.
39. Ibid.
40. Alair Townsend, interview by Jeffrey L. Rodengen, digital recording, 28 October 2004, Write Stuff Enterprises.
41. Townsend, interview.
42. Ibid.
43. George Bugliarello, interview by Jeffrey L. Rodengen, digital recording, 10 June 2004, Write Stuff Enterprises.
44. Bugliarello, interview.
45. "Poly Swings for the Fences," *Polytechnic Cable*, Fall 1988, 1.
46. "Poly Breaks Ground for New Building," *Polytechnic Cable*, Summer 1990, 3.
47. "High Honors for Poly's Electromagnetic Research," *Polytechnic Cable*, Summer 1991, 3.

48. "Dedication Day," *Polytechnic Cable*, Summer 1992, 1.
49. Ibid.
50. Ibid.
51. Ivan Frisch, interview by Jeffrey L. Rodengen, digital recording, 23 August 2004, Write Stuff Enterprises.

CHAPTER NINE SIDEBAR:
HERMAN MARK REMEMBERS
ALBERT EINSTEIN

1. "Memories of Einstein: Dr. Mark Reminisces," *Polytechnic Cable*, September 1979, 18.

CHAPTER NINE SIDEBAR:
ACCOMPLISHMENTS
AND ACHIEVEMENTS

1. National Inventors Hall of Fame, "Gordan Gould," http://www.invent.org/ hall_of_fame/69.html.
2. "Professor D.F. Othmer Awarded SCI's Perkin Medal," *Polytechnic Cable*, February 1978, 3.
3. "First Woman Polytechnic PhD Recipient Awarded Carl Neuberg Medal," *Polytechnic Cable*, May 1978, 6.
4. "High Honors for Poly's Electromagnetic Research," *Polytechnic Cable*, Summer 1991, 3.

CHAPTER NINE SIDEBAR:
CLASS OF 1983
MAKES MEDIA HISTORY

1. "Class of 1983 Makes Media History," *Polytechnic Cable*, Summer 1983, 1.
2. Ibid.

CHAPTER NINE SIDEBAR:
STAR WARS

1. Michael Hanrahan, "Star Wars Research $ to Polytechnic," *Daily News*, 18 March 1986.
2. "Polytechnic Dedicates 'Star Wars' Center," *Long Island Business*, 26 March 1986.

CHAPTER NINE SIDEBAR:
BERN DIBNER

1. George Rostky, "Bern Dibner, Founder of Burndy, Dies at 90,"

Electronic Engineering Times, 18 January 1989.
2. Ibid.
3. Ibid.
4. "Dedication Day," *Polytechnic Cable*, Summer 1992, 1.

CHAPTER NINE SIDEBAR:
POLY ALUMNA WINS NOBEL PRIZE

1. "1988 Nobel Prize Shared by Former Poly Grad Student," *Polytechnic Cable*, Winter 1989, 1.
2. Ibid.
3. Ibid., 8.
4. Ibid.

CHAPTER NINE SIDEBAR:
MORE KUDOS

1. Polytechnic University, "Charles Strang," http://www.poly.edu/ trustees/strang.cfm.
2. "Jacobs Chair in Chemical Engineering Established," *Polytechnic Cable*, Fall 1990, 1.

CHAPTER NINE SIDEBAR:
METROTECH—A VISIONARY
DREAM MADE REAL

1. Kim Strosnider, "A Research Park Grows in Brooklyn," *Chronicle of Higher Education*, 12 December 1997.

CHAPTER TEN

1. David Doucette, interview by Jeffrey L. Rodengen, digital recording, 28 October 2004, Write Stuff Enterprises.
2. "Polytechnic Wins Major Technology Reinvestment Awards," *Polytechnic Cable*, Winter 1994, 1.
3. Robert Flynn, interview by Jeffrey L. Rodengen, digital recording, 9 September 2004, Write Stuff Enterprises.
4. "Promise Fund Dinner Sets New Record," *Polytechnic Cable*, Spring 1994, 1.
5. "Alumni Profiles: Henry J. Singer," *Polytechnic Cable*, Winter 1994, 5.
6. "Martinez Elected Chairman of the Board," *Polytechnic Cable*, Spring 1994, 1.
7. "Jacobs Elected to NAE," *Polytechnic Cable*, Spring 1994, 2.

8. "Alumnus Named NYC Buildings Commissioner," *Polytechnic Cable*, Spring 1994, 5.
9. "Dr. David Chang Elected Polytechnic's New President," *Polytechnic Cable*, Summer 1994, 1.
10. "From George Bugliarello," *Polytechnic Cable*, Summer 1994, 4.
11. "Tribute Dinner," *Polytechnic Cable*, Summer, 1994, 1.
12. Ibid., 4.
13. Joseph Jacobs, interview by Jeffrey L. Rodengen, digital recording, 25 August 2004, Write Stuff Enterprises.
14. "Joseph J. and Violet J. Jacobs College of Engineering and Science Announced," *Polytechnic Cable*, Summer 1994, 1.
15. Ibid.
16. "Poly 1000 Wall Dedicated," *Polytechnic Cable*, Fall 1994, 1.
17. "Inauguration of the Center for Technology and Financial Services," *Polytechnic Cable*, Winter 1995, 1.
18. "Wireless Lab Established," *Polytechnic Cable*, Winter 1995, 4.
19. Henry Bertoni, interview by Jeffrey L. Rodengen, digital recording, 6 June 2004, Write Stuff Enterprises.
20. "Institute for Applied Technology," *Polytechnic Cable*, Fall 1995, 7.
21. "Money Magazine Kudos to Polytechnic," *Polytechnic Cable*, Winter 1995, 6.
22. "Academic Restructuring Announced," *Polytechnic Cable*, Summer 1995, 3.
23. "Polytechnic's New Student Center," *Polytechnic Cable*, Fall 1996, 1.
24. Ibid.
25. "The Legacy of Donald F. Othmer," *Polytechnic Cable*, Winter 1996, 1.
26. Ibid.
27. Ibid.
28. Ibid.
29. "President Emeritus Ernst Weber Dies," *Polytechnic Cable*, Spring 1996, 1.
30. Polytechnic University, "S. Steve Greenfield '43 Honored with Polytechnic Alumni Achievement Award," *News at Poly*, 5 December 2003, http://www.poly.edu/news2/ view_story.cfm?id=1841.

31. "Arthur C. Martinez '60 ME," *Polytechnic Cable*, Spring 1996, 3.
32. Mel Horwitch, interview by Jeffrey L. Rodengen, digital recording, 16 September 2004, Write Stuff Enterprises.
33 "Polytechnic Launches $150 Million Capital Campaign," *Polytechnic Cable*, Winter 1997, 1.
34. Ibid.
35. William Murray, interview by Jeffrey L. Rodengen, digital recording, 15 September 2004, Write Stuff Enterprises.
36. "More Than 1,000 Receive Degrees at Polytechnic's 142nd Commencement," *Polytechnic Cable*, September 1997, 1.
37. Ibid.
38. Polytechnic University, "Polytechnic Launches $275 Million Campaign," http://media.poly.edu/ dream/polycampaign.asp.
39. "A Year of Progress and Promise, An Extraordinary Opportunity for Transformation," *Report of the President*, Polytechnic University, 1997-1998, 1.
40. Ibid.
41. Stewart Nagler, interview by Jeffrey L. Rodengen, digital recording, 14 November 2004, Write Stuff Enterprises.
42. "Polytechnic Prepares for the New Century: Launches Strategic Planning 2000 to Transform University," *Polytechnic Cable*, Fall 1998, 1.
43. "IEEE Honors Provost Ivan T. Frisch," *Polytechnic Cable*, Winter 1998-99, 6.
44. "Gregory Smith Named New VP for Finance," *Polytechnic Cable*, Spring 1998, 6.
45. "Martinez Receives Gold Medal Award," *Polytechnic Cable*, Spring 1998, 6.
46 "Polytechnic Trustee Joseph J. Jacobs Challenges Alumni With $10 Million Matching Gift," *Polytechnic Cable*, Spring 1999, 2.
47. Ibid.
48. Ibid.
49. "Polytechnic Wins Coveted $2.6 Million Federal Grant To Develop Environmental Bioagent Detection," *Polytechnic Cable*, Summer 1999, 8.

CHAPTER TEN SIDEBAR: THE CHUDNOVSKY BROTHERS

1. "New Institute for Mathematics and Advanced Supercomputing," *Polytechnic Cable*, Winter 1997, 1.
2. Ibid.
3. Ibid.
4. Ibid.

CHAPTER TEN SIDEBAR: POLY GRADUATE AWARDED 1995 NOBEL PRIZE IN PHYSICS

1. Stanford Linear Accelerator Center, "Martin Perl Wins Nobel Prize in Physics," http://www.slac.stanford. edu/slac/feature/951011/ mperl95.html.
2. "Polytechnic Graduate Awarded 1995 Nobel Prize in Physics," *Polytechnic Cable*, Fall 1995, 1.
3. The Nobel Foundation, "Martin L. Perl— Autobiography," http://nobelprize.org/ physics/laureates/1995/ perl-autobio.html.
4. "Polytechnic Graduate Awarded 1995 Nobel Prize in Physics," *Polytechnic Cable*, Fall 1995, 1.
5. Ibid.

CHAPTER TEN SIDEBAR: POLY GRADUATE SPACE BOUND

1. "Alumni Profile: Charles J. Camarda '74," *Polytechnic Cable*, Summer 1996, 5.
2. Spaceflight Now, "STS-114 Mission Specialist 5 Charles J. Camarda," 19 December 2004, http:// www.spaceflightnow.com/ shuttle/sts114/crew/ camarda.html.
3. Ibid.
4. About.com, Nick Greene, "Preflight Interview: Charlie Camarda," Space/Astronomy, http://space.about.com/ cs/spaceshuttles/a/ camardaint1.htm.

CHAPTER TEN SIDEBAR: THE KING OF PATENTS

1. The Lemelson Foundation, "Jerome L. Lemelson," http://www.lemelson.org/ about/bio_jerry.ph.

2. Ibid.

CHAPTER TEN SIDEBAR: EUGENE KLEINER

1. Michael Liedtke, "Silicon Valley Pioneer, Kleiner Dies at 80," 27 November 2003, http://slick.org/deathwatch/ mailarchive/msg01175.html.
2. Ibid.
3. Ibid.
4. Ibid.
5. Ibid.
6. Ibid.

CHAPTER ELEVEN

1. "Strategic Planning 2000: A Blueprint for Excellence," *Polytechnic Cable*, Winter 1999-2000, 11.
2. "David Dibner Announces Two Large Gifts to Polytechnic," *Polytechnic Cable*, Summer 2000, 2.
3. "University Signs Biotech Deal with SUNY Downstate Medical Center," *ePoly Briefs*, January 2001, http://www. poly.edu/wwwpoly/ebriefs/ ebriefs_archive2001/ JanBriefs.cfm#University% 20Signs%20Biotech%20 Deal%20with%20SUNY%20 Downstate%20Medical% 20Center.
4. Ibid.
5. Ibid.
6. "CATT Awarded $1.5 Million to Expand Research Activities," *ePoly Briefs*, April 2001, http:// www.poly.edu/wwwpoly/ ebriefs/ebriefs_archive2001/Apr ilBriefs.cfm.
7. "ITE Hosts First High-Tech Conference in Israel," *ePoly Briefs*, January 2001, http://www.poly.edu/ wwwpoly/ebriefs/ ebriefs_archive2001/ JanBriefs.cfm.
8. "Tuition Increases for 2001-02 School Year," *ePoly Briefs*, April, 2001, http://www.poly.edu/ wwwpoly/ebriefs/ebriefs_archive 2001/AprilBriefs.cfm#Poly%20 in%20the%20News.
9. "Polytechnic Breaks Ground for New Building; Jacobs and Othmer Honored During

Ceremony," *Polytechnic Cable*, Summer 2000, 4.

10. Ibid.

11. Ibid.

12. Ibid.

13. "Board Of Overseers Named For Othmer Institute," *ePoly Briefs*, September 2001, http://www. poly.edu/wwwpoly/ ebriefs/ebriefs_archive2001/ SepBriefs.cfm#2.

14. "Professors Named Othmer Fellows," *ePoly Briefs*, November 2001, http:// www.poly.edu/wwwpoly/ ebriefs/ebriefs_archive2001/Nov Briefs.cfm#2.

15. "Poly Dedicates Two Buildings on MetroTech Campus," *ePoly Briefs*, June 2002, http://www. poly.edu/wwwpoly/ebriefs/ ebriefs.

16. Ibid.

17. Henry Singer, interview by Jeffrey L. Rodengen, digital recording, 13 September 2004, Write Stuff Enterprises.

18. "Poly Dedicates Two Buildings on MetroTech Campus," *ePoly Briefs*, June 2002, http://www.poly.edu/ wwwpoly/ebriefs/ebriefs.

19. "University Enters Phase 2 to Reduce Deficit," *ePoly Briefs*, February 2003, http://www.poly.edu/ wwwpoly/ebriefs/ebriefs.

20. Ibid.

21. Ibid.

22. Ibid.

23. Ibid.

24. Ibid.

25. Eli Pearce, interview by Jeffrey L. Rodengen, digital recording, 9 September 2004, Write Stuff Enterprises.

26. "Strategic Plan 2004-2007 Moves Forward," *ePoly Briefs*, April 2004, 1, http://www.poly.edu/ wwwpoly/ebriefs/ebriefs.

27. Ibid.

28. Christopher Hayes, interview by Jeffrey L. Rodengen, digital recording, 10 June 2004, Write Stuff Enterprises.

29. Therese E. Tillett, interview by Jeffrey L. Rodengen, digital recording, 10 June 2004, Write Stuff Enterprises.

CHAPTER ELEVEN SIDEBAR: PETER REGNA, DISTINGUISHED ALUMNUS AND BENEFACTOR

1. "Regna Lounge Is Dedicated," *ePoly Briefs*, September 2003, http://www.poly.edu/ePoly_

Briefs/Sept03.htm<http:// www.poly.edu/ePoly_Briefs/ Sept03.htm>.

2. Ibid.

3. Ibid.

4. Ibid.

CHAPTER ELEVEN SIDEBAR: SEPTEMBER 11, 2001

1. "Poly Mourns WTC Losses, Establishes Scholarships," *Polytechnic Cable*, Fall 2001, 2.

2. Ibid.

3. Ibid.

4. National Hazards Center, "Beyond September 11th: An Account of Post-Disaster Research," http://www. colorado.edu/hazards/sp/ 911book.html.

5. "Poly Mourns WTC Losses, Establishes Scholarships," *Polytechnic Cable*, Fall 2001, 2.

6. Ibid.

CHAPTER ELEVEN SIDEBAR: POLYTECHNIC UNIVERSITY NAMES NEW PRESIDENT

1. News release, Polytechnic University, 25 May 2005.

2. Ibid.

INDEX

Page numbers in italics indicate photographs.